Elements of
Shipping

BOOKS BY THE SAME AUTHOR:

(1984) *Elements of Export Marketing and Management,* 1st edn, Chapman and Hall, London.

(1984) *Dictionary of Commercial Terms and Abbreviations,* 1st edn, (6000 entries), Witherby and Co. Ltd, London.

(1985) *Elements of Export Practice,* 2nd edn, Chapman and Hall, London.

(1986) *Dictionary of Shipping/International Trade Terms and Abbreviations* (9000 entries) Witherby and Co. Ltd, London.

(1986) *Elements of Port Operation and Management,* 1st edn, Chapman and Hall, London.

(1988) *Economics of Shipping Practice and Management,* 2nd edn, Chapman and Hall, London.

(1988) *Dictionary of English–Arabic Shipping/International Trade/ Commercial Terms and Abbreviations,* (4400 entries), 1st edn, Witherby and Co. Ltd, London.

(1989) *Import/Export Documentation,* 1st edn, Chapman and Hall, London.

(1989) *Dictionary of Multilingual Commercial/International Trade/ Shipping Terms in English/French/German/Spanish* (13 000 entries), 1st edn, Witherby and Co. Ltd, London.

Elements of Shipping

Sixth edition

Alan E. Branch
F.C.I.T., F.I.Ex.

Senior Lecturer and Chief Examiner
in Shipping and Export Practice,
Shipping and Export Consultant
Export and Shipping Director

CHAPMAN & HALL

London · Glasgow · New York · Tokyo · Melbourne · Madras

& Hall, 2-6 Boundary Row, London SE1 8HN

Boundary Row, London SE1 8HN, UK

Professional, Wester Cleddens Road, Bishopbriggs, UK

mbH, Pappelallee 3, 69469 Weinheim, Germany

USA., One Penn Plaza, 41st Floor, New York,

ll Japan, ITP - Japan, Kyowa Building, 3F, 2-2-1 Chiyoda-ku, Tokyo 102, Japan

Hall Australia, Thomas Nelson Australia, 102 Dodds th Melbourne, Victoria 3205, Australia

& Hall India, R. Seshadri, 32 Second Main Road, CIT East, 00 035, India

dition 1964
d edition 1970
edition 1975
th edition 1977
h edition 1981
printed 1983
ixth edition 1989
Reprinted 1991, 1992, 1993, 1994

© 1964, 1970, 1975, 1977, 1981, 1989 Alan E. Branch

Typeset in 10/12pt Times by Photoprint, Torquay, Devon
Printed in Great Britain by St Edmunsbury Press Ltd, Bury St Edmunds, Suffolk

ISBN 0 412 32240 4

A Catalogue record for this book is available from the British Library
Library of Congress Cataloging-in-Publication Data available

To my wife
Kathleen

Contents

Acknowledgements

The author wishes to acknowledge the generous assistance provided by the following companies and institutions:

Alcatel
Alsthom
Baltic and International Maritime Conference
Baltic Exchange
Baltic International Freight Futures Exchange (BIFFEX)
British Shipbuilders Ltd
Bureau Veritas
Department of Trade and Industry
Freight Transport Association
General Council of British Shipping
HM Customs and Excise
International Association of Independent Tanker Owners
International Cargo-Handling Co-ordination Association
International Chamber of Commerce
International Labour Organization
International Maritime Organization
International Maritime Satellite Organization
Lloyd's Register of Shipping
Maersk Line
MAT Shipping Ltd
P & O Containers Ltd
Royal Caribbean Cruise Line
Sea Containers Ltd
Simpler Trade Procedures Board
Suez Canal Authority
United Nations Conference on Trade and Development

Preface to the sixth edition

Some 25 years has passed since the first edition of this book was published. Today it is regarded by many as standard work on the subject, and is retailing in over 175 countries. It is appropriate the sixth edition should be published at a time of great change in the international shipping industry.

Opportunity has been taken particularly to enlarge the chapters on bills of lading, chartering, ships and their cargoes, containerization, and the international consignment. Additional illustrations have been provided especially on ship types.

The sixth edition will be useful specifically for students taking courses sponsored by the Institute of Chartered Shipbrokers, Institute of Freight Forwarders, Institute of Export, Institute of Transport Administration, Institute of Physical Management, Chartered Institute of Transport, Institute of Bankers, Institute of Marine Engineers, Institute of Marketing, Institute of Road Transport Engineers and Chambers of Commerce. It will also be ideal for students taking shipping, export, import, international trade and transport examinations/research courses at degree/diploma level at universities and polytechnics, not only in the UK, but also in Hong Kong, Nigeria, Malaysia, Jamaica, Jordan, USA, the Middle East, Europe, Pacific Rim Nations and Third World countries. The book remains compulsory reading on the Foundation Course in Overseas Trade – subject 'International Physical Distribution' – for which I was one of the four subject specialists responsible for the course's development under the aegis of HM Government in 1975 through the British Overseas Trade Board.

Elements of Shipping treats the subject in a practical, professional way and is an ideal *aide-mémoire* to the shipping/export/import executive. It provides the reader with a basic understanding and knowledge of the shipping industry internationally, with particular emphasis on the salient economic, political, commercial and operating aspects of the subject.

The book reflects the author's many years of experience in ship and port management and international trade, both in the UK and overseas. To the person who wishes to know more about export practice the reader should also study my companion volume *Elements of Export Practice*. Similarly the reader who wishes to know more about ship management techniques should study my book *Economics of Shipping Practice and Management*, and the seaport operator/executive the book *Elements of Port Operation and Management*.

I am greatly indebted to the various organizations listed in the acknowledgements for the assistance they have so enthusiastically given me. The fact that an increasing number are situated overseas is reflected in the international content and market of the book.

Finally, in common with earlier editions, I would like to acknowledge with grateful thanks the generous secretarial help given by my life-long friends Mr and Mrs Splarn, and Maurice Hicks with proof-reading, and as always my dear wife Kathleen for her forbearance, encouragement and help in this task especially with proof-reading.

A.E.B.

	Course Director
19 The Ridings	International Trade/Shipping
Emmer Green	Basingstoke College of Technology
Reading	Worting Road
Berkshire, RG4 8XL	Basingstoke
May 1989	Hampshire RG21 1TN

Preface to the first edition

This book has been written with the aim of introducing shipping to those who have little or no knowledge of the subject. It is written in simple language and outlines the main economic, commercial, operating and political aspects of this very wide subject. The reader should master this book before tackling more advanced textbooks.

It is intended not only for the student preparing for shipping examinations, but also for the shipping employee who wishes to further his general knowledge of the subject.

The book is particularly commended to students studying the shipping examinations sponsored by the Institute of Chartered Shipbrokers, Institute of Freight Forwarders Ltd, Institute of Export, Institute of Materials Handling, Institute of Traffic Administration, Port Working Education scheme, the University of London Diploma in Transport Studies, Institute of Transport, Industrial Transport Association, Society of Shipping Executives Ltd, Royal Society of Arts, City of London College shipping certificate sponsored by Chamber of Shipping, City of Liverpool College of Commerce shipping certificate, and London Chamber of Commerce.

In writing this book I am greatly indebted to the various shipping institutes and organizations. To all who have helped me so generously I am deeply grateful.

My greatest debt is to a fellow tutor of the Transport Tutorial Association Ltd, Mr J.R. Basham, A.M.Inst.T., ASF. He gave me much useful advice and was a constant source of inspiration and enthusiasm.

At my request, Mr Basham was responsible for Chapter 7 on maritime canals, Mr M.N. Doig, M.A. (Oxon.) and Mr G.C. Killby have also read the draft and the book has benefited greatly from their comments. I am also indebted to Mr D.A. Rollinson who was responsible for the diagrams, and to my wife for help in reading the proofs.

East London College of Commerce   A.E.B.
May 1964

CHAPTER 1

Introduction

1.1 SCOPE OF BOOK

This book is written chiefly for the student who knows little or nothing of the shipping industry, and aims to give him/her a basic knowledge and understanding of the way in which it works. With this in mind, it will cover the economic, political, commercial, and operating aspects of the subject. Particular emphasis will be given to ship management and the practical aspects of the subject. It will examine the subject on an international basis.

1.2 FUNCTION OF SHIPPING AND ITS RELATIONSHIP TO INTERNATIONAL TRADE

Generally speaking, the demand for transport is derived from the demand for other things. Certain forms of transport, such as pleasure cruises and holiday travel, may be regarded as 'consumer services'; but the basic function of transport, involving economic, social or military needs, is the creation of utilities of place, i.e. the carriage of goods from places where their utility is low to places where it is higher. The value of a little more oil at Kuwait is relatively low, while the value at a UK oil refinery is correspondingly higher.

Since about 1870 technical improvements in sea transport have brought about a worldwide trading network, and have made it possible for whole regions to specialize in a single commodity for export. Thus the production of coffee in Brazil, or oil in Kuwait, is dependent on a cheap and efficient system of transport.

While ships have been used from the earliest time for ocean transport, the goods involved were largely luxuries or necessities unobtainable at home. The comparatively modern system of international exchange and specialization was made possible by the advent of the steamship, with its ability to maintain regular schedules enabling merchants' business to become less speculative and more a matter of supply and demand.

The most significant factor in the development of international trade was the cheapening of ocean transport largely by economy in propulsion. In 1840, the first Cunarder *Britannia* consumed 4.7 lb coal per horse-power per hour: by 1910 consumption of coal had fallen to 1.4 lb. Technical improvements in propelling machinery and fuel are continually making for increased speed at economical cost and increased space available for cargo, thus cheapening the cost of sea transport and permitting raw materials and foodstuffs of relatively low value to enter international trade. Modern communications have made it possible to put ships to better use and have been responsible for the conditions of almost perfect competition, under which the world's tramp tonnage carries the vast quantities of food and bulk raw materials, in accordance with market requirements.

As we progressed through the 1980s vessels had become more specialized and with improved ship management techniques were more intensively used. Fuel cost had risen substantially in the early and late 1970s and this had tended to place less emphasis in attaining high speed schedules and more on increasing ship capacity utilization. Vessels were tending to become more multi-purpose in their design and operation to counter trade fluctuations.

Politics by the late 1980s tended to play an increasing role in international shipping. More and more governments were following a policy of nationalism and protectionism in shipping and trade policies. There were increases in flag discrimination, operating and ship building subsidies, plus the implications of the developing nations mercantile fleets and similarly those of Eastern Bloc countries. Furthermore, the Flags of Convenience fleet continues to expand. As we progress through the 1990s it will be interesting to trace the growing impact of international organizations in the world trade and shipping scene. UNCTAD strongly advocates the need for less developed countries to increase their maritime fleets. Also maritime technology will continue to improve. Ship operation will become more integrated with inland distribution to facilitate the development of combined transport operation thereby improving the level of efficiency in international distribution in both bulk and general merchandise (container/Ro/Ro) markets.

CHAPTER 2

The ship

2.1 MAIN FEATURES OF HULL AND MACHINERY

There are two main parts to a ship: the hull and the machinery. The hull is the actual shell of the ship including her superstructure, while the machinery includes not only the engines required to drive her, but also the ancillary equipment serving the electrical installations, winches and refrigerated accommodation.

The hull is virtually the shell of the ship and usually designed for a particular trade in accordance with a shipowner's specification. A vessel is constructed of a series of transverse frames, which extend from the fore to aft of the vessel, rising at right angles to the keel. In reality they form the ribs of the ship. Statutory regulations exist regarding the distance between each frame. Each vessel, depending on her classification – passenger, container, tanker, bulk carrier – must have a number of bulkheads which are virtually steel walls isolating various parts of the vessel. This is necessary in the interests of containing a fire or flooding following a collision. Ocean-going vessels must have at the fore end a collision bulkhead installed at a distance of not less than 5% of the ship's length from her bow. The obligatory after-peak bulkhead function is to seal off the stern tubes through which run the tailshaft driving the propeller.

Figs 2.1 and 2.2 are mostly self-explanatory. The rear portion of the ship is termed the after end or stern. When moving stern first, the vessel is said to be moving astern. The front portion of the ship is termed the fore end, whilst the extreme forward end is called the bows. When moving bow first, the vessel is said to be moving ahead. Fore and aft are generally used for directional purposes. The area between the forward and aft portions of the vessel is called amidships. The maximum breadth of the vessel, which is found in the amidships body, is known as the beam.

The engine room houses both the machinery required to drive the vessel and the generators required for lighting, refrigeration and other auxiliary loads. Since 1950 there has been a tendency for all types of vessels to have their engines situated aft, thus releasing the amidships space – at the broadest part of the vessel – for cargo and passenger accommodation. The ship's funnel, painted in the shipping line colours, is situated above the engine room. In modern passenger liners, it is specially designed to keep fumes and smuts clear of the passenger accommodation. The propeller shaft, linking the propeller with the engines, passes through a shaft tunnel. The ship's anchors and the windlasses used to lower and raise them are found in the bow section. Additional anchors might also be provided on a large ship.

Modern tonnage, particularly tankers, container ships and passenger liners, have a transverse propulsion unit in the bows. Its purpose is to give greater manoeuvrability in confined waters, e.g. ports, and so reduce or eliminate the need for tugs. The rudder which enables the vessel to maintain her course, is situated aft. Some ships have an additional rudder in the bows for easier manoeuvrability in port. Stabilizers are in appearance similar to the fins of a fish, and are fitted to modern passenger liners and container ships to reduce rolling in heavy seas. They are fitted in pairs, and when in use protrude at right angles from the hull, deep below the water line. Their number depends on the size of the vessel. The provision of a bulbous bow can also improve passenger comfort, as it can reduce pitching in heavy seas and has also been provided in tankers, bulk carriers and modern cargo liners to increase speed when in ballast.

The modern tendency is to have large unobstructed holds with electrically operated hatch covers, for the speedy handling of cargo, and to reduce turn-round time to a minimum.

Their actual design and the number of decks will depend on the trade in which the ship plies. A vessel comprises various decks with the uppermost decks being called the navigational, boat and promenade decks. A continuous deck in a ship would run throughout the length of the vessel from fore to aft.

The transverse bulkheads run from the tank tops or floors of the hold to the deck. The longitudinal framing consists of steel sections running the length of the ship into which are fixed the skin plates forming the hull. Nowadays, with the development of the welded construction as opposed to the former riveted hull, many vessels are constructed on the combined system which uses the longitudinal system in the double bottom, and at deck level uses transverse framing for the sides. Basically the combined system is better for welded construction.

Scantlings basically are the dimensions of the structural parts of the ship embracing size of frames, beams, steel plating, bulkheads and decks. A vessel built to the full scantlings would be based on the maximum draught when the freeboard measured from the loadline to the deckline (the upper side of the continuous maindeck or freeboard deck which is equipped with permanent means of closing all openings to the elements) is at its minimum. Single deck vessels fall within this category such as an ore carrier which needs the strongest type of ship construction to convey such heavy deadweight cargoes with low stowage factors. Such vessels are built to the highest specification of the classification societies such as Lloyd's Register of Shipping, American Bureau of Shipping, Bureau Veritas etc., as regards strength of the component parts of the structure.

As already established the basic construction of all dry cargo vessels consists of a skeleton of steelwork to which is fixed the outer plating or skin of the ship's hull. The structure involves a girder construction which extends to the whole length of the ship and takes the form of an 'H' laid on its side. From the centre of the keel rises the keelson at right angles and in the top of it is fixed the foundation plate. The latter is extended outwards towards the sides of the vessel and forms the floor of the holds. Between the floor of the holds and the bottom of the ship is a clear space between which is the double bottom. Its dual function is to act as a second bottom to the vessel and thus help prevent serious damage to the vessel and cargo in the event of the ship grounding or striking a submerged object. Its other role is for water ballast or fuel as required on the voyage.

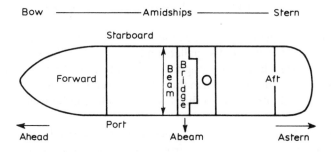

Fig. 2.1 Plan of steamship.

To give access to cargo holds, openings are cut into the deck of the vessel which are termed hatchways and are surrounded by coamings which are like steel walls rising from the deck. The height of these coamings is regulated by statute or classification society regulations.

Each mercantile type vessel has a certain number of various types of tanks for a variety of purposes and the following are the more salient ones:

(a) The forepeak tank is situated in the bows of the vessel between the bows and the collision bulkhead.

(b) Conversely the aft peak tank is situated in the stern of the vessel. It forms the aftermost watertight bulkhead.

(c) The wing tank is located at the side of the holds designed for carrying water ballast. These are found particularly in specialized bulk carriers.

(d) The deep tanks are situated one in each of the holds at the two ends of the ship. Such tanks are used for carrying water ballast and can be used to carry dry cargo. In modern vessels they are constructed to convey oil, either as bunkers, or wood or palm oil.

A tramp, carrying shipments of coal or ore, will be a single-deck vessel with large unobstructed hatches to facilitate loading and discharge. A vessel, conveying a variety of cargo in relatively small consignments, would have 'tween decks to facilitate stowage (See Fig. 3.3). If such a vessel also conveyed wool and other commodities of a high stowage factor, a shelter deck would be provided. Additionally, container ships are equipped with specially designed holds to facilitate speedy container handling using shore-based lifting apparatus. A description of the various types of vessel follows in Chapter 3.

The handling of cargo will be mechanized as far as possible with the use of conveyor belts, pallets and containers. The holds of a modern cargo liner are designed to facilitate dealing with such modern methods of cargo handling. Flush 'tween deck hatch covers are frequently provided so that fork lift trucks can be used in the holds.

The derricks are the ship's cranes, and are electrically operated. Their lifting capacity can vary from 3 to 50 tonnes. If heavy items

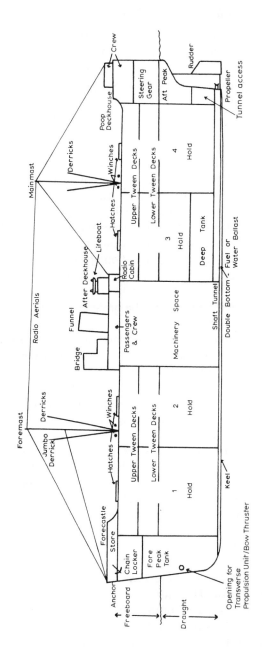

Fig. 2.2 Profile of ship.

such as locomotives or boilers are commonly carried, jumbo derricks capable of lifting up to 120 tonnes are provided (see Fig. 4.7). The decks are strengthened to accommodate such heavy lift cargoes.

A modern vessel called a Combi carrier (see Fig. 4.7) has superseded the 'tween deck tonnage in trades unable to invest in container tonnage and its infrastructure of port facilities and distribution overland network.

The bridge of a vessel is the navigating centre of the ship where her course is determined. Most modern tonnage today has the navigating bridge and machinery situated aft thereby facilitating the naval architect's designing the vessel of the maximum cargo capacity. The engines are bridge controlled and the navigating officer on watch makes use of a bridge computer to steer the vessel, to work out her course, and give position reports etc. More recently vessels use the maritime satellite system explained on pp. 142–6. Included in the navigating bridge accommodation is the helm, and also a large amount of nautical equipment, including radar sets, gyrocompass, radio, direction finder, etc. The bridge is in direct communication with all parts of the vessel.

Crew accommodation on modern cargo ships and tankers is situated aft in close proximity to the machinery. Standards of accommodation are high, and are controlled by various statutory regulations.

In the late 1960s the development of the container ship became evident in many cargo liner trades. Such vessels are usually free of derricks and the fourth generation have a capacity of up to 4000 high capacity ISO containers TEUs (Twenty Foot Equivalent Units). Their speed is between 16 and 22 knots and the more sophisticated type of container vessel is called a cellular ship. Such a vessel is built in the form of a series of cells into which the containers are placed, usually by sophisticated shore-based cranes. The most recent container vessel tends to be multi-purpose in design with ramp facilities for transhipping vehicle cargo. This improves the general cargo mix flexibility of the vessel.

Passenger accommodation will be either one-class with different grades of cabin comfort, as on an hotel basis, or two-class, incorporating first class and tourist. This ensures that the most economical use is made of the cubic capacity of the ship. In a cruise passenger liner, it is common to find a swimming pool, cinema, shops, hospital, nursery and numerous other amenities and recreational facilities.

There are various statutory provisions concerning the quantity and type of life-saving apparatus carried on a vessel. Broadly, it is determined by the type of vessel, crew establishment and passenger certificate (authorized number of passengers permitted to be carried). Life-saving apparatus includes lifeboats, inflatable rubber liferafts, lifebuoys and individual lifejackets.

The draught of a vessel is the vertical distance from the keel to the waterline. The maximum permitted draught varies according to the seasons and waters in which she plies. The markings are given in Fig. 2.3 and all ships must be loaded so that the loadline corresponding to the zone in which they are steaming must not be submerged. The seasons to which the markings apply are Tropical (T), Summer (S), Winter (W) and Winter North Atlantic (WNA). The world has been mapped off into sections showing where those sections apply. These are broadly detailed below:

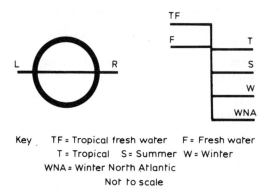

Key TF = Tropical fresh water F = Fresh water
T = Tropical S = Summer W = Winter
WNA = Winter North Atlantic
Not to scale

Fig. 2.3 International loadline of cargo vessel. Passenger and timber vessels have additional lines.

Tropical Venezuela to Costa Blanco and Rio de Janiero to Walvis Bay, Somalia via Saigon to Guatemala and Diego Suarez via Darwin to Coquimbo

Summer All areas between the lower line of the foregoing tropical area down to a line passing through Bahia Blanca, Cape Town, Durban, Launceston, Dunedin and Valparaiso

It must be appreciated that some areas change from summer to winter with different dates applying.

Given below is the seasonal winter situation:

Bergen to Greenland including the centre of the North Atlantic; Prince Rupert and the North Pacific to Yokohama – winter loadlines apply from 16th October to 15th April and summer loadlines from 16th April to 15th October.

All areas below the line between Bahia Blanca, Cape Town, Durban, Launceston, Dunedin and Valparaiso – winter loadlines apply from 16th April to 15th October, and summer loadlines from 16th October to 15th April.

Continent Baltic and North Atlantic – winter loadlines from 1st November to 31st March and summer loadlines from 1st April to 31st October.

Mediterranean and Black Sea – winter loadlines from 16th December to 15th March and summer loadlines from 16th March to 15th December.

Sea of Japan – summer loadlines from 1st March to 30th November and winter loadlines from 1st December to 28–29th February.

Seasonal Tropical (Arabian Sea – above Muscat and Karachi) – tropical loadlines from 1st August to 20th May; summer loadlines from 21st May to 31st July.

Arabian sea, below Muscat and Karachi to a line from Somaliland to Colombo – tropical loadlines from 1st December to 20th May; summer loadlines from 21st May to 15th September.

Tropical loadlines from 16th September to 15th October; Summer loadlines from 16th October to 30th November.

Bay of Bengal – tropical loadlines from 16th December to 15th April and summer loadlines from 16th April to 15th December.

China sea – tropical loadlines from 16th December to 15th April and summer loadlines from 1st May to 20th January.

The foregoing regulations/zones must be strictly followed as vessels are not permitted to operate submerged above their seasonal loadline marking. Alterations in the zones are made by the timber cargo regulations.

Freeboard is the distance measured amidships from the water line to the main deck of a vessel. This is normally the uppermost continuous deck in a ship with one or more decks. However, in a shelter deck vessel it would be the next deck below.

2.2 TYPES OF PROPULSION

The type and economics of propulsion has changed radically following the escalation in fuel cost in 1973 and 1979. Hitherto there was a trend towards faster vessels but nowadays shipowners have tended to encourage slower schedules to conserve fuel costs. Moreover, there has been a tendency to have the type of machinery which burns the cheaper fuel. Hence the bulk of the world mercantile fleet is diesel-engine operated. Meanwhile, research continues both in the diesel and steam turbines to improve performance not only in fuel consumption terms but also in maintenance costs.

The shipowner has a fairly wide range of propulsion units from which to choose. The steam reciprocating engine, even with modern refinements such as superheated steam and reheat cycle, is now obsolete. The steam turbine with its smoothness and reliability of operation is a choice for some large fast passenger liners.

The diesel engine has become increasingly popular for practically all vessels, as its low fuel consumption gives added deadweight and cubic capacity for cargo. It is almost exclusively used in river and short sea trades. A number of ships has also been built with diesel-electric or turbo-electric drive. In these ships the power units, steam turbine or diesel, are used not to drive the propellers directly, but to generate electricity for the driving motor coupled to the shaft. These units have greater flexibility; but against this must be set the increased costs of installation, maintenance and operation.

Today more than 85% of the world fleet is propelled by diesel engines. They have good performance at efficient propeller speeds and can be readily reversed for astern operation. Moreover, it is the most efficient prime mover from the standpoint of overall thermal efficiency. Fuel consumption is lower than with the steamship and consequently less bunker space is required. Additionally, compared with the steamship, it offers a reduction in size/weight ratio which facilitates the diesel machinery being placed aft. Conversely, however, although the diesel engine is less expensive to build it is more costly to maintain; it creates more vibration and noise and finally tends to have a shorter life compared with the steam turbine engine. The favourable size/ weight ratio plus lower fuel consumption which improves the vessel payload potential are very important aspects in favour of diesel propulsion. Moreover, extensive research is being undertaken to lessen the vibration aspect, reduce maintenance and overall to prolong the life of the diesel engine investment. Much has been achieved in these areas during the past ten years.

The choice of the propulsion unit is governed by many factors. These include initial cost; required speed; cost and availability of fuel on the route used; cargo-carrying capacity required; length and duration of voyage and operational expenses.

Improvements in marine engineering and in the efficiency of fuel are constantly reducing costs. For example, many shipowners in recent years have adapted their diesel engines to enable them to use cheaper, heavier boiler oil, instead of the more costly diesel oil for which they were originally designed. Of course, the use of heavy fuel oil for diesel engines raises the cost of maintenance, due to its action on pistons and cylinder linings. Meanwhile, the tendency to produce larger, more powerful diesel engines continues, thereby widening the scope of this type of propulsion in larger tonnages.

Speed is determined by the value set upon it by shippers. A high speed is subject to increasing marginal cost and is only economically possible where the trade can generate the cargo business. On short voyages, higher speeds and consumption are possible because a smaller quantity of fuel has to be carried in fuel tanks and less cargo space is taken up. On long voyages, high consumption would mean more fuel space, and less cargo capacity, so that an engine with a lower consumption is more economic for such voyages. The space required for fuel will also depend on steaming distances between ports where fuel can be replenished at reasonable cost. The modern engine room and wheelhouse is very much automated and the larger vessel is provided with computer facilities to operate at optimum speed and automatic navigation. Such measures aid conservation of fuel cost and lower crew levels.

Factors which will tend to influence a growing movement

towards diesel propulsion and possibly the development of coal-fired-pulverized propulsion are given below:

(a)   High oil cost.

(b)   Lower fuel consumption of the diesel unit compared with steam propulsion. For example a VLCC powered by steam turbine consumes 170 tons of heavy fuel oil per day. Conversely a diesel-driven equivalent consumes over 100 tons. Hence, not only does consumption fall with diesel propulsion, but also the cost per ton is much cheaper, plus a longer steaming distance before rebunkering.

(c)   Technical trends of the 1990s suggest the future propulsion unit will be primarily either the slow or medium/high-speed diesel engine. The cost savings outweigh the advantages of reliability, easy maintenance and compactness usually inherent with the steam turbine.

(d)   A growing shift in new tonnage terms from large ships to smaller vessels, and the maximum power of diesel engines offers up to 55 000 bhp with a single slow-speed diesel and 65 000 bhp with two medium speeds.

(e)   A large number of engine transplants took place in the 1980s from steam turbine to diesel propulsion. This includes, for example, container ships being equipped with the slow-speed diesel unit whilst the tanker transplant involves the medium-speed unit. It will be recalled the slow-speed diesel unit is one with less than 250 r/min and is usually better able to cope with low quality bunker fuel. It is usually a two-stroke engine and does not require a gearbox thereby generating more efficiency. Less cylinders are involved and likewise maintenance and lubrication. The medium-speed engine diesel unit is one above 900 r/min and can burn fuel just as low-grade as the slow-speed diesel engine.

(f)   By 1983 new coal-fired tonnage involving bulk carriers was in operation under the Japanese flag. Much experience is being gained from the operation of such tonnage and it remains to be seen whether it will herald the start of a new era of coal-fired propulsion.

The future predicts largely an era of diesel propulsion with continuing research into improving the performance of the diesel unit. Nuclear or gas-fired propulsion is unlikely to be developed for a variety of reasons. Nevertheless, a possible growth area is coal-fired propulsion. Much will depend on the research outcome of developing a modern economical technically efficient coal-fired propulsion unit with no significant additional crew cost/complement. A further factor will be the cost relationship between oil and coal. Long term it looks as though the world mercantile fleet will be largely diesel powered.

2.3 TYPES AND METHODS
OF TONNAGE MEASUREMENT

There are five main kinds of tonnage in use in shipping business. These are deadweight, cargo, displacement, gross and net tonnages.

Deadweight tonnage (dwt) expresses the number of tons (of 2240 lb) a vessel can transport of cargo, stores and bunker fuel. It is the difference between the number of tons of water a vessel displaces 'light' and the number of tons of water a vessel displaces when submerged to her loadline. Deadweight tonnage is used interchangeably with deadweight carrying capacity. A vessel's capacity for weight cargo is less than its total deadweight tonnage.

Cargo tonnage is expressed in terms of a weight or measurement. The weight ton in the US and sometimes in the UK is the American short ton of 2000 lb, or the English long ton of 2240 lb. A measurement ton is usually 40 ft^3, but in some instances a larger number of cubic feet is taken for a ton. Most ocean package freight is taken at weight or measurement (W/M) ship's option. With the growth in use of the metric system the metric ton of 1000 kg, or cubic metre is becoming more widely used. The freight ton is a mixture of weight and measurement tons and can lead to confusion in the collection and analysis of statistics.

Displacement of a vessel is the weight in tons of 2240 lb of the ship and its contents. It is the weight of water the ship displaces. Displacement light is the weight of the vessel without stores, bunker fuel or cargo. Displacement loaded is the weight of the vessel plus cargo, passengers, fuel and stores.

Gross tonnage applies to vessels, not to cargo. It is determined by dividing by 100 the volume in cubic feet of the vessel's closed-in spaces, and is usually referred to as the gross registered tonnage (GRT). The spaces exempt from the measurement include light and air spaces; wheelhouse; galley; lavatories; stairways; houses enclosing deck machinery; hatchways to a maximum of 0.5% of the gross tonnage and open shelter deck. A vessel ton is 100 ft^3. It is used as a basis for pilotage and dry-dock dues, and sometimes tonnage dues. Additionally, it is employed for official statistical purposes, when comparing ship's sizes, and as a basis for Protection and Indemnity club entries.

Net tonnage is a vessel's gross tonnage after deducting space occupied by crew accommodation including facilities for the master and officers; spaces used for navigation; boatswain's store room; water ballast and fresh water spaces including forward and aft peak tanks, deep tanks provided only fitted with manholds and not employable for carriage of liquid cargo; propelling and machinery space which does not represent earning capacity of the ship. A vessel's net tonnage expresses the space available for the accommodation of passengers and stowage of cargo, and is usually referred to as net registered tonnage (NRT). A ton of cargo in most instances occupies less than 100 ft^3: hence the vessel's cargo tonnage may exceed its net tonnage, and indeed the tonnage of cargo carried is almost always greater than the gross tonnage. It is the cubic capacity of all earning space, and it is on this tonnage figure that most harbour dues and other charges are calculated. The aim of the average shipowner is to achieve a low net tonnage consistent with a maximum cubic capacity for cargo and/or passengers.

The Suez and Panama tonnage regulations make it obligatory for vessels to be measured for tonnage if they require to use the canals. The equivalent gross and net tonnage are somewhat lower than the British standard, where one ton equals 100 ft^3. Where vessels proceed to ports in countries which do not accept the British tonnage rules, dues will also be levied on tonnages assessed under local conditions.

2.4 RELATIONSHIP BETWEEN DEADWEIGHT TONNAGE AND CUBIC CAPACITY

The relationship between net, gross and deadweight tonnage varies according to the type of vessel. In the case of cargo liners built for trades with high measurement cargoes like cotton, hay, wool or esparto grass, a lower ratio of deadweight to gross registered tonnage will be evident compared with ships built to carry heavy cargoes such as ore or coal. The deadweight of ULCC is approximately twice its GRT.

Passenger vessels have relatively little deadweight capacity, and in some cases this is lower than the net registered tonnage. It is difficult to give a rough guide to the various ratios of their different tonnages, as passenger vessels vary so much in their allocation of cubic capacity to cargo.

In assessing the overall stowage factor of a cargo vessel, it is best to use the total cubic bale or grain capacity, divided by the cargo deadweight tonnage. For example, the ship with 499 000 ft^3 grain of hold accommodation and 10 500 dwt, has a stowage factor under 50 – very suitable for coal. Grain cubic capacity is the total amount of cargo hold space available for the carriage of bulk cargo. It incorporates all space available, including the gaps between the frames and the beams in the holds. Bale cubic capacity is the total amount of cargo space available for the carriage of bags, bales or boxed cargo, and does not include the space between the frames and beams which would be accessible to baled cargo. The bale cubic capacity of a vessel, is therefore always slightly less than the grain cubic capacity.

Tonnage measurement and relationship between deadweight tonnage and cubic capacity are important factors in establishing the economic characteristics of a vessel capacity. It is very relevant in use in the chartering market when the merchant is seeking a suitable vessel to convey his cargo.

In 1982 IMO recommended a change in the gross and net registered tonnage measurement which is now in the process of adoption in new tonnage: this will become a mandatory requirement on July 18th, 1994.

CHAPTER 3

Ship design and construction

3.1 GENERAL PRINCIPLES AND FACTORS INFLUENCING DESIGN, TYPE AND SIZE OF SHIP

In his choice of the type of ship to be built, the shipowner must consider primarily the trade in which she is to operate. His decision as to size and propelling machinery will be governed by the factors involved in his particular trade, such as the nature of the cargo mix to be moved, the cost and availability of fuel, the minimum carrying capacity required, the length and duration of the voyages and the required speed. Economic, technical, statutory and safety considerations will all influence his choice.

So far as the building and operating costs are concerned, within certain limits, the larger ship is a cheaper proposition. For example, the cost of the propelling machinery for a 100 000 tonner is less than the cost for two 50 000 tonners developing the same power. The larger ship costs less to crew than two smaller ships and her operating costs per ton are lower. In the bulk trades, where the nature of the cargo calls for large roomy holds, the economics of size alone favour the employment of large ships. However, increased size implies deeper draught, and if a general trader is to be operated economically, she must be able to proceed anywhere where cargo is offered. On one voyage she may be going to Bombay which permits vessels with a maximum draught of 16 m, while her next employment may be in the River Plate where the draught is limited to about 9 m. She may have to load from an ore jetty off the coast of Chile where safety considerations prohibit the large ship. All these considerations have to be balanced, and today the modern tramp has developed into a handy-sized vessel of the Freedom type found in Fig. 3.3 of 14 000 dwt with a speed of 14 knots.

Recently the cellular container ship features more prominently in cargo liner trades. Additionally, more purpose-built tonnage is becoming available for carrying such products as liquefied methane, cement, sugar, wine, bananas, trade cars, etc. Such ships – often owned or on charter to industrial users – are designed for a particular cargo and are frequently involved in a ballast run for part of the round voyage. Purpose-built tonnage requires special terminals – often situated away from the general port area – frequently involving expensive equipment to ensure quick transhipment. The mammoth oil tanker up to 500 000 dwt with a draught of over 29 m comes within this category. Such vessels together with the OBOs and ore carriers of 100 000 dwt and over, are very restricted in their ports of call due to their size, particularly draught. There is every reason that purpose-built tonnage will continue to increase in size subject to economic and technical developments being favourable in particular trades, and it remains to be seen what other types of purpose-built tonnage other than those described elsewhere in this book will reach 100 000 dwt during the next decade. More emphasis is being placed on the multi-purpose vessel to lessen the impact of trade depression as when a market is low the ship can move into one which is more buoyant.

Where the vessel to be constructed is intended for long-term charter to industrial users, as in the case of many oil tankers, ore carriers and other specialized cargo ships, the limits of size are dictated by terminal facilities or by obstacles of the voyage – such as arise, for example, in the Panama canal or St Lawrence Seaway. Such vessels may be sometimes 400 000 dwt which cannot use the St Lawrence Seaway.

Much of the foregoing analysis applies equally to cargo liners, except that flexibility of operation is not so important. A factor tending more to limit their size is the importance of providing frequent sailings which the market can support. The overseas buyer pays for his goods when the seller can produce bills of lading showing that the consignment has been shipped. Under such conditions the merchant demands frequent sailings and, if the ship-owner does not provide these, his competitors will! Hence, he must operate a larger fleet of smaller ships, and therefore few cargo liners are as economically large as they might be. This was particularly so with 'tween deck tonnage, but with containerization emphasis is placed on speed coupled with the benefits of quick port turnround, fewer ports of call, but more reliance on feeder services (see pp. 382–94). Such vessels are able to take advantage of economies of scale, thereby permitting the shipowner to operate a more economically sized ship. Moreover, the container shipment is able to offer the combined transport transit embracing rail or road as the collector/distributor with shipping undertaking the trunk haul.

3.2 SAFETY AND OTHER REGULATIONS

Associated with the provision of new tonnage, there is the obligation to comply with statutory regulations, classification society rules and international agreements affecting ship design, and these vary according to the requirements of the different flags, particularly in matters relating to accommodation.

Vessels registered in the UK have to be built to the statutory requirements imposed by the Department of Trade. The regulations concern all life-saving apparatus, navigational aids, the hull and machinery, crew and passanger accommodation, watertight and fireproof bulkheads, gangways, emergency escapes, anchor cable and hawsers, shell plating, etc. The basis of these requirements is included in the Merchant Shipping Act of 1894. Various amendments and additions to these regulations have reached the Statute Book to meet new conditions and developments. The most recent are the Statutory Instruments of 1965 giving effect to the SOLAS (Safety of Life at Sea) convention of 1960.

3.3 STATUTORY REGULATIONS

International conventions, codes and protocols concerning ship safety and marine pollution are agreed by the member states of the United Nations Agency, the International Maritime Organization (IMO – see pp. 127–42). In the past 25 years IMO has promoted the adoption of some 30 conventions and protocols and adopted well over 500 codes and recommendations. The conventions and codes usually stipulate inspection and the issuance of certificates as part of enforcement. Most member countries and/or their registered shipowners authorize classification societies to undertake the inspection and certification on their behalf. For example more than 120 member states have authorized Lloyd's Register to undertake such inspection and certification.

IMO conventions define minimum standards but member states can instigate national regulations which incorporate IMO standards and apply equally well to their own fleets and visiting foreign ships. Classification societies participate in the work of IMO as technical advisers to various delegations. Their key function is to provide inspection and certification for compliance and advice on these complex regulations.

Given below are a selection of statutory marine surveys:

(a) *International Convention on Load Lines 1966.* This involves the vessel being surveyed for the issue of Load Line Certificate under the terms of Article 13 of the Convention which came into force in July 1968. An initial survey ensures that all arrangements, materials and scantlings fully comply with the requirements of the Convention before the ship goes into service. Freeboards are computed, marked on the hull and verified by a surveyor. Periodical surveys are required at least every five years together with annual inspections on the anniversary of Load Line certification. Every new ship must be supplied with loading and stability information in an approved form. For tankers which require Type A freeboards and Type B ships that require reduced freeboards the classification society verifies compliance with the minimum stipulated stability requirements after damage.

(b) *International Conventions for the Safety of Life at Sea* (SOLAS). SOLAS 1960 came into force in May, 1965 and remains in force for those signatories who have not ratified SOLAS 1974, which came into force in May, 1980. SOLAS 1974 was amended by the Protocol of 1978, which became effective for contracting states from 1st May, 1981. The Protocol introduced additional requirements for radar, inert gas systems and steering gear for tankers, as well as new requirements for mandatory annual and intermediate surveys amendments agreed in 1981, which entered into force in September 1984, replace Chapters II–1 (Construction – Subdivision and Stability, Machinery and Electrical Installations) and II–2 (Construction – Fire Protection, Fire Detection and Fire Extinction). There are editorial changes to Chapter III (Lifesaving Appliances) and amendments to Chapters IV (Radiotelegraphy and Radiotelephony), V (Safety of Navigations) and VI (Carriage of Grain).

Further amendments agreed in 1983, which entered into force in

July 1986, replace Chapter III (Life-saving Appliances) and VII (Carriage of Dangerous Goods). There are editorial changes to Chapter II–1 (Construction – Subdivision and Stability, Machinery and Electrical Installations) and amendments to Chapters II–2 (Construction – Fire Protection, Fire Detection and Extinction) and IV (Radiotelegraphy and Radiotelephony).

A number of classification societies are authorized by many states under the terms of Regulation 12(a) (vii) of SOLAS 1974 to undertake the inspection and survey of ships and to issue the relevant certificates.

Cargo Ship Safety Construction Certificate. Under the terms of the 1960 and 1974 Conventions, any cargo ship of 500 tons gross and over engaged on international voyages, requires a Cargo Ship Safety Construction Certificate, and Cargo Ship Safety Equipment, Radiotelegraphy and Radiotelephony Certificates. Those of 300 tons gross and over, but less than 1600 tons gross, must have a Cargo Ship Safety Radiotelegraphy or Radiotelephony Certificate. Ships of 1600 tons gross and over require a Cargo Ship Safety Radiotelegraphy Certificate.

Passenger Ship Safety Certificates. This involves the initial and periodical inspection and survey of passenger ships for the issue of a Passenger Ship Safety Certificate following compliance with the requirements of the 1974 SOLAS convention. This includes approval and survey of arrangements for sub-division, damage stability, fire safety, life-saving appliances, radio equipment and navigational aids.

Grain Loading. Ships which carry grain must comply with the requirements of Chapter VI of the SOLAS Convention. It is essential that grain carrying ships carry the relevant approved loading manuals and plans for the authorities at grain loading ports to permit the ship to be loaded. Delays may result if approved documentation cannot be produced.

(c) *Convention on the International Regulations for Preventing Collisions at Sea 1972.* This Convention, which came into force in July 1977, superseded Annex B of SOLAS 60. Compliance is required by Regulations 7 and 8 of Chapter I of SOLAS 74, amended by the 1978 Protocol and the 1981 Amendments to the COLREGS that came into force in June 1983. The Convention deals with steering and sailing rules, lights, shapes and sound and light signals. Compliance is a condition for the issue of Passenger

Ship Safety Certificates and Cargo Ship Safety Equipment Certificates.

(d) *International Convention for the Prevention of Pollution from Ships, 1973,* as modified by the Protocol of 1978 relating thereto (MARPOL 73/78). This Convention, which aims to minimize ocean pollution, contains five annexes, each dealing with a particular pollution hazard as follows:

Annex I – Oil,

Annex II – Noxious liquid substances in bulk (categorised A, B, C, or D),

Annex III – Harmful substances in packaged form or in freight containers, portable tanks or tank wagons,

Annex IV – Sewage,

Annex V – Garbage.

Annex I entered into force in October 1983. Annex II entered into force in April 1987 and requires full implementation of the IMO Bulk Chemical Code or the International Bulk Chemical Code applicable to category A, B and C substances (See item (f)). Annexes III, IV, and V are to be ratified separately and are not yet in force. Nearly 40 countries have acceded to Annexes I and II. Overall the Convention involves the processing of surveys and issues Certificates of Compliance.

Possession of the Certificate of Compliance, which includes all the information and features to be found on the Convention Certificate, including the provision for annual and intermediate surveys, should ease the difficulties encountered in some ports by ships otherwise unable to produce documentary evidence of compliance with the Convention.

(e) *Tonnage measurement regulations.* A Tonnage Measurement Certificate is required by a national administration to secure permanent registration. This involves the process of undertaking tonnage measurement surveys and issue of Tonnage Certificates. The International Convention on Tonnage Measurement of Ships 1969 came into force in July 1982 and applies to ships under the flag of signatories to this Convention as follows: new ships; existing ships which undergo alteration or modification which the administration deems to be a substantial variation in their gross tonnage; existing ships, if the owner so requests and all existing ships by 18th July, 1994. For ships of administrations that are not signatories to the Convention, and for existing ships of those administrations which are signatories, the main systems of measurement in force are the British, United States and International (Oslo Convention) Tonnage Regulations. These were revised to take into account IMO Resolution A48 (III), generally referred to as the Tonnage Mark Scheme, and have been adopted by the majority of leading maritime nations.

(f) *IMO Code for the Construction and Equipment of Ships Carrying Dangerous Chemicals in Bulk.* This Code, known as the Bulk Chemical Code, provides safety standards for the design, construction, equipment and operation of ships carrying noxious liquid substances in bulk. Some countries have implemented the Code and others use it on a voluntary basis; some require foreign chemical tankers trading in their waters to possess a Certificate of Fitness issued either by the flag administration or a recognized organization, such as a classification society, on their behalf. Statements of Compliance are also provided at the request of owners for the flag administration to issue a Certificate of Fitness.

Under the provisions of the 1983 Amendments to SOLAS 74, compliance with an updated version of the Code, known as the International Bulk Chemical Code, became mandatory for new ships in July 1986. Annex II of MARPOL 73/78 made compliance with the Bulk Chemical Code, or the International Bulk Chemical code, mandatory from April 1987, for the carriage of pollution category A, B, and C substances and those category D substances assessed as presenting both pollution and safety hazards.

Crew accommodation. Minimum crew accommodation standards have been developed by the International Labour Organization. These standards are used by some governments and adopted by others into their own crew accommodation. This involves the regular survey of crew accommodation in accordance with the requirements of the ILO conventions or national crew accommodation regulations.

IMO code for the construction and equipment of ships carrying liquefied gases in bulk. This Code known as the Liquefied Gas Carrier Code requires that the design, constructional features and equipment of new ships minimise the risk to the ship, its crew and environment. There is an additional Code applicable to existing ships delivered on or before 31st October, 1986. Some countries implement these Codes or apply them on a voluntary basis; some require foreign liquefied gas carriers trading in their waters to possess a Certificate of Fitness. The 1983 Amendments to SOLAS 74, which came into force in July 1986, make compliance with a slightly amended version of these Codes, the International Gas Carrier Code, mandatory.

In 1988 at the IMO headquarters a major international conference in maritime safety was held and it considered the following aspects:

1. amend Chapter IV of the SOLAS Convention to recognize the Global Maritime Distress and Safety System (GMDSS);

2. amend both the SOLAS and the Load Line Conventions to incorporate the provisions of the harmonized system of survey and certification (HSSC); and

3. adopt internationally agreed amendments to the Load Line Convention which have not entered into force due to the recognized deficiency of the explicit amendment procedure.

3.4 SURVEY METHODS

The traditional way of surveying a vessel was to bring her to a shipyard where items to be surveyed were opened up, cleaned, inspected and reassembled. This method is both time consuming and expensive, and is still practised widely for a variety of reasons. However, a number of alternative survey methods exist today which have been developed by the classification societies and in time will become increasingly popular. Details are given below:

(a) Voyage Survey
The surveyor is in attendance during the ship's voyage, and carries out the required surveys. If requested, he prepares specifications in co-operation with the owner on items to be repaired.

(b) BIS-Notation
Although docking a vessel is still necessary for a number of reasons, the interval between docking has been increased considerably. This extended interval may come into conflict with the 'normal' class rules. However, by arranging minor modifications to the hull and its appendages, a notation 'bis' (built for in-water surveys) may be obtained which allows a docking interval of 5 years.

(c) Continuous survey

Classification Rules require that the surveys of hull and machinery are carried out every 4 years. Alternatively continuous survey systems are carried out, whereby the surveys are divided into separate items for inspection during a 5-year cycle. For the machinery survey the rules provide that certain of these items may be surveyed by the chief engineer. Furthermore, for vessels carrying out machinery maintenance in accordance with a fixed maintenance schedule, this system may replace the continuous machinery survey system, thereby reducing the class survey to an annual survey.

(d) Planned maintenance system

This is subject to a type approval and may thereafter be used as a basis for a special survey arrangement for individual ships at the owner's request.

Today, most cost-conscious shipowners operate advanced planning systems and maintenance procedures in order to meet increasing demand for cost-effective operation.

To avoid unnecessary opening up of machinery and duplication of work, many classification societies have introduced an alternative survey arrangement for the machinery. The arrangement is based on the owner's planned maintenance system already in operation 'on board'. It involves the following sequence of survey programme.

(i) classification society approves the owner's maintenance programme;
(ii) initial survey onboard by classification society surveyor;
(iii) continuous machinery survey to be in operation;
(iv) chief engineer to be approved by classification society.

The annual survey inspections carried out by the chief engineer are accepted as class surveys. However, the annual audit survey must be carried out in conjunction with the ordinary annual general survey (AGS). The audit survey is to verify that the arrangement meets agreed procedures. At the annual audit survey, the surveyor reports the class items requested by the owner.

(e) Harmonization of surveys

Hitherto surveys were spread throughout the year indiscriminately and several visits on board were necessary by the surveyor. A number of classification societies have now developed 'harmonization of surveys' whereby the relevant surveys may be harmonized or sychronized with those required by the maritime authorities. Each survey must be carried out with a tolerance time band and there are three categories as detailed below:

(1) annual surveys with a time band of 3 months before and after the due date;

(2) 2, and 2½-year surveys to be undertaken within 6 months before and after due date;

(3) special periodical survey every 4 years with a permitted 1-year extension.

As we progress through the 1990s the implications of the *Herald of Free Enterprise* accident which capsized in the precincts of the port of Zeebrugge in 1987 will manifest themselves through new legislation to decrease the risk of such accidents. It resulted in the loss of nearly 200 lives. The major cause was that the bow doors gaining access to the vehicle deck were not closed. New legislation emerging from the IMO could involve modifications to the vehicle and passenger decks to improve passenger emergency access and design of the bow and stern doors.

3.5 RECENT TRENDS IN SHIP DESIGN

During the past decade the trend has been towards faster vessels of increased size with improved machinery and cargo-handling equipment, while standards of accommodation have been raised for both passengers and crew. However, as we progress through the 1990s more attention in ship design will be given to producing a versatile vessel with optimum capacity and speed – the latter having regard to increasing fuel cost. Additionally, it will reflect the need to reduce crew complement; further extension of high technology in shipboard equipment; improved maintenance/survey techniques (see Fig 3.1); development of more computerized techniques in all areas; improved port turn-round time to compensate for slower transits involving combined transport development, and improve marine technology.

Cargo liners have increased in speed from about 15 to 22 knots, mainly because of market forces and the desire to reduce the

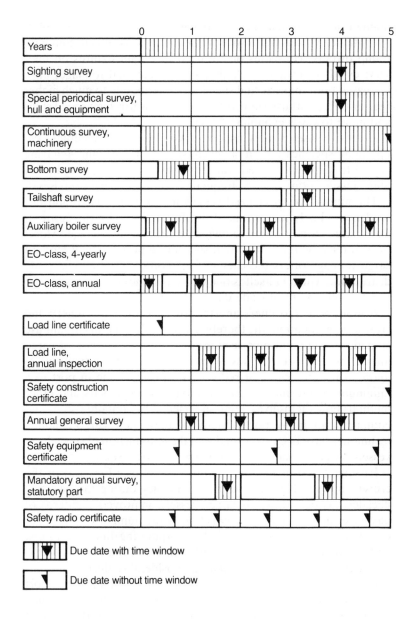

Fig. 3.1 Non-harmonized ship survey program. (Reproduced by kind permission of Det Norske Veritas)

number of vessels in a fleet by introducting faster ships, particularly container vessels often with rationalized ports of call. Similarly tramp owners, conscious of the need to obtain fixtures on liner services where owners seek short-term additional tonnage, have increased both ship size and speed. Long term, due to much higher fuel cost, less enthusiasm will be directed towards high speed ships and more towards economic design.

Extensive use is now made of computers to facilitate the optimum specification in a given set of circumstances having regard to ship type, speed, capacity, draught, beam, length, etc. Ship classification societies frequently feature in such exercises.

The number of specialized vessels has also increased, and this tendency is likely to continue. It is often linked with the desire of many large cargo owners to own or charter such tonnage. Moreover, it must be recognized that specialized purpose-built modern cargo tonnage offers the cheapest method of international trade distribution which in itself is one of the paramount reasons for the rapid development of trade during the 1980s.

Nowadays, cargo liners and tramps have their machinery and crew accommodation aft, thereby ensuring that the maximum use is made of the amidships section for cargo. In the case of cargo liners, improved techniques of cargo handling have been introduced, with the object of reducing turn-round time in port to a minimum. These include palletization, conveyor belts and other methods now themselves being superseded by container ships and equipment in many ports. Many of these new cargo-handling techniques have been associated with the introduction of specialized vessels. A good example is the Combi Carrier (see Fig. 4.7).

Passenger vessels may be the ferry vessel (see Fig. 4.5) or the cruise ship (see Fig. 4.4), and the tendency during the past two decades has been towards larger vessels, improved standards of passenger accommodation, reduction in the number of passenger classes to either two-class vessels incorporating first and tourist and for the cruise tonnage the development of the hotel concept.

Passenger tonnage has increased considerably during the past decade especially in the ferry division as, for example, in the Short Sea Trades particularly UK/Continental. The vessels are designed to be as versatile and functional as possible to the market operational requirement and are called multi-purpose ships with vehicular capacity – cars, lorries, trailers, containers, and caravans. Many have a passenger certificate of 2000, with about 200 to 300 berths depending on the route. Some have less than 50 cabins on the shorter voyages. The ships are designed for economic operation with both bow and stern ramp loading to facilitate quick turn-round, and a mezzanine deck so that the car/lorry combination capacity can be varied to meet seasonal traffic variations. Such tonnage may have a car capacity of 400 or for 80 lorries/trailers. More recently vessels with two decks of up to 120 lorry/trailer capacity have been introduced. This permits simultaneous loading/discharging at either deck, thereby speeding up turn-round time in port. During peak season some vessels operate eight trips during the 24 hours on the shorter routes. Passenger facilities are to a high standard together with the catering. The passenger may be the foot passenger, served by connecting rail port services or motor coach, the lorry driver, or the motorist accompanied by his family. The voyage time varies from 2½ to 8 hours, with some longer crossings extending to 36 hours. Entertainment including films, discos, coin-operated amusement machines etc. are becoming prominent on the long-distance ferry ships. The vessels are functionally designed to a high aesthetic standard with emphasis on cleaning aids and maximum utilization of available cubic capacity. An example of a modern ferry vessel is the MV *Pride of Dover* operating on the Dover/Calais route. This market will expand and the accompanied car market is unlikely to be adversely affected by air competition.

Navigational aids to cater for the needs of INMARSAT (see pp. 142–6) will be provided.

As we progress through the 1990s the application of ergonomics to ship design will become paramount particularly in the interest of reducing crew complement. A good example is bridge design and the increasing emphasis on unmanned machinery spaces. This involves the concept of the ship control centre which embraces navigation, ship control and engine and cargo control functions. A further example of the influence of ergonomics involves ship systems concerned with how people get aboard and leave ships and how they move around the ship once aboard. This involves stairways; lifts and hoists; machinery spaces; ladders – fixed and portable; mast and radar platforms; lifeboats; holds and tanks; emergency escapes; watertight doors; stores and workshops and sick bay and hospital rooms.

Ergonomics can play an influential role in the panel instrument and display layout and configuration both in the bridge/wheelhouse and machinery room. This involves the central choice and disposition, the design of alarm and warning signals, and the overall philosophy of both the control and maintenance panel layout. The influence of ergonomics may extend to the written word in the organization and preparation of manuals, check lists and fault-finding guides and in the provision of on-board computer-aided systems run on an interactive basis.

The modern engine room is computer-controlled and electrically operated through a series of panels on the bridge. Undoubtedly, in the future, further emphasis will be placed on computer technology in ship design and operation.

3.6   GENERAL STRUCTURE OF CARGO VESSELS

Cargo vessels can be classified according to their hull design and construction.

Single-deck vessels have one deck, on top of which are often superimposed three 'islands': forecastle, bridge and poop. Such vessels are commonly referred to as the 'three-island type'. These islands help to protect the main deck by preventing heavy seas from sweeping the length of the ship and save deck cargo, such as timber or esparto grass, from damage by sea water. It also gives the vessel added buoyancy.

This type of vessel is very suitable for the carriage of heavy cargoes in bulk, as easy access to the holds (with only one hatch to pass through) means that they are cheap to load and discharge. A modern single-deck vessel is found in Fig. 3.3 with all the accommodation and machinery aft. It is of the Freedom-type design and ideal for grain, packaged lumber, etc. Such a vessel of four holds would have a 19 000 dwt displacement, a draught of 9.05 m, and cargo capacity of 14 500 tonnes.

A large number of single-deck vessels, particularly colliers (coal carriers) have very large hatches and are known as 'self-trimmers', as the cargo can be loaded into all corners of the hold. This reduces loading costs and improves turn-round time in port. Such vessels normally have their machinery aft. There is, however, one disadvantage with such vessels in that their large hatches are more liable than small hatches to be broken open by heavy seas, and it is

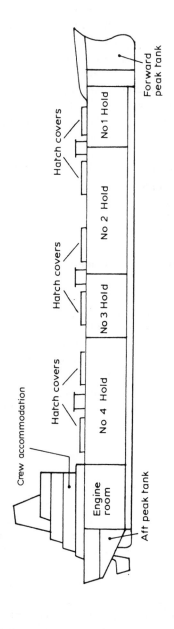

Fig. 3.2 Single-deck vessel.

for this reason that self-trimming vessels are not permitted to load so deeply as similarly constructed vessels with smaller hatches.

The most suitable cargoes for single-deck vessels are heavy cargoes carried in bulk, such as coal, grain and iron ore. However, these vessels also customarily carry such light cargoes as timber and esparto grass, which are stowed on deck as well as below, the large clear holds making for easy stowage and the three islands affording protection for the deck cargo. This type of vessel is not suitable for general cargo, as there are no means of adequately separating the cargo.

There are a number of variations in the single-deck type of vessel. Some vessels, for example, may be provided with a short bridge while others have a longer bridge. The latter has an advantage in that it extends over the holds and so helps to provide extra cargo space. Sometimes the space between two of the islands is filled in, leaving one space only. Vessels of this type are referred to as being of the 'well-deck type'. This method of construction also provides additional space for cargo.

The 'tween-deck type of vessel has other decks below the main deck, and all run the full length of the vessel. These additional decks below the main deck are known as the 'tween decks; some vessels in the liner trades often have more than one 'tween deck, and they are then known as the upper and lower 'tween decks.

A vessel with 'tween decks is very suitable for general cargo, as not only is the cargo space divided into separate tiers, but also the 'tween deck prevents too much weight from bearing on the cargo at the bottom of the hold. This type of vessel also makes for better stowage of heavy bagged cargo, such as sugar and cement, as the weight pressure in the lower holds, which sometimes causes the bags to split, is reduced. Moreover, if a heavy cargo is loaded, the 'tween decks enable it to be distributed throughout the ship. This has the effect of raising the centre of gravity thereby lessening the stability of the ship. A 'tween deck vessel of modern design is found in Fig. 3.3. Again it is the Freedom type and has machinery and accommodation aft. It has four cargo holds and is of 14 000 dwt. Its speed is 14 knots.

An example of a modern products carrier is found in Fig. 3.4. It has an overall length of 182.5 m and a draught of 11.0 m. The service speed is 14 knots. The vessel has a twin-skin double bottom hull structure to give clean, smooth cargo tanks permitting easy

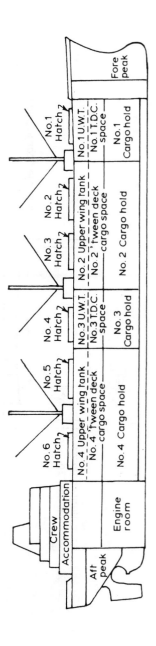

Fig. 3.3 Freedom-type ship with 'tween-deck accommodation.

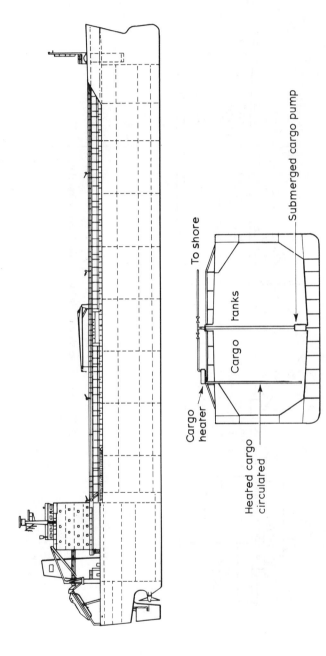

Fig. 3.4 Tango products carrier of 47 300 dwt and ideal for bulk shipment of gasoline, aviation gasoline, jet fuel, naphtha, diesel fuel, fuel oil, caustic soda, ethanol, B-T-X, molasses and vegetable oil. (Reproduced by kind permission of British Shipbuilders Ltd)

and rapid cleaning from one cargo to another with reduced heating and coating maintenance costs; individual tank-mounted cargo pumps which strip the tanks efficiently without the problems of long suction lines thereby obviating the need to have a shipboard pump room; deck-mounted heat exchangers for efficient control of cargo temperature; and versatility of cargoes embracing all of the common oil products and a range of easy chemicals including gasoline, aviation gasoline, jet fuel, naphtha, diesel fuel, fuel oil, caustic soda, ethanal, B-T-X, vegetable oil and molasses. It has a total deadweight tonnage of 47 300 and a cargo capacity of 50 000 m^3 which for example would be sufficient for a 30 000 tonne cargo of naphtha. The vessel has 9 tanks and crew accommodation for 25 persons.

The vessel is suitable for worldwide trading in the bulk product markets. It is built by British Shipbuilders and called the Tango Products carrier. An example of a modern container vessel is found in Fig. 3.5. It has an overall length of 162 m and draught of 9.75 m. It has a total deadweight tonnage of 21 800 and a container capacity of 1739 TEUs. The service speed is 18 knots. It has eight hatches. All are unobstructed to provide full width 40-ft length openings and closed by lift on/lift off pontoon-type hatch covers. All the holds are designed for 40-ft containers; 20-ft boxes can be stowed using a combination of cell guides, side bars and stacking cones without the use of portable guides or dedicated holds. Three electro-hydraulically operated slimline deck cranes are provided, each of 36 tonnes capacity.

The vessel is suitable for worldwide trading in containerised markets. It is called a Compact containership and built by British Shipbuilders Ltd in a size range from 600 to 2100 TEUs. Sometimes such tonnage is described as cellular cargo vessels when the holds have been designed to form a series of cells into which the containers are placed.

Although the larger container vessels now have a capacity of 2500 containers, it is quite possible during the next decade, as tonnage and port facilities are modernized/enlarged, that ships approaching 3000/3500 container capacity will be available. A feature of container ships is the quick turn-round time in port which, when one has 1700 to both discharge and load, involves a highly organized operation usually involving both road and rail. On average one unit of lifting equipment takes 3 minutes to complete the cycle of lifting the container from the ship's hold, placing it on

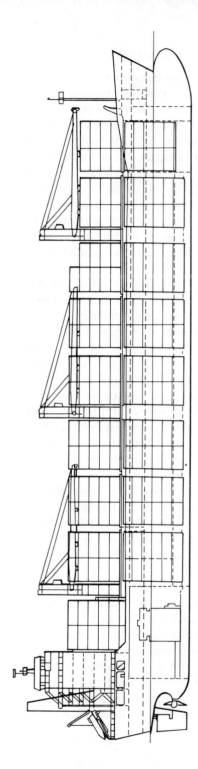
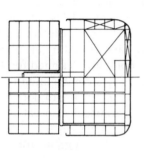

Fig. 3.5 Compact containership of 21 800 dwt, and capacity of 1739 TEUs. The paramount feature is its flexibility and fuel economy, as it can hold both 20 ft and 40 ft containers, plus the maximum earning capacity with higher container numbers for the hull envelope. It is ideal for worldwide container trading. (Reproduced by kind permission of British Shipbuilders Ltd)

the quay or railway wagon, lorry etc. and returning to collect the next container. Usually the lifting equipment operates in pairs depending on ship size. Many of the containers are cleared through container bases/inland clearance depots/container freight stations, situated usually in industrial areas and conveyed to and from the port 'under bond' by road or rail. Many major container operators now make extensive use of the computer particularly in the overall transit control arrangements and ship stowage. The latter involves the formulation of the stowage plan.

3.7 TRANSFER OF CLASS FROM ONE CLASSIFICATION SOCIETY TO ANOTHER

An increasing number of shipowners are now transferring their classification tonnage class from one ship classification society to another. This arises from a variety of situations particularly under transfer of ownership which may involve a transfer of flag.

To undertake a transfer of class from one classification to another involves a specific criterion to all societies which are full members of the International Association of Classification Societies (IACS). Full IACS members include American Bureau of Shipping, Bureau Veritas, Germanischer Lloyd, Lloyd's Register of Shipping, Nippon Kaiji Kyokai, Det Norske Veritas, Polsk Rejestr Statkow, Registro Italiano Navale and USSR Register of Shipping.

Insofar as vessels seeking transfer to the Lloyd's Register the first stage is the submission of a limited number of essential plans for appraisal and retention for record purposes. This includes plans for Hull and Machinery. Additional plans are required for oil tankers/ore-oil ships; gas carriers; chemical tankers; and oil tankers. Additional data may be required for Swedish, Norwegian or Liberian flag vessels. The Society appraises the plans bearing in mind they already have been accepted by another IACS member society. However, where any feature of the design is found to prove detrimental to the ship or its machinery, or where arrangements contravene the applicable International Maritime Organization Convention requirements, the society will advise the owner accordingly and if necessary to require that modifications be carried out as a condition for classification.

The second stage enables the current status of the ship assigned by the previous classification society to be obtained by Lloyd's Register directly from that society, once the owner's permission has been received. If all classification surveys are found to be up to date, it should only be necessary for the surveyors to carry out an examination equivalent to no more than the requirements of an annual survey and verification of arrangements as shown on the plans. Where, however, the examination of a ship's hull or machinery has been carried out on a continuous survey basis, a detailed check of all survey records must be carried out to establish that individual items of hull and machinery have been surveyed in accordance with requirements during the previous 5-year period. This precaution is considered absolutely essential if Lloyd's Register is to be responsible for issuing any Safety Construction Certificate on behalf of the country under whose flag the ship is registered.

The final stage involves the process of completing the documentation and issuing fresh classification certificates together with any statutory certificates required. In general terms, if the applicable statutory certificates are issued by the national authority of the flag state, these will remain valid on transfer of class. If they were issued by the previous society on behalf of the national authority, and are still valid, these certificates are acceptable, until such time as the requirements for transfer of class have been completed and the previous class withdrawn.

These general terms are not applicable in those cases where a change of flag is involved, as specific instructions regarding the procedure to be adopted will be forwarded.

3.8 ECONOMICS OF NEW AND SECOND-HAND TONNAGE

The most decisive factor influencing the shipowner's choice between new and second-hand tonnage is the availability of capital and its cost.

The economics of new and second-hand tonnage now forms an important part of ship management. Moreover, with ship costs continuing to rise, the economics of buying a relatively modern ship of up to 5 years in age proves an attractive proposition despite the conversion cost especially with countries experiencing hard currency problems. For example, a number of oil tankers have been converted to dry cargo bulk carriers. The cost is modest when related to new tonnage, and particularly when shipyards are hungry for work with a depressed new tonnage order book. Furthermore, it permits the vessel to be quickly introduced to meet the market trade demand. The latter point is very significant in cash flow terms as the vessel starts to earn money sooner than a new one involving up to a 3-year time scale. If the shipowner has sufficient capital available, he will in all probability prefer new to second-hand tonnage – its most distinct advantage being that he can have a vessel built to his own specification in the matter of type, design and speed.

Among the disadvantages inherent in buying new tonnage is the adequate depreciation of the vessel during her normal working life to provide funds for replacement. At present, in some countries, depreciation is based on initial and not on replacement cost, which because of inflation, is likely to be considerably higher. Further disadvantages include the risk of building delays; uncertain costs at time of delivery, if the vessel is not being built on a fixed price; and lastly a possible recession in the market when she is ready to trade. Further advantages/disadvantages of buying new tonnage are given below:

(a) The vessel is usually built for a particular trade/service and thereby should prove ideal for the route in every respect, i.e. speed, economical crewing, ship specification, optimum capacity, modern marine engineering technology, ship design etc. In short, it should be able to offer the most optimum service at the lowest economical price.

(b) It usually raises service quality and such an image should generate additional traffic.

(c) It facilitates optimum ship operation particularly if there is a fleet of sister ships aiding minimum stock of ship spares/replacement equipment to be provided.

(d) Service reliability should be high.

(e) Maintenance and survey cost should be somewhat lower than older second-hand tonnage particularly in the early years.

(f) New tonnage presents the opportunity to modernize terminal arrangements particularly cargo transhipment, cargo collection and distribution arrangements etc. Overall it should improve the speed of cargo transhipment arrangements and reduce ship port turn-round time to a minimum. This all aids making the fleet more productive.

(g) A significant disadvantage is the time-scale of the new tonnage project which can extend up to 3 years from the time the proposal was first originated in the shipping company until the vessel is accepted by the shipowner from the shipyard following successful completion of the trials. During this period the character and level of traffic forecast could have dramatically adversely changed. In such circumstances it may prove difficult to find suitable employment for the vessel elsewhere.

(h) Annual ship depreciation is substantially higher than the vessel displaced whilst crew complement would be much lower.

With second-hand tonnage, the shipowner has the advantage of obtaining the vessel at a fixed price, which would be considerably lower per deadweight ton in comparison with a new vessel. Furthermore, the vessel is available for service immediately the sale is concluded. Conversely, the shipowner will have to face higher maintenance costs, lower reliability, generally higher operating cost and a quicker obsolescence. It can create a bad image on the service. He is also unlikely to benefit from any building subsidies or cheap loans – available for the new tonnage in certain countries – despite the fact that the shipowner may be involved in a conversion of the second-hand tonnage. Nevertheless, it may be ideal to start a new service to test market potential and thereby involve the shipowner in a low risk capital project.

Other significant advantages and disadvantages of second-hand tonnage are detailed below:

(a) On completion of the purchase the vessel is basically available for service commencement. However, usually the new owner wishes to have the ship painted to his own house flag colours plus undertake ship alterations to facilitate the economic deployment of the vessel. For example, a new section could be inserted in the vessel to lengthen her and increase cargo accommodation. The extent of such alterations will depend on the trade, age and condition of the vessel and capital availability. The paramount consideration will be the economics of the alterations and capital return of the investment.

(b) Second-hand tonnage is ideal to start a new service and in so doing enable the operator to test the market in a low-risk capital situation. In the event of the service proving successful, new tonnage can be introduced subsequently. Likewise, to meet a short-term traffic increase extending over 18/24 months, it may prove more economic to buy second-hand tonnage rather than charter. The advantage of charter is the vessel is ultimately returned to the owner to find employment although with some charters one can have an option to purchase on completion of the charter term.

(c)   Second-hand tonnage tends to be costly to operate in crewing and does not usually have the ideal ship specification, i.e. slow speed, limited cargo capacity, poor cargo transhipment facilities. Such shortcomings can be overcome by ship modification, but it is unlikely to produce the optimum vessel for the service. Ship insurance premium is likely to be high with older vessels, particularly over 15 years.

(d)   The vessel is likely to have a relatively short life and maintenance/survey/operating costs are likely to be high. If the ship registration is to be transferred from one national flag to another, this can prove costly as standards differ. Moreover, it is not always possible to assess accurately the cost involved until conversion work is in progress. Conversely depreciation is likely to be low.

(e)   Service quality could be rather indifferent whilst reliabilty/ schedule punctuality could be at risk. For example, the engines may be prone to breakdown and additional crew personnel may be required to keep them maintained to a high reliable standard.

An example of a new build/conversion is the Ro/Ro – container vessels of up to 16 000 dwt capacity. Moreover, tankers with no long-term employment prospects are being converted to bulk carriers and bulk carriers of modest size are being converted to other specialized dry cargo specifications.

Emerging from the *Herald of Free Enterprise* and *European Gateway* casualties, IMO work on revising the SOLAS Convention requirements for watertight doors in passenger ferries is nearing completion. Meanwhile, the revised Merchant Shipping (Closing of openings in hulls and in watertight bulkheads) Regulations came in to force in November, 1988.

Often when a vessel is uneconomical to operate in one trade, it can be converted for other uses. This may involve lengthening the ship by inserting a portion amidships. In the past decade many oil tankers, too small and slow for the petroleum trade, have been lengthened and converted to ore carriers and other trades. This trend also involving other cargo tonnage, will continue as the economics of higher capacity ships becomes increasingly attractive. More recently some ore carriers have been fitted with demountable skeleton decks and ramp facilities to convey trade cars.

Study also Chapter 3 of *Economics of Shipping Practice and Management* (see also pp. 443–4).

CHAPTER 4

Ships and their cargoes

4.1 TYPES OF SHIPS

The type of merchant vessel employed on a trade route is determined basically by the traffic carried. Broadly speaking there are three main divisions: liners, tramps and specialized vessels such as tankers.

On occasions, and in particular when merchant vessels in one division are underemployed, a number may be transferred to another division. For example, a tramp may be put on a liner berth to compete for liner cargoes. Conversely, liners may at times carry tramp cargoes, either as full or part cargoes.

During the past decade there has been a trend towards the development of the multi-purpose vessel and the combined transport system. The need for the multi-purpose vessel has arisen to combat trade fluctuations and enable the vessel to become more flexible in her operation. Not only can the vessel vary the cargo

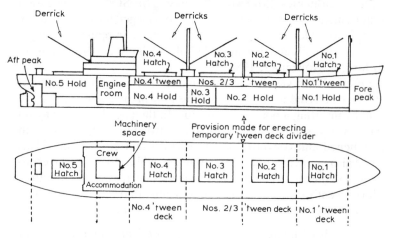

Fig. 4.1 SD-14 Mark IV 15 000 dwt general cargo vessel.

Table 4.1 World and UK owned and registered fleets (100 GRT and above) and average age at 31 December 1986 and 30 June 1988

Type	World 1986 No.	000 dwt	Average Age	World 1988 No.	000 dwt	Average Age	UK 1986 No.	000 dwt	Average Age	UK 1988 No.	000 dwt	Average Age
Cellular container	1 053	21 451	8.9	1 075	22 978	9.5	47	1 298	12.1	43	1 265	14.9
Ore/bulk carrier	4 945	194 889	9.9*	5 117*	230 744	10.8	62	2 234	7.8*	47*	2 174	8.7
Combination carrier	363	39 113	11.9	–	–	–	2	455	12.5	–	–	–
Other dry	21 833	108 706	–	21 325	104 512	–	428	1 333	–	401	1 069	–
Total Dry Cargo	28 194	364 160	–	27 517	358 234	–	539	5 320	–	491	4 509	–
Tanker	7 495	252 039	10.3	7 631	251 358	12.4	189	5 263	10	160	4 070	12.8
Liquefied gas carrier	765	9 995	–	772	9 999	–	11	204	–	12	173	–
Total Tanker	8 260	262 034		8 403	261 358	–	200	5 467	–	172	4 242	–
Total Fleet	36 454	626 194	11.6	35 920	619 592	12.2	739	10 787	10.5	663	8 751	12.3

Sources: GCBS
* Includes combination carriers

mixture capacity on a particular voyage, but also she can switch from one trade to another. Such tonnage, although more expensive to build, should enable the volume of laid-up tonnage to fall. Examples of multi-purpose tonnage are found particularly in the vehicular ferry (Fig. 4.5, p.61), and container vessel plus an increasing number of combination bulk cargo vessels including the tramp vessels as found in the SD-14s (Fig. 4.1) and Freedom-type tonnage (Fig. 3.3).

The escalation in bunkering cost particulariy in 1973 and 1979 gave new impetus to the development of the international combined transport system. This includes the through international road haulage operation, the train ferry and containerization. This trend is likely to continue in a period of developing unitization of transport on an international scale.

In examining the type of vessels available, it is appropriate to consider the world fleet in 1986 and 1988 by type and age (see Table 4.1). A description of each division follows.

4.2 LINERS

These are vessels that ply on a regular scheduled service between groups of ports. The student should note that it is this function, and not the size or speed, which defines the liner. Liner services offer cargo space to all shippers who require them. They sail on scheduled dates, irrespective of whether they are full or not. Hence, in liner operation the regular scheduled service is the basis of this particular division, and it is vitally important to the ship-owner that everything is done to have punctual sailing and arrival dates, otherwise his prestige will quickly decline. Liner operation involves an adequately sized fleet, and a fairly large shore establishment. The liner company therefore tends to be a large concern and in more recent years operating container tonnage on a consortia basis. However, there still remains a small volume of 'tween-deck break-bulk cargo vessels in service particularly in the sub-Continent, Orient area, the developing countries, and COMECON.

Cargo liners, or freighters as they are often called, are ships designed to carry general cargo. Such vessels operate on fixed routes, serving a group of ports and operate on fixed sailing schedules – the vessel departing whether she is full or not. This division constitutes one of the most important and largest categories of world tonnage, and provides a network of services throughout the world. The vessels which convey general cargo operate not only in deep sea and Mediterranean trades, but also in the short sea and coastal trades. Their capacity varies from 200 dwt with two holds in the short sea and coastal trades, to 20 000 dwt with six holds or more, in the Mediterranean and deep sea trades. Their speed varies from 13 to 22 knots in the deep sea and Mediterranean trades where the majority of the liners are found. A large volume of such tonnage is container vessels or Combi carriers capable of conveying containers, unitized cargo, vehicular cargo, liquid bulk cargo in deep tanks and so on. Such vessels require specialized berths and efficient port infrastructure much of which is computerized.

In the short sea trades, vehicular ferries often described as roll-on/roll-off ships carrying cars, passengers and road haulage vehicles are prominent.

4.3 TRAMPS

The tramp, or general trader as she is often called, does not operate on a fixed sailing schedule, but merely trades in all parts of the world in search of cargo, primarily bulk cargo. Such cargoes include coal, grain, timber, sugar, ores, fertilizers, copra etc., which are carried in complete shiploads. Many of the cargoes are seasonal. The tramp companies are much smaller than their liner cargo counterparts, and their business demands an intimate knowledge of market conditions.

Tramps are an unspecialized type of vessel with two to six holds, each with large unobstructed hatches, and primarily designed for the conveyance of bulk cargoes. Some ships are built with special facilities particularly suitable to the five main tramp trades: grain, coal, bauxite, phosphates and iron ore.

A typical modern tramp vessel is the SD-14. She has a crew of 30, a speed of 15 knots and has 'tween deck accommodation. The ship is of 9100 GRT, with a NRT of 6100 and a loaded mean draught of 8.84 m. The vessel's length is 140 m and she has a beam of 21 m. Five holds are provided with the accommodation amidship aft. Each hold is served by derricks and total grain cubic capacity exceeds 764 000 ft^3. The total cargo deadweight tonnage is approximately 14 000. This vessel is very versatile both

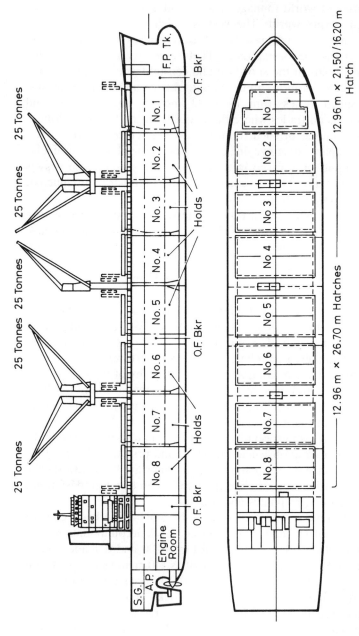

Fig. 4.2 Combi King 45 – flexible container/bulk carrier. This vessel of 45 000 dwt has a grain capacity of 58 700m³ or a container capacity of 2127 TEUs. It is suitable for worldwide trading in the bulk carriage of grain, coal, ore, bauxite, phosphates, packaged timber, standard pipe lengths and containers. (Reproduced by kind permission of British Shipbuilders Ltd)

operationally, and to the acceptance of the traditional tramp bulk cargoes, i.e. grain, timber, ore, coal etc.

Another example of a modern tramp vessel and of Japanese build is the Freedom-type tonnage. This vessel combines the essential features of a single deck bulk cargo carrier with those of a closed shelter deck ship. It is able to operate efficiently in dry cargo trades such as grain, coal, potash, phosphate rock, bauxite and iron ore cargoes, as well as general cargoes, palletized and container cargoes. The vessel has four holds with accommodation aft and crew of 30. She has a speed of 14 knots, an overall length of 145 m, a beam of 21 m and loaded mean draught of 9 m. This ship has a grain cubic capacity of 705 000 and a cargo deadweight tonnage of 15 000. Both the SD-14s and 'Freedom'-type vessels are multi-purpose dry cargo carriers and a specification of each is found in Figs 3.3 and 4.1 (pp. 33 and 42).

An example of a modern flexible container/bulk carrier ship is found in Fig. 4.2. It has eight holds and a deadweight tonnage of 45 500 with a draught of 12.2 m. The service speed is 14 knots and the ship's overall length is 194.30 m. The cargo hold grain capacity is 58 700 m^3. Container capacity totals 2127 TEUs of which 1069 TEUs are above deck. It has one single 25 tonnes and two twin 25 tonnes electro hydraulic deck cranes all of which are fitted with grabs. The crew accommodation complement is 25 of which 9 are officers.

The vessel is suitable for worldwide trading in the bulk carriage of grain, coal, ore, bauxite, phosphates, packaged timber, standard pipe lengths and containers. The vessel is built by British Shipbuilders and called the Combi King 45-flexible Container/ Bulk carrier.

Tramp vessels are engaged under a document called a charter party, on a time or voyage basis.

The number of tramp vessels has fallen during the past decade and similarly the number of tramp companies, as such companies, often family-owned, have tended to merge. Nevertheless the total volume of tramp tonnage remains fairly stable as larger capacity vessels are introduced. The trend to have long-term time charters of 5 to 10 years' duration is becoming more popular. The tonnage involved is usually modern, purpose-built, of high capacity such as 100 000 dwt and involves a bulk cargo such as oil, ore, etc. An example of a modern multi-purpose general cargo ship is found in Fig 4.3.

4.4 SPECIALIZED VESSELS

A number of cargo ships are designed for carrying a particular commodity, or group of commodities. Such specialization is the result of demand, but its provision may also create a new demand depending on the extent of the market. Examples of such specialized vessels are ore carriers and sugar carriers. A description follows of the more usual types of ship, and in view of the preponderance of tankers in this group, these will be examined first.

During the period 1970 to 1978 there was a substantial increase of the world *tanker fleet* rising from 150 million dwt in 1970 to 352 million dwt in 1980 from which time it has started to rapidly decline. The latter trend is likely to continue through a world policy of conservation of energy resources, inflation of oil prices and substantial over-tonnaging of the world tanker fleet. By 1988 it was 261 million dwt or 42% of the world merchant fleet deadweight tonnage. This figure is likely to fall as the world dry cargo fleet grows through containerization (see Table 4.1). Nevertheless, the world tanker fleet will continue to remain very formidable. Some of the world's largest vessels are tankers, a number of which exceed 400 000 dwt.

The world's tanker fleet is divided between tramp operators, which operate under a charter party, and those owned by the oil companies. By far the larger proportion is owned and operated by the oil companies and employed on regular routes, so that operation in this respect is similar to a liner operator. Most independently owned tankers are on long-term charter to the oil companies.

Crude oil is transported from the oilfields to refineries, and petroleum and fuel oil from refineries to distribution centres and bunkering ports, so that there is worldwide network of tanker routes.

In more recent years the oil producing countries have tended both to own and operate their own tanker fleet thereby having complete control over the distribution arrangements and costs. Moreover, they are shipping it as refined oil and not as they previously did, allowing major importing industrial nations to refine it and re-export it. Their income is thus improved.

The tanker is provided with two or three longitudinal bulkheads and many transverse bulkheads dividing the hull into numerous tanks. Each tank has a watertight hatch and ventilator, and is connected by pipeline to pumping rooms. Machinery and crew accommodation are aft together with the navigating bridge. Extensive shore equipment is provided involving pumping apparatus.

A crude-oil tanker of 300 000 tonnes would have seven tanks and a draught of 22 m. The service speed would be of 16 knots and the overall vessel length 350 m with a breadth of 56 m.

The tanker is thus a very specialized vessel. It is designed to deal with bulk liquid cargoes permitting quick loading and discharge, thereby ensuring the fast turn-rounds so essential to good utilization. Vessels return in ballast as it is seldom possible to obtain return cargoes. During recent years, however, a number of ships have been built capable of carrying ore and oil, and therefore the vessel is able to be loaded in both directions, i.e. in one direction oil and in another iron ore. These vessels are somewhat limited in their operations, as such trades exist on only a few routes, and generally cannot compete with the specialized ship – where the ultra large crude carrier (ULCC) has emerged.

The long-term development is likely to be in the specialist oil product carrier field between 30 000 and 80 000 dwt range. There is unlikely to be any new building in the foreseeable future of ULCC (ultra large crude carrier) and VLCC (very large crude carrier), particularly the latter.

(a) Barge carrier

An increasing number of ocean-going barge carriers are now in operation throughout the world and we will examine three: Baco liners, LASH and SEABEE.

The Baco liner concept in common with the other similar types has been introduced to reduce port delays and is in operation between Europe and West Africa. The vessel has a capacity of 21 000 dwt and may convey 500 TEUs including some refrigerated containers, and twelve barges all accommodated below deck. The Baco liner has a length of 205 m, and breadth of 29 m, with a speed of 15 knots and draught of 6.7 m. The barge deck is divided into two by a watertight centre line bulkhead, loading six of the barges each 24 m long, 9.5 m breadth and 800 dwt capacity. Each vessel has three sets of twelve barges. Containers are carried on the upper deck. A 40–tonne gantry crane is provided for heavy lifts conveyed on deck.

The LASH (lighter-aboard-ship)-type of vessel emerged in the late 1960s and a limited number are now operating throughout the world. The ship is of 44 000 dwt and has a capacity of 73 barges with about 27 000 tons of cargo – each lighter has a capacity of about 400 tons of cargo. This new type of ship enables lighters to be carried from one port to another, thus combining inland waterway with ocean transportation. Each lighter is hauled on board over the stern by a 510–ton travelling gantry crane and then dropped into the desired position on the ship. The holds can be converted overnight so that the LASH vessel can carry up to 1400 standard ISO 20-ft containers. The vessel has a speed of 19 knots and two such ships would serve a fleet of 400 barges. After off-loading in the ports the barges are towed along the various inland waterways, providing a form of door-to-door service with a high-speed delivery. Advantages of the service include through rates/ bills of lading; no intermediate handling during transfer to and from the ship, thereby reducing cost and permitting competitive rates to be quoted and faster transits attained; lower insurance premiums; less risk damage/pilferage; low risk of cargo delay as the barges are lowered into water immediately on arrival at each port and likewise the barges are loaded on the LASH vessel, thus reducing time spent in port or its environs to a minimum. Moreover, through the individual barges serving a variety of ports, it permits the LASH vessel to rationalize severely the ports of call to maintain good ship utilization.

The SEABEE vessels accommodate containers on the upper deck and the barges below deck. The concept is similar to the LASH system.

(b) Coal carriers
Coal carriers are designed to convey such cargo in bulk in deep-sea trades. An example of modern tonnage is the 75 000 tonne carrier in the Australian trade. It is likely vessels of 100 000 tonnes dead-weight could be operative in some deep-sea trades by the early 1990s.

(c) Coasters
These are all-purpose cargo carriers, operating around our coasts. They are normally provided with two holds, each supplied with derricks to handle a variety of cargoes. Machinery and crew accommodation are aft. In common with the colliers, described in

the next paragraph, the coasters are subject to severe inland transport competition.

(d) Colliers

These are designed to convey coal around our coasts. They have two unobstructed holds. No derricks are provided and the mast and funnels are frequently hinged, to permit the vessel to go under bridges when travelling upstream. Engines and crew accommodation are usually aft. In recent years, the number of colliers has sharply declined, due to the reduced volume of coastal coal traffic.

(e) Combi carrier

To cater for the need to improve ship turn-round time, versatility of vessel employment and to contain operating cost, an increasing number of vessels are now being introduced called Combi carriers as illustrated in Fig. 4.7. Such vessels are superseding 'tween-deck tonnage and essentially are a unitized type of cargo carrier combining container and vehicular shipments including Ro/Ro.

The Combi vessel in the diagram is operated by the DFDS Norland Line in the US Gulf – US East Coast – Mediterranean/ Central American trade and is called an Omni carrier. The ship has an overall length of 135 m and beam of 25 m with an NRT of 1714 and GRT of 4496. Her draught is 6.68 m and dwt (metric) 8000. The vessel has a container capacity of 516 TEUs with 264 TEUs on the upper deck, 216 TEUs on the main deck and 36 TEUs on the lower deck. The ship has a lane capacity of 563 m on the upper deck, 603 m on the main deck, and 250 m on the lower hold. The car deck area totals 212 m^2 on the main deck and 293 m^2 in the lower hold. The cargo conveyed will vary by individual sailing and be a mixture of containers and vehicle traffic as illustrated in the diagram. This aids flexibility of ship operation and ensures the best use is made of the available vessel capacity having regard to market demand.

The vessel is equipped with two derricks of 36 tons and 120 tons thereby aiding the transhipment of heavy indivisible loads which are much on the increase. By using a medium/heavy duty mobile crane on the quay it is possible to load and discharge at the same time with the vessel using its own gear for loading/discharging through the lift hatch. Loading containers or other cargo is through the aft hatch. A high capacity fork lift is available for stowing on the main deck. The vessel has a crew of 30.

The stern ramp is 14 m long and has a flap of 4.2 m. The width of the ramp is 8.5 m at the shore-based end. It can be used for fast loading/discharging of containers on trailers or by heavy fork lifts operating with 20-ft containers athwartships.

The spacious main deck may be used for awkward shaped goods, e.g. building cranes, offshore and refinery equipment, pre-fab building components etc. The clear height of 6.3 m on the main deck allows double stacking of containers each up to 9 ft 6 in high.

Special suspension hooks underneath the lift provide an additional lifting facility of 60 tons for the transfer of units onto trailers. Containers are placed on trailers for transfer by lift to the lower hold. The lift hatch when required serves as a third point of access for loading/discharging cargo by use of the shore crane.

A side door of 7.5 × 4.0 m width is provided which allows simultaneous operation by two fork lifts handling palletized cargo. The wide side door also allows truck loading or the discharge of large items. Containers of 20 ft length can also be handled through the side door.

Advantages of the Combi carrier can be summarized as follows:

(a) It has a versatile cargo mixture permitting a variation of unitized cargo to be conveyed plus the awkward shaped cargo. This is a major advantage in the cargo liner field where more consignments are indivisible loads.

(b) The range of cargo transhipment facilities on the vessel, i.e. derricks, stern ramp, side doors etc., aid quick transhipment and is virtually independent of quay transhipment facilities. This improves the ship versatility particularly in ports where cargo transhipment facilities are virtually non-existent. It also reduces the cost of using port equipment.

(c) Good shipboard cargo transhipment facilites quicken the ship turn-round time and improve ship utilization/efficiency.

(d) The vessel specification, i.e. draught, beam, length is an optimum ideal for a wide range of ports and thereby generates versatility of ship employment and operation world wide.

(e) The vessel is able to convey a wide variety of cargo at economical cost including particularly ease of handling.

(f) The ship's specification facilities reduce port congestion as the vessel is independent with her handling equipment. Furthermore, for example, the 200 ton capacity stern ramp requires only 30 m of quay space.

The foregoing explanation of the Combi carrier specification as illustrated in the diagram demonstrates the versatility of the vessel and undoubtedly it will become more common as we progress through the 1990s particularly in the liner cargo deep-sea trades involving less-developed nation's seaboards.

(f) Container vessels

These are becoming increasingly predominant in many cargo liner trades and such tonnage has been described in Chapter 4 together with Fig. 3.5. The merits of containerization are described in Chapter 16. There is no doubt that this type of tonnage which permits complete integration with other forms of transport, thereby offering a door-to-door service, will become more popular annually and by the early 1990s maybe 95% of the tonnage on liner cargo services will be containerized. In the long run they should help to keep costs to a minimum and somewhat below the displaced 'tween-deck tonnage, thereby helping to stimulate international trade.

A modern container vessel today would have a capacity of 2000 containers of which 60% would be conveyed under deck and the residue on deck. A substantial proportion of the containers may be refrigerated for which under-deck hold accommodation facilities would be provided. The vessel would be of 33 300 tonnes and have an overall length of 250 m with a beam of 33 m. Her draught would be 12 m and service speed 22 knots.

More recently the multi-purpose type of container vessel has been developed with an integral ramp being provided as part of the ship's equipment. This permits both container and vehicular cargo to be conveyed and enables flexibility of berth/port operation as no portal is required.

(g) Fruit carriers

These are similar in design to refrigerated vessels. Cool air systems are installed in the holds to keep the fruit from over-ripening. Such vessels convey apples, oranges, bananas, and are often owned by the cargo owners. Fast voyage times are essential, otherwise the fruit over-ripens and deteriorates.

(h) LNG

The development of the liquefied natural gas (LNG) carrier in the past few years has been very significant. A typical vessel has crew accommodation and machinery aft. Cargo is contained in maybe nine prismatic internally insulated aluminium tanks, three of which are fitted into each of the three holds. To keep the gas in liquid form, it must be kept down to a minus 161°C (–258°F). The inside of the holds are insulated with panels of balsa wood lined with plywood. The plywood lining keeps the gas from escaping if a tank leakage should occur. The tanks are constructed of aluminium or nickel steel. Some vessels are equipped with self-supporting rectangular or spherical-shaped independent tanks (Fig. 4.3). Others incorporate a semi-membrane type fleet tank. The tanks jut out above the deck and about 40% of the cargo is carried above this level. In these carriers the gas 'boiling off' can be used to fuel the ship's boilers. Such vessels have very high initial cost. A modern LNG carrier of 125 000 m³ would have a draught of 11 m, a length of 277 m and a breadth of 42 m. This ship would have a speed of 20 knots. By 1988, there were 772 LNGs of total dwt 9 999 000.

(i) Multi-purpose general cargo ship

An example of a modern multi-purpose general cargo ship is found in Fig. 4.3. It has four holds and a deadweight tonnage of 21 500 with a draught of 10.75 m. The vessel's overall length is 155.5 m and the service speed is 15.3 knots. The cargo hold grain capacity is 30 340 m³ and bale capacity 27 950 m³. The container capacity is 746 TEUs of which some 408 TEUs is above deck. The crew accommodation complement is 25 of which 9 are officers. The vessel has two single 25 tonnes and one twin 25 tonnes electro-hydraulic deck cranes.

The vessel is suitable for worldwide trading in general cargoes, dry bulk, long steel products, grain cargoes and containers. The vessel is built by British Shipbuilders and called the Multi King 22-multi purpose general cargo ship.

(j) OBO

Ore/bulk/oil ships are multi-purpose bulk carriers designed for switching between bulk shipments of oil, bulk grain, fertilizer and ore trades. They were first introduced in the mid-1960s and many of them exceed 200 000 dwt. This type of vessel with engines aft is growing in popularity and will have a profound effect on tramping

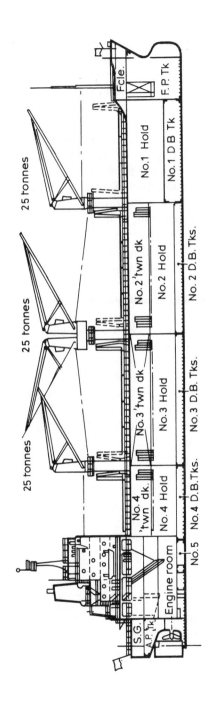

Fig. 4.3 Multi King 22—multipurpose general cargo vessel. The vessel is of 21 500 dwt. It has a cargo hold grain capacity of 30 340m³, a bale capacity of 27 950m³ or container capacity of 746 TEUs. The vessel is suitable for worldwide trading in general cargoes, dry bulk, long steel products, grain cargoes and containers. (Reproduced by kind permission of British Shipbuilders Ltd)

as it will probably bring a new and more profitable era to this important shipping division. A typical vessel would have an overall length of 280 m, draught of 17 m and of 270 000 dwt. Her dry cargo capacity would be 170 000 m^3 whilst her oil capacity totals 224 000 m^3. Cargo space is provided in eleven holds to carry oil of which seven can ship dry cargo or ore as an alternative shipment. Crew accommodation and machinery – much automated – is situated aft. Such vessels although of high initial cost are very flexible in their use, keeping ballast voyages to a minimum and of course ideal for modern day requirements in international trade, which demand high capacity (optimum-sized) vessels to move world bulk shipments at a very low cost per ton. The development of the combination bulk carrier is likely to continue through the 1990s.

Ore carriers are provided with long wide hatches over the self-trimming large holds. By using longitudinal bulkheads, wing holds or tanks are provided which are used for water ballast when the vessel is returning light to the loading areas. The depth of the double-bottom tanks is greater than in other vessels, so as to raise the centre of gravity, because a low centre of gravity will give a 'stiff' effect in heavy seas. The machinery is situated aft, together with crew accommodation and navigation bridge. Cargo-handling gear is not provided, as loading and discharging is undertaken by mechanical shore-based gear. This may be in the form of conveyor belts (self-unloaders), magnetic loaders, or grabs. These vessels are particularly renowned for speedy loading and discharging, permitting a quick turn-round. Today some of the largest ships afloat are ore carriers and frequently exceed 100 000 dwt. Specialized terminals are required which are frequently away from the general port area or situated at a private terminal. Such vessels are often integrated with an industrial process programme demanding a reliable regular shipment schedule, without which industrial production is jeopardized; at modern terminals they can be loaded at the rate of 3500 tons per hour.

(k) Parcel tankers

This type of ship is designed to carry shipments including chemicals, petroleum products, edible oils and molasses. Vessels of this type vary in size but have a capacity range between 30 000 and 80 000 dwt.

(l) Passenger vessels
These fall into two distinct divisions. There are those which
operate in the short sea trade and have limited cabin accommodation. They also convey motorist and Ro/Ro (roll-on/roll-off)
units. This type of vessel of up to 9000 GRT is described on p. 29.

The other division concerns the cruise market where vessels of
up to 30 000 GRT are found. Such passenger liners are designed
with each passenger allocated a cabin or berth. Adequate lounges,
entertainment, restaurant, etc. facilities are provided. Italy has the
largest passenger fleet. An example of a modern passenger cruise
liner built in 1987 is the MV Star Princess; she has a capacity of
2 600, and is illustrated in Fig. 4.4.

(m) Pure car and truck carriers (PCTC).
This type of tonnage is designed for the conveyance of cars,
lorries/trucks and other wheeled units. A modern PCTC has
thirteen decks and can convey between 5 500 and 5 800 cars or a
permutation of 3 200 cars and 600 trucks. Such tonnage can also
convey containers on 20 ft (6.10 m) or 40 ft (12.2 m) long Mafi
trailers. A major operator in this field is Wallenius Lines Ltd
which has a 19-vessel fleet of PCTC providing a worldwide service
embracing Far East, North America and European markets.

(n) Refrigerated vessels
These are designed for the carriage of chilled or frozen* meat,
butter or eggs. Such vessels operate on liner cargo services, and
are provided with large insulated holds with refrigerating machinery to maintain the cargo in good condition.

(o) Ro/Ro vessels
A Ro/Ro type of vessel was developed after the Second World
War, and is frequently termed a vehicle ferry. It was designed for
the conveyance of road haulage vehicles and private cars. At each
terminal, a ramp or link span is provided enabling the vehicle to
drive on or off the vessel. This, of course, eliminates cranage and
permits a quick turnround. It also permits through-transits,
eliminates cargo-handling, and reduces pilferage to a minimum.
This type of vessel operates primarily in the short sea trade, and is
growing in popularity. Such vessels, when designed to carry private

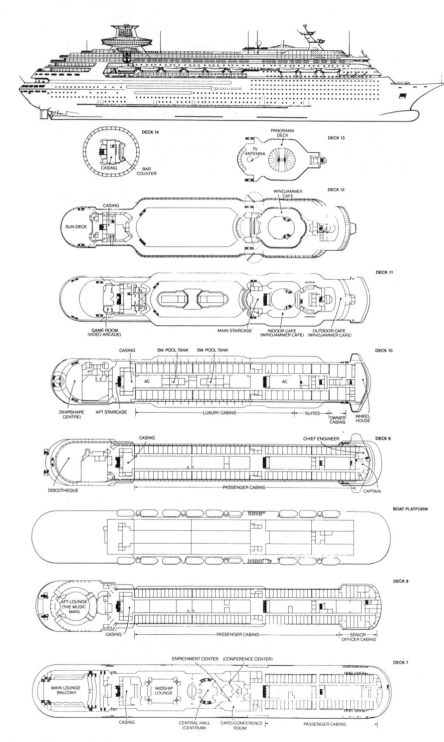

Fig. 4.4 Profile and general arrangement plans of the 74 000 grt RCCL cruise ship. The vessel, owned by the Royal Caribbean Cruise Line, has a

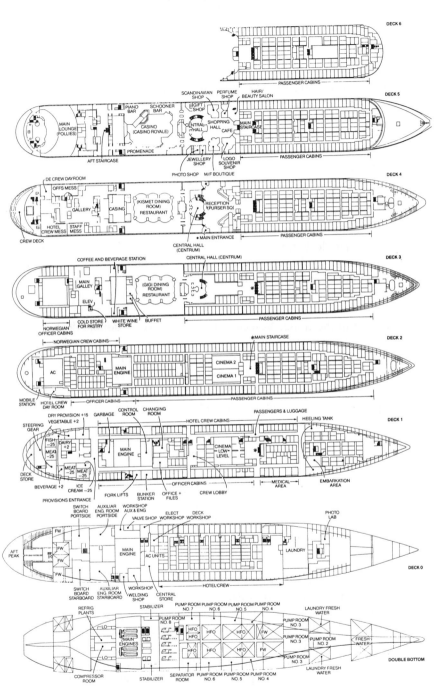

passenger certificate of 2600, and 1140 passenger cabins. The ship has an overall length of 269 m a moulded breadth of 33 m and a draught of 7.5 m. The vessel was launched in 1987 and has thirteen decks. The vessel serves the Caribbean cruise market, and is called the MV *Star Princess*. (Reproduced by kind permission of Alsthom and the Royal Caribbean Cruise Line) cars with their passengers, coaches, road-haulage vehicles and non-motorist passengers, are called multi-purpose vehicular ferries.

There is no doubt as we progress through the 1990s Ro/Ro tonnage or a combination with other types of vessel will increase, thereby exploiting the economics of the combined transport system concept. An example of a Ro/Ro vessel is found in Fig. 4.5 and such vessels have two decks to permit simultaneous loading/unloading. In some deep sea trades there are four decks or more.

An example of a typical vehicular ferry is the MV *St. Anselm* (Fig. 4.6) operative in the Dover/Calais trade and commissioned in late 1980. She has a passenger certificate of 1000 passengers. Her vehicular deck capacity is 309 cars or 62 × 12 m road haulage vehicles or a mixture of the two. Cargo transhipment takes place at both deck levels simultaneously thereby aiding quick turnround of vessels which can be achieved in about one hour. The two deck levels are a feature of this tonnage and represent a new breed of vessel in the trade. Vehicles are loaded over a double deck shore ramp through doors located in the bow or stern of the ship. The MV *St. Anselm* has a service speed of 19 knots and length of 129.4 m with breadth of 21.6 m. She has a crew of 72 and tonnage details include 8200 GRT, 3170 NRT, and 1920 dwt. Details of the ship specifications are found in Fig. 4.6 featuring athwartship section at frame 120.

Ro/Ro combination is now found in the container vessel field as found in Fig. 4.7, p. 64. This particular vessel termed an Omni carrier has a length overall of 140 m, a beam of 23 m and capacity of 8000 dwt. It can accommodate some 516 TEUs, and has a Ro/Ro deck lane capacity of 1416 m. Car deck area totals 505 m². The ramp, which is hydraulically operated, is situated at the stern and has a load capacity of 200 tons. The crane is of 36-tons lifting capacity and the mast/derrick is of 120-tons lifting capacity. A lift of 60-tons capacity is provided to permit inter-deck movement/stowage of cargo within the vessel.

Another example of a Ro/Ro (roll-on/roll-off) – Lo/Lo (lift-on/lift-off) vessel is one of 17 000 dwt, with an overall length of 140 m. The moulded breadth is 23 m and she has a speed of 16 knots. The ship has a Ro/Ro lane capacity of 1300 m and 600 TEUs container capacity. Hold capacity totals 27 000 m³. The vessel has a stern ramp, internal fixed ramps, electro-hydraulic cranes, and hydraulically operated hatch covers. Liquid cargoes (latex or similar) can be

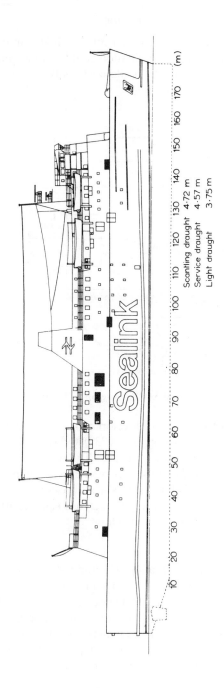

Scantling draught 4·72 m
Service draught 4·57 m
Light draught 3·75 m

Fig. 4.5 Vehicular ferry

conveyed in the foretanks. Such a vessel offers a high cargo mix versatility. Hence such a cargo combination could include general break bulk cargo, which could be palletized; bulk cargo, containers, trailers, cars and Ro/Ro cargo.

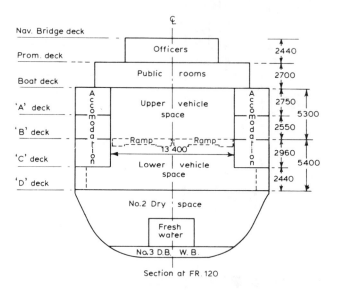

Fig. 4.6 Athwartships section of MV *St Anselm*, a Ro/Ro vessel.

A further example of the Ro/Ro development in the deep sea sector and of a combination carrier, is the 33 000 dwt Ro/Ro ship operative in the Canadian/Japanese trade. The vessels convey packaged timber from Canada whilst Japanese cars are conveyed on the return leg. The vessels have a 3600-car capacity.

All the three vessels types are likely to increase significantly in many liner cargo trades in the next decade.

(p) Sugar ships

These are designed with self-trimming longitudinal sub-divisions with wing holds, the latter being used for ballast purposes. Such vessels are served by special mechanical shore gear incorporating grab equipment capable of handling up to 20 tons per minute, which ensures quick turn-round. The engines are situated aft to provide additional cargo space, and also to prevent the sugar drying out in after-holds, due to heat from machinery spaces.

(q) Timber carriers

These are provided with large unobstructed holds and large hatches to facilitate cargo handling. They are frequently called three-island vessels and incorporate a raised forecastle, bridge and poop, thereby facilitating stowage of deck cargo which is now packaged.

(r) Train ferries

These have been aptly described as floating moveable bridges. In design, they are in many ways similar to the Ro/Ro type of vessel, except, of course, that they carry railway passenger and freight rolling stock. Railway track is provided on the main deck. At each terminal a link span is provided, which enables the rolling stock to be propelled on or drawn off the vessel. This eliminates cranage and facilitates a quick turn-round. Additionally, it permits through-transits, dispenses with cargo-handling and reduces damage and pilferage to a minimum.

(s) Very large crude carriers (VLCCs)

Such oil-carrying vessels exceed 200 000 dwt of which there were in 1980 in excess of 140 tankers. Subsequently vessels in excess of 350 000 dwt have emerged which classify as the ultra large crude carrier (ULCC). Such tanker tonnage has presented numerous problems over many fields embracing safety/operation/structural. Nevertheless these have been largely overcome and the trade has benefited economically from such tonnage. Crew accommodation and machinery is situated aft and there may exist a fully integrated manoeuvring and navigating system. Many such vessels are equipped with bow and stern thrusters to improve manoeuvrability.

Our study of ship types would not be complete without mention of the hovercraft, hydrofoil and jetfoil type of craft which are primarily orientated towards the passenger market involving the estuarial and short sea trades.

(t) The hovercraft

This was developed in the early 1960s and operates on a cushion of air above the water. Early versions were primarily confined to estuarial services and land/river exploration work. As technical improvements were realized, general operational reliability improved and the craft became of larger capacity. Particular

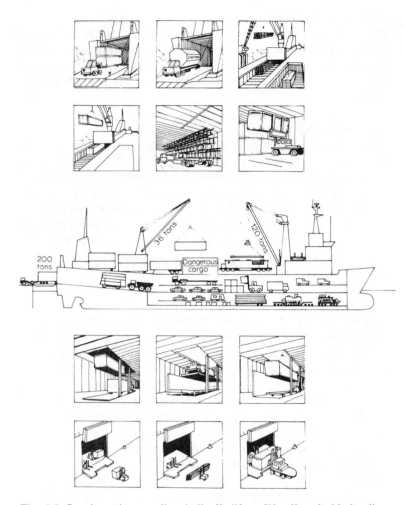

Fig. 4.7 Omni carrier – roll-on/roll-off, lift-on/lift-off and side-loading Combi carrier.

attention has been given to improving the skirt of the hovercraft. The largest ones operate in short sea trade as found on the Dover/Calais–Boulogne routes and carry passengers and cars. A typical craft would have a 450-passenger, and 60-car capacity with a service speed of 65 knots.

(u) The hydrofoii
This was developed in the early 1960s and is propelled by water jet with fully submerged foils and an automatic control system to provide a jet-smooth ride at 40 knots even in rough water. A modern craft would have two decks with an overall passenger capacity of 300 and speed of 50 knots. Many operate between the Greek islands.

(v) The jetfoil
This craft emerged in the early 1970s as a commercial craft. It is an advanced design high-speed hydrofoil. Basically it is a ship whose weight is supported by foils which produce lift by virtue of their shape and forward velocity through the water in the same manner as an airplane wing. There are two types of hydrofoils; those with surface-piercing foils and those with fully submerged foils. The surface-piercing foil has inherent stability but it is greatly affected by wave disturbances. The fully submerged foil is affected to a much smaller degree by wave disturbances and produces a much more comfortable ride as a result.

The passenger capacity can range from 150 to 400 passengers depending on the craft range. On a 36-mile schedule the capacity would be 260 passengers which would fall to 190 passengers on a 100-mile route.

Present indications suggest that the hovercraft is not likely to improve on its operational performance in terms of faster schedules, whilst the hydrofoil could attain a speed of up to 60 knots. However, new generations of the hovercraft should produce more simple design, much increased capacity and substantially reduced overall operating cost. Reliability should also be much improved.

The hydrofoil offers great passenger comfort but less reliability in terms of operating in adverse weather conditions.

The impact of these developments must be viewed against the conventional passenger vessel operating in such estuarial and short sea trades. It is possible these developments would reduce the passenger and to some extent the motorist carryings on such vessels. It would not affect the Ro/Ro tonnage market.

4.5 CALIBRATED AUTOMATIC PILOTING SYSTEM

It is perhaps appropriate to conclude our examination of ships of the previous three chapters by looking at the calibrated automatic piloting system (CAPS). It enables ships and other floating vessels to follow a set track or to keep on station with high accuracy. It also provides computer-aided control functions.

The control system is based on state-of-the-art automatic control engineering techniques. An optimized track is first computed, allowing for all ship-originated constraints. A complete model of the ship and propulsion system is then used to evaluate the effect of a series of command vectors on the displacement of the vessel relative to the optimized track. Finally, the vessel is piloted on the basis of selected command vectors in real time, and with continuous interaction with the immediate positioning data input. The use of models, which include non-linear variations of the system parameters, enables the autopilot to operate under a wide range of operating conditions without operator intervention.

The performance of a given ship and propulsion system is greatly improved, and high accuracy of tracking or station-keeping is achieved.

With this system it is also possible to keep control of the ship after complete loss of position data, during the time necessary to introduce emergency procedures in all safety.

The dynamic positioning can be fitted with all kinds of position reference sensors: taut wires, acoustic radio, radio navigation, satellite or inertial navigation systems.

CAPS also provides: continuous calculation of the most favourable heading in station-keeping mode; a control system for manoeuvres in manual-assisted mode, with forces and moment instructions input to the console; and automatic checks facilitating maintenance procedures. This system has been developed by Alcatel.

CHAPTER 5

Manning of vessels

The manning of vessels is an extensive subject, and this chapter is intended only to cover its most important aspects. Ship manning today forms a very important part of the shipping industry complex in an increasingly competitive cost-conscious situation. New technology is being introduced whilst economic change is continuous. Moreover, seafarers' standards both in ship accommodation terms and navigation/engineering/catering techniques are rising. Overall seafarers' shipboard living standards are improving.

A major factor influencing manning cost is the change in the disposition of the world mercantile fleet as Table 5.1 reveals. It confirms the rapid rise of the Liberian, Panamanian and Cypriot fleets all of which are flags of convenience.

A major problem internationally is the differing wage scales offered to seafarers worldwide which makes it very difficult to compete on equal crew cost terms. On the one hand one has the Eastern hemisphere countries like Russia, the Philippines, India and China offering low wage scales, whilst the industrialized nations of West Germany, Holland, UK, USA, etc. offer much higher salaries.

To counter this an increasing number of shipowners are flagging out their fleets. This includes UK, Japan, Greece, Norway, US and West Germany. This involves transferring the flag to a nation which has lower crew cost and fringe benefits plus overall tax benefits to the Shipping Company. This tends to counter the very high competitive crew cost in high labour cost maritime fleets. Such offshore registries are situated in the Isle of Man, Bermuda or Hong Kong. The shipowner either negotiates 'offshore' agreements with the British seafarers unions through foreign associate companies or hands over the manning of their ships to international manning agencies. By the end of 1986 over 50% of

Table 5.1 Ten largest fleets 1983 to 30th June 1988 (100 gross registered tonnes and above)

Flag	Position 1983	1984	1985	1986	1988	31 Dec 83 m dwt	31 Dec 84 m dwt	31 Dec 85 m dwt	31 Dec 86 m dwt	30 Jun. 88 m dwt	1983 % of World	1984 % of World	1985 % of World	1986 % of World	1988 % of World
Liberia	1	1	1	1	1	123.0	118.1	113.1	97.8	93.6	18.3	17.7	17.3	15.6	15.1
Panama	4	2	2	2	2	57.7	64.4	66.1	69.0	70.6	8.6	9.7	10.1	11.0	11.4
Japan	3	3	3	3	3	63.2	62.0	62.1	55.8	47.0	9.4	9.3	9.5	8.9	7.6
Greece	2	4	4	4	4	65.8	59.5	55.2	46.0	39.6	9.8	8.9	8.4	7.3	6.4
Norway	5	5	5	–	–	31.5	27.5	25.2	–	–	4.7	4.1	3.8	–	–
USA	6	6	6	5	6	25.0	24.9	24.9	25.1	26.4	3.7	3.7	3.8	4.0	4.3
USSR	8	7	7	6	7	22.4	23.1	22.9	23.4	23.8	3.3	3.5	3.5	3.7	3.8
UK (owned and registered)	7	8	8	–	7	23.2	19.7	19.0	–	10.3	3.5	3.0	2.9	–	1.7
China	–	–	9	8	8	–	–	15.5	17.9	18.9	–	–	2.4	2.9	3.1
Cyprus	–	–	10	7	5	–	–	14.3	23.4	32.8	–	–	2.2	3.7	5.3
Hong Kong	–	–	–	9	–	–	–	–	13.7	–	–	–	–	2.2	–
Philippines	–	–	–	10	9	–	–	–	13.7	15.4	–	–	2.5	2.2	2.5
Bahamas	–	–	–	–	10	–	–	–	–	14.9	–	–	–	–	2.4

Source: GCBS

UK tonnage was registered to offshore registries. A further partial solution is being sought by some industrial nations through reduced manning levels, but the scope is limited and one must bear in mind the continuing rising standards in seamanship competency certification. This expresses itself in the most recent agreement reached by IMO as detailed on p. 133 to raise the number of certificated crew personnel and dealt with elsewhere in this chapter. An example occurred in 1979 when IMO adopted at the convention on *standards of training*, the certification and watch-keeping for seafarers. Such international regulations ensure the man on the ship meets the standards required of him. The Convention received worldwide support and is further evidence of measures designed to raise seafaring navigation standards.

In attaining such crew complement reductions, one must reconcile the fact that vessels have tended to increase in size/capacity, and there has been greater automation particularly in the engine room/navigation aids. On the catering side many owners are using pre-prepared foods to aid catering crew reduction. These factors have tended to favour maritime nations who can finance new tonnage. Such crew reductions can only be attained without impairing safety standards. Moreover in some industrial maritime nations' fleets studies are being conducted in the field of ship maintenance, with a view to transferring the ship maintenance functions which were previously done ashore. This aids improved ship utilization, less time spent in port, more productive use of the crew and overall lower cost to the shipowner. Additionally the need to encourage more crew diversification continues. This has tended to eliminate the traditional demarcation lines found in the engineering, catering and deck departments. This is very common in modern container tonnage and foreign-going tankers. Moreover, the CGBS have revised the designation of certain rating personnel to raise productivity and status as described on p. 79.

An example of crew reductions being sought by industrial nations such as West Germany include new container tonnage introduced in the early 1980s of between 15 000 and 25 000 GRT. A crew of 25 would normally be associated with such tonnage but one of 13 seafarers is being sought. Each man will be versatile in job activity and the crew complement proposed would be composed of a master, two navigational and two technical officers, an electrician, four crew members, a cook, a steward and a radio operator. The officers and ratings would be trained in both deck and engine-room procedures. Machines would provide their morning coffee, wash and iron their clothes, wash the dishes and do much of the catering. Engines will be bridge controlled, and the officer on watch then would make use of a bridge computer which will also steer the vessel, work out the course, give position reports, warn of danger, collision, etc.

With the rising cost of fuel and need to contain ship operating cost the crew and fuel expenses now represent between 50 and 70% of voyage costs. The tendency is to encourage slower schedules where economic or practicable and quicker port turn-round times to lessen the impact overall. This means more pre-planning or cargo transhipment and less time for the crew to undertake their customary 'in-port' shipboard assignments, particularly ship maintenance.

Many more operators now have up to three crews assigned to a vessel and fly out and back crew personnel to all ports of the world to ensure the ship is in continuous operation. Modern ships have accommodation for wives to accompany their officer husbands. Again all these factors add to crew cost in an era of rising living standards.

In an era when shipowners are endeavouring to reduce their crew costs the following options exist other than flagging out as earlier described:

(i) Reduction of the crew to the minimum number required under legislation. This increases the workload on remaining crew personnel but ship maintenance and operation may suffer as a result. Further training to ensure the crew are familiar with automation can also be undertaken with a subsequent reduction in crew numbers.

(ii) Increase the voyage length and shortening leave periods. The utilization of crew can be improved by lengthening the duration of trips and shortening leave periods. This is particularly relevant to westernized tonnage crews. It can also extend to lower fringe benefits from which the seafarers can make his own arrangements for medical insurance and pension contributions. In the early and mid-1980s European crews enjoyed a two days on and one day off work/leave ratio which compared with Third World countries such as Philippines and North Korea having a 12-month continuous voyage contract. This not only provided longer trips but also reduction in repatriation cost: i.e. airflights, agency fees, etc – of crew per year. Hence much westernized tonnage has two crews in the short sea trade business.

(iii) An increasing number of shipowners are employing more low cost non-domiciled seafarers with their European crews. Often the officers would be European and the ratings Filopinos or North Koreans. Hence a vessel may have a ratings crew of 1.1/1.2 compared with an officer crew of 1.5/1.8.

(iv) The process of greater integration of crew personnel duties is likely to accelerate in the 1990s as the need to reduce crew cost becomes more significant and shipboard automation further develops. The duties of the ship Master and first mate, and chief engineer and second engineer could be integrated on tonnage where circumstances so allow.

In conclusion one must bear in mind the lower the crew complement and number of crews per ship, plus the longer the voyage length, the greater the cost savings. This applies to fringe benefits especially.

In studying this chapter one must bear in mind the foregoing arises at a time when it is vital for shipping costs to remain competitive to aid international trade development: crew cost has a vital role to play in this situation.

5.1 DUTIES AND RESPONSIBILITIES OF THE MASTER

It is a common but very wrong belief that the person in charge of a vessel is the Captain. This term is simply a naval rank. The correct term to be applied to the person in absolute charge of the vessel, which may be a large passenger liner like the *Queen Elizabeth II* or a relatively small cargo ship engaged in our coastal trade, is the Master.

The Master's duties and responsibilities are many, varied and extensive. He is the owner's personal representative, and bears the ultimate responsibility for the safe navigation of his vessel and for the efficient loading, stowage and discharge of cargo. Further- more, he has the power to act as a lawyer, a doctor and even to bury people. The Master may arrest members of the crew or passengers, if they constitute a nuisance during the voyage. In certain circumstances, particularly if the person is dangerous to other members of the ship, the Master may place the individual under restraint. In the event of any mutiny, any act of the Master is regarded as one entirely of self-defence, and he has the power to call on persons on board to render assistance. Similarly, if the ship is imperilled in any way, the Master may call upon all persons on board to give assistance.

In days past, he was also responsible for transacting the business of the ship in ports abroad. Nowadays, modern communications have enabled the owner to assume more direct supervision of the ship and her business abroad, so that the Master's responsibilities in this respect have narrowed.

Wide authority is vested in the Master and, under maritime law, acts done within the scope of his authority are binding on his owners. Under very rare circumstances, he is empowered by a 'bottomry bond' to pledge the vessel, and likewise by a 'respondentia bond', her cargo so that funds may be secured to permit the voyage to proceed.

It is therefore readily apparent that the Master's responsibilities and duties are very diverse. To hold the position of a Master, especially on a large passenger liner, is a much coveted appointment, and is the culmination of years of sea experience. He is required to hold a Master's Certificate (see p. 78), which is obtained by examination, and issued by the Department of Trade. Furthermore, in common with the deck officers from which department he is promoted, he must be thoroughly competent in navigation matters including the use of such navigational aids as the gyrocompass, radar, direction finder, echo-sounding device, and position-fixing device.

In the 1990s the traditional watch-keeping crew manning system will change radically as is evident in many modern maritime fleets today. The present modern tonnage provides automation in the engine room coupled with extensive computerization and minimum of crew personnel outside the normal working day of 0800/1800 hours. This reduces crew costs especially in the engineer and deck departments. A further significant aspect is that the departmental system of deck and engineers will become more integrated and more productive in manpower, especially in deep-sea tonnage.

An example of integrated crew manning system is given below which involves a 16-man complement of a Danish registered 'Omni carrier' vessel of 8 000 dwt operating on the route Gulf of

Mexico/US East coast – Mediterranean – Caribbean/Central America/Mexico.

Master	Second engineer
Chief mate	Third engineer
First mate	Electrician
Second mate	Purser
Radio officer	Cook
Chief engineer	Four trainees
First engineer	

The ship has a total container capacity of 516 TEUs and vehicular deck space of 1416 m^2; heavy lifting gear for loads up to 120 tonnes is also provided.

The integrated crew is especially common with Scandinavian and West German registered tonnage crews.

A brief description of the departments, responsibilities and composition follow; but it is stressed that this manning system is becoming less and less common as integration takes place to attain more productive use of the crew.

5.2 SHIP'S OFFICERS AND CREW MANNING

(a) Deck department

The running of this department is the responsibility of the chief officer or first mate who supervises the handling of cargo and is responsible for the upkeep of the ship and her equipment, excluding the engine room and auxiliary power gear. In addition, he also acts as a semi-chief of staff to the Master. He is assisted by two, three or more mates on larger vessels. These deck officers have to be duly certified by Department of Trade examination after the appropriate qualifying sea time has been completed. There are five certificates of competency for deck officers as fully described on p. 78. It is the practice in many vessels for both the chief and second officers to hold Master's Certificate of competency command endorsement. The statutory requirements for British vessels are fully described on p. 75.

The deck department also includes chief petty officer (deck), petty officers (deck) and a carpenter, together with a number of deck-hands, including junior seamen, seamen grade II and seamen grade I. The duties of the bosun are such that he acts as a foreman of the deck-hands. The carpenter's responsibilities include attendance at the forward windlass during berthing and unberthing operations. In common with the officers, the seamen grades I and II are watch-keepers, taking their turn at steering and look-out duties, while the remaining deck-hands are day workers employed at sea in general duties. The deck department in port usually works cargo watches in 8-hour stretches.

In the case of a large passenger liner, it is the frequent practice to have a Staff Captain, who is primarily responsible for looking after passengers' administration.

(b) Radio Officers

These are specialists, whose duties involve radio watch-keeping and maintenance of the radio transmitters and associated generators, receivers, batteries, lifeboat transmitters and receivers. Statutory provisions stipulate that for British vessels exceeding 500 tons gross and under 1600 tons gross, either a radio telephony or radio telegraphy installation is required. A radio telegraphy facility is necessary in all vessels exceeding 1600 tons gross. The operational part of the radio officer will change and the job, as at present constructed, will disappear when Future Global Maritime Distress and Safety System comes into operation in the 1990s (see page 142).

(c) Engine room department

The engine room is the charge of the chief engineer, who is responsible to the Master both for the main propulsion machinery and to auxiliaries comprising electrical plant, cargo winches, refrigerating machinery, steering gear, ventilating system, etc. He is also responsible for fuel, maintenance and repairs. He is assisted by a number of engineer officers, according to the size of the vessel. For example, a motorship requires more engineers than a steamship of equivalent power, while a turbo-electric or diesel-electric ship would require more electricians. Minimum manning scales of certified marine engineer officers are given on p. 79.

The ratings of the engine room department comprise junior motorman, motorman grade II, motorman grade I, petty officer (motorman) and chief petty officer (motorman). The complicated machinery of the modern ship has made the engine room department a very important one and much of it is computerized in modern tonnage.

(d) Catering department

This department is under the control of the chief steward, or catering officer, who is responsible for catering and the galley, for galley stores, and for ship's linen. He is assisted by cooks, bakers, and assistant stewards. In deep sea passenger ships and those engaged in multipurpose passenger tonnage in the short sea trades, this is a very large and important department. As such it is usually in the charge of the Purser.

(e) Manning

'Manning scales' are laid down for vessels flying the British flag, and every vessel must carry a minimum number of duly certificated deck officers and engineers, while more detailed requirements are often agreed jointly between employers and unions.

The number of personnel in each of the various departments depends on the type and size of vessel, and the trade in which she is engaged. For instance, a cargo vessel of 10 000 dwt would have a very small catering department compared with a vessel engaged in deep-sea cruising carrying 750 passengers.

The Merchant Shipping Act 1970 introduced new regulations regarding the certification of deck officers and marine engineer officers. They are contained in the *Merchant Shipping (Certification of Deck and Marine Engineer Officers) Regulations 1977*, which became operative from 1st September, 1981.

This involves UK-registered ships of 80 gross register tonnage or over and passenger ships in carrying a specified number of deck officers determined according to the tonnage of the ship and the voyage to, from or between locations in specified trading areas in which it will be engaged. Similar requirements are prescribed for ships registered outside the UK which carry passengers between places in the UK, or between the UK and the Channel Islands or Isle of Man or on voyages which begin or end at the same place in the UK and call at no place outside the UK. Provision is made for the exceptional circumstance when one deck officer cannot be carried because of illness. Special requirements are prescribed for tugs and sail training ships. Certificates of competency will be issued to deck officers who satisfy the requisite standards of competency as determined by the Department of Trade. Additional training is required for certain deck officers in ships carrying bulk cargoes of specified dangerous chemicals or gases. The same applies to certain marine engineer officers. Overall the new standards of certification reflect broadly the outcome of discussions at IMO.

Given below is the minimum number of Deck Officers to be carried as prescribed in the *Merchant Shipping (Certification of Deck Officers) Regulations 1977*. These must be regarded as the minimum manning scales and this equally applies to the marine engineer officers dealt with on p. 79. From January, 1988, the

Table 5.2 Minimum number of deck officers to be carried in ships of 80 GRT and over, other than passenger ships and tugs

Trading Area	Description of Ships	Minimum Number of Certified Deck Officers to be carried				
		Class 1 Cert.	Class 2 Cert.	Class 3 Cert.	Class 4 Cert.	Class 5 Cert.
Unlimited	1600 GRT and over	1	1	1	1	–
	80 GRT but under 1600 GRT	1	1	1	–	–
Middle Trade	5000 GRT and over	1	1	1	1	–
	1600 GRT but under 5000 GRT	–	–	1*	1	1
	Under 1600 GRT	–	–	–	2*	1
Near Continental	10 000 GRT and over	1	1	1	–	–
	5000 GRT but under 10 000 GRT	1	–	1	1	–
	16000 GRT but under 5000 GRT	–	–	–	2*	1
	800 GRT but under 1600 GRT	–	–	–	–	3*
	200 GRT but under 800 GRT	–	–	–	–	2*
	80 GRT but under 200 GRT	–	–	–	–	1*

* Subject to special provisions

syllabuses for Classes I and II Deck Officer Certificates of Competency, combined into a single sullabus examined at the Class II stage, came into effect.

Differing scales apply to passenger vessels which are much higher. This is also applicable to the other table found on p. 79.

The 'Near Continental' is any location within the area bounded by a line from a point on the Norwegian coast in latitude 62° North to a point 62° North 02° West; thence to a point 51° North 12° West; thence to Brest, but excluding all waters which lie to the east of a line drawn between Kristiansand, Norway and Hanstholm lighthouse on the north Danish coast.

The 'Middle Trade' is any location not within the near Continental trading area but within an area (which includes places in the Baltic Sea) bounded by the Northern shore of Vest Fjord (Norway) and a line joining Skemvaer lighthouse to a point 62°: North 02°: West; thence to a point 58° North 10° West; thence to a point 51° North 12° West; thence to a point 41° 9′ North 10° West; thence to Oporto. Basically the unlimited trading area is any location not within the Middle Trade or Near Continental trading areas. These trading areas apply to the relevant table found on p. 79.

Table 5.3 gives details of Certificates of Competency in regard to a ship's Master appointment as prescribed in the regulations.

The new five classes of Certificate of Competency (Deck Officer) is such that Class I is the Master Mariner level. In broad terms the new Class I certificate is equivalent to the Master Foreign Certificate as prescribed under the Merchant Shipping Act 1894. Likewise a First Mate Foreign-Going certificate and Second Mate Foreign-Going certificate is equivalent to the new Classes II and III respectively.

Differing Certificates of Competency and Command Endorsements exist for tugs. With regard to the regulations of marine engineer officers these involve UK registered ships having registered power of 350 kW or more, including all sail-training ships with a propulsion engine. It embraces the voyage to, from or between locations in specified training areas. Similar requirements are prescribed for a specified number of Engineer Officers for ships registered outside the UK, which carry passengers between places in the UK or between the UK and the Channel Islands or Isle of Man or on voyages which begin and end at the same place in the UK and call at no place outside the UK. Provision is made for

Table 5.3

Certificate of Competency (Deck Officer) or Certificate of Validity	Command Endorsement	Description of Ship
Class 2 or Class 3	Master (Middle Trade)	Ships (other than passenger ships) of less than 5000 GRT going between locations in the combined Near Continental and Middle Trade trading areas
Class 4	Master (Middle Trade)	Ships (other than passenger ships) of less than 1600 GRT going between locations in the combined Near Continental and Middle Trade trading areas
Class 2, Class 3 and Class 4	Master (Near Continental)	Ships (other than passenger ships) of less than 5000 GRT going between locations in the Near Continental trading area. Passenger ships of less than 1000 GRT going between locations in the Near Continental trading area
Class 5	Master (Near Continental)	Ships (other than passenger ships) of less than 1600 GRT going between locations in the Near Continental trading area. Passenger ships of less than 200 GRT going between locations in the Near Continental trading areas.

the exceptional circumstance when one Engineer Officer cannot be carried because of illness or incapacity. Special requirements are prescribed for sail-training ships.

Overall there are four classes of Certificate of Competence and related to the First Class Engineer Certificate as prescribed under the Merchant Shipping Act 1894 it will be the Marine Engineer Officer Class 1. Certificates of Competency of Class 1, 2, or 4 shall be issued for motor or steam machinery, or for combined motor and steam machinery. Class 3 certificates shall be issued for motor machinery only.

Given below is the minimum number of marine engineer officers to be carried as prescribed in the *Merchant Shipping (Certification of Marine Engineer Officers) Regulations 1977.*

Table 5.4

Area	Registered Power (kW) of Ships Including Sail Training Ships	Minimum Number of Certificated Marine Engineer Officers To Be Carried			
		Class 1 Cert.	Class 2 Cert.	Class 3 Cert.	Class 4 Cert.
Unlimited or Middle East	3000 and over	1	1	–	2
	746 or more but under 3000	–	1*	1	1
	350 or more but under 746	–	–	1*	1
Near Continental	6000 and over	1	1	–	1
	3000 or more but under 6000	–	1*	1	–
	746 or more but under 3000	–	–	1*	1
	350 or more but under 746	–	–	–	1 and 1*

* Subject to special provisions

In an attempt to raise the status of ratings both in the deck and engineer departments, plus the need to facilitate the productivity and diversification of rating work load on UK vessels, a new structure has been introduced to a number of posts. Brief details are given below of the new structure:

Deck Department *New Designation*	*Marine Engineer Department* *New Designation*
Junior Seaman	Junior Motorman
Seaman Grade II	Motorman Grade II
Seaman Grade I	Motorman Grade I
Petty Officer (Deck)	Petty Officer (Motorman)
Chief Petty Officer (Deck)	Chief Petty Officer (Motorman)

Given below are details of Certificates of Competency in regard to the chief engineer officer appointment of a specified vessel as prescribed in the regulations:

Table 5.5　Certificates of Competency or Service

Class of Certificate of Competency or Service	Service Endorsement	Description of Ship
Class 2	Chief Engineer Officer	In ships of 746 or more but under 3000 kW registered power going to, from, or between any locations. In ships of 3000 or more but under 6000 kW registered power going between locations in the Near Continental trading area.
Class 3	Chief Engineer Officer	In ships of 350 or more but under 746 kW registered power going to, from or between any locations. In ships of 746 or more but under 3000 kW registered power going between locations in the Near Continental trading area.
Class 4	Chief Engineer Officer	In ships of 350 or more but under 746 kW registered power going between locations in the Near Continental trading area. In sail training ships of less than 350 kW registered power going to, from or between any locations.

A similar restructuring has taken place on the catering side.

In the late 1990s, it is likely the concept of crew manning will further change to reflect the greater technology now found in modern tonnage. Radical changes could emerge in manning scales, particularly in the increased number of certificated personnel. This has already been evidenced in the UK *Merchant Shipping (Certification of Deck and Marine Engineer Officers) Regulations 1977* described earlier.

5.3 INTERNATIONAL CONFERENCE ON TRAINING AND CERTIFICATION OF SEAFARERS 1978

At the International Conference on Training and Certification of Seafarers 1978 involving the International Maritime Organization, new regulations were adopted.

It is generally accepted that many accidents at sea can be attributed to human errors. Whilst such accidents can never be completely eliminated, IMO recognized that one of the most important factors affecting maritime safety, efficiency of navigation and the prevention and control of marine pollution from ships, is the education and training of seafarers.

In 1971, the IMO Council decided that further action was necessary to strengthen and improve standards of training and qualifications and requested the Maritime Safety Committee to give urgent consideration to the preparation of international standards of training, certification and watch-keeping for seafarers.

The International Conference on Training and Certification of Seafarers was held in London in 1978 and was attended by 72 States and a total of 541 participants, including observers.

Details of the IMO requirements related to watch-keeping, training, certification and continued proficiency and up-dating of knowledge are given below:

(a) Master – deck department

(a) Basic principles to be observed in keeping a navigational watch.

(b) Mandatory minimum requirements for certification of masters and chief mates of ships of 200 gross register tons or more.

(c) Mandatory minimum requirements for certification of officers in charge of a navigational watch and of masters of ships of less than 200 gross register tons.

(d) Mandatory minimum requirements for certification of officers in charge of a navigational watch on ships of 200 gross register tons or more.

(e) Mandatory minimum requirements to ensure the continued proficiency and up-dating of knowledge for masters and deck officers.

(f) Mandatory minimum requirements for ratings forming part of a navigational watch.

(g)   Basic principles to be observed in keeping a watch in port.

(h)   Mandatory minimum requirements for a watch in port on ships carrying hazardous cargo.

(b) Engine department

(a)   Basic principles to be observed in keeping an engineering watch.

(b)   Mandatory minimum requirements for certification of chief engineer officers and second engineer officers of ships powered by main propulsion machinery of 3000 kW propulsion power or more.

(c)   Mandatory minimum requirements for certification of chief engineer officers and second engineer officers of ships powered by main propulsion machinery between 750 kW and 3000 kW propulsion power.

(d)   Mandatory minimum requirements for certification of engineer officers in charge of a watch in a traditionally manned engine room or designated duty engineer officers in a periodically unmanned engine room.

(e)   Mandatory minimum requirements to ensure the continued proficiency and up-dating of knowledge for engineer officers.

(f)   Mandatory minimum requirements for ratings forming part of an engine room watch.

(c) Radio department

(a)   Mandatory minimum requirements for certification of radio officers.

(b)   Mandatory minimum requirements to ensure the continued proficiency and up-dating of knowledge for radio officers.

(c)   Mandatory minimum requirements for certification of radio-telephone operators.

(d) Special requirements for tankers

(a)   Mandatory minimum requirements for the training and qualifications of masters, officers and ratings of oil tankers.

(b)   Mandatory minimum requirements for the training and qualifications of masters, officers and ratings of chemical tankers.

(c)   Mandatory minimum requirements for the training and qualifications of masters, officers and ratings of liquefied gas tankers.

(e) Proficiency in survival craft

(a) Mandatory minimum requirements for the issue of certificates of proficiency in survival craft.

Details of the resolutions adopted by the Conference are given below:

(f) Master – deck department

(a) Operational guidance for officers in charge of a navigational watch.

(b) Principles and operational guidance for deck officers in charge of a watch in port.

(c) Additional training for ratings forming part of a navigation watch.

(d) Additional training for masters and chief mates of large ships and of ships with unusual manoeuvring characteristics.

(e) Radar simulator training.

(f) Training in the use of collision avoidance aids.

(g) Engine department

(a) Operational guidance for engineer officers in charge of an engineering watch.

(b) Principles and operational guidance for engineer officers in charge of an engineering watch in port.

(c) Minimum requirements for a rating nominated as the assistant to the engineer officer in charge of the watch.

(h) Radio Department

(a) Basic guidelines and operational guidance relating to safety radio watch-keeping and maintenance for radio officers.

(b) Basic guidelines and operational guidance relating to safety radio watch-keeping for radio-telephone operators.

(c) Radio operators.

(d) Training for radio officers.

(e) Training for radio-telephone operators.

(i) Tankers and ships carrying dangerous and hazardous cargo other than in bulk

(a) Training and qualifications of officers and ratings of oil tankers.

(b) Training and qualifications of officers and ratings of chemical tankers.

(c) Training and qualifications of masters, officers and ratings of liquefied gas tankers.

(d) Training and qualifications of officers and ratings of ships carrying dangerous and hazardous cargo other than in bulk.

(j) Miscellaneous

(a) Training of seafarers in personal survival techniques.

(b) International certificate of competency.

(c) Human relationships.

(d) Technical assistance for the training and qualifications of masters and other responsible personnel of oil, chemical and liquefied gas tankers.

(e) Promotion of technical co-operation.

The resolutions are in process of adoption throughout the world.

5.4 ENGAGEMENT AND DISCHARGE OF THE CREW

We have already established that the person in sole charge of the vessel is the Master. The conditions of employment of seamen are the subject of statutory legislation and regulations under the Merchant Shipping Act, 1970. A voyage is still a venture subject to many hazards and difficulties. To complete the venture successfully, relative rights, duties and restraints must be enforced on all who share the venture. These special circumstances have given rise to legislation in most countries to restrict and protect seamen in their employment.

The Merchant Shipping Act 1970 brought into effect the first major change for many years in the legislation relating to the employment of seamen. It repealed parts of the 1894 and 1906 Merchant Shipping Acts. The new Act deals with crew agreements; crew lists; engagement and discharge of crew; seamen's documents; discipline; wages and accounts; seamen left behind abroad; deceased seamen, and medical treatment and expenses. The more salient aspects are now examined.

The contract of employment is made between the shipowner and the crew. It is called a crew agreement, and a number of clauses are taken directly from the Merchant Shipping Act 1970 whilst other derive from National Maritime Board agreements. The shipowner is the contracting party, but seamen must sign the crew agreement prior to the intended voyage. It is not necessary for the superintendent or proper officer to be present during the signing on or discharge but in some Commonwealth countries this practice is obligatory under their legislation involving Shipping Masters/Superintendents.

A standard form of crew agreement is provided by the Department of Trade or non-standard editions as prepared by employers and approved by the Department of Trade may also be used. The crew agreement contains a voyage clause giving the geographical limits of the voyage, and notice/termination clauses which vary by the trade in which vessel engaged, i.e. foreign-going voyage or home trade. If a seaman wishes to terminate his employment in contemplation of furtherance of an industrial dispute, 48 hours' notice must be given to the Master, when the vessel is securely moored at a safe berth in the UK.

It will be recalled that in many maritime countries the employment agreement between the seamen and shipowner is called the Articles of Agreement. Indeed it is still referred to as such in UK tonnage rather than the 'crew agreement' and applies to individual crew members.

A maritime conference of the International Labour Office in 1926 adopted a convention on seamen's Articles of Agreement, and prescribed the form and conditions of such agreements. This convention was ratified by 25 countries. Later, at an international conference at Seattle, many provisions regarding minimum wages and standards of accommodation were adopted.

The 1970 Act requires the ship's master to maintain a crew list and this must be produced on demand to the Registrar-General of Shipping and Seamen, a superintendent or proper officer, or an officer of Customs and Excise.

The crew list embraces reference; name of seaman; discharge book number or date/place of birth; Mercantile Marine Office where registered; name of ship in which last employed – if more than 12 months since last ship, actual year of discharge; address of seaman; name of next kin; relationship of next of kin; capacity in which employed; grade and number of certificate of competency; date of commencement of employment on board; date of leaving ship; place of leaving ship; rate of wages; if discharged – reason for discharge; signature of seaman on engagement, and signature of seaman on discharge.

The crew list remains in being until all the persons employed under the crew agreement have been discharged. A copy must be kept with all the changes by the UK shipowner, and any change in the crew list must be notified to a superintendent or proper officer within two days of the change.

Before seamen are engaged on a new crew agreement and before they are added to an agreement which is already current, at least 24 hours' notice must be given to the appropriate superintendent or proper officer. The notice of engagement must include name of ship; port of registry; official number; whether a new crew agreement is to be made or whether a person(s) is to be added, and the capacity in which each person to be engaged is to be employed.

When a seaman is present at his discharge it must be before (a) the master, or (b) the seaman's employer, or (c) a person so authorized by the master or employer. The person before whom the seaman is discharged must enter in the official log book the place, date and time of the seaman's discharge and in the crew list the place, date and reason for the discharge. The seaman must sign the entry in the crew list. In the event of the seaman not being present at the time of discharge, similar entries must be made in the official log and in the crew list. All entries in the official log must be signed by the person making the entry and by a member of the crew. The seaman can request a certificate either as to the quality of his work or indicating whether he has fulfilled his obligations under the agreement.

The detailed requirements of seamen's documents are contained in the *Merchant Shipping (Seamen's Documents) Regulations (Statutory Instrument 1972 No. 1295)*. This embraces a British seaman card valid for 5 years, and a discharge book.

The Act also deals with discipline and embraces stowaways and their prosecution; aiding and abetting stowaways, and Master's power of arrest. This indicates that where the Master considers it necessary for any person on board to be placed under restraint in the interest of safety or for the preservation of good order or discipline on board the ship, the Master is empowered to do so.

The Act makes provision for payment of seaman's wages including at the time of discharge. Additionally provision is made for allotment of his wages up to two persons and not more than 50% of his income both of which may be varied only in exceptional circumstances. This arrangement is concluded at the time when the crew agreement is signed.

The Act also places on the employer the primary responsibility and the cost of providing for the relief and repatriation of seaman left behind. This embraces the following relating to employer or his agent responsibility to the seaman:

(a) Maintenance and cost of repatriating seamen who are left behind.

(b) Provision of their surgical, medical, dental and optical treatment.

(c) Provision of their accommodation.

(d) Making arrangements for their repatriation.

(e) Applying, if necessary, to the proper officer for the issue of a conveyance order.

Basically the regulations relating to the relief and repatriation of seamen left behind and conveyance orders are found in the *Merchant Shipping (Repatriation) Regulations 1972.*

Provision in the Act is also made regarding deceased seamen which places the obligation on the Master to inform the next of kin within 3 days. Mention is also made regarding the deceased seaman's wages and property.

A radical change in shipboard disciplinary procedures emerged under the Merchant Shipping Act 1979. It was the result of an agreement involving employers, unions and Department of Trade and laid down a contractual system of discipline by consent based on a Code of Conduct. This involved the abolition of fines imposed by ship Masters for disciplinary offences laid down in statutory regulations. It involved agreed disciplinary procedures culminating in joint shore-based committees with power to debar a serious offender from further employment at sea. The code gives particular emphasis on safety and recognizes the common interest of employers and seafarers in dismissing from their ships members whose conduct endangers their shipmates or is prejudicial to their social well-being.

The Merchant Shipping Act 1988 amended the law relating to Crew Agreements to bring the payment of seamen into line with that for other categories of employee.

Our examination of the manning of vessels would not be

complete without considering the function and responsibilities of
the National Maritime Board, General Council of British Shipping
and International Shipping Federations, which follows.

5.5   THE NATIONAL MARITIME BOARD

The National Maritime Board (NMB) exists as a joint negotiating
body, and is divided into six separate panels, each representing a
seagoing department with its own special problems and requirements. There are 24 members to each panel, and membership is
apportioned equally between shipowners and employees, with a
chairman for each side.

The object of the NMB is simply to provide a form of machinery
for joint negotiation between owners and seafarers, on matters
affecting pay, hours of duty, manning, leave, and travelling
expenses. Each panel has authority to negotiate on any of these
matters, and its decisions are binding. The six panels cover
masters, navigating officers, radio officers, engineer officers,
catering staff, seamen and firemen. The NMB is administered by a
permanent independent staff, and it is financed by a proportionate
levy on shipowners and seafarers representatives. The NMB issues
annually a book detailing minimum rates of pay and conditions of
employment. Overall the scheme is administered by the GCBS.

In the longer term it is likely there will be a gradual replacement
of the NMB agreements on pay and conditions by individual company agreements with consequent wage bargaining at company
level. It is considered that company bargaining may be more
closely related to the economic circumstances of the company on
the one hand and to the real needs of the employees on the other.
It could also provide more scope for genuine productivity
bargaining than could be achieved in a national negotiation. The
flagging out of much UK tonnage has undoubtedly contributed to
the situation.

In 1986 there was a merger of three of the officers unions namely
the Merchant Navy and Airline Officers' Association, the Mercan-
tile Marine Service Association and the Radio and Electronic
Officers Union: a new union was formed which was called the
National Union of Marine Aviation and Shipping Transport
Officers (NUMAST). Consequently the merchant navy officers

are now represented by two unions NUMAST and the Amalgamated Union of Engineering Workers.

5.6 GENERAL COUNCIL OF BRITISH SHIPPING

The General Council of British Shipping (GCBS) took over the role of the UK Chamber of Shipping and British Shipping Federation in March 1975 – the latter's origins date back to 1890. The Council, undertaking the former role of the Federation, is a central organization representing all UK shipowners in all matters affecting seagoing personnel.

In addition to representing the views of shipowners in these matters to the government and other outside interests, including international bodies, the Council provides the employers' side of the National Maritime Board. Its offices throughout the country recruit seafarers, administer the Established Service Scheme, and act as employment exchanges in supplying crews to ships. They also provide medical services. In conjunction with other interests, through the Merchant Navy Training Board, the Council determines training policy.

The many other matters with which it is concerned include pensions, redundancy payments, personal injury claims, racial discrimination, safety and welfare. The Council also provides a recruitment and selection service for companies wishing to train deck and engineer cadets.

In latter years the GCBS has been endeavouring to rationalize and provide more cost effective services at a time of great change in the industry. This involves for example to integrate the separate companies found in GCBS/MNE (Merchant Navy Establishment) into a group structure relative to pensions etc.

5.7 INTERNATIONAL SHIPPING FEDERATION (ISF)

This organization is a federation of national shipowners' organizations on the same basis as the International Chamber of Shipping. It is, however, administered by the General Council of British Shipping.

Founded in 1909, much of its work at that time was concerned with indemnifying shipowners for losses incurred through labour disputes and it was exclusively a European organization.

The creation of the International Labour Office in 1919 radically altered both the membership and the practical scope of the Federation. It became and remains a worldwide organization and it is concerned primarily with the whole and ever-widening field of industrial relations for shipping. It is a consultative and advisory organization and in no way infringes national autonomy. Its present membership consists of the national organizations of shipowners of the following 19 countries:

Australia	Greece	Norway
Belgium	India	Portugal
Canada	Italy	Spain
Denmark	Japan	Sweden
Finland	Netherlands	United Kingdom
France	New Zealand	United States of
Germany		America

Since 1919 the principal function of the International Shipping Federation has been to give shipowners of different countries an opportunity of exchanging views upon all social and personnel problems affecting the shipping industry. In particular it acts as a medium of preparation for international labour (maritime) conferences and provides the secretariat of the shipowners' group. It acts in the same way for the shipowners' side of the Joint Maritime Commission of the ILO (International Labour Organization).

CHAPTER 6

Customs House and ships' papers

During the past century Customs cargo clearance has become a very complicated procedure. In the UK this has been due to the existence of five major factors. These include strict government control of exports and imports; the licensing of exports and imports; financial considerations for Revenue purposes embracing currency; statistics of export and import trades; and lastly, the documentation requirements for all exports and imports arising out of the other four factors. The accession of the UK to the European Common Market has resulted in the increasing complexity of import documentation, introducing controls for Common Agricultural Policy (CAP) levy and compensatory payments.

One must bear in mind that Customs entries are necessary for the following reasons:

1. To provide a record of exports and imports, and so enable the government to assess and thereby control the balance of trade.

2. To ensure that no dutiable goods enter the country without paying duty.

3. To bring all imports 'to account' by perfected entries prepared by importers or their agents.

4. In so far as dutiable cargo is concerned, to provide a valuable form of revenue through the government and European Community imposition of certain duties and levies on certain goods imported into a country.

6.1 ORGANIZATION AND WORKINGS OF CUSTOMS & EXCISE

HM Customs & Excise is one of the two main tax collecting departments in the United Kingdom. It has origins in one of the oldest Departments of State, the Board of Customs, which was appointed in 1671. The Department of Customs & Excise was established in 1909. The Board of Customs & Excise, composed of Commissioners individually appointed by the Sovereign under the Great Seal of the UK, is responsible to Treasury Ministers for the work of the department.

The work of HM Customs & Excise may be divided into two broad areas:

(a) The control of imported and exported goods for the purpose of duties, statistics and the prevention of importation of prohibited goods, especially drugs.

(b) The administration and collection of most of the taxes on consumer expenditure (indirect taxes) levied in the United Kingdom. In 1985/86, Customs & Excise receipts were just under £37.4 billion and represented 39.2% of the total revenue from central government taxation. Mostly, Customs & Excise revenue is made up of Value Added Tax (VAT), duties on hydrocarbon oils, tobacco products, alcoholic drinks and car tax. Other indirect taxes collected by Customs & Excise are betting and gaming duties and duties on matches and lighters. Vehicle licence duties and stamp duties are not the responsibility of the department.

Like most government departments, HM Customs & Excise has been affected by UK membership of the EC (European Community). All EC Member States use a common customs tariff to charge the same rates of duty on imported good from outside the Community. Goods from within the EC generally move free of Customs' duties between the member states (Belgium, Denmark, France, Greece, Ireland, Italy, Luxembourg, the Netherlands, Portugal, Spain, the UK and West Germany). The EC is constantly seeking greater harmonization in the field of indirect taxation with a view to achieving a genuine common internal market with no barriers to trade between member states.

While the department's main functions are the collection of revenue and the control of imports and exports, by arrangement with other government departments it also undertakes a variety of non-revenue work which includes collection of external trade statistics; prohibitions and restrictions, and investigation regarding fraud, imports and exports cargo processing.

The principal functions of the Customs side of the department have traditionally been the assessment and collection of customs duties on imported goods and the control of smuggling. But one of the results of EC membership has been a change in the nature of customs duties. They no longer accrue to national treasuries but are paid over to the EC as 'own resources' (i.e. they form part of the EC budget revenue). The department collects customs duties on goods coming from countries outside the EC which do not qualify for relief under any preferential trade agreements made with the EC. In addition, Customs collect and control the other charges which may be levied at import and remitted at export, such as excise duty and VAT, and the levies payable on agricultural products under the EC Common Agricultural Policy (CAP).

6.2 IMPORTATION AND EXPORTATION OF GOODS

(a) Commercial importations

General
Customs procedures for commercial importations vary according to the type of traffic involved but the principles remain broadly the same:

(i) goods may be imported legally only through places approved by Customs (e.g. wharves, airports and approved routes across the Land Boundary with the Irish Republic);

(ii) ships and aircraft must lodge a report, including a cargo list, with Customs on arrival (usually before unloading begins);

(iii) all goods must be properly 'entered' and any duty (or levies on goods subject to the Common Agricultural Policy (CAP)) and other charges due must normally be paid before they are released from Customs control; this usually takes place at a wharf or airport of importation but the requirements can be completed at inland clearance depots or, under a special scheme, at the importers premises;

(iv) Customs officers have the right to examine all goods to confirm that they correspond with the 'entry' made for them.

Import entry procedure
The importer is responsible for preparing an 'entry' for all the

goods he is importing. The 'entry' is a document on which he declares the description, value, quantity, rate of duty and various other details about the goods. When presented to Customs it is normally accompanied by supporting documents such as copies of commercial invoices and packing lists to provide evidence of the nature and value of the goods, but frequently also by an official document to prove their status for duty purposes; this may be a Community Transit document authenticated by the exporting member state for goods imported from elsewhere in the EC, a single administrative document (SAD) or a certificate of origin if preference is being claimed. Since accession to the EC, Customs are responsible for controlling goods received from other member states under the Community transit system and for returning the Community transit document to the issuing member state. Any appropriate claim for free admission for goods under the various special EC tariff regimes is made on the entry. In the case of goods which may be imported only under a licence issued by a government department (e.g. the Department of Trade or the Home Office) the licence must normally accompany the entry. Detailed descriptions of goods for duty and statistical purposes necessary for the preparation of an entry are shown in HM Customs & Excise Tariff and Overseas Trade Classification ('The Tariff') published by HM Stationery office. The importer or his agent present the completed entry with its supporting documents to the appropriate Customs office. It is checked for accuracy and any duties or other charges due are then paid, or deferred under special arrangements.

A number of consignments are selected for examination; in these cases it is the responsibility of the importer or his agent to produce the goods for examination as required by the officer. Much of the information given on the entry is also used in compiling the overseas trade statistics.

Variations in procedure – variations in entry procedure include the following:

1. *Suspension of duty and reliefs*. There are procedures for suspending the payment of duty or for relieving goods of duty provided that certain conditions are met and, usually, that the goods remain under Customs control. One example is where goods are moved to an approved warehouse; other examples

include goods imported under a variety of temporary importation reliefs, goods imported by certain traders to undergo an authorized process before being re-exported, and goods claiming 'end-use' relief from duties under EC regulations which allow free entry only if the goods are used for a specified purpose such as shipbuilding. Goods being transhipped (i.e. imported for re-export either from the port of importation or from another port) are also relieved of duty.

2. *Local import control.* Traders who regularly import repetitive traffic and who can satisfy specific conditions may make entry of their goods locally and have them cleared at their premises.

3. *Period Entry (imports).* Traders who use computers for stock control and accounting purposes and whose import trade is repetitive and on a large scale may apply to submit a simplified entry at the time of import supplemented by periodic schedules in a computer medium such as magnetic tape.

4. *Sea traffic.* The system of direct trader input has also been introduced at over twenty seaports and inland clearance depots.

5. *Postal consignments.* Goods imported by post are subject to the same duties, taxes, prohibitions and restrictions as other imports. Postal packages enter the country through postal depots where they are subject to Customs scrutiny. In most cases any charges due are assessed on the basis of the Customs declaration by the sender and/or examination and are collected by the postman when he delivers the package.

6. *Inward processing relief.* Goods imported by authorized traders for process and exportation outside the EC may be relieved of customs duty and other import charges but not VAT. Officers visit processors for control purposes and ensure that duty is paid on any goods diverted to use within the EC.

7. *Free zones.* The Department is also responsible for the control and administration of the free zones which have been set up on an experimental basis at a number of ports and airports. A free zone is an enclosed area into which goods may be moved without payment of customs duty and similar import charges, including Value Added Tax charged at importation. Such charges become payable only if goods are brought out of the zone into the UK market or are consumed within the zone. In addition, duty (but not VAT) is payable if goods are processed other than for export outside the EC.

Commercial exportations

General

Exported goods are relieved of excise duties and VAT although some agricultural products may be liable to export levies or entitled to refunds under the CAP. Since accession to the EC, Customs are responsible for authenticating community transit documents for exports to (or through) other member states of the community including the Single Administrative Document. These documents indicate whether or not the goods are Community goods (i.e. either goods wholly produced in the Community or goods on which duty has already been paid) and therefore entitled to free entry, or whether duty remains to be paid on entry into another member state. Customs also control the issue of Certificates of Origin for goods exported to a number of countries outside the EC which give preference to EC goods.

Export Entry procedures

Goods may be exported only through approved wharves, airports, inland clearance depots, etc. Exporters must declare their goods for export and these declarations are examined by Customs to check that all details required are included. The export declarations are used both for control purposes and for the compilation of external trade statistics. Regular exporters may register to use a simplified clearance procedure under which a commercial document may be presented at the time of exportation and the entry submitted retrospectively. For entries submitted retrospectively there is a facility known as HMC80 Exports which is similar to that available at import whereby traders are able to input their entries from their own VDUs direct to computerized departmental entry processing system.

Entries required to be received before exportation are sent to the officer at the place of loading who is responsible for ensuring that the goods are actually exported and that reliefs have been claimed correctly, or that levies due have been properly declared. Finally, the shipping company (or airline) submits a manifest detailing all the cargo loaded.

Local export control is an optional procedure under which, subject to prior approval, export control and clearance may be effected at the trader's premises.

Period Entry (exports) enables appropriate traders to submit periodic schedules of their exports instead of individual export declarations for each consignment.

The Harmonized Commodity Description and Coding System (HS)
There is a need to classify and code commodities which enter into international trade, for a variety of reasons: for customs duty purposes, for trade statistics, for transport operations, etc. Various attempts have been made over the years to produce standardized systems for such purposes. The most successful has been the Customs Co-operation Council Nomenclature (CCCN) for tariff purposes and the United Nations Standard International Trade Classification (SITC) both of which date from 1950.

However, some years ago it was recognized that the CCCN had not kept pace with the rapid changes in technology and patterns of trade which have taken place in recent years, particularly in high-tech areas, such as micro-electronics. There was also a growing awareness amongst those concerned with international trade of the need to bring into line the various separate systems for classifying goods for different purposes. Work on a new updated classification system culminated in the 1983 CCC International Convention on the Harmonized Commodity Description and Coding System (HS). The HS is based on the revised 4-digit CCCN expanded to a 6-digit code intended to cover both tariff and trade statistics requirements and hopefully will be adopted by all the major trading nations of the world. The HS will be of particular benefit in respect of EC trade with Canada and the USA which do not currently use the CCCN.

Use of the HS as a common system on a worldwide basis for describing and coding goods for tariff and statistical purposes should greatly facilitate Customs clearance and the exchange and utilization of information about international trade transactions. Moreover it should help to simplify trade and tariff negotiatons e.g. in the General Agreement on Tariffs and Trade (GATT).

The Community Integrated Tariff (TARIC)
The fruits of many years' work which have gone into devising an integrated tariff of the EC came into effect on 1st January, 1988. The object of the exercise has been to provide for each description

of goods, in just one place in the the tariff, an indication of all the EC tariff related measures to which they could be subject.

Hitherto in the UK most of the information required for tariff related measures affecting imports from non-Community countries, such as preferential rates of duty, are contained in separate annexes to the tariff. Integration of these measures in the tariff will be achieved, in the most part, by the provision of an extended numerical code which will indicate whether they can benefit from, for instance, preferential rates of duty, tariff suspensions or end-use relief.

The implementation of HS and TARIC in the EC

With effect from 1st January, 1988, the EC uses a Combined Nomenclature (CN) which is based on the HS and replaces the existing tariff (CCT) and statistical (NIMEXE) nomenclatures. The CN will comprise 8 digits, the first 6 of which will be the HS code and the last 2 will cater for EC statistical needs not covered by the HS. The CN will include some 9500 lines identified by the 8 digit code which will be common throughout the EC and, together with the relevant duty rates, will form the common external tariff of the EC.

To provide for the national statistical needs of the EC member states for which the 6-digit HS code and the 8-digit CN will not suffice there will be a ninth digit.

Intra-Community movements of goods and exports outside the Community will generally be identified by this 9-digit code. To identify the various Community tariff measures to which goods

Combined Nomenclature		National Statistics Classification	TARIC Sub-headings
HS	EC Statistics		
123456	78	9	10 11

(additional 4 digit code for, e.g. CAP goods)

imported from third countries may be subject a tenth and eleventh digit will be added. These, together with the relevant duty rates form the Community's integrated tariff known as TARIC and will comprise some 13 000 lines.

Member states will be free to add to the code at the twelfth, thirteenth and fourteenth digit level to integrate national measures, e.g. VAT or excise duties if they wish. The UK will not be using these in the foreseeable future.

In a very limited number of cases, an additional 4-digit code will be used to provide the nomenclature breakdowns necessary for certain CAP measures and anti-dumping duties.

Single Administrative Document (SAD)

Movements of goods, both within the EC and imported into or exported from the Community have to be documented for Customs purposes. Importers and exporters have to complete written import, export and, for intra-Community trade, Community Transit forms. For EC trade, most of the information required by each member state is the same. In order to facilitate trade and to overcome the duplication of effort, the Single Administrative Document, was introduced on 1st January 1988. It combines into a single format the requirements of over a hundred different forms for use in both EC and non-EC trade.

The SAD has been designed essentially as an 8-part document combining three functions: export, transit and import. It can be prepared in one operation as a single set of documents or it can be split into its component sections and each of these sections can be completed separately – by different people if necessary. These options allow the adoption of new procedures or the continuation of existing arrangements according to the needs of particular businesses.

When a full 8-part SAD is completed in one operation for an EC export it can be used for what is called the full procedure. The exporter or his agent will produce a full set of documents to Customs at the place of export clearance. Customs will retain the top two copies and return the remainder. The third copy is for retention by the Principal to the Community Transit (CT) movement and the rest will move forward with the goods.

The fourth copy provides evidence to Customs in the import country that the goods are (or are not) in free circulation and the fifth will be returned to the UK to provide evidence that the goods reached their destination. Copies 6 to 8 comprise the import declaration, although copy 7 may also be used for transit control purposes as well.

It is important to understand, that when a SAD originating in the export country is being used as an import declaration, there is information that must be added to the form before it can be presented to Customs. As the form's self copying properties do not apply to most of these boxes carbon paper has to be inserted at this stage.

The four copy version of the SAD in which each copy has two functions can also be used for the full procedure in which case two sets of this version are needed. It is then important to ensure that the second set only contains the information which would normally appear on copy 6 in a full 8-copy set.

The full procedure is also being used when the goods are not moving in transit through EC countries – for example when they are being flown between two EC airports, but copies are being provided for export and import purposes as well as to provide evidence of the free circulation status of the goods. In this situation copy 5 should be removed from the set(s) before presentation Customs at export.

Split use means that the form is not being used for all three of its functions, but only one or two of them. The need to use it will arise in a number of different situations. Several special sets containing selected copies of the SAD are being made available to cater for these situations and to avoid the need to discard unwanted copies from full sets.

For example, an exporter may wish to prepare his own export declarations but prefer to leave it to a transport operator to complete transit forms. In this situation the exporter would complete an export SAD while the transport company would prepare a transit SAD. Similarly an import agent may not wish to await the arrival of the SAD in order to add information to complete it as an import declaration and may prefer to use a fresh SAD and present it to Customs before the goods arrive. In these circumstances the SAD arriving with the goods would then serve only as evidence of the duty status of the goods. For goods imported from or exported to non-Community countries direct simple import or export SADs alone are required.

Two points are worth bearing in mind. First, for exports to or through other EC countries, using the form at least as a combined export and CT declaration is considerably more efficient from both Customs and commercial points of view than the use of separate SADs, but exporters and their agents need to agree that this option is most suitable for them.

Secondly, groupage operators will need to use separate full SADs for each consignment in the groupage load if the form is to be used as an import declaration at the other end of the journey, but when this is not the case a single SAD with continuation sheets – or CT loading lists when the form is being used solely for transit purposes – could be used instead. Other commercial factors will also influence the decision between these two options, but it needs to be remembered that the more SADs that are produced in this situation the longer it will take for the goods to be cleared through Customs at export.

The SAD is operative throughout the EC, Scandinavia and USA. It is possible other countries worldwide will use it as it enables extensive rationalization of customs documentation to be realized.

Report (or entering in) and inward clearance
On arrival of a ship in a UK port from a place outside the UK, it is necessary for the vessel to be 'entered in' with HM Customs in accordance with the provisions found in sections 35 and 64 of the Customs & Excise Management Act 1979. This is the responsibility of the Master or his appointed agent who must report to the Customs House or other designated place.

The report must embrace the following:

(a) *Form C 13 – Master declaration.* This gives general information about the ship, the voyage, and details of ships stores including duty free stores. It must be signed by the Master.

(b) *Form C 142 – Crew declaration.* This form gives details of goods owned by crew members including the ship's Master for presentation and clearance by Customs. It will have regard to prohibited and restricted goods.

(c) *A declaration of cargo.* A complete declaration of cargo on board the vessel. It can be undertaken in four ways as under:
  (i) On a cargo manifest giving details of each consignment and embracing the following:
    – the maritime transport document reference, e.g. the bill of lading number;
    – the container identification/vehicle registration number;
    – the number, kind, marks and numbers of the packages;
    – the description and gross weight/volume of the goods;

- the port or place where the goods were loaded on to the ship;
- the original port or place of shipment for goods on a through maritime transport document.

(ii) If there is no manifest or other suitable document, Customs will accept a cargo declaraion on the model form produced by the International Maritime Organization.

(iii) If the vessel is carrying a single commodity bulk cargo, details can be given in box 13 of form C 13 of the Master declaration.

(iv) Most UK ports now operate a computerized inventory control system termed Direct Trader Input, in which case the Master must endorse form C 13 in box 13 that the cargo declaration will be undertaken in this manner.

(d) *Form SUR 238*. Declaration of deck tonnage if applicable.

(e) *PAS 15 (arrival)*. Passenger return – if applicable.

The customs officer may visit the vessel on arrival in which case the report will be submitted to him/her. If such a visit does not take place, the report must be submitted not later than 3 hours after the vessel has reached its place of loading or unloading, or 24 hours after arrival within port limits.

Customs require to have details of passengers disembarking and crew members being paid off. Passengers must not be allowed ashore until they have been cleared by an immigration officer or under local arrangements approved by an immigration officer. The latter would include passenger ports where immigration procedures are undertaken ashore. All relevant immigration documents must be completed.

When the foregoing has been completed, the vessel may commence discharge and/or loading.

Entry outwards and outward clearance

For a vessel sailing outwards the following procedure applies:

The Master or his appointed agent must report to the Customs House or other designated place and present the following:

(a) *Form C 13* – Master's declaration detailing cargo on board the vessel. Additionally Customs require the following – if applicable.

(i) The cargo declaration copy – form C 13 which was

submitted at the time of ship's arrival under inward clearance. Customs require to have details of any imported goods remaining on board for export.

(ii) Details of any clearance given previously at a UK port for the same voyage.

(b) *Form SUR 238* – declaration of deck cargo tonnage – if applicable.

(c) *PAS 15 (Departure)* – passenger return – if applicable.

Additionally Customs will check the following ship's papers to confirm they are valid and correct:

  (i) loadline certificate or loadline exemption certificate;
 (ii) cargo ship safety equipment construction certificate (if less than 500 tons gross);
(iii) safety certificate;
 (iv) passenger certificate (if a passenger ship);
  (v) ships register or certificate of registry;
 (vi) lights certificate – to confirm any light dues which fall for payment have been paid.

When all these formalities have been completed the ship may sail on her voyage.

6.3 SHIP'S PAPERS

UK registered ships, where so required, should carry the following documents, including those required by international regulations, and it is obligatory for the Master to produce them to any person who has authority to inspect them.

1. Charter party or bills of lading.

2. Cargo manifest. This contains an inventory of cargo carried on board the vessel giving details of cargo description, consignee/consigner, destination port, container number, etc. The data are despatched by the telex/airmail to the ship/port agent by the shipowner to give details to port authority importers, customs, etc. It enables the agent to prepare for the ship's arrival.

3. List of dutiable stores.

4. Loadline certificate or loadline exemption certificate.

5. Cargo ship safety equipment construction certificate ship licence (if less than 500 tons gross).

6. Safety certificate.

7. Passenger certificate (if a passenger ship), or cargo ship safety radio certificate or exemption certificate (if 300 tons or more).

8. Ship's register or certificate of registry. This is the ship's official certificate of registration and is issued by the authorities of the country in which the ship is registered. It gives the registration number, name of vessel, port of registry, details of the ship and particulars of ownership.

9. Official log.

10. Radio log book if required.

11. De-ratting certificate in accordance with Regulation 19 of the Public Health (Ships) Regulations 1970.

12. Deck log book.

13. Oil record book.

14. Crew list.

All these documents have been described elsewhere in this book, with the exception of the official log. This is in reality the ship's diary, and is required to be compiled in a form laid down by the Department of Trade. Entries found in the official log include any births, deaths and marriages; a record of the crew's conduct, wages, and any fines; any unusual incident or mishap to the ship (such as going to the aid of another vessel in distress); fire in the engine room, adverse weather conditions causing the ship to reduce speed or even shelter in an estuary, and so on. All entries in the log book are admissible as evidence in a court of law. Furthermore, all entries recorded must be made as soon as practicable after the actual incident and signed by the Master and by a senior member of the ship's crew on duty at the time of the occurrence. Apart from the official log, ships also keep deck, engine and radio logs.

6.4 SHIP'S PROTEST

The Master, on arrival at the port, may decide to make a protest before a consul or notary public, declaring that he and his officers have exercised all reasonable care and skill during the voyage to avoid damage to ship and cargo, and that any actual loss is due to extraordinary circumstances beyond their control. Protest is a formality, but in cases where damage or loss has occurred, extending protest is made within 6 months of noting, and sworn declaration may be supported by members of the ship's crew. In the UK there is no legal necessity to note protest, but noting of protest assists the defence against claims by consignees. In other countries protest is necessary before certain legal remedies can be obtained.

In the event of any casuality to the ship, the Master and/or his officers would be required to give depositions under oath before a receiver of wreck, who is a senior Customs officer.

6.5 INLAND CLEARANCE DEPOTS

Inland Clearance Depots (ICDs) are situated at convenient points – usually in industrial and commercial areas often outside the limits of any port or airport. They are operated by a consortium or other approved body and provide facilities for the entry, examination and clearance of goods imported or exported in containers, railway train ferry wagons, unit loads or other approved methods. This facility has been inaugurated in recent years to reduce to a minimum the formalities that have to be observed at the ship's side. It enables importers and exporters to gain full advantage of the use of such services as 'Roll-on/Roll-off', vehicular carrying ships, and containerization generally.

CHAPTER 7

Maritime canals and inland waterways

The geographical position and economic importance of artificial waterways must be considered by all concerned in the shipping industry. In fact it is a subject of growing importance in the shipping industry with the development of the combined transport operation and the escalation in price of bunker oil in 1973 and 1979 causing owners to use shorter voyage routes.

The real economic importance of maritime international canals has, however, changed in recent years, due in the main to the introduction of larger capacity vessels with deeper draught, such as the mammoth oil tankers. Maritime canals must therefore keep pace with new tonnage developments, otherwise ships will follow alternative routes due to the sheer inability of the canal to accommodate their draught, beam or length. One must therefore judge individual maritime canals in terms of their economic importance, seen in the light of their physical ability to accept modern tonnage currently or potentially available.

Since 1973 there has been a radical change in shipping practice much of which stems from the escalation in fuel cost. The era of building the most mammoth-sized vessel particularly tankers and bulk carriers has virtually ceased for the foreseeable future. Ships are more multipurpose in their design to counter trade fluctuations and some shipowners are placing less emphasis on attaining fast schedules especially when conveying lower value cargoes. Moreover, with many shipping companies in a depressed financial situation, greater emphasis is on cost consciousness and operating the most economic schedules. All the foregoing factors must be reconciled with the international role of artificial waterways.

A glance at a map will indicate the vital importance of the Suez Canal not only to those countries with a Mediterranean coastline, or bordering on the Arabian Sea, but also to the countries of North West Europe – the UK, Holland and Germany – which have extensive and long-established commercial connections with countries of the Far East.

Similarly, the opening of the Panama Canal has accelerated the development of the North Pacific coast of the USA and Canada. The canal is 51 miles long and in 1987 handled 1.3 million TEUs representing 14% of its annual 150 million tonnes of total traffic. It has a traditional role of conveying a sizeable volume of the US intercoastal trade linking the East and West coast ports. It is also very popular with shipments from the Asian Pacific Rim and the US East Coast.

In addition to these examples, there are many other instances where distances have been reduced on trade routes. A recent example is the new canal of about 60 km which runs wholly across Romanian territory to connect Cernavoda on the Danube with the port of Constanza on the Black sea which opened in 1982. The waterway width is 70–90 m and it is lock-free. It provides a considerable stimulus to Danube trade and reduces the distance between Regensburg in the Federal Republic of Germany and Constanza from 2500 to 2100 km.

Other considerations in an owner's mind when routing his vessel are the price and availability of fuel at the alternative bunkering ports, and the complexities of the International Loadline Regulations (varying with the time of year) which limit the amount of both freight-earning cargo and bunkers. With regard to fuel cost, which now forms a substantial portion of the daily operating expense of a vessel, the bunker savings realized by choosing the canal route will have a major bearing on the evaluation.

A liner operator has the same basic problem of routing to face, but additional consideration has to be given to the amount of cargo likely to be shipped to and from the intermediate ports of call on the alternative routes. Thus a liner company in the Australian trades can participate also in trade with Egypt, the Red Sea, and Colombo if their ships proceed via Suez. Otherwise, if they sail via South Africa they can also carry cargo between such ports and Australia. Of course, the schedule of liner services is complicated by the fluctuations in cargo offerings and the profitability to those operators concerned.

Table 7.1 Suez Canal dues tabulation

| Type of Vessel | Canal Toll Rates, 1987 | | | | Suez Canal Net Tonnage | | | | | |
| | First 5000 tonnes Per SDR | | Next 15 000 tonnes Per SDR | | Next 20 000 tonnes Per SDR | | Next 45 000 tonnes Per SDR | | Rest of the tonnage Per SDR | |
	Laden	Ballast	Laden	Ballast	Laden	Ballast	Laden	Ballast	Laden	Ballast
1. Tankers of crude oil	5.10	4.08	2.70	2.16	1.25	1.00	1.20	0.96	1.10	0.88
2. Tankers of petroleum products	5.10	4.08	2.70	2.16	1.45	1.00	1.45	0.96	1.45	0.88
3. Bulk carriers	5.10	4.08	2.70	2.16	1.0	0.80	0.80	0.64	0.80	0.64
4. Combined carriers										
(i) if carrying crude oil only;	5.10		2.70		1.25		1.20		1.10	
(ii) if carrying petroleum products only;	5.10		2.70		1.45		1.45		1.45	
(iii) if carrying dry bulk cargo only;	5.10		2.70		1.0		0.80		0.80	
(iv) if carrying more than one kind of cargo;	5.10		2.70		1.45		1.45		1.45	
(v) if in ballast;		4.08		2.16		1.00		0.96		0.88
5. Other vessels – including gas carriers (LPG – LNG)	5.10	4.08	2.70	2.16	2.15	1.72	2.15	1.72	2.15	1.72

Reproduced by kind permission of Suez Canal Authority

7.1 SUEZ CANAL AUTHORITY

The Suez Canal was opened in 1869 linking the Mediterranean with the Red Sea. Its overall length between Port Said and Port Thewfik is 192 km and its breadth at water level is 300 m. The maximum permissible draught of ships is 53 ft and the depth of the canal is 19.5–20 m.

The canal is navigable throughout the 24 hours and operates on a single lane basis with four bypass points at Port Said, Ballah, Timsah and Deversoir. A ship takes on average 14 hours to transit the canal. Three convoys transit the canal daily departing from Port Said at 0100 hours and 0700 hours, and from the Suez at 0600 hours. Pilotage is compulsory for all ships of more than 300 tons. A speed limit is imposed varying from 13 to 15 km/h according to the category and tonnage of ships.

The Suez Canal has recently introduced a vessel traffic control system which is a comprehensive system to ensure safety of transit in the Canal as well as increasing the Canal throughput capacity. The system consists of the following:

(a) A three-station radar network at Port Said–Bitter Lakes–Port Thewfik.

(b) A wireless Loran C. position fixing network (Port Said–Tenth of Ramadan City–Raas Sedre).

(c) Digital computer network which displays accurate and comprehensive data about the traffic situation on visual display units in the control room.

(d) Several wireless communication networks all along the Canal network. Details of the Canal toll rates are given in Table 7.1.

Table 7.2

From	To	Distance in Miles		
		Via Cape of Good Hope	Via Suez Canal	Difference in Miles
Rotterdam	Bombay	10 850	6 337	4 513
Piraeus	Jeddah	11 410	1 320	10 090
New York	Singapore	12 430	10 169	2 261

Reproduced with kind permission of Suez Canal Authority

The geographic position of the Suez canal has made it the shortest navigable route between the East and West as compared with the route of the Cape of Good Hope, thus offering considerable savings in cost of operating, voyage time and fuel oil as in the examples given in Table 7.2.

The number of ships passing through the Canal is falling and in 1986 totalled 18 500 – a decline of 7% whilst the net tonnage increased to 13.5 million tons – an increase of 4%. Hence the average size vessel using the Canal is increasing and in 1986 the daily number was 50 ships.

Details of types of vessel which used the Canal in 1986 are given Table 7.3.

The volume of merchandise including oil which transited the Suez Canal in 1986 was 262 million tonnes – an increase of 4 million tonnes. An analysis of the main areas involved are given in Table 7.4.

The foregoing pattern of trade is likely to continue into the 1990s.

7.2 THE ECONOMIC EFFECT OF CANALS AND THE LEVEL OF DUES CHARGED

Few, if any, canals are built purely with the profit motive in view. It will be realized that the political and naval importance of such waterways as Panama and Kiel were at least partly responsible for their construction. Once the canal is built, however, its administrators (within the framework of their powers) are actuated by economic motives to secure traffic. In general, dues cannot be more than the cost of sending a vessel the 'long way round'. Of course, some canals are much more open to this sort of competition than others. Vessels in the Baltic trades often use the Kiel Canal only if they have reason to believe that bad weather on the Skaw route may delay their passage.

A good example of the economical effect a canal may impose on a region is the St Lawrence Seaway which was opened in 1959. Overall it is a deep waterway extending some 2340 miles from the Atlantic Ocean to the head of the Great Lakes, at the heart of North America. The St Lawrence Seaway extends from Montreal to Lake Erie and includes the Welland Canal (usually referred to as the Western section) and in the east of Montreal–Lake Ontario

Table 7.3

	Net Tonnage	Total No. of Vessels	No. of Vessels Loaded
Tankers	138 559	3 659	2 024
Combined carriers	24 186	429	246
Dry cargo vessels	54 930	2 895	2 593
Container ships	56 020	2 468	2 335
General cargo ships	43 557	7 224	6 090
Ro/Ro ships	16 238	984	803
Car carriers	23 511	637	111
LASH ships	3 482	119	106
Passenger ships	602	51	38
Warships	749	139	–
Other	4 242	1 081	796

Table 7.4

Areas North of Canal	*Loaded and Unloaded Goods Quantities (000 tonnes)*
Ports of European Seaboard and UK	85 529
Baltic sea ports	6 649
North Mediterranean ports	71 779
East and south east Mediterranean ports	19 419
Black Sea ports	33 050
American ports	21 952
West and south west Mediterranean ports	21 252
Others	2 822
Areas South of Canal	
Red Sea ports	70 610
East African ports and Aden	7 930
India, Pakistan, Burma, Sri-Lanka	31 441
Arabian Gulf ports	64 188
East Asian ports and Sunda Islands	28 110
Far East ports	48 705
Australian ports	11 228
Others	240

section which extends from the St Lambart Lock, the upbound entrance of the Seaway, to Lake Ontario just beyond the Iroquois Lock.

Vessels 222.5 m long, 23.0 m wide and loaded to a draught of 7.9 m now travel through the Seaway locks. These large 'lakers' may carry more than 27 000 tonnes of iron ore or 36 000 m³ of wheat. Iron ore and wheat constitute the most important cargoes carried through the canal and the two-way nature of their movement is significant to the economy of the Great Lakes region, and indeed of the entire continent. It is rather doubtful that the rapid expansion of the Quebec–Labrador mining complex would have taken place without the Seaway, of which the Welland Canal was the forerunner. One can also well imagine the difficulties Canada would have encountered in meeting delivery commitments on its massive wheat sales were it not for the efficient and inexpensive shipping facilities provided by the waterway. Mine products together with an increasing number of manufactured goods are growth areas in the canal trade.

7.3 THE INFLUENCE OF CANALS ON SHIP DESIGN

The construction of artificial waterways, and any necessary locks, is very costly and therefore the size of ships which can use them is often restricted. Bearing such limitations in mind, the ship designer therefore limits the dimensions of the vessels so that they are able to navigate the particular waterways likely to be used. Such limitations affect the draught in the case of many canals, and length and beam in respect of locks, while, to deal with overhead obstructions, retractable top masts and removable funnel tops may be needed.

To get the longest possible sized vessel through various locks the designer uses all his skill, sometimes resulting in the compromise of vessels with inferior sea-keeping qualities and added cost per deadweight tonne.

Canal authorities charge their dues on the tonnage of the vessels using their waterways; major canals such as Suez and Panama have their own system of tonnage measurement.

The development in recent years of inland waterways in certain European countries has fostered the development of major ports such as Antwerp, Rotterdam, Hamburg, Dunkerque and Calais.

7.4 CANAL AREAS AS POINTS OF ECONOMIC GROWTH

Not all ships pass directly through canals; the ports at their entrances become important transhipment ports through the regular services traversing the waterway. Other activities concerned with shipping such as bunkering also develop. Such areas offer flat land with excellent port facilities for private quays and a position on the ocean trade routes; all these are very important factors in the location of modern large-scale industry.

This final aspect is observed more in those artificial waterways as yet hardly mentioned – those which lead to an important trade centre or industrial area. Ports like Dunkerque and Rotterdam can only be reached by ocean vessels through their own canals, and it is on the banks of these that modern industrial installations are constructed, with all the benefits arising from deep water quays on the actual site. Refineries, iron and steel works, paper mills and chemical installations all come into this category.

However, the most important example in modern ocean transport is the St Lawrence Seaway allowing deep-sea vessels to reach the heart of industrial (and agricultural) North America clustered around the Great Lakes. The Great Lakes themselves formed an important artery of water transport before ocean ships could reach them, and developed their own form of vessel, the 'laker'. These ships can now reach the Lower St Lawrence to tranship to ocean vessels there, but they face competition from deep-sea vessels (albeit limited in their draught) able to load direct from railheads and warehouses.

7.5 INLAND WATERWAYS

Shipping is becoming more integrated with inland waterways as the concept of the combined transport system develops. The provision of LASH, BACO and SEABEE liner concepts as explained in Chapter 4 are facilitating such developments. Other types of tonnage exploiting the combined transport system include containers, Combi carriers, train ferries and Ro/Ro vessels. Such ships rely primarily on rail and road as a distributor.

As the energy situation encourages countries endeavouring to conserve their energy source import bill, it will strongly favour the development of inland waterways where favourable physical situations obtain. This position is evident for example in Western Europe particularly France, West Germany and Holland. In West Germany, 27% of freight is conveyed by inland waterway whilst the figure in France was 10% and Holland 42% in 1980. Moreover, modernization of the system in such countries continues to increase the capacity of the barge using the network and extend it operationally where economic to do so. An example due for completion in 1990 is the Rhine/Rhone project involving the widening of the 229-km canal length between the Saône and the Rhine to connect Fos (Marseilles) and Rotterdam. Meanwhile the project Rhine/Main/Danube connection opened in the late 1980s linked Rotterdam to the Black Sea. Another scheme under consideration is the Seine-Nord and Est Region to the Moselle in North East France.

In considering Inland waterways one must give particular emphasis to the role they play in many less developed and developing countries. The infrastructure in such countries tends to be inadequate in many areas especially in the area of transportation/distribution to and from the ports. Hence lighterage remains an important distributor especially of primary products and other non-containerized cargoes. It is economical and aids the quicker port turn-round of vessels. Moreover, it reduces the level of congestion in the port/quay. In the longer term it is likely to become more popular on an international scale particularly where the traffic volume and capital infrastructure favours it such as, for example, in Western Europe and Third World countries.

7.6 EUROTUNNEL

The Eurotunnel currently under construction is a 31 mile route subterranean rail tunnel between Folkestone (UK) and Frethun near Calais (France). It is being built below the sea bed in the English Channel and will have three tunnels – two of which will be 7.6 m diameter to convey trains and one of 3.3 m which will be a service tunnel. Terminals with road and rail access will be provided at both portals (Ashford and Calais).

Two types of trains will use the tunnel. Cars and coaches at the portals will drive onto a special shuttle train service. Cars will use double-decker wagons, and coaches single deckers. Passengers will stay with their vehicles or stroll around the train. Road haulage vehicles will drive onto a separate single decker shuttle train service. The other type of train will be the through intercity international express passenger which will run from London (and eventually other major UK cities) to European destinations such as Paris, Brussels and so on. Journey time through the tunnel will be 35 minutes providing an overall journey time of 3 hours 15 minutes between London and Paris. Completion of the Euro-tunnel is scheduled for 1993 at a cost of £2100 million (1987 prices). Eurotunnel is an Anglo-French company.

This project will have a major impact on the existing shipping routes operating between Newhaven/Dieppe; Folkestone/Bou-logne; Dover/Boulogne/Calais/Dunkerque; Ramsgate/Dunkerque, and Dover/Ostend. It is very likely the bulk of such traffic conveyed on the foregoing services to/from French ports will transfer to the Eurotunnel if the market conditions are favourable. This includes road haulage vehicles (Ro/Ro), coaches, cars, and passengers. Air traffic between London and Paris will also be adversely affected. Much additional traffic is likely to be generated by the Eurotunnel especially in the passenger market. Present market growth on the shipping routes is between five and seven percent per year according to type of traffic. Overall traffic volume between 1988 and 2003 is likely to double.

A number of reasons exist for the development of the project which are given below:

(a) Growth in tourism and trade between UK and Europe following UK admission into EEC in 1973.

(b) Development of UK and Continental motorway network have favoured strongly the growth of Ro/Ro, cars and coaches to and from the Continent.

(c) Higher capacity Ro/Ro units through legislation – currently 38 tonnes gross – and improved technology of the road haulage vehicle favour the economics of European road operation growth.

(d) Port modernization and higher capacity ships with lower unit cost have aided market development coupled with quick customs clearance at the ports.

(e) Decline in UK/Commonwealth trade markets and continu-ing integration with EEC which will be further developed when the political country boundaries disappear in 1992 thereby permitting freedom of movement of goods throughout the Community.

The provision of the Eurotunnel will further raise the profess-ional standards of international distribution between UK/EEC and should aid UK trade and tourism expansion on an accelerated scale.

A further rail tunnel completed in 1988 was the Seikan tunnel linking the main island of Honshu with Hokkaido. The tunnel is 32.3 miles long and links the Japanese and Asian mainland railway systems. Traffic hitherto was conveyed on the ferries across the Tsugaru Straits. It cost £46 000 million.

Services performed by principal shipping organizations

It is indeed appropriate at a time when international shipping is becoming more influenced by international and national organizations that this chapter is enlarged with the sixth edition of this book.

8.1 GENERAL COUNCIL OF BRITISH SHIPPING

The General Council of British Shipping (GCBS) is the representative body of the British shipping industry, nationally and internationally, on all aspects of corporate policy affecting it. The scope of its activities is wide and varied, ranging from consultations with government departments on policies affecting the interests of its members and negotiations with seafarers' unions on industrial relations and manpower questions, to the provision of services to its members in the recruitment and training of seafarers and the provision of crews. The GCBS became operative on 1st March 1975 when it took over the roles of the Chamber of Shipping of the United Kingdom and the British Shipping Federation, both established for nearly a century. It is an incorporated company limited by guarantee and not having a share capital.

Overall there are three classes of members, namely:

(a) Members, who are persons resident in the UK or bodies corporate registered in the UK owning or managing UK registered ships. Members cover the entire UK merchant fleet consisting of some 200 or so shipping companies owning or managing about 50 million dwt of shipping.

(b) Associate Members, who comprise associations of shipowners established in the UK who represent the interests of shipowners in a particular area or in respect of a particular type of ship and also Protection and Indemnity Associations or similar bodies of which UK shipowners are members.

(c)   Honorary Members, who may be admitted at the discretion of the General Council.

The primary object of the GCBS is to promote and protect the interests of the owners and managers of British ships and to take appropriate action, nationally and internationally, to achieve that end. It is not directly involved in the commercial affairs of individual companies but tries to set the climate in which shipping can best serve trade and operate as a free enterprise competitive industry.

The GCBS is closely connected with legislation which affects or could affect shipping and while maintaining a position of strict political neutrality it advises, consults, negotiates and, where necessary, takes issue with the government of the day on policies which directly or indirectly can affect the interests of the shipping industry. Although this work is done in discussion with ministers and their officials there is also liaison with members of all parties of both Houses of Parliament to ensure that they are kept well informed of developments within the shipping industry and of its achievements and problems.

There are links too with industry and commerce generally in the UK and overseas.

On sea-going personnel matters, the GCBS represents British shipowners and managers on bodies such as the National Maritime Board, the Merchant Navy Training Board, the Seafarers' Pension Funds and the Merchant Navy Welfare Board. It provides an advisory service to its members on the development of industrial relations policies.

It is responsible for the recruitment, selection and shore training of most of the rating personnel employed in the Merchant Navy. It also plays an important part in the recruitment of deck and engineer cadets, and in the formulation and co-ordination of policy on the training of officers. Moreover it administers the Merchant Navy Established Service Scheme.

Shipping being an international business, effective working relationships are important with the many organizations concerned with trade and shipping throughout the world. Accordingly the GCBS is linked with the work of the International Maritime Organization (IMO), the International Labour Organization (ILO), United Nations Conference on Trade and Development (UNCTAD), United Nations Commission on International Trade

Law (UNCITRAL), the International Chamber of Shipping (ICS), the International Shipping Federation (ISF), the Council of European and Japanese National Shipowner's Association (CENSA), the International Chamber of Commerce (ICC), the British and European Shippers' Councils, the EEC Shipowners Association (CAACE), the Customs Co-operative Council (CCC), the Economic Commission for Europe (ECE), the Baltic and International Maritime Conference (BIMCO), the International Association of Independent Tanker Owners (INTERTANKO), and many others of direct concern to the industry. The GCBS is also linked with the many professional and similar bodies concerned with shipping in the UK. The GCBS provides the secretariat for the ICS and ISF.

The governing body of the GCBS is the General Council which comprises all members and meets at least once a year. The conduct of the business of the GCBS is vested in a General Policy Committee (GPC) of not more than forty persons, some elected – including the President and Vice-President – and some co-opted. The GPC, which meets at regular intervals, is in effect the organization's 'Board of Directors' and as such is its top policy-making body. It is supported by a carefully integrated organizational structure comprising Sections (each representing a different category of shipping), Districts and Functional Committees. These cover every phase of work of the GCBS and are composed of persons drawn from the senior management of member companies and members of their staff who voluntarily give their time, knowledge and experience for the benefit of the industry as a whole.

The work at headquarters based in London is administered on a divisional basis as follows:

(a) industrial relations, covering all aspects of this subject;

(b) manning, covering manning policy, manning scales, manpower planning, recruitment of seafarers (British Shipping Careers Service), supply of seafarers (MNE), non-UK domiciled seafarers and National Sea Training Trust;

(c) training, covering seafarers' and shore staff-training courses, the Merchant Navy Training Board, defence training;

(d) marine, covering safety, navigation, radio-communications, life-saving appliances, ship construction, prevention of occupational accidents, prevention of marine pollution, carriage of dangerous goods, technical research management services;

(e) foreign shipping policy, covering liner conferences, documentation and customs, containers, insurance, EEC matters;

(f) legal and general, covering ports, port labour, pilotage, lighthouse administration, ship building, ship repairing, prosecution machinery, personal injury claims, maritime law, parliamentary, press and information;

(g) economics and statistics, covering economics including policy research, taxation, shipping finance and statistics;

(h) administration and accounts, covering staff, accounts, office administration, accommodation and ancillary services;

(i) central secretariat, covering constitution and membership, servicing meetings of the General Council, General Policy Committee, Executive and Sections; consultative machinery within the organization, charter parties, library, defence of merchant shipping, annual report and hospitality. In 1987, the GCBS, BST and ICS were formed into a single group.

8.2 INTERNATIONAL ASSOCIATION OF INDEPENDENT TANKER OWNERS (INTERTANKO)

The International Association of Independent Tanker Owners with headquarters in Oslo, is an organization of tanker owners from all major maritime nations. Today INTERTANKO membership comprises more than 270 tanker companies controlling over 170 million dwt tankers and combined tonnage. Oil company and government owned tanker tonnage is not eligible for membership.

INTERTANKO started with the tanker crisis in the 1930s which initiated a closer co-operation in an otherwise competitive industry. The successful tanker lay-up pool commonly known as the Schierwater plan, was administered by the International Tanker Owners Association Ltd. (INTERTANKO) established in the spring of 1934.

When the tanker market improved towards the end of the 1930s the organization slowly went into hibernation where it remained until it was formally dissolved in 1954.

The successful experiment of the Schierwater plan fostered an atmosphere of international co-operation, and INTERTANKO was once more established in London in the mid-1950s under its former name. This organization did not, however, gain the support and momentum necessary to further its members' interests effectively and subsequently fell into a semi-dormant state.

In 1970, a group of independent tanker owners congregated in Oslo. Delegates from ten maritime nations then instituted the International Association of Independent Tanker Owners, again called INTERTANKO. The new organization started its work in January 1971, with secretariat and headquarters in the Norwegian Shipowners' Association building in Oslo.

Although the new INTERTANKO was given a broader mandate, it was agreed that it should not participate in lay-up schemes. The aims of the organization were that the association should be a non-profit body whose aims are to further the interest of independent tanker owners. The scope and objectives were to promote internationally the interests of its members in matters of general policy; to co-operate with other technical, industrial or commercial interests or bodies on problems of mutual concern to its members and to take part in the deliberations of other international bodies as far as may be necessary for the attainment of its objectives.

INTERTANKO's vigorous participation in international forums has produced its reputation for effective promotion of the interests of independent owners and works closely with the following organizations:

(a) IMO: INTERTANKO is represented at all relevant IMO meetings. It has stressed the problem of lack of shore reception for oily wastes; promoted further ratification of MARPOL – particularly by the oil exporting countries – to ensure a fair division of liability for oil pollution compensation between cargo and shipowning interests.

(b) UNCTAD: Increased pressure for protectionist measures; cargo sharing in the bulk trades and elimination of open registries has been firmly resisted by INTERTANKO. As always, INTERTANKO's case has been based on the sound economic facts which, taken together, reveal the benefits of free competition.

(c) Worldscale: Close links are maintained between INTERTANKO and the Worldscale Association. There is continuous dialogue on both basic principles and updating of freight schedules. INTERTANKO's Port Office provides crucial information for the updating of freight schedules.

In addition, INTERTANKO maintains close liaison with the International Chamber of Shipping, the Baltic and International

Maritime Council, the Oil Companies, International Marine Forum and other national and international organizations.

INTERTANKO places much emphasis to ensure that its services are of practical value to members. The services include:

(a) Port information office
Members receive monthly bulletins including the latest data on port conditions and costs. INTERTANKO's comprehensive service includes prompt action on behalf of members where overcharging is demonstrated, and expert advice on port costs, agency arrangements, freight taxes, etc.

(b) Freight and demurrage information pool
A service designed to combat the growing problem of late or non-payment by charterers and oil traders. The Pool succeeded in collecting or speeding up settlement of over USD 1.5 million in its first 2 years of operation.

(c) Charter party conditions
INTERTANKO has produced model clauses and documents for all forms of tanker chartering. Its experts provide members with practical advice on chartering problems.

(d) Market research
INTERTANKO's market research brings an independent view of basic trends in tanker supply and demand. Recent publications include: *The Outlook for Product Tankers; VLLCCs Present and Future;* and *Alternative Tanker Opportunities.*

(e) Commercial/safety information
INTERTANKO members receive regular bulletins, providing the latest data on port and bunker costs, charter party news, market trends, information on regulatory developments affecting operation of tankers and safety at sea and other vital information.

8.3 INTERNATIONAL CARGO HANDLING CO-ORDINATION ASSOCIATION

The aim of the International Cargo Handling Co-ordination Association is to facilitate improved handling techniques in the world transport system. The concept of a worldwide body to achieve this aim was inaugurated in 1951 and ICHCA was established with its headquarters, the International Secretariat, in London.

The new Association expanded rapidly, and in the first 4 years of its life, eight national committees were established in Western European countries, backed up by a strong local membership in the transport field. While maintaining an overall international participation through close links with the International Secretariat, these national committees dealt primarily with problems peculiar to their own countries, organizing meetings and seminars which often attracted participation from beyond their frontiers. Today ICHCA's links have further developed with members in some 90 countries worldwide and there exists some 21 national committees.

The prime function of ICHCA is co-ordination. This is achieved by including in its worldwide membership and activities the diverse disciplines that have an impact on cargo handling efficiency; by stimulating interest and cross-fertilization of ideas through technical meetings, seminars and technical publications; by gathering and disseminating pertinent technical, conceptual and procedural information; and by identifying trends and evolving concepts in the science of cargo handling thus crystallizing ideas in this field. ICHCA has pursued this crystallizing function since its inception, as a brief survey of its major activities shows. In the mid-1950s, the Association was discussing the packaging of timber and the handling of sugar in bulk, while Ro/Ro operations were first debated at the 1957 Biennial Conference in Hamburg. The container was the subject of a conference in the same decade, and the continuing development of this unit-load device was followed by ICHCA in the 1960s. Barge carriers and computer operations in cargo handling were examined in 1969 and 1970. Further work continued with computer operations etc, as a result of which ICHCA published *Electronic Data Processing and Computer Involvement in Container Handling Operations* in 1986.

In 1973, the Technical Advisory Sub-Committee (TASC) was formed; it is composed of representatives from national sections of ICHCA worldwide and seventeen nations are at present represented. TASC normally meets four times a year, the gatherings being held in different participating countries; the major part of its work, however, is done by correspondence which is co-ordinated by the ICHCA Technical Officer, located in the International Secretariat in London. TASC was formed to monitor technical matters of concern to ICHCA and is considered of particular interest to the Association's membership.

Since its inception, the work of TASC has resulted in a number of significant reports published by the International Secretariat as follows:

(i) *Condensation in Containers.* This was originally published in 1974 and quickly became known as the standard work on this topic. It won widespread approval throughout the industry and was recommended by the International Union of Marine Insurance as mandatory reading. Further work was subsequently carried out and culminated in the publication in 1986 of *Condensation in Containers: an Interim Report.*

(ii) *Cargo Security in Transport Systems* (1976). This was a two-part project; the first concerned pilferage, while the second examined the incidence and prevention of major theft. The reports formed the basis of two conferences on cargo security, held in London and Amsterdam.

(iii) *Preslinging and Strapping of Cargo* (1977). This examined simple low-cost methods of unitizing cargo and aroused considerable interest, particularly from developing countries.

(iv) *Ro/Ro Shore and Ramp Characteristics* (1978). This brought together for the first time details of over one thousand Ro/Ro ramps in ports and on ships throughout the world. The data, initially intended to assist the International Standards Organization in harmonizing the Ro/Ro ship-to-shore connection, have transcended the initial purpose and proved of value to ship operators, naval architects, equipment manufacturers, terminal managers and shippers.

(v) *The Securing of ISO Containers: Theory and Practice* (1981). This was the first major study of the costs of securing containers and was based on extensive enquiries and personal visits to the ship operators, stevedores, terminal managers and others.

(vi) *The Handling of ISO Containers in Low Throughput Situations* (1982). This provides a well illustrated insight into the solutions available for handling containers in a variety of limited throughput situations, outside the context of large ports.

(vii) *An International Survey on Handling Iron and Steel Prod-*

ucts (1982). This surveys the handling, storage and transport of semi-finished and finished iron and steel products from mill to consumer. It highlights international practice and provides guidance on equipment, tackle, methods and approaches, with a view to minimizing the risk of injury to those who handle the cargo and of damage to products.

(viii) *Containers the Lease-Buy Decision* (1983). This picks out the key factors which a shipping company must examine before deciding between container ownership and the leasing option.

(ix) *The Safe Handling of Flexible Intermediate Bulk Containers (FIBCs).* (1985). This was published as a result of the increased use of FIBCs since ICHCA first produced the results of its survey into the use of IBCs in 1979. This guide gives a description of FIBCs covering the forms of construction and lifting arrangements together with dock safety and legal requirements.

(x) *Multilingual Glossary of Cargo Handling Terms* (1987). This has so far been published in three editions, with the third edition incorporating nine languages: Dutch, Finnish, French, Italian, German, Portuguese, Spanish, Swedish and English.

The ICHCA Container Panel also meets regularly and, in conjunction with the Technical Officer, have produced a number of publications:

(i) *Handling Containers in Small Ports* (1985 & 1987). These two seminars covered the initial port operation and the gradual development of the facility to optimum operational and economic efficiency, taking into account climate, local terrain and ground conditions.

(ii) *Equipment Availability, Downtime and Utilization.* This paper sets out to discuss performance indices with a view to clarifying them and to demonstrate ways in which they can be of use.

(iii) *Safe Handling of ISO Freight Containers by Hooks and General Guide to the Container Safety Convention* (1987). This gives a brief guide on these topics which were identified when undertaking a survey on the handling of containers with hooks. The answers to the questionnaire revealed that containers are often handled with wire slings and hooks, sometimes rigged in combination with a variety of different spreaders or lifting beams, many of which impose compressive forces on the container. With the tendency to lift heavier loads there is the need to improve slinging methods in many small ports. In addition there are numerous conference proceedings and other fully illustrated publications covering the handling of cargo by all modes of transport: road, rail, sea, waterway and air.

Besides crystallizing and stimulating views, ICHCA is a catalyst for the cargo-handling industry and is always seeking means of involvement in training and the development of the Third World countries. Although the structure of the Association does not lend itself easily to the establishment of training courses, much has been done in the past in conjunction with educational and other organizations in various parts of the world to arrange projects, and ICHCA will continue to take an active role in training at all levels. The Henri Kummerman Foundation offered to fund a research project in the 1979/80 biennium, and the first 6-month handling project was undertaken in conjunction with the International Secretariat in 1980. The advantages of this type of assistance is two-fold: the general bank of cargo-handling knowledge is improved, and the experience of those undertaking the projects will be widened by exposure to an international environment.

The threads of ICHCA's activities are drawn together at the biennial Conference and the General Assembly held in different countries at the invitation of the local national committee or section. The themes of the conferences epitomize the Association's work, and the differing venues provide a unique opportunity for the worldwide membership to meet and exchange views and expertise.

Another major activity of the International Secretariat is the monitoring of the many governmental, inter-governmental and non-governmental organizations that are liable to influence new legislation, devise new rules and regulations or generally impinge upon the smooth working of the day-to-day operational life of the people in the industry. This activity of monitoring allows intervention during the discussion on appropriate items on the agenda where ICHCA is granted the status of a participant.

By these means, and through the combined experience and expertise of its members, ICHCA plays a vital role in the field of cargo handling today and in the future.

8.4 INTERNATIONAL CHAMBER OF SHIPPING (ICS)

Formed in 1921 as the International Shipping Conference, and renamed in 1948, this body is an association of national organizations representing predominantly private shipowners in the following 23 countries:

Australia	Greece	Portugal
Belgium	India	Spain
Canada	Ireland	Sweden
Columbia	Italy	Switzerland
Denmark	Japan	UK
Finland	Netherlands	United States
France	New Zealand	Yugoslavia
Federal Republic of Germany	Norway	

Through these organizations, membership of the ICS embraces some 50% of the world's active trading fleets.

ICS deals with shipping policy in its broadest sense, primarily in the technical and legal spheres; it is not concerned with personnel relations, which are handled by the International Shipping Federation.

The objects of ICS as set out in its constitution, are:

(a) To promote internationally the interests of its members in all matters of general policy.

(b) With that end, to exchange views and frame policies for international and national application by way of representations through the governments of the countries represented in ICS or otherwise.

(c) To co-operate with other technical, industrial or commercial interests or bodies on problems of mutual concern to its members and to such interests.

(d) To take part in the deliberations of other international bodies so far as it may be necessary for achievement of its objectives.

8.5 INTERNATIONAL MARITIME ORGANIZATION (IMO)

The IMO is a specialized agency of the United Nations concerned solely with maritime affairs. Its interest lies mainly in ships used in international services. Altogether 131 states are members of IMO including ship-owning nations, countries which use shipping services and countries in the course of development.

The objectives of IMO are to facilitate co-operation among

governments on technical matters affecting shipping, particularly from the angle of safety of life at sea, and the prevention of marine pollution from ships. This entails providing an extensive exchange of information between nations on technical maritime subjects and the concluding of international agreements.

The Convention establishing IMO was drafted by the United Nations Maritime Conference at Geneva in 1948, and it reflected the wish of maritime nations to consolidate the diverse forms of international co-operation which had grown up over the years in the world of shipping. The IMO Convention required acceptance by twenty-one states, including seven with at least one million gross tonnes of shipping each. This requirement was met on 17 March 1958 and the first IMO Assembly met in London in January 1959.

The Assembly consists of representatives from all member states; it decides upon the work programme, approves all recommendations made by IMO, votes the budget to which all member states contribute on an agreed scale of assessments, approves financial regulations, elects the IMO Council and Maritime Safety Committee, and approves the appointment of the Secretary General. The Assembly normally meets in London and regular sessions are held every 2 years.

The Council consists of representatives of thirty-two member states elected by the Assembly for a term of two years; it normally meets twice a year and is IMO's governing body between Assembly sessions.

The Council has established Committees on Maritime Safety, Protection of the Marine Environment, Law, Technical Co-operation and Facilitation, the latter dealing with simplifying formalities and paperwork connected with the arrival and departure of ships.

The Maritime Safety Committee is the most important one and deals with navigation aids, construction and equipment of ships, rules for preventing collisions at sea, dangerous cargoes, life-saving appliances, marine radio-communications, standardization of training, watch-keeping and qualifications of officers and crew, search and rescue. It also deals with subdivision and damage stability, intact stability, loadlines, safety of fishing vessels; ship design and equipment; fire protection of ships; automation in ships; tonnage measurement of ships; novel types of craft; special trade passenger ships, and nuclear ships. The Facilitation Committee work aims to reduce and simplify governmental formalities, documentary requirements and procedures connected with the arrival, stay and departure of ships. It also considers all matters concerning facilitation of international maritime travel and transport, and deals with the formulation, circulation, adoption and implementation of facilitation measures expediting maritime traffic and preventing unnecessary delays.

The role of IMO within international shipping grows annually and given on pages 130–40 is a list of Conventions formulated by IMO.

The adoption of a convention marks the conclusion of the first stage of the process, but the adoption by itself is hardly enough. Before the convention comes into force, i.e. before it becomes binding upon governments, it has to be accepted formally, through the procedure of ratification by individual governments.

Each convention includes appropriate provisions stipulating conditions which have to be met before it enters into force. These conditions vary from convention to convention, but generally speaking the more important and more complex the document, the more stringent are the conditions for its entry into force. For example, the International Convention for the Safety of Life at Sea 1974, provides that entry into force requires acceptance by 25 states owning not less than 50% of the world's gross merchant shipping tonnage; for the International Convention on Tonnage Measurement of Ships, 1969, the requirement is acceptance by 25 states owning not less than 65% of world tonnage.

When the appropriate conditions have been fulfilled, the convention enters into force for the states which have accepted – generally after a period of grace intended to enable all the states to take the necessary measure for implementation.

In the case of some conventions which affect a few states or deal with less complex matters, the entry into force requirements may not be so stringent. For example, the Convention Relating to Civil Liability in the Field of Maritime Carriage of Nuclear Material 1971, came into force ninety days after being accepted by five states; the Special Trade Passenger Ships Agreement 1971, came into force 6 months after three states (including two with ships or nationals involved in special trades) had accepted it.

For the important technical conventions, it is necessary that they be accepted and applied by a large section of the shipping community. It is therefore essential that these should, upon entry into force, be applicable to as many of the maritime states as possible.

Table 8.1 IMO's conventions as at March 1987

Title of Convention	Date of Adoption	Conventions Requirements for Entry into Force	Period between Fulfilment of Requirements and Entry into Force	Date of Entry into Force	Contracting Parties at 1 Mar. 1987	Amendments and Protocols (P) Is Tacit Acceptance Procedure Included?	Year of Adoption	Date of Entry into Force	Contracting Parties at 1 Mar. 1987	Notes
a	b	c	d	e	f	g	h	i	j	k
Maritime Safety										
International Convention for the Safety of Life at Sea (SOLAS)	1 Nov. 1974	25 States whose combined merchant fleets constitute not less than 50% of world gross tonnage	1 year	25 May 1980	97 96%	Yes	1978 (P) 1981 1983	1 May 1981 1 Sept 1984 1 July 1986	62 89% – –	The adopted amendments to SOLAS 1960 are incorporated in this instrument
International Convention on Load Lines (LL)	5 Apr. 1966	15 States including 7 with not less than 1 million gt of shipping	1 year	21 July 1968	110 97%	No	1971 1975 1979 1983		46 41 37 17	The amendments will enter into force 12 months after being ratified by 2/3 of Contracting Parties (73)

a	b	c	d	e	f	g	h	i	j	k
Special Trade Passenger Ships Agreement (STP)	6 Oct. 1971	3 States (including at least 2 in whose territory are registered ships engaged in special trades or whose nationals are carried in ships engaged in these trades)	6 mths	2 Jan. 1974	13	No	1973 (P)	2 June 1977	11	
International Convention for Safe Containers (CSC)	2 Dec. 1972	10 States	1 year	6 Sept. 1977	44	No	1981	1 Dec. 1981	–	The amendments are concerned with Annex I, regulations for testing, inspection, approval and maintenance of containers
							1983	1 Jan. 1984	–	

	Conventions					Amendments and Protocols (P)				
Title of Convention	Date of Adoption	Requirements for Entry into Force	Period between Fulfilment of Requirements and Entry into Force	Date of Entry into Force	Contracting Parties at 1 Mar. 1987	Is Tacit Acceptance Procedure Included?	Year of Adoption	Date of Entry into Force	Contracting Parties at 1 Mar. 1987	Notes
a	b	c	d	e	f	g	h	i	j	k
Convention on the International Regulations for Preventing Collisions at Sea (COLREG)	20 Oct. 1972	15 States with not less than 65% of world fleet by number of ships or g+t	1 year	15 July 1977	97 95%	Yes	1981	1 June 1983	–	These regulations replace those adopted in 1960 and annexed to the Final Act of the 1960 SOLAS Conference
Convention on the International Maritime Satellite Organization (INMARSAT) and Operating Agreement	3 Sept. 1976	States representing 95% of initial investment shares	60 days	16 July 1979	48	No	1985	–	11	Amendments to Convention and Operating Agreement will enter into force 120 days after acceptance by ⅔ of Parties/ Signatories representing ⅔ of total intestment shares

a	b	c	d	e	f	g	h	i	j	k
Torremolinos International Convention for the Safety of Fishing Vessels (SFV)	2 Apr. 1977	15 States with not less than 50% of world fishing fleet of 24 m in length and over	1 year	–	15	Yes	–	–	–	
International Convention on Standards of Training, Certification and Watchkeeping for Seafarers (STCW)	7 July 1978	25 States with not less than 50% of world gt	1 year	28 Apr. 1984	56 71%	Yes	–	–	–	
International Convention on Maritime Search and Rescue (SAR)	27 Apr. 1979	15 States	1 year	22 June 1985	27	Yes	–	–	–	

	Conventions						Amendments and Protocols (P)				
a	b	c	d	e	f	g	h	i	j	k
Title of Convention	Date of Adoption	Requirements for Entry into Force	Period between Fulfilment of Requirements and Entry into Force	Date of Entry into Force	Contracting Parties at 1 Mar. 1987	Is Tacit Acceptance Procedure Included?	Year of Adoption	Date of Entry into Force	Contracting Parties at 1 Mar. 1987	Notes

Prevention of Marine Pollution

International Convention Relating to Intervention on the High Seas in Cases of Oil Pollution Casualties (CSI)	29 Nov. 1969	15 States	90 days	6 May 1975	50	No	1973 (P)	30 Mar. 1983	21	

a	b	c	d	e	f	g	h	i	j	k
Convention on the Prevention of Marine Pollution by Dumping of Wastes and Other Matter (LDC)	29 Dec. 1972	15 States	30 days	30 Aug. 1975	61	Yes	1978 (disputes); 1978 (incineration); 1980 (list of substances)	–; 11 Mar. 1979; 11 Mar. 1981	9	This Convention was adopted under the auspices of the United Kingdom but IMO performs Secretariat functions
International Convention for the Prevention of Pollution from Ships, 1973 as modified by the Protocol of 1978 (MARPOL 73/78)	2 Nov. 1973 (Conv); 17 Feb. 1978 (Prot)	15 States with not less than 50% of world gt of merchant shipping; As above	1 year; As above	2 Oct. 1983	43; 80%	Yes	1978 (P); 1984; 1985	7 Jan. 1986*; 6 Apr. 1987*		The 1978 Protocol absorbs the parent Convention: States which ratify the Protocol automatically ratify the Convention as modified, but entry into force of Annex II was deferred until 6 April 1987 * Under tacit acceptance.

	Conventions						Amendments and Protocols (P)			
Title of Convention	Date of Adoption	Requirements for Entry into Force	Period between Fulfilment of Requirements and Entry into Force	Date of Entry into Force	Contracting Parties at 1 Mar. 1987	Is Tacit Acceptance Procedure Included?	Year of Adoption	Date of Entry into Force	Contracting Parties at 1 Mar. 1987	Notes
a	b	c	d	e	f	g	h	i	j	k
Liability and Compensation										
International Convention on Civil Liability for Oil Pollution Damage (CLC)	29 Nov. 1969	8 States including 5 with not less than 1 million gt of tanker tonnage each	90 days	19 June 1975	58	No	1976 (P)	8 Apr. 1981	24	
							1984 (P)	–	1	
Convention Relating to Civil Liability in the Field of Maritime Carriage of Nuclear Material (LNM)	17 Dec. 1971	5 States	90 days	15 July 1975	11	No	–	–	–	

a	b	c	d	e	f	g	h	i	j	k
International Convention on the Establishment of an International Fund for Compensation for Oil Pollution Damage (IFC)	18 Dec. 1971	8 States, which have received at least 750 m tons of contributing oil during previous calendar year	90 days	16 Oct. 1978	35	No	1976 (P) 1984 (P)	–	14	
Athens Convention Relating to the Carriage of Passengers and Their Luggage by Sea (PAL)	13 Dec. 1974	10 States	90 days	28 Apr. 1987	10	No	1976 (P)	–	–	
Convention on Limitation of Liability for Maritime Claims (LLMC)	19 Nov. 1976	12 States	1 year	1 Dec. 1986	13	No	–	–	–	

	Conventions						Amendments and Protocols (P)			
Title of Convention	Date of Adoption	Requirements for Entry into Force	Period between Fulfilment of Requirements and Entry into Force	Date of Entry into Force	Contracting Parties at 1 Mar. 1987	Is Tacit Acceptance Procedure Included?	Year of Adoption	Date of Entry into Force	Contracting Parties at 1 Mar. 1987	Notes
a	b	c	d	e	f	g	h	i	j	k
Other Matters										
Convention on Facilitation of International Maritime Traffic (FAL)	9 Apr. 1965	10 States	60 days	5 Mar. 1967	56	Yes, since entry into force of 1973 amendments	1969 1977 1973 1986	1971 1978 1984 1 Oct. 1986*	– – –	The 1969 and 1977 amendments only concern the Annex. Those adopted in 1973 affected article VII, and introduced 'tacit acceptance' into the Convention

* Under tacit acceptance. |

a	b	c	d	e	f	g	h	i	j	k
International Convention on Tonnage Measurement of Ships (TM)	23 June 1969	25 States with not less than 65% of world gt of merchant ships	2 years	18 July 1982	75 94%	No	–	–	–	

Instruments which are in force or applicable but which are no longer fully operational because they have been superseded by later instruments

Prevention of Marine Pollution

a	b	c	d	e	f	g	h	i	j	k
International Convention for the Prevention of Pollution of the Sea by Oil (OILPOL)	12 May 1954	10 States including 5 with not less than 500 000 gt of tanker tonnage	1 year	26 July 1958	72	No	1962 1969 1971 (Great Barrier Reef) 1971 (Tank size)	1967 1978 –	28 27	This Convention was adopted under the auspices of the UK but depository functions were transferred to IMO when the Organization came into being in 1959. As far as Parties to MARPOL 73/78 are concerned, this Convention has been superseded

	Conventions					Amendments and Protocols (P)				
Title of Convention	*Date of Adoption*	*Requirements for Entry into Force*	*Period between Fulfilment of Requirements and Entry into Force*	*Date of Entry into Force*	*Contracting Parties at 1 Mar. 1987*	*Is Tacit Acceptance Procedure Included?*	*Year of Adoption*	*Date of Entry into Force*	*Contracting Parties at 1 Mar. 1987*	*Notes*
a	b	c	d	e	f	g	h	i	j	k
Maritime Safety										
International Convention for the Safety of Life at Sea (SOLAS)	17 June 1960	15 States including 7 with not less than 1 million gt of merchant shipping each	1 year	26 May 1965	100	No	1966 1967 1968 1969 1971 1973 general 1973 grain		46 36 37 26 18 9 10	The amendments to this instrument have been incorporated in SOLAS 1974. It has been superseded as far as Contracting Parties to SOLAS 1974 are concerned
International Regulations for Preventing Collisions at Sea	17 June 1960	Individual acceptances	—	Applied from 1 Sept. 1965	73	No	—	—	—	The regulations were adopted at the 1960 SOLAS Conference and annexed to the Final Act

Otherwise they would tend to confuse, rather than clarify, shipping practice since their provisions would not apply to a significant proportion of the ships they were intended to deal with.

Accepting a convention does not merely involve the deposit of a formal instrument: a government's acceptance of a convention necessarily places on it the obligation to take the measures required by the convention.

Often national law has to be changed to enforce the provisions of the convention; in some cases, special facilities may have to be constructed – such as the reception facilities outlined in the International Convention for the Prevention of Pollution from Ships 1973, as modified by the Protocol of 1978 relating thereto (MARPOL 73/78); an inspectorate may have to be appointed or trained to carry out functions under the convention, and adequate notice must be given to shipowners, shipbuilders and other interested parties in order to ensure that they take account of the provisions of the convention in their future acts and plans.

At present IMO conventions enter into force within an average of 5 years after adoption. This compares favourably with the record of other organizations. Nevertheless, member governments of IMO are not satisfied with the situation and have been considering possible measures to speed up the process wherever possible.

IMO works through its committees and sub-committees composed of its own members, and with the collaboration of representatives of other specialized agencies. It has agreements or arrangements for co-operation with many inter-governmental organizations. In consultative status with IMO are 43 non-governmental international organizations representing maritime, legal and environmental interests.

Basically IMO is a forum where its members can exchange information on and endeavour to solve problems connected with maritime, technical and legal matters. It makes recommendations on maritime questions submitted by its member states or by other members of the United Nations family. IMO is responsible for convening and preparing international conferences on subjects within its sphere of action, for the purposes of concluding international conventions or agreements. Its headquarters is in London.

The International Maritime Organization was formerly the Inter-Governmental Maritime Consultative Organization – the change taking place in 1982.

8.6 INTERNATIONAL MARITIME SATELLITE ORGANIZATION (INMARSAT)

The International Maritime Satellite Organization (INMARSAT) operates a system of satellites to provide telephone, telex, data and facsimile, as well as distress and safety communications services, to the shipping, aviation and offshore industries.

It is based in London. INMARSAT began operations on 1st February 1982. Users of its system include oil tankers, liquid natural gas carriers, offshore drilling rigs, seismic survey ships, fishing boats, cargo and container vessels, passenger liners, ice-breakers, tugs and cable-laying ships, among others. The system is also used to provide emergency transportable communications at times of human disaster and natural catastrophe. By late 1987 almost 6200 ship earth stations or transportable versions were commissioned for use with the INMARSAT system.

INMARSAT is now developing systems and equipment to enable it to begin providing satellite communications to aircraft and the aeronautical community in 1988 and beyond. These systems are compatible with the requirements of the Airlines Electronic Engineering Committee and the International Civil Aviation Organization's Special Committee on Future Air Navigation Systems (FANS). Services with include operation flight data and passenger telephone facilities.

INMARSAT leases the MARECS A and B2 satellites from the European Space Agency, maritime communications subsystems (MCS) on several INTELSAT V satellites from the International Telecommunications Satellite Organization and contingency capacity on three MARISAT satellites from COMSAT General of the United States. The system is currently configured as follows:

Ocean Region	Atlantic	Indian	Pacific
Operation Location:	MARECS B2 26W	INTELSAT MCS-A 63E	INTELSAT MCS-D 180E
Spare Location:	INTELSAT MCS-B 18.5W	INTELSAT MCS-C 66E	MARECS A 178E

INMARSAT is now in the process of procuring a second

generation of satellites. The INMARSAT-2 spacecraft, the first of which is scheduled to be delivered in mid–1988, will have approximately three times more capacity than the most powerful satellite in the present INMARSAT system.

Another component of the INMARSAT system is the coast earth stations, which provide the link between the satellites and the international telecommunications networks. Coast earth stations are generally owned and operated by the Signatories – organizations nominated by their countries to invest in, and work with, INMARSAT – of the countries in which they are located. By 1987 there were 20 coast earth stations: Tangua (Brazil), Maadi (Egypt), Pleumeur Bodou (France), Thermopylae (Greece), Fucino (Italy), Ibaraki and Yamaguchi (Japan), Umm-al-Aish (Kuwait), Eik (Norway), two stations at Psary (Poland), Jeddah (Saudi Arabia), Singapore (Singapore), Goonhilly (UK), Southbury and Santa Paula (USA), two stations at Odessa and two stations at Nakhodka (USSR). Several of these are equipped to provide aeronautical services.

INMARSAT comprises three bodies: The Assembly is composed of representatives of all member countries, each of which has one vote. It meets once every 2 years to review the activities and objectives of INMARSAT and to make recommendations to the Council. The Council functions in a similar fashion to the Board of a company. It consists of representatives of the 18 Signatories with the largest investment shares and four others elected by the Assembly on the principle of a just geographical representation and with due regard for the interests of developing countries. It meets at least three times a year and each member has a voting power equal to its investment share. It oversees the activities of the Directorate, the permanent staff of INMARSAT. Comprising 202 people of 35 different nationalities and working under the Director General, the Directorate carries out the day-to-day tasks of INMARSAT.

The organization is financed by the Signatories of the 53 member countries, each of which has an investment share based on its actual usage of the system.

A major development relative to the role of INMARSAT is the IMO decision in 1987 to replace the present maritime distress and safety system with what is called the 'Global Maritime Distress and Safety System' (GMDSS). This will rely heavily on automation and will use INMARSAT's satellites for rapid and reliable communications.

Maritime distress and safety communications today rely primarily on the capability of a ship in distress to alert another ship in the vicinity. The present requirement, under the 1974 Safety of Life at Sea (SOLAS) Convention, consists of morse radiotelegraphy on 500 kHz for ships above 1600 gross registered tonnes and radiotelephony on 2182 kHz and 156.8 MHz for all ships above 300 gross registered tonnes. This system has many limitations and disadvantages – such as short range of 100 to 150 nautical miles, manual distress alerting and aural watchkeeping. With this in mind, and noting the major technological advances in radio communications, including satellite capabilities, IMO members decided that a new distress and safety system should be developed.

The GMDSS is being designed to ensure a combination of safety and efficiency. Consequently, it will be a largely automated system and will require ships to carry a range of equipment capable of simple operation. IMO approached this task by defining communications functions which needed to be performed by all ships and then specifying what equipment would meet these functional requirements in defined ocean areas of the world. The communications functions encompass all distress, safety and general communications needs and include distress alerting: ship-to-shore; shore-to-ship; ship-to-ship; search and rescue co-ordination; bridge-to-bridge communications; on-scene communications; signals for locating; marine safety information, and general radio-communications.

The oceans of the world have been divided into operational sea areas, which recognize the capabilities and limitations of various communications techniques as detailed below:

Sea Area A1 – within coverage of Very High Frequency (VHF) coast radio stations (25–30 mm range) providing digital selective calling (DSC) alerting;

Sea Area A2 – within coverage of Medium Frequency (MF) coast radio stations providing continuous availability of DSC alerting (excluding Sea Area A1);

Sea Area A3 – within coverage of geostationary satellites (excluding Sea Areas A1 and A2);

Sea Area A4 – the remaining sea areas outside Sea Areas A1, A2 and A3 (generally, the extreme polar areas).

With the communications functions and the operational areas defined, IMO specified the communications equipment to be carried for each of the areas of operation. All ships over 300 grt are required to carry a common minimum set of communications equipment as below:

1. VHF installation capable of transmitting and receiving DSC on channel 70 and radiotelephony on channels 6, 13 and 16;
2. equipment able to maintain continuous DSC watch on VHF channel 70;
3. radar transponder operating in the 9 GHz band;
4. NAVTEX receiver, capable of receiving Marine Safety Information, if the ship operates in any area where NAVTEX is provided;
5. float-free satellite EPIRB capable of transmitting a distress alert through Cospas-Sarsat polar – orbiting satellites operating at 406 MHz;
6. equipment capable of being manually activated for transmission of a distress alert via satellite if the EPIRB cannot be manually as well as automatically activated.

(a) Additional requirements for ships operating entirely in Sea Area A1

1. The VHF installation shall be capable of general radiocommunications using telephony on working frequencies in the band 156–162.05 MHz;
2. (Optionally), a float-free EPIRB capable of transmitting a distress alert using DSC on VHF channel 70, in lieu of a satellite EPIRB;
3. A second radio system to transmit the distress alert from the navigating position, either by: VHF; Manual activation of a VHF EPIRB; Manual activation of a 406 MHz satellite EPIRB; MF using DSC; HF using DSC; HF using DSC; or an INMARSAT ship earth station.

(b) Additional capability for ships operating in Sea Areas A1 and A2

1. An MF installation capable of telephony on 218 kHz and DSC on 2187.5 kHz;

2. Equipment capable of maintaining continuous DSC watch on 2187.5 kHz;
3. Equipment capable of general radio communications on working frequencies in the MF band 1605–4000 kHz, or INMARSAT ship earth station.
4. A second radio system to transmit the distress alert from the navigating position, either by: manual activation of a 406 MHz satellite EPIRB; HF using DSC; or an INMARSAT ship earth station.

(c) For ships operating in Sea Areas A1, A2 and A3
(within coverage of INMARSAT satellites):
These have the option of carrying an INMARSAT ship earth station – either Standard-C or Standard-A – or adding an HF (voice, narrow-band direct printing, DSC) radio installation. Facilities must include at least two of the following radio systems for transmitting the distress alert from the navigating position: INMARSAT ship earth station (Standard-A or Standard-C); Manual activation of a 406 MHz satellite EPIRB; HF radio installation.

(d) For ships which operate beyond the INMARSAT system, in Sea Area A4
An MF/HF radio installation is required in addition to the common minimum for all ships:
1. Capability of transmitting and receiving on all distress and safety frequencies in the band 1605–27 500 kHz using DSC, telephony and NBDP. It shall also be capable of general communications using telephony or direct-printing in the band 1605–27 500 kHz;
2. Equipment capable of maintaining DSC watch on 2187.5 kHz, 8375 kHz and at least one additional distress and safety frequency in the band 4000–27 500 kHz.
3. A second radio system to initiate the distress alert from the navigating position through the polar orbiting satellite system on 406 MHz; this may be manual activation of a 406 MHz satellite EPIRB.

8.7 INTERNATIONAL LABOUR ORGANIZATION

The International Labour Organization (ILO) was set up in 1919 to bring governments, employers and trade unions together for united action in the cause of social justice and better living conditions everywhere. It is a tripartite organization, with worker and employer representatives taking part in its work on equal status with those of governments. The number of ILO member countries now stands at 150. The Organization was awarded the Nobel Peace Prize in 1969.

Historically, the ILO is an outgrowth of the social thought of the nineteenth century. Conditions of workers in the wake of the industrial revolution were increasingly seen to be intolerable by economists and sociologists. Social reformers from Robert Owen onwards believed that any country or industry introducing measures to improve working conditions would raise the cost of labour, putting it at an economic disadvantage compared to other countries or industries. That is why they laboured with such persistence to persuade the powers of Europe to make better working conditions and shorter hours the subject of international agreements.

The first concrete result of these efforts was an international conference held in Berlin in 1890 and attended by representatives of 14 countries. In 1900 an international conference in Paris succeeded in creating the International Association for Labour Legislation. This forerunner of the ILO, with its headquarters in Basle, undertook the translation and publication of labour laws of many countries. The *Legislative Series* begun then was taken over by the ILO and is still published.

Toward the end of the First World War a new opportunity for positive action arose. At the request of trade unions in several countries, the Peace Conference of 1919 set up a Labour Commission. It agreed on a document which on 11 April 1919 became Part XIII of the Treaty of Versailles. With amendments, it remains to this day the charter under which the ILO works.

In its preamble the ILO Constitution declares that universal and lasting peace can be founded only on the basis of social justice. At Philadelphia in 1944 the International Labour Conference adopted a Declaration, now an annex to the Constitution, which embodies an even more dynamic concept. It proclaims the right of all human beings 'to pursue both their material well-being and their spiritual development in conditions of freedom and dignity, of economic security and equal opportunity'. It further states that 'poverty anywhere constitutes a danger to prosperity everywhere'.

The first International Labour Conference was held in Washington in October 1919.

Between the two World Wars the ILO was an autonomous part of the League of Nations. The most urgent problems of the time, on which its first decisions were made, included the promotion of the 8-hour working day, the struggle against unemployment, maternity protection and the working conditions of women and the young.

In 1946, the ILO became the first specialized agency associated with the United Nations. Since then, a system of close co-operation has grown up between international organizations which attempt to deal with the grave inequalities and imbalances among the world's various regions. In the field of social policy the ILO plays an active part in one of the most striking changes since the Second World War: the large-scale development of international technical co-operation. New problems continue to arise as a result of technological, economic and social change. While improved working and living conditions and the promotion of full employment remain central aims of the ILO, it now has to deal also with such matters as migrant workers, multi-national corporations, the working enviornment and the social consequences of monetary instability.

The ILO remains a standard-setting body, but today there is also marked emphasis on operational programmes and on educational work, in the broadest sense. This led to the creation of the International Institute for Labour Studies (Geneva) in 1960 and the International Centre for Advanced Technical and Vocational Training (Turin) in 1965, and to the launching of the World Employment Programme. The operational programmes have also been largely responsible for the decentralization of responsibilities from Geneva headquarters to the various regions of the world.

The ILO has 150 member States, compared with 42 in 1919 and 58 in 1948. Its regular budget has grown from $4.5 million in 1948 to $325 million for 1988/89. Growth has been accompanied by considerable changes in policy and geographical representation. The former preponderance of industrial countries with market economies has given way to a more varied mixture in which the centrally planned economies of eastern Europe, the newly independent lands and the Third World in general also play an important part.

The ILO is composed of a yearly general assembly, the International Labour Conference; an executive council, the Governing Body; and a permanent secretariat, the International Labour Office. The Organization also works through subsidiary bodies such as regional conferences, industrial committees and panels of experts.

The International Labour Conference elects the Governing Body; adopts the ILO's budget, financed by contributions from member States; sets international labour standards; and provides a world forum for the discussion of social and labour questions. Each national delegation is composed of two government delegates, one employers' delegate and one workers' delegate, accompanied as necessary by technical advisers. Employers' and workers' delegates have a free voice; they can, and often do, disagree with their governments and with each other.

The governing body normally holds three sessions a year at Geneva to decide questions of policy and programme. It is at present composed of 28 government members, 14 employer members and 14 worker members. Ten states of chief industrial importance have permanent government representatives, and the others are elected every three years by the Conference.

The ILO is headed by a Director-General (Mr Francis Blanchard since 1974) elected by the governing body. The staff includes more than 100 nationalities. The number of officials has grown from 500 in 1948 to some 1900 in 1987, plus more than 660 experts serving on technical co-operation programmes around the world. In addition to its operational activities ILO engages in research and publishes documents on a wide range of labour and social matters.

The main task of the ILO at the outset was to improve conditions of life and work by building up a comprehensive code of law and practice. The Organization's founders felt that standards laid down through the joint efforts of governments, management and labour would be realistic, solid and widely applicable.

This standard-setting function is one that the ILO still performs. The number of international labour instruments – Conventions and Recommendations – adopted by the International Labour Conference since 1919 has now reached 340 (166 Conventions and 174 Recommendations).

Each Convention is a legal instrument regulating some aspect of labour administration, social welfare or human rights. Its ratification involves a dual obligation for a member State; it is both a formal commitment to apply the provisions of the Convention, and an indication of willingness to accept a measure of international supervision. A Recommendation is similar to a Convention except that it is not subject to ratification, and provides more specific guidelines. Both Conventions and Recommendations define standards and provide a model and stimulus for national legislation and practice in member countries.

ILO Conventions cover a wide field of social problems, including basic human rights matters (such as freedom of association, abolition of forced labour, and elimination of discrimination in employment), minimum wages, labour administration, industrial relations, employment policy including women workers, working conditions, social security, occupational safety and health and employment at sea.

With regard to the latter, it embraces international regulations and agreements affecting working conditions at sea and on inland waterways. Recommendations and conventions through ILO are shaped by tripartite delegations made up of representatives of government, of employers and of the work force. An international code for seafarers has been set by ILO, and special sessions of the main ILO conference, prepared for by its Joint Maritime Commission, are regularly held to study applications for new items for this code and for extensions of it.

The technical co-operation programme of the ILO assists countries in process of establishing, developing or improving their maritime industries to apply in practice the organization's international maritime labour standards.

The ILO, within the framework of the Programme of Industrial Activities, has also become actively concerned with problems encountered in the offshore petroleum industry, including related offshore construction and diving activities.

ILO is concerned with the protection of seafarers, fishermen and dock workers, the establishment and updating of international minimum standards concerning various maritime labour questions such as recruitment (including minimum age, medical examinations, and articles of agreement), repatriation, vocational training, decasualization of employment, occupational safety and health, crew accommodation, labour problems arising from technological change, wages, hours of work and manning, holidays, health and welfare facilities, and maritime industrial relations. It undertakes research, analysis, and the publication of information on economic, technical, labour and social developments in the maritime industry, both ashore and afloat.

Several ILO instruments concern exclusively maritime fishermen. A Committee on Conditions of Work in the Fishing Industry was convened in May 1988 to set the future programme in this field. A number of other instruments deal with dockworkers. The final text of a Convention dealing in the occupational safety and health of dockworkers was adopted in June 1979.

Recent ILO developments in the field of shipping include the adoption, at the 74th (Maritime) Session of the International Labour Conference in Geneva in September 1987, of the following international labour standards:

1. A Convention and a Recommendation concerning seafarers' welfare at sea and in port. The Convention lays down clear responsibilities for governments to ensure that adequate facilities and services are provided for seafarers both in port and on board ship, and that the necessary arrangements are made for financing these facilities and services. The Recommendation contains more detailed guidelines on the provision of these facilities and services including access to public transport, availability of medical treatment, dissemination of information to visiting seafarers, as well as the protection of seafarers stranded in foreign ports or detained by local authorities.

2. A Convention concerning social security for seafarers under which ratifying States are bound to provide for social security protection no less favourable than that enjoyed by shore workers and to apply minimum or superior standards in at least three of the following branches of social security: medical care, sickness benefit, unemployment benefit, old-age benefits, employment injury benefit, family benefit, maternity benefit, invalidity benefit, and survivors' benefit. This Convention should promote the improvement of social security provisions for seafarers and their dependants, especially when these seafarers are sailing on ships flying the flag of a country other than their own.

3. A Convention on health protection and medical care for

seafarers, which provides for wide-ranging measures to ensure that seafarers benefit from health protection and medical care comparable to those available to workers ashore. These measures include preventive measures, access to a doctor without delay in ports of call, standards of medical care facilities on board ship, and international co-operation in areas such as search and rescue, as well as optimum use of doctors and hospital facilities available at sea.

4. A Convention and a Recommendation concerning the repatriation of seafarers. The Convention provides that seafarers are entitled to be repatriated under certain conditions after a period of shipboard service which shall be less than 12 months. It also lays down the responsibilities of competent authorities in the event of shipowners' failure to exercise their duty to repatriate a seafarer. The Recommendation also supports this concept of repatriation in the last resort by the country of nationality or the country from which the repatriation is to be effected with the expenses being claimed from the shipowner.

The ILO's standards put into effect many of the principles affirmed in the Universal Declaration of Human Rights by incorporating them in agreements of worldwide scope.

Although the ILO cannot, of course, dictate action by member countries, it does keep a careful eye on the way governments carry out their obligations under ratified Conventions through an independent Committee of Experts on the Application of Conventions and Recommendations. In addition to these procedures another system has been set up, in consultation with the Economic and Social Council of the United Nations, to examine complaints concerning freedom of association.

The Conventions and Recommendations form the International Labour Code. The standards embodied in the Code transcend the significance of the particular matters covered: they represent a common pool of accumulated experience which is available to countries at any stage of development. The Code is an international standard for social justice; it has an important influence on the development of social legislation throughout the world.

Given the universal nature of the goals set before it at the start – given also a specific obligation under its Constitution to participate fully in the war against want – the ILO has joined with other organizations of the United Nations to improve world economic and social well-being. The ILO co-operates closely with other UN organizations as regards questions of common interest notable among which is the training and certification of merchant seafarers, dealt with continually by a standing joint IMO/ILO committee on training, and on the health of seafarers dealt with by the joint ILO/WHO committee on the health of seafarers.

Operational programmes are expanding rapidly, in close collaboration with United Nations bodies, particularly the United Nations Development Programme (UNDP), which still provides the major part of financing for ILO technical co-operation projects. Of some $102 million spent on ILO technical co-operation in 1986, $45 million came from the UNDP. The ILO also finances technical co-operation from its own regular budget, and carries out programmes financed by other sources. Under this last heading, there is an increase in multi-bilateral aid (where the ILO executes a co-operation programme on behalf of an industrialized country). Expenditure of this type amounted to $40 million in 1986.

ILO technical co-operation programmes are to be found in Africa, Asia, Latin America, the Middle East and, to a lesser extent, in Europe. There are also inter-regional projects. Co-operation is concentrated in the following major areas:

(i) development of human resources, including vocational training and management development;

(ii) employment planning and promotion;

(iii) labour relations, trade union development and the growth of social institutions;

(iv) conditions of work and life.

Many of the ILO's technical co-operation projects help countries develop, train and employ their workers for national economic development. Vocational training and management development are particularly important because the basic problem in many of the developing countries is the disparity between the great abundance of manpower and the acute shortage of modern skills. The ILO also helps countries in such fields as co-operatives, small-scale industries, social security, workers' education, labour administration, labour statistics, and the safety and health of workers. In addition, a rural development programme is designed to help raise rural incomes and improve living standards in developing countries.

ILO research work is intended to throw new light on labour problems, to suggest ways of solving them and to indicate means by which these solutions can be put into effect. Research of this kind is undertaken in the preparation of reports for consideration by the International Labour Conference and for other meetings. Many studies and research projects are related to activities in the field, as has been the case for example under the World Employment Programme, which is a major ILO contribution to the current Second Development Decade of the United Nations. Employment strategy missions sent by the ILO to several member states have led to the publication of policy reports which are of interest to development specialists as well as to the governments of the countries concerned.

The ILO is both a storehouse and a clearing house for information on social and economic policy. Its library has more than 15 000 books in this field, and it publishes a great deal of original work.

The exchange of ideas takes place at a large number of meetings. Regional conferences concentrate on labour and social matters of particular interest to a given group of countries; industrial committees and tripartite technical meetings review developments in specific sectors of the world economy. Other bodies are concerned with such matters as the conditions of seafarers and the improvement of labour statistics; sometimes these are held in conjunction with other UN agencies such as the World Health Organization, the United Nations Educational, Scientific and Cultural Organization and the Food and Agriculture Organization.

The International Institute for Labour Studies, created by the ILO in Geneva in 1960, specializes in higher education and research in the fields of social and labour policy. The International Centre for Advanced Technical and Vocational Training in Turin, established in 1965, provides key personnel with training at a higher level than they can obtain in their home countries in vocational training and in management development.

The traditional standard–setting activities of the ILO and its newer technical co-operation activities complement one another and are inseparable from its research and publishing work. With the modernization of social structures and increasing economic development of production, ILO standards would be only a distant hope in many of the emerging countries rather than reasonable and immediately applicable measures.

To conclude our review of the ILO few could have forecast in 1976 that we were seeing the beginning of the end of 50 years' consistent growth in seaborne trade, and the emergence of unparalleled overcapacity in virtually every sector of world shipping. It would seem that few persons, if any, recognized the structural changes that were taking place, and changes that were coinciding with the 'normal' cyclical downturn the industry was experiencing. The accumulated effects of energy conservation, industrial stagnation, the diversification of energy sources, the development of new oil producing areas and the technological changes affecting traditional heavy industry were to lead to unprecedented overcapacity in all sectors of the shipping industry. A great excess of oil tankers was to be succeeded by a gross overcapacity of ships engaged in dry-bulk trading; eventually even the liner trades (that is, ships on particular routes with regular sailings) would meet with the same fate.

This overtonnage is at the root of virtually all handicaps that have affected the shipping industry and those who work in it during the past decade. Coupled with the recession in the demand for shipping services, it has led to measures to contain costs; it has resulted in many of the problems associated with substandard shipping and poor management; it has caused unemployment ashore and afloat in the shipping industry and threatened many of the hard fought improvements in working conditions gained over the years. While the difficult trading conditions have been the death-knell for many shipping companies, for others they have provided an enormous challenge, a test of their ingenuity in the design and operation of ships. Serious adverse conditions have encouraged the acceleration of technological change and spurred both designer and operator to develop advanced shipping capable of operating at a fraction of yesterday's costs. The commercial advantages which encouraged the development of the very large crude carrier (VLCC) have been extended to most other types of shipping. Moreover, advances in automation have enabled owners to operate their modern tonnage with fewer crew members than was possible a decade ago. Port improvements and the improvement in ships' cargo-handling equipment, the refinement of Roll-on/Roll-off, container techniques and high capacity bulk-handling facilities have greatly reduced the time a ship needs to stay in port.

Though these are considered important advances by the ship operating community, that have led to further erosion of the seafarer's employment opportunities; it might also be argued that modern ship operation has in many ways diminished his enjoyment of seafaring. Certainly there is a need to reconcile technological progress with job satisfaction, just as there is a need to educate and train seafarers and shore operators to deal with the more sophisticated ships they are expected to run. These are some of the challenges that must be faced in the future if the shipping industry is to recover and provide employment opportunities to future generations of seafarers.

Owing to the evolution which has taken place in the shipping industry, today's seafarers are faced with circumstances substantially different from those existing in 1976, and as these circumstances continue to change so may the problems which arise. It is the task of the ILO to come to grips with certain of the current problems of seafarers and also to look ahead, since the changes that have taken place in recent years will surely lead to future challenges.

8.8 COUNCIL OF EUROPEAN AND JAPANESE NATIONAL SHIPOWNERS' ASSOCIATIONS (CENSA)

(a) Composition, objectives and structure

The Council of European and Japanese National Shipowners' Associations (CENSA) comprises the National Shipowners' Associations of thirteen major maritime nations, namely Belgium, Denmark, Finland, France, Germany, Greece, Italy, Japan, the Netherlands, Norway, Spain, Sweden and the UK.

Individually these associations are concerned with all aspects of shipping policy, whether in the liner, tramp, bulk carrier or tanker sectors. Collectively the work of CENSA also extends to these areas.

The primary objective of CENSA is the promotion and protection of the interests of its membership through the development of sound shipping policies including in particular:

(a) the elimination of restriction on, and interference with, international transport and trade;

(b) the promotion of a system free, so far as possible, from governmental discrimination or regulation and which preserves for shippers the freedom of choice of vessel;

(c) the development of a system of fair trading between providers and users of shipping services on the basis, as far as possible, of self-regulation.

CENSA is administered by a secretariat in London which is international in character, its members being drawn from the constituent countries. Over the years, CENSA has absorbed and carried on the work of two other bodies with related but more specialized objectives: the Committee of European Shipowners (CES), a body of individual liner owners, whose primary objective was to secure and maintain a fair and effective conference system in the US trades; and the Committee of Liner Operators of South America (COMLOSA) another body of individual interests which provided a forum for discussion and co-ordinated action regarding the shipping policies and practices of South American countries.

CENSA's main policy organ is its Council which meets four or five times a year. It consists of two representatives from each member Association, from which it elects a Chairman and two Vice-Chairmen.

Worldwide developments are kept under review by four sections consisting of representatives from national associations and, in the case of one, the US section, also individual liner companies and national or international container consortia. The sections work through the medium of specialist committees and sub-committees, and report to the Council.

These sections are concerned respectively with: (i) US affairs, (ii) UN affairs, (iii) legislation and general policy and (iv) conference/shipper issues.

The US affairs section keeps under review developments in US Shipping policy and in the regulatory fields which are likely to affect the member associations of CENSA and individual lines and container consortia. It makes submissions to Congress, to the regulatory agencies and elsewhere where necessary.

The UN affairs section monitors developments within the United Nations, in particular, the UN Conference on Trade and Development (UNCTAD) and its Committee on Shipping, in order that CENSA can be informed, and also the governments of CENSA countries advised of the views of their shipowners. CENSA has consultative status with UNCTAD.

The legislative and general policy section surveys the national legislation and policy of countries worldwide which may have an impact on members whether in the liner, tramp, or tanker sections.

The conference/shipper affairs section is concerned with the furtherance of consultation between shipowners and shippers on a collective basis and with CENSA's relationship with European-based liner conferences.

The work of CENSA through these sections falls broadly under two heads. Relations with governments and relations with shippers' councils, conference etc., namely matters pertaining to commercial relations.

(b) Liaison with other international bodies

It is part of CENSA's function to maintain close contacts with other international bodies notably the International Chamber of Shipping (ICS) and the Organization of the Shipowners' Associations of the European Communities (CAACE) and the Sea Transport Commission of the International Chamber of Commerce (ICC).

8.9 INTERNATIONAL COMMITTEE OF PASSENGER LINES

Although not a component of CENSA, another international shipowners' body is administered by the CENSA 'International' secretariat namely the International Committee of Passenger Lines (ICPL).

The function of this Committee is to provide a forum for discussion of developments in the USA, whether of a legislative, regulatory, or other character, which may affect the interests of its members, with the object of co-ordinating any action necessary to protect those interests. Membership of the Committee is open to owner operators providing passenger services into or out of the USA. In practice these are largely cruise operators.

8.10 INTERNATIONAL COMMITTEE ON THE ORGANIZATION OF TRAFFIC AT SEA (ICOTAS)

This Committee functions under the authority of the British, French and German Institutes of Navigation, with the Royal Institute of Navigation in London providing the secretariat. Its main object is to advise shipping interests and government authorities responsible for shipping on measures to improve the organization of traffic at sea.

Membership of the Committee is international and, so far as possible, composed of personnel from various nations who, in the opinion of the Institutes, are able to offer the best professional advice on the organization of traffic at sea.

The Committee makes its recommendations, as appropriate, through the national governments to the Maritime Safety Committee of the International Maritime Organization (IMO), or to the shipping industry through the International Chamber of Shipping.

The Committee has powers to co-opt members and membership of the Committee is reviewed at least every 2 years.

8.11 LLOYD'S REGISTER OF SHIPPING

Lloyd's Register of Shipping is an independent society, staffed by engineers, naval architects and other professionals, which for over 200 years has inspected ships to ensure that they are seaworthy. Originally, a small team of surveyors, retired sea captains and the like, were employed to examine ships and 'classify' them according to their condition.

Today, rules for ship construction and maintenance are laid down by Lloyd's Register and ships must conform to these rules if they are to be classed, i.e. built and maintained under survey, by the Society. As no responsible shipowner would consider owning or operating a ship that had been built to anything but the highest class, there is now only one standard of construction for ocean-going ships, symbolized by the Lloyd's Register notation '100A1'. Details of the world's merchant ships of 100 tonnes gross and above are published in the Lloyd's Register of Ships, the ships classed having this notation beside their name.

Lloyd's Register's knowledge of marine engineering problems has led in recent years to an ever-increasing demand for inspection services onshore. Lloyd's Register Industrial Services Division undertakes inspection work for many land-based industrial projects, such as oil refineries and power stations.

Lloyd's Register takes its name from a coffee house run by Edward Lloyd in Lombard Street, London, during the last years of the seventeenth century. Merchants, marine underwriters and other concerned with shipping business congregated there to exchange information and gossip, and Lloyd increased the popularity of his shop by circulating to patrons as much shipping news as he could lay his hands on.

Although Edward Lloyd died in 1713, and the coffee house passed on to his daughter and then out of the family, it continued for many years to be known by the name Lloyd's. In 1760 a group of marine underwriters who met there regularly formed themselves into a committee and set about producing a list of ships for which they might be asked to provide insurance cover, although little would be known about their condition. This list, the first Register of Ships, was published in 1764.

The Register Book contained details of each ship's owner, builder, master, size, and, most important of all, an indication of the condition of both hull and equipment, as assessed by those first surveyors. This early system of classification was somewhat rough and ready. The condition of the hull was indicated by the vowels A, E, I, O or U in descending order of merit, and the equipment (masts, rigging, etc.) by the letters G, M or B which stood for Good, Middling or Bad. This system lasted for some years, and then the G, M and B were replaced by numbers, the Register for 1775–76 being the first to show the famous 'A1' symbol.

The major fault of this method of classification soon became apparent. The men employed by the underwriters to examine the ships were not necessarily expert in the art of surveying. As there were at first no properly defined standards, it was left to each surveyor to exercise his own judgement in assessing a ship's condition, and results obtained were inevitably inconsistent. It was also the practice to limit the number of years for which a ship could hold the highest class. The term of years varied according to where the ship had been built and this naturally angered shipowners as they could see no reason why a ship built on the Thames, for example, should remain in the highest class longer than one built, say, on the Wear. This disagreement led to shipowners producing a register of their own which was published in competition with the underwriters' register for many years, causing both to lose income and eventually reach the verge of bankruptcy. The two registers were rescued just in time and joined forces to become 'Lloyd's Register of British and Foreign Shipping'. The new constitution, drawn up in 1834, established a General Committee, composed of underwriters, owners and merchants, who were responsible for the grading of ships into classes, using surveyors' reports as a basis for their decisions.

The General Committee also took over responsibility for the formulation of rules for ship construction and maintenance until in 1890, a Technical Committee was set up with the specific job of making recommendations to the General Committee for changes in existing rules or for the adoption of new ones.

As Lloyd's Register began to establish itself in Great Britain, so its reputation became known overseas and soon requests were received for surveyors to be posted in other countries. In 1852 a surveyor was appointed to Quebec and from then on a network of surveyors was steadily built up all over the world.

As laid down by the constitution of 1834, direction of the Society's affairs is in the hands of the General Committee, composed nowadays of underwriters, shipowners, shipbuilders, marine engineers, steelmakers, and representatives of various shipping and ship-building organizations, all of whom serve voluntarily. In certain countries Lloyd's Register is advised and assisted in managing its affairs by National Committees, each similar in composition to the General Committee and represented on that body by its Chairman. The Society has no shareholders or owners of any kind and income derived from survey fees and sales of publications is used to improve services and facilities for its clients, and to offset the costs of running a complex international organization.

Lloyd's Register's technical staff now consists of more than 1600 surveyors stationed at ports, shipyards and industrial centres all over the world. Those designated 'ship surveyor' have qualifications in naval architecture and may be recruited after service in

1	2	3	4	5	6	7
LR NUMBER / Call Sign / Official No. / Navigational aids	SHIP'S NAME / Former names / Owners / Managers / Port of Registry / Flag	TONNAGE / Gross / Net / *Deadweight (Gross / Net / *tonnes)	CLASSIFICATION / Special Survey / Hull / Machinery / Refrigerated cargo installation / Equipment Letter / Fee Numeral	HULL / Date of build / Shipbuilders - Place of build / Yard Number / Length overall (m) / Breadth extreme (m) / Draught maximum (m) / Length B.P. (m) / Breadth moulded (m) / Depth moulded (m) / Superstructures / Decks / Riveted/Welded / Rise of floor (mm) / Keel (mm) / Water ballast / Alterations / Bulkheads / Conversion	SHIP TYPE/CARGO FACILITIES / Propulsion / Ship type / Shelter deck / Passengers / Holds & lengths (m)/Cargo tanks & types / Grain/Liquid (m³) / Bale (m³) / Insulated spaces (m³) / Containers & lengths (ft) / Hatchways & sizes (m) / Heating coils / Winches / Cranes/Derricks (SWL tonnes)	MACHINERY / No. & Type of engines / Bore × stroke (mm) / Power / Enginebuilders / Where manufactured / Boilers Pressures Heating surface Furnaces / Aux. electrical generating plant & output / Special propellers / Fuel bunkers (tonnes) / Speed

REGISTER OF SHIPS 1988-89

923 · LJUBIJA

7383920 / LŽDS / 1875 / Df Esd / Gc Rdr / RT	**LIVIO S.** / ex Falstaff-86 ex Lyspol-81 / **Yerimar S.r.l.** / Napoli — Italy	1 599 / 934 / 2 950	Ri (NV)	**1974** Stocznia Gdańska im. Lenina—Gdańsk (B431/501) / 84.16 / 13.62 / 5.315 / 80.47 / 13.59 / 6.41 / P 21.1 F 8.6 1 dk / rf 51	**M General Cargo** / Ice strengthened / 2 Ho 27.8 27.7 ER / G 3 862 B 3 559 / 2 Ha (stl) (each 23.3 × 8.0) ER / 4W Der 2(10) 2(5)	Vee Oil 4SA 12Cy 300 × 450 / 2 500bhp (1 839kW) / H. Cegielski — Poznan GMT / Gen 3 × 110kW 380V 50Hz a.c. / Fuel 156.5t (d.o.)-7.0pd 12.75kn
5406849 / UKMB / M-3205 / Df Esd / Gc Pfd / Rdr RT	**LIVNY** / **U.S.S.R.-Novorossiysk Shipping Co. (NOVOSHIP)** / Novorossiysk — U.S.S.R.	22 463 / 12 607 / 36 653	RS / ✠Classed LR until 4/65	**1963-1** Ishikawajima Harima Heavy Ind. (IHI)—Aioi (594) / 207.04 / 27.06 / 11.070 / 195.00 / 27.01 / 14.46 / 1 dk / rf 51	**M Tanker** / Ice strengthened / 1 Ho 22 Ta ER / G 1 450 L(oil) 47 556 / 1 Ha (3.9 × 3.9) / 1W Der 1(2.5)	Oil 2SA 9Cy 900 × 1550 / 18 000bhp (13 240kW) / Ishikawajima Harima Heavy Ind. (IHI) Aioi Sulzer / Fuel 179.0t (d.o.) 2 379.5t (hvf)-61.0pd 16.5kn
5196555 / IPLV / 587 / Df Esd / Rdr RT	**LIVORNO** / ex Kraustand-66 / **Fratelli Neri S.a.s.**	650 / 297 / 850	(GL) (RI)	**1957** Schlichting-Werft G m b H —Travemuende (1277) / 62.62 / 8.95 / 3.201 / 57.00 / 8.91 / 3.54 / P 21.4 B 6.1 F 9.5 1 dk	**M Tanker** / 8 Ta ER / L(oil) 1 227	Oil 4SA 6Cy 400 × 460 / 700bhp (515kW) / Masch. Augsburg-Nuernberg (MAN) Augsburg / Fuel 35.5t-2.5pd 10.5kn
7338733 / Esd RTh	**LIWA** / **Government of Abu Dhabi (Department of Development & Public Works)** / Abu Dhabi — United Arab Emirates	156 / 0 / 59	✠Classed LR until 31/7/85	**1974-4** Karachi Shipyard & Eng. Works Ltd.—Karachi (S142) / 28.12 / 7.70 / 2.896 / 25.38 / 7.68 / 3.81 / RAD 1.6 1 dk / rf 569 BK 76	**M Tug**	Oil 4SA 6Cy 260 × 368 reverse reduction geared to sc. shaft / Ruston Paxman Diesels Ltd Lincoln / Gen 1 × 40kW 1 × 30kW / 415V 50Hz a.c.
7740544 / Gc Rdr / RT	**LIWIA** / **Zegluga Szczecinska** / Szczecin — Poland	142 / 93 / —	PR	**1978** S. Ordzhonikidze Works—Poti (S-684) / 35.21 / 6.02 / 1.150 / 30.38 / / 1.81 / 1 dk	**Aluminium Alloy TM Hydrofoil Ferry**	2 Vee Oil 4SA each 12Cy 180 × 200 geared to sc. shafts / 2 000bhp (1 471kW) / Zvyezda Works Lenningrad / Gen 1 × 6.5kW 1 × 5.5kW 24V d.c. 32kn
7638234 / 9VPO / 3835.8 / Df Esd / Gc Pfd / Rdr RT	**LIYANG** / ex Mirasol-86 ex Polsund-86 / ex Mirasol-82 ex Hornsund-81 / ex Torasund-78 / ex Nortrans Tora-77 / ex Torasund-77 / **Ocean Navigation Pte. Ltd.** / Singapore — Singapore	6 016 / 3 263 / 9 478 / 9 580 / 5 831 / 13 753	NV	**1977** VEB Warnowwerft Warnemuende —Warnemuende (303) / 152.63(BB) / 20.35 / —/9.330 / 140.47 / 20.31 / 9.53 / P - F - 2 dks / rf 102	**M General Cargo** / 3 Ho ER 1 Ho / G 21 312 B 19 307 / TEU 307 C. 307/20′ / 6 Ha (stl) (13.0 × 8.4) (21.2p&s / 19.7p&s × 7.7) ER (13.0 × 10.9) / Der 1(80) 3(22) 1(8) 4(-)	Oil 2SA 8Cy 700 × 1200 / 11 200bhp (8 238kW) / VEB Dieselmotorenwerk Rostock (DMR) MAN Rostock / Gen 3 × 452kW 380V 50Hz a.c. 17kn
8418708 / Gc Rdr / RT	**LIYVI LACHT** / **U.S.S.R.**	150 / 50	RS (Class cont.)	**1986** Stocznia "Wisla"—Gdansk (KP2/7) / 37.88 / 11.85 / 2.701 / 33.02 / / 4.42 / 1 dk	**TM Ferry** / Twin Hull / 429dk P	2 Oil 4SA 6Cy 200 × 240 geared to sc. shafts / 1 140bhp (839kW) / H. Cegielski Poznan Sulzer

7941679 **LIZA CHAYKINA**
U.S.S.R.
4 136 / 1 736 / 4 987 — U.S.S.R.
1980 Volgograd Shipyard—Volgograd
125.61 / 120.61 / 1 dk
4 201 / 6.91
RS
TM Tanker
Ice strengthened
Mchy.aft
2 Oil
6 000bhp (4 413kW)

7943536 **LIZANNA**
WSX3 / 191 / 605578
Trawler Gulf Master Inc.
Tampa, Fl — United States of America
112 / 76 / —
1979 Bayou la Batre, Al
20.46 / 6.71
1 dk
3.43
M Fishing
Oil
365bhp (268kW)
U.S.A.

8821597 **LIZIE FOLMER**
OZOO / D1633 / Df Esd / Pfd Rdr / RTm/h/v
ex Lize Frem-82
ex Birthe Junior-74
Seacarriers I/S Rederiet
H. Folmer & Co.
Kobenhavn — Denmark
T Mk / 299 / 162 / 715
1968 A/S Nordsovaerftet—Ringkobing (40)
BV
49.71 / 8.41 / 3.480
44.30 / 8.31 / 5.52
2 dks
rf nil
M General Cargo
1 Ho 30.4 ER
G.1 312 B.1 159
1 Ha (25.6 × 5.0) ER
2W Der 2(2.5)
Oil 2SA 5Cy. 260 × 400
500bhp (368kW)
Alpha-Diesel A/S — Frederikshavn
Gen 2 × 48kW 1 × 20kW
280V 50Hz a.c.
Controllable pitch propeller
Fuel 76.0t (d.o.)5.5pd
10.5kn

7827237 **LIZONIA**
GBJN / 364574 / Esd Gc / Pfd Rdr / RT
J. Wharton (Shipping) Ltd.
F. T. Everard & Sons Ltd.
Goole — United Kingdom
798 / 554 / 1 315
SS 2/84 1980-2 Cochrane Shipbuilders Ltd—Selby (109)
✠100A1
✠LMC
UMS
ELK 35.5/28.0U2
FN 886
60.30 / 11.28 / 3.896
56.01 / 11.21 / 4.60
P 11.3 F 6.1 1 dk
rf nil
3BH WB485T
M General Cargo
1 Ho 39.0 ER
G.1 781 B.1 633
1 Ha (stl) (30.9 × 8.5) ER
Oil 4SA 8Cy. 222 × 292 reverse reduction
geared to sc. shaft
999bhp (735kW)
Mirrlees Blackstone (Stamford) Ltd. — Stamford
Gen 2 × 80kW 415V 50Hz a.c.
Fuel 62.0t
12kn

7311965 **LJOSAFELL**
TFHV / 1277 / Df Esd / Gc Pfd / Rdr RT
Hradfrystihus Faskrudsfjardar H/f
Faskrudsfjordur — Iceland
462 / 146 / 366
✠100A1 M 6/86-21mos 1973-4 Narasaki Zosen K.K.—Muroran (809)
stern trawler
Ice class 3
✠LMC
EL (I) J 1"U2
FN 662
47.10
41.23 / 9.53 / 4.566
B & F 18.3 2 dks / 6.51
rf 787 BK 305
Coll BH to U dk 3 to 2nd dk WB nil
M Fishing
Stern Trawler Ref
Oil 4SA 6Cy. 310 × 380
2 000bhp (1 471kW)
Niigata Eng. Co. Ltd. — Niigata
Gen 2 × 200kW 380V 50Hz a.c.
Fuel (d.o.)
12kn

7129570 **LJOSAFOSS**
TFXI / 1370 / Df Esd / Pfd Rdr / RT
ex Utstraum-74
H/f Eimskipafelag Islands (The Iceland Steamship Co. Ltd.)
Reykjavik — Iceland
T Mk / 200 / 128 / 594 / 702 / 452
1972 G. Eides Sonner A/S—Hoylandsbygd (92)
NV
55.15 / 10.55 / 3.017/3.341
51.11 / 10.51 / 5.87
2 dks
rf 597
M Refrigerated Cargo
2 Ho ER
In.1 048
2 Ha (14.4 11.7 × 6.4) ER
2W Der 2(3)
Oil 2SA 8Cy. 260 × 400
800bhp (588kW)
Alpha-Diesel A/S — Frederikshavn
Gen 2 × 96kW 1 × 29kW
220V 50Hz a.c.
Controllable pitch propeller
Fuel 45.5t (d.o.)4.0pd
12kn

8019942 **LUBICA C**
396257
Lucky S Fishing Co. Ltd.
S. Skoljarev
Port Adelaide, S.A. — Australia
204 / 167 / —
1981 Colan Shipbuilders Pty Ltd—Port Adelaide, S.A. (40)
(NV)
28.20 / 7.51 / 3.92
27.77
1 dk
rf 1148
M Fishing
Side-fishing Tuna Seiner Ref
Mchy.fwd
8 Ho
In.90 L.110
8 Ha (stl)
Vee Oil 4SA 12Cy. 159 × 203 with
clutches & sr reverse geared to sc. shaft
850bhp (625kW)
Caterpillar Tractor Co. — Peoria, Illinois
Gen 1 × 125kW 1 × 80kW
415V 50Hz a.c.
11kn

5209924 **LJUBIJA**
YTJI / Df Esd / Gc Pfd / Rdr RT
RO Dalmatinska Plovidba
Dubrovnik — Yugoslavia
12 847 / 8 792 / 19 175
SS 8/84 1981-10 Brodogradiliste i Tvornica Dizel Motora "Uljanik"—Pula (232)
✠100A1
strengthened for heavy cargoes
✠LMC
EL it 2½"SQ
FN 5614
173.56 / 22.18 / 9.335
161.55 / 22.10 / 12.65
P 32.0 F 14.1 1 dk
rf 76
NS 7BH WB7835t incl. topside tanks
JR 2068t
M Bulk Carrier
7 Ho 27.0 4.8Upr 25.0 4.8Upr
25.0 4.8Upr 26.0 ER
G.27 706
7 Ha (stl) (18.0 9.6 12.8 9.6 12.8 9.6 16.0 × 8.6) ER
Cr. 5(3)
4bth P 4.8Upr
Oil 2SA 6Cy. 740 × 1600
7 500bhp (5 517kW)
R.O. Tvornica Dizel Motora "Uljanik" — Pula
2 AuxB (1 o.f. 1 exg) 100lbf/in² (6.9bar)
Gen 4 × 168kW 440V a.c.
Fuel 1 020.0t (hvf)
15kn
B&W

Fig. 8.1 Lloyd's Register of Shipping – a sample page with key. (Reproduced by kind permission of Lloyd's of London)

shipyards or straight from university when suitable training and experience is provided to C.Eng. standard. 'Engineer surveyors' have normally spent some time at sea as marine engineers and also have practical and academic qualifications again, where they are recruited straight from university, suitable training and experience is provided to C.Eng. standard. Many surveyors qualify to act in both capacities after acquiring appropriate experience with Lloyd's Register.

In addition to experts in such subjects as stress analysis, electricity, automation, refrigeration, metallurgy, and computer mathematics, Lloyd's Register has in recent years also recruited specialists in structural engineering, soil mechanics, plastics, and quality control procedures. In order to give surveyors the opportunity of discussing modern developments in their field, technical and management courses are run regularly at Lloyd's Register Training Centre which are led by senior Lloyd's Register staff and by outside instructors. A similar centre was opened in Yokohama in 1972 to facilitate training of staff serving in Japan and the Far East.

The shipowner's motives today in seeking to class his ship with Lloyd's Register are probably little different to a century ago. If he is buying new, he naturally wants to be sure that he is getting value for money in terms of a sound ship which he can operate economically in his chosen trade. He is aware that classification with a recognized classification society will assist him in arranging insurance and in fixing charters, and he knows the value of the technical back-up which will be available to him during the life of the ship. If he decides to sell her, he will find that a ship with class maintained is a more marketable commodity than one without class.

Having decided that he wants a new ship built to Lloyd's Register class, the owner specifies this in his contract with the shipbuilder, and it is the builder who makes a formal request for Lloyd's Register's services and accepts the responsibility for the payment of fees. It is also the builder who submits plans of hull and machinery to Lloyd's Register's surveyors for approval as required by the Rules. Until recently, almost all plan approval work was done in headquarters but as demand increased, some of this work was transferred to offices in major shipbuilding ports around the world. This decentralization has developed to the point where the same plan approval facilities using computer techniques are available in the major shipbuilding countries as in London headquarters. Plans are scrutinized at the approval office and an analysis of the ship's structure with regard to stress resistance is made using Lloyd's Register's computer and specially developed programs. The builder must then ensure that any amendments stipulated by the surveyors are incorporated into the final plans.

The steel is tested by surveyors at the maker's works, which must be on the Lloyd's Register's approved list. Forgings and castings are also inspected and tested. Alternatively, steel sections for the hull, or steel forgings, may be manufactured by a works approved under Lloyd's Register's recently introduced quality assurance scheme for materials. Under this scheme, a works having suitable quality control procedures of its own may be granted an approval certificate for the manufacture of certain items by specified processes, which can be renewed each year subject to satisfactory performance.

Each stage of construction of the ship's hull and machinery is supervised by surveyors to ensure that the approved plans are being followed and that the standard of workmanship is satisfactory. On completion of acceptance trials, the surveyors submit a detailed report of the survey to London headquarters. Provided the report confirms that all classification requirements have been met, the General Committee will authorize the issue of classification certificates, and assign class to the ship, details of which will then appear in the Register Book.

In order to maintain class the ship must be surveyed at regular intervals during its service life, and all repairs, whether arising from general wear and tear or from damage, must also be carried out under survey. In principle a major survey must be held every 4 to 5 years. However, as such as thorough inspection is too time consuming and therefore expensive, the shipowner may elect to spread the survey over a period of 5 years, each item being checked in rotation. In addition to this major survey, the ship also has to undergo 'intermediate' surveys, for example of hull, boilers and tailshafts.

Although it is the shipowner's responsibility to see that these surveys are held when due, Lloyd's Register assists the owner in planning a maintenance schedule for his ship or fleet by automatically notifying him regularly of the dates by which surveys must be carried out. This service is made possible by the computerization of all classification records.

In recent years Lloyd's Register has offered a worldwide service distinct from classification, which provides pre-contract technical advice and detailed supervision for a shipbuilding or engineering project to ensure that the agreed specification is being met. This service, co-ordinated by the specification services department, can be provided for ships and machinery of all types, docks, lock gates, buoys, offshore structures, etc.

In the advisory field there are many forms of the service ranging from a broad indication of the suitability of hull and/or machinery for a specific purpose to detailed advice on either the whole or part of a project. Included in the supervisory services are an examination of the specification and its associated plans, supervision during construction and installation, attendance at all shop tests and the issue of periodic progress reports and a final report on completion of satisfactory trials. The service is of particular benefit to clients with limited technical resources or who require additional technical staff for supervision duties.

Lloyd's Register has a special unit, the Technical Investigations Department, whose surveyors operate worldwide as a team of on-the-spot trouble-shooters. They attend to ships in trouble, anywhere in the world, to investigate causes of machinery failure and to recommend ways to remedy them. Frequently necessary is the examination of marine machinery under service conditions and for this purpose the department has built up a wide range of sophisticated equipment, of which the strain gauge is probably the most often used. The greatest part of the department's work is on the ship but the surveyors also investigate the machinery, structural and habitability problems, on offshore installations and inshore-based plant.

An important section of Lloyd's Register's marine activity is the statutory survey work undertaken by the International Conventions Department. General shipping standards, concerning for example tonnage measurement, loadlines and ship safety, are laid down in the form of international or national conventions which come into effect when a specified number of maritime governments officially accept the conditions and requirements contained in them. Lloyd's Register is authorized by many governments to carry out the necessary survey work and issue certificates for ships registered in these countries.

Lloyd's Register has had a long association with the marking of loadlines. Even before Samuel Plimsoll's well-known campaign against 'coffin ships' in the middle of the nineteenth century, Lloyd's Register had developed a simple rule for calculating the position of a loadline on the side of a ship, beyond which ships could not be safely loaded. It soon became obvious, however, that a more accurate method of calculation was needed, and so in the early 1880s the Chief Ship Surveyor of Lloyd's Register set about producing a set of tables which later, with only minor amendments, formed the basis for international loadline regulations. Present regulations were formulated by the International Loadline Convention, 1966, promoted by the UN agency IMO.

Lloyd's Register has made a significant contribution to the work of IMO through its surveyors, who attend their meetings as members of a number of national delegations, thus making their expertise available.

Lloyd's Register plays a prominent part in the deliberations of IACS (International Association of Classification Societies) of which it is a founder member. IACS was set up in 1968 with the purpose of promoting by collaboration and consultation the aims which its members hold common, and to provide for consultation and co-operation both national and international.

Lloyd's Register takes part in the main work of IACS dealt with in its working parties which cover such subjects as tanker safety, sub-division and stability, strength of ships, mooring and anchoring, marine engines, propellers and containers.

Safety regulations are laid down by the International Convention for the Safety of Life at Sea 1960, and include those covering ship construction, propelling machinery, electrical installations, safety equipment (fire protection, life-saving appliances, etc.), and radio-telegraphy and radio-telephony installations.

Computer programs have been developed to calculate loadlines, tonnages, and information necessary for the approval of grain-loading arrangements. Special programs have also been written to deal with the stability problems associated with drilling rigs and floating platforms which cannot be resolved by normal ship-type calculations.

The development of new types of ships and materials naturally means that amendments may from time to time have to be made to existing conventions. Lloyd's Register is closely connected with any changes through its representation on various IMO sub-committees. IACS also takes an interest in this work through its various working parties.

Today's Register Book looks very different from the slim, 7½ × 5 in. volume that covered the years 1764–66. It is now published annually in 3 volumes, totalling over 5400 pages, with a cumulative supplement issued every month, and contains extensive details of over 76 000 sea-going merchant ships, of 100 GRT and above. An example of the entries in the Register, and the key to the Register of Ships is found on pp. 162–3. Approximately 23% of the tonnage listed is to Lloyd's Register class.

Associated publications to the Register include an *Appendix* listing details of wet and dry docks, shipbuilders and telegraphic addresses; *List of Shipowners,* with postal addresses and fleets and a *Register of Offshore Units, Submersibles and Diving Systems.*

The Society also annually publishes the *Statistical Tables,* analysing the merchant fleets of the world: comprehensive figures on ships on order and under construction are published quarterly, with an annual summary and annual casualty returns are issued, for ships totally lost and sold for scrap.

In the spring of 1976 Lloyd's Register of Shipping and Lloyd's of London Press Ltd, the publishing subsidiary of Lloyd's of London, entered into a joint exercise to market shipping information, based mainly on five of their computerized files. These files cover ship movements; ship characteristics; new ship building; shipowners with postal addresses; and casualties. These files can be accessed to answer enquiries. Also, data can be supplied, on magnetic tape if a user wishes to analyse the raw data on his own computer. This subsidiary company called Lloyd's Maritime Information Services operates from Drewster House, Mark Lane, London EC2.

In addition to rules for ship construction, Lloyd's Register also publishes rules for yachts to be built in various materials, for inland waterway vessels, floating docks, mobile offshore drilling units and submersibles. Guidance notes and requirements for many other types of craft and machinery are also issued, together with a number of lists of approved equipment. All LR publications are printed at the Society's printing house.

Each week some 400 reports arrive at headquarters from surveyors around the world, containing detailed particulars of ships classed or being built to class. Of these generally over half contain information which is of use to the Technical Records Office – information concerning defects and damage to the structure or any part of the machinery of a ship. These data are extracted, coded and fed into the Lloyd's Register's computer. They form the basis of an information bank, valuable to both surveyors and outside clients, which can detect trends of defects and of service problems, and even predict, by statistical probability ratings, the possible rate of failure of a given item. All information is confidential to Lloyd's Register, but if a definite pattern of defect should emerge for a certain component, it may be necessary to inform the manufacturer of the Society's findings.

For almost twenty years now, Lloyd's Register has been involved in the classing of oil-drilling rigs and other offshore equipment. In view of the increasing variation in the types of structure, materials, and equipment being produced, Lloyd's Register set up a special department to deal with this work, the Ocean Engineering Department, now part of the Offshore Services Division.

The discoveries of oil deposits in the North Sea have resulted in great expansion in offshore work, particularly since Lloyd's Register was appointed by the British Government as a certifying authority for drilling units operating in the UK sector.

The Group is responsible for the certification and classification of drilling and production platforms, supervision of their assembly on site and inspection during service, as well as classification or design appraisal of submersibles, under-water habitats, diving chambers, sea-bed vehicles and other specialized offshore craft.

Lloyd's Register's computer, understood to be the most powerful in the European shipping industry, is used for a wide variety of applications, some of which have already been mentioned. These include the analysis of complex ship and offshore structures; the maintenance of classification records showing the state of survey of every classed ship; the storage of information on damage trends prepared by the technical records department; the processing of statistical shipping information; and the handling of data for more conventional purposes, such as calculation of staff salaries.

In addition to the main computer installation, Lloyd's Register has facilities for the visual display of data. Advanced equipment, given the information in the form of cards, will display a diagrammatical plot of the information on its screen.

Although primarily designed for internal use, many of Lloyd's Register's technical computer programs are of value to the ship-building, marine and non-marine industries, and the computer centre offers facilities for the use of these proven programs with clients' data.

The metallurgical section receives damaged components regularly from all over the world for testing, and, using experience built up over many years, is generally able to assess the cause of failure. Equipment includes microscopes, hardness testing machines, impact machines, creep testing equipment and torsional fatigue machines.

Investigations of an engineering nature are made by experts in stress and vibration analysis. Causes of machinery failure are assessed, and examinations of new designs are carried out prior to approval. Structural research often involves the use of scale models of ship sections or offshore structures, built of plastics or thin sheet steel, to which various stresses can be applied and measurements taken.

Equipment is also available at the laboratory for non-destructive testing. In addition to work done on the premises, specialist surveyors also give approval to testing establishments to carry out NDT examinations on equipment being manufactured under LR survey.

As a result of the increasing 'batch-and line' production of certain items of marine machinery, Lloyd's Register introduced a scheme in 1968 for the certification of mass-produced machinery items. As with the quality assurance scheme for materials, surveyors inspect manufacturers' processes and quality control procedures, and, if satisfied, issue an approval certificate. These procedures are subsequently audited on a regular basis, but do not require continuous inspection.

Yachting services are organized by the Yacht and Small Craft Services department. Wood, steel, alloy and reinforced plastic yachts may be classed provided they have been built according to the appropriate LR rules. An alternative to full classification is the Lloyd's Register Building Certificate (LRBC), which is granted to a yacht moulded or constructed under survey in an accepted establishment. Under this scheme subsequent periodical surveys are not necessary but, should it be required, full technical advice is available at the owner's request during the service life of his craft. Consultancy services on computer-aided structural analysis, advanced fibre technology and general specification aspects of yacht construction are also carried out.

Other services include the supervision of glass-reinforced plastic hull mouldings and fitting out, series production surveys of small yachts produced in large numbers, and condition surveys of Lloyd's Register classed yachts of all types.

Although the Society was originally established and maintained for the benefit of the shipping and shipbuilding communities, other industries in time became aware that they too could make use of technical expertise available. Today Lloyd's Register Industrial Services Division provides an international inspection service for many kinds of land-based undertakings, including nuclear power projects, hydro-electric and thermal power stations, oil refineries and chemical plant, pipelines, glass-reinforced plastic fabrication, pre-stressed concrete constructions, mining equipment, etc. Inspection can be carried out according to the terms of any code or specification agreed between purchaser, manufacturer and Lloyd's Register, in conjunction with any special requirements the client may have. This service is used by government departments and municipal authorities, as well as by private industrial concerns such as the major international oil companies.

Many contracts require very skilled and careful co-ordination. A hydro-electric scheme, for example, may call for the survey of components manufactured in several different countries for final installation in yet another. The very wide geographical spread of Lloyd's Register's staff gives it a special capability for such work.

In many cases survey of components at the point of manufacture is followed by supervision of erection of plant and equipment on site. When the installation stage has been completed and the plant has come into operation, surveyors may then be asked to inspect the equipment at regular intervals, either on a visiting basis or by being permanently attached to the operating company.

Inspection services such as these have been provided for projects under the British nuclear power programme since the programme's origin in 1950. In addition, Lloyd's Register has been concerned with nuclear plants for India, Italy, Japan, Spain, Sweden and the USA, and with nuclear research in the UK.

The Industrial Services Division also operates a freight container certification scheme, which covers approval of manufacturers' works, container types, materials, line production and quality control facilities. The service may also include condition surveys of used containers and re-certification after damage.

In 1986 Lloyd's Register introduced an on-line classification and statutory survey display system designed specifically to benefit owners of LR-classed ships. It is called LR CLASSDATA and uses modern communication, technology and computer techniques. LR CLASSDATA is available free of charge and offers shipowners direct and quick 24-hour on-line access on a worldwide basis to LR classification files held on an IBM 3081K mainframe computer. Public data network (PDN) facilities are available in a number of Latin American Countries using extended line links to Telenet/Tymnet services. A telephone connection also to the LR CLASSDATA provides up-to-date survey details of LR-classed ships direct to the visual display unit in the shipowners office. Overall some 40 countries specifically support the PDN services whilst 160 countries have direct dialled access via the public switched telephone network.

Examples include the following:

(a) *Master list of surveyable machinery items.* This will feature the due date, overdue indicator and any postponements granted will be shown for all continuous survey items.

(b) *Classification surveys.* This features surveys that need or will shortly need attention. It will feature ships name, LR number, assigned and due dates of surveys, including overdue surveys.

(c) *Statutory surveys.* The periodical statutory surveys and their assigned, due and range dates.

(d) *Machinery items due for survey.* This gives items due for examination within the next twelve months under the continuous machinery survey arrangements.

(e) *Hull items due for survey.* When a main survey such as the Special Survey is partially held, the items remaining to complete the survey are indicated on the visual display unit.

(f) *Master list of surveyable hull items.* This provides a master list of hull surveyable items. A complete list can be obtained by paging through a series of visual display screens.

(g) *Conditions of class.* The final display gives details of the three hull conditions of each class.

On page 173 is found a diagram of Lloyd's Register of Shipping Data Communication Services (see Fig. 8.2).

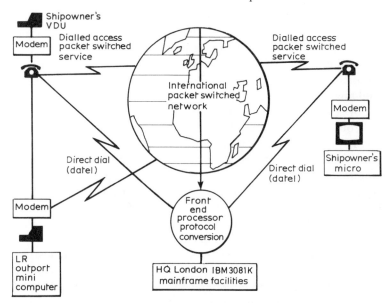

Fig. 8.2 Lloyd's Register of Shipping Data Communication Services. (Reproduced by kind permission of Lloyd's of London)

In the course of its development and expansion, Lloyd's Register has acquired experience in a wide variety of fields, some quite unconnected with the original business of ship classification. Lloyd's Register has grown from a handful of inexperienced surveyors, with no accepted standards to guide their judgement, to today's vast international network of specialists who are able to carry out technical inspection work calling for knowledge of many different engineering disciplines. Whatever the nature of the job, the prime concern of Lloyd's Register will always be to give service, while guarding closely its reputation for impartiality and integrity.

8.12 BUREAU VERITAS CLASSIFICATION SOCIETY GROUP

From a modest information agency for maritime insurance companies, set up in Antwerp in 1828, Bureau Veritas has grown into an International Group of Companies, based in Paris with activities ranging all over the main sectors of the economy. Establishment of rules, classification, testing, inspection and surveying are the historical aspects of the work of the Bureau Veritas Group. The applications of these skills into a diverse range of industries has resulted in the formation of five main Branches including Marine, Aeronautical and Automobile, Products and International Trade, Building Civil Engineering Safety and Industrial.

For several years now, Bureau Veritas has been engaged in a vigorous diversification policy, using its subsidiaries to move into sectors such as: non-destructive testing (Veritest); technical assistance (Tecnitas); software security and quality (Veridatas); commodities and food inspection (Controle Technique and Labs. de Bromatologie de France); inspection of inland navigation vessels in Belgium (Unitas); motor vehicle testing in Belgium (Auto Inspection Bureau Veritas); certification of quality management systems (BVQI); and inspection of containers (BVCS).

In 1986 the Bureau Veritas International workforce was 3380 of which 1569 were engineers and other technical staff, providing a permanent research potential and capacity for innovation. If the staff of subsidiaries is included the total workforce of the Bureau Veritas Group at the end of 1986 amounted to 3823. Group turnover for 1986 was 1.2 billion francs.

While marine activities remain the cornerstone of Bureau Veritas it is significant in 1986 income from the marine activities branch was surpassed by that from Building and Civil Engineering as detailed below:

	%
Building and civil engineering	34.3
Marine	32.6
Aeronautical	10.6
Industrial and international trade	22.5

One of the main features of Bureau Veritas is its international scale of operations. With 62 branches, 65 agencies and 14 subsidiaries, Bureau Veritas currently has 385 operational centres, in 123 countries on all five continents.

(a) Marine activities

Classification, in the first place, consists of checking design parameters against established rules by studying the design and construction drawings of the hull, machinery and equipment. This is followed by inspection of material and equipment at the manufacturers, supervision of the building at the yard to check that work is done in compliance with approved drawings, verification of procedures and the qualifications of the personnel and finally to attend dock and sea trials. After satisfactory completion of these operations, Bureau Veritas issues a classification certificate to the ship, valid for 5 years. The ship's name is then added to the 7000 or so already entered in the Bureau Veritas Register.

All ships classed by Bureau Veritas are regularly surveyed, throughout the world, by the marine branch surveyors. The purpose of such surveys is to ensure that the ship's condition remains in compliance with the rules, thus validating the class assigned during classification.

Statutory surveys
While classification operations deal with the safety of ships and cargoes, governments themselves establish the regulations for crew and passenger safety. Almost all of the maritime countries have delegated Bureau Veritas the authority to carry out statutory surveys, to check that ships comply with the regulations laid down by governments in conformity with International Maritime Conventions. Bureau Veritas is empowered to issue, upon conclusion of these surveys, the certificates relative to the safety of life and pollution prevention.

Inland navigation
The development of river transport led the Group to extend its classification activities to inland navigation and to prepare rules applicable to the building of inland navigation vessels. Four thousand vessels, navigating today on large rivers throughout the world, some more than 100 m in length, carry the seal of Bureau Veritas or its subsidiary Unitas.

Offshore
Offshore, has seen, in recent years, such a spectacular development that the offshore division today accounts for 20% of the activities of the marine branch.

To classify mobile offshore drilling platforms and underwater production units calls for proficiency in many fields (hydrodynamics, naval achitecture, mechanical engineering) and knowledge of the behaviour of various structures and materials.

The versatility of Bureau Veritas permits it to solve the various problems raised, to keep under control all the tasks relative to regulations and inspections and to issue certificates of fitness or conformity to offshore units, on behalf of the many states from which delegation has been obtained.

Aeronautics
Principal author of the first French aeronautical regulations, Bureau Veritas continues today to take part in the preparation of safety specifications on behalf of foreign governments. France became the first country to commission Bureau Veritas to check compliance with airworthiness regulations for civil aircraft. Since then, more than 20 other States, from Luxembourg to Togo, and from Algeria to Senegal, have delegated their authority to Bureau Veritas to check aeronautical safety.

Commodities and international trade branch
The development of international trade has created a gulf between operators and the products they are dealing with. Goods are loaded or unloaded hundreds or even thousands of miles away, their existence confirmed only by the exchange of a few telexes, and bank documents. This has increased the possibility of error or deception. One way of reducing such risks is to arrange for third party inspection, to ensure that transactions are carried out properly.

Bureau Veritas answers these needs professionally. Its worldwide network, its financial independence from all banking groups, governments or other authorities, enable Bureau Veritas to provide such a trade inspection service.

It operates in fields as diversified as agriculture and food, consumer goods, pharmaceuticals and health care products, chemicals, minerals and petroleum products, and in the evaluation of the appropriate costs of goods and services (see also pp. 427–8).

Bureau Veritas has established an import and export supervision programme for governments. As a basic tool for the implementation of economic policies, this programme enables a country's trade flows to be monitored in order to improve the balance of trade, and consequently the balance of payments. Several States have already recognized Bureau Veritas, thereby displaying their confidence in the approach adopted by the Commodities and International Trade Branch, in its relationships with government authorities, and guaranteeing its integrity. This programme is structured using important computer and communication tools.

The interventions are as follows:

(a) determination of appropriate price;

(b) checking the quality of the goods;

(c) checking the quantities: weight, volume, number;

(d) checking the legal documents related to the commercial transaction.

Industry

The industrial branch is involved in a diversity of tasks throughout the world such as the examination of pipelines, survey of radioactive waste treatment plants and the inspection of railway equipment.

Within the scope of such contracts, the Industrial Branch deals with the specification, standardization and inspection of industrial equipment; more recently it has carried out inspections of consumer goods and computer products, drafted the necessary regulations, when required, and applied to the industrial world the qualities that have meant success for the society – specialization, independence and worldwide coverage.

Building, civil engineering, safety

In 1929 Bureau Veritas created the Department for the Inspection of Buildings. By diversifying its activities over the years according to new developments in social and economic organization, technology and legislation, this Department has now become the Civil Engineering and Safety Branch.

Beyond the inspection of houses and buildings, Bureau Veritas tasks cover inspections and technical assistance for the following:

(a) major sectors of construction: hospitals, hotels, large sport and cultural centres;

(b) major civil engineering works: water supply, treatment and purification; roads, bridges, dams, airports, underground railways, port infrastructures, etc.;

(c) industrial plants: refineries, nuclear plants, cement factories etc.;

(d) floating structures;
(e) defence installations.

In France (where the Spinetta law defines the responsibility of each corporation involved in construction works) technical inspection is one of the main activities of the Civil Engineering and Safety Branch.

Recognized by the French government within the scope of this legislation, Bureau Veritas carries out inspections to check the strength of structures, at each building stage from the project up to completed work; checks drawings and plans; examines engineering documents and supervises the work in progress.

The Civil Engineering and Safety Branch now carries out such inspections in other parts of the world for prime contractors and builders, whether for the construction of or existing buildings, plants or other works.

Quality management systems

Spurred by the publication in 1987 of the ISO 9000 – series standards, Bureau Veritas established a new subsidiary – Bureau Veritas Quality International.

This company specializes in the assessment and certification of companies' Quality Management Systems. This is seen as a logical extension of the parent society's traditional role in the certification of products (ships and aircraft) into assessment of the way a company arranges its internal management to ensure that stated standards of quality are being met and maintained.

8.13 THE CORPORATION OF LLOYD'S

Marine insurance* is of great importance in the shipping industry because ships are expensive and subject to many natural perils and hazards. A ship may suffer total loss with all her cargo, or be seriously damaged by fire, storm or collision. As such a disaster could financially cripple the owners, it has long been the practice for owners to insure their vessels in order to cover the risk of the voyage.

---

* Marine insurance is a separate subject which is really beyond the scope of this book. For a detailed survey the reader is advised to study one of the many textbooks available.

There are no fixed rates in marine insurance and the actual premium for a particular ship or cargo is assessed on the incidence of losses in that trade and the risks that the ship is likely to undergo. This process of assessing the premium is known as underwriting and the marine insurance contract is embodied in a document called a policy. Marine insurance is undertaken by insurance companies or by Lloyd's underwriters.

Lloyd's of London is an association of insurers specializing in the insurance of marine and similar risks. It has its origin in the seventeenth century when shipowners and merchants meeting at Lloyd's Coffee House in London began to underwrite risks among themselves. Lloyd's was incorporated by Act of Parliament in 1871 and is governed by an elected committee.

The Corporation of Lloyd's, which incidentally has no connection with Lloyd's Register of Shipping, does not accept insurance or issue policies. All the underwriting business is transacted by members of Lloyd's trading as individuals. Briefly, the Corporation provides the facilities and the members transact the business. Lloyd's underwriters are individually liable under Lloyd's policies and their liability is absolutely unlimited. Although Lloyd's underwriters transact their business as individuals, it is usually found they associate with one another in groups of varying size, known as syndicates, with an underwriter acting for each group.

The Corporation of Lloyd's owns the premises and provides the various departments necessary for the conduct of such a large organization. Separate departments are maintained for the signing of policies, the settlement of claims, the collection of general average refunds*, salvage and recoveries from third parties, and for the payment of claims abroad. The Corporation is also responsible for the chain of signal stations on the trade routes of the world, and the maintenance of a Lloyd's Agent in every port of importance. Other important activites include the publication of *Lloyd's List*, a daily shipping paper and many other technical publications.

The part played by the broker in the process of underwriting is a

---

* A general contribution of money is paid by all parties concerned in the voyage in direct proportion to their several interests, when a voluntary and deliberate sacrifice has been made of one or more of the party's goods with a view to saving the remainder of the property, e.g. jettisoning under-deck cargo to lighten the ship or prevent fire from spreading.

leading one. The public have no direct access to the underwriter. Business is brought to him by the broker who, having learnt the needs of his client, prepares the 'slip' which is the basis of the policy to be, presents it to likely underwriters and secures the best terms for insurance, collecting the initials of various underwriters until the 'item' is completely insured. Thus for a hull insurance of £9 million there may be over six underwriters who have agreed by initialling the slip to underwrite certain portions of this risk. When the item is completely insured, the broker informs his client and subsequently a policy is issued on behalf of the underwriters involved.

8.14 PROTECTION AND INDEMNITY ASSOCIATIONS

These associations, known as P & I Clubs, were formed in the UK from 1855 onwards by the shipowners for mutual protection against those risks for which they were not covered under ordinary marine insurance. Today their function is the insurance of shipowners against third party liability, which is not covered by the usual hull and cargo policies obtained in the marine insurance markets at Lloyd's or elsewhere. The main items concerned are personal injury to passengers and crew, damage to or loss of cargo, and claims arising from collision with another ship or other object.

There are over a dozen P & I Clubs in the UK, and others are found in the USA, Japan and Scandinavia. In the UK the Clubs are run on a non-profit-making mutual basis and account for about 20% of premium income from marine insurance. They are controlled by committees of representatives of the shipowner members and managed by experts who collect the premiums and deal with claims as they arise. The claims on these associations – of which the majority are in connection with passengers, crew and cargo – are met by financial calls on members, based on the gross registered tonnage entered. Calls are made at regular intervals, and when the liabilities of a particular year have been ascertained, a further call or refund may be made. Thus in one year the liabilities may be heavy and in consequence the calls will be high. This differs from the American system where the majority of the business is done at fixed rates. P & I Club membership in the UK includes shipowners in all parts of the world. Foreign companies are represented on the controlling committees. Most of the business placed with the Clubs is direct, involving no payment of brokers' commission.

The UK P & I Clubs are arranged geographically and it is normal for the same type of shipowner to be found in each Club. In all there are four groups, details of which are as follows:

1. Group I *Protection*. This covers loss of life, collision or damage to another vessel or fixed object, crew expenses including sickness, funerals, etc; the cost of Department of Trade inquiries and raising wrecks.

2. Group II *Indemnity*. This covers shipowners' liabilities through their contracts, liabilities to cargo interest, Customs fines for innocent breach of regulations, cost of fighting cases and the ship's proportion of general average when in excess of the insured value.

3. Group III *Freight, Demurrage* (compensation paid to a ship-owner for delay to a vessel beyond the agreed time in a charter party for loading or discharge), and *Defence* (this covers only the legal costs of recovering freights, etc).

4. Group IV *War Risks* This covers mines' risk and, in event of hostilities, would cover a shipowner until the vessel reached a port of refuge, and a government war-risk scheme could be introduced.

An example of a typical P & I Club is found in the North of England P & I Associations Ltd whose entered tonnage by area of Management and claim payments by type during ·1982/83 is recorded below:

Entered tonnage by area of Management (%)		*Claim payments by type (%)*	
UK	53	Loss of life, personal injury	25.3
Yugoslavia	27	Collision	1.8
Far East	10	Fixed objects	5.8
Europe	8	Cargo	32.1
Others	2	Pollution	28.8
		Fines	0.7
		Others	5.5

Given below is a commentary on a number of P & I Clubs which emphasizes the extent of the range of services provided.

The American Club
The American Steamship Owners Mutual Protection and Indemnity Association, Inc. (the American Club) is the only mutual P & I Club in the United States. The Club was founded in 1917 solely for the benefit of American owners but has expanded its scope to provide full P & I Coverage and services to vessels of all flags.

The club has headquarters in New York and is managed by Shipowners Claims Bureau, Inc. Operations are subject to the control and inspection of the New York State Department of Insurance.

Britannia Steam Ship Insurance Association Ltd
This association was founded in 1855 and is the oldest of the P & I Clubs. About 2600 ships having a gross tonnage in excess of 40 m, are presently entered in the Association. The membership is worldwide, although the areas most strongly represented are the UK, Spain and the Far East including Japan. The Association covers shipowners' third party liabilities, and the extent of cover is adjusted to meet the requirements of individual members. As a mutual, non profit-making organization, the annual cost depends upon the total claims recovered by its members.

British Marine Mutual
British Marine Mutual has maintained its policies of providing insurance services to operators of smaller ships, especially those in UK and northern Europe, for Hull, P & I and the other usual classes. In northern Europe the economic pressures on its traditional members have been severe, resulting in greater efforts having been made by the Association to keep premiums at the lowest possible level, to reduce office costs to the minimum and to avoid the disruptive effect of unexpected supplementary calls on members. The Association is reinsured entirely in London and is still independent of the main P & I group of clubs; it is one of the few remaining clubs operated entirely from London. There is no management company, the directors themselves supervising the club's work.

The Canadian Shipowners' Mutual Assurance Association
The Canadian Shipowners Mutual Assurance Association was incorporated in 1953 by a special Act of the Canadian Govern-

ment. The Association provides war risks insurance for Canadian vessels of all types.

The Chartered Shipbrokers' Protection & Indemnity Association Ltd

Chartered Shipbrokers and Agents engaged in chartering, sale and purchase, liner and port agency as well as in secondary activities such as Air and Bunker Broking, Freight Forwarding and Travel Agency, Ship Management, Providing Crews, P & I Club Representation etc. benefit from cover for errors and omissions, including Breach of Warranty of Authority with and without negligence (without for the main activities any deductible) and a preventive advisory service, often after hours, to help to avoid negligent mistakes. This is a service unique in the market.

The Far East Club

The Far East Club was established in 1978, in order to provide P & I cover for shipowners and operators exclusively based in South East Asia. Membership is currently drawn from Hong Kong, Singapore, Malaysia, Thailand, Taiwan, Philippines and Indonesia.

German Shipowners' Defence Association

Founded in 1901, the Association has vessels entered which are either owned or managed by German companies and are tramp or liner vessels of all categories, i.e. coasters, dry cargo vessels, tankers and some types of specialized ships. The Association covers freight, demurrage and defence risks excluding collision risks.

International Ship Brokers' & Agents' P & I Club Ltd (Isbaclub)

The Club's two classes are as follows:

(a) *Protection.* This includes free assistance to recover money paid out for disbursements, stores, repairs, etc. in respect of vessels in a members' agency as well as to recover brokerages and commissions due to members for a fixture or sale etc.

(b) *Indemnity.* This is to provide members with cover or indemnification for claims which arise as a result of errors and omissions or negligence occurring in the course of members' business as shipbrokers or agents or for acting in excess of authority.

The Club also handles indemnity for loss of brokerages or omissions or negligence occurring in the course of members' pollution or damaged port installations by vessels in members' agency. The club also deals with enquiries from its members for marine insurance cover including charterers' liability (voyage or time charter).

Newcastle P & I Association
The Association was founded in 1886 and is proud of its long record of moderate and relatively stable calls and of accurate cost forecasting. Cover is also available for losses arising out of shore and crew strikes.

North of England
The North of England Protecting & Indemnity Association Ltd, founded in 1886, offers P & I, F.D. & D. and War Risks cover for hull and machinery, freight, etc. Membership of the Association can be obtained in any, or all, of the P & I, F.D. & D. and War Risks Classes.

Although traditionally an Association catering for British owners, vessels of other flags are accepted and now constitute an important part of the membership.

The Pan American Club
This section of Pacindat Mutual Protection & Indemnity Association Ltd, was introduced on 1 July 1981, as a separate entity to the Far East Club, specifically designed to accommodate the localized needs of Latin America with the same Pacindat philosophy of uniting shipowners and managers from a specific area and specializing in their particular problems and needs.

Post & Co (P & I) B.V.
Serving shipowners, charterers as well as their agents and insurance brokers, this company has developed the expertise and experience to know in what respect P & I can be adapted to the needs of owners and charterers in their different trades and locations. It also has the market contacts to put this into practice by finding the right club or market in order to obtain the required security at a competitive rate.

The same specialized attention can be given to claims handling where required. Some owners, with their own claims department, prefer to deal directly with the clubs. Others avail themselves of an outside full claims handling service. This need not be restricted to the handling of cargo and crew claims only, but can be extended to the whole range of claims of a P & I nature as well as those of a defence nature like freight and demurrage disputes.

A further service can be provided to those who are interested in an independent opinion on their present P & I insurance coverage, without wanting to commit themselves to a new intermediary.

The Shipowners' Loss of Hire Insurance Association Ltd

This Association is known in the market as 'The Loss of Hire Club' and offers insurance to shipowners against the loss of charterhire or lost earnings of an entered vessel arising out of a marine casualty. Entry is available to all types of vessel ranging from coasters to ocean-going bulkers and tankers. The cover offered is basically similar to that of the ordinary market but a full study of the Association's rules would show one or two positive advantages. As a mutual association, tangible cost savings are also offered.

The Shipowners' Mutual Strike Insurance Association (Bermuda) Ltd

The Association, known worldwide as 'The Strike Club' remains unchallenged as the world leader for this type of insurance and premiums remain at a modest level. The Strike Club basically covers members' loss of daily running cost/charter hire arising from 'shore strikes' such as stevedores, tug crews, pilots, customs officers, crane drivers, railmen, lorry drivers, miners, warehousemen and others but Class III, which covers the owners' loss of daily running cost when crews strike, has become an even more attractive proposition and necessary form of insurance.

The Standard Steamship Owners' Protection & Indemnity Association

The Club, managed by Charles Taylor & Co., (Bermuda), has grown considerably since its inauguration in February 1970, and continues to welcome approaches from potential new members of high quality.

Steamship Mutual

The Steamship Mutual Underwriting Association (Bermuda) Limited has been operating snce 1975 and includes substantial tonnage from Italy, Germany, Brazil, India and the Far East. General investment policy is to match currency assets to expected currency needs with the majority of the fund in long-term fixed interest securities, but an active Finance Committee has taken advantage of all opportunities to improve income which have been considered to be compatible with maximum security of capital.

Sunderland Steamship P & I Association

The Association was founded in 1879 by local shipowners. It now provides a full P & I and F.D. & D. service to an international membership. The Club's policy has been to build up a unified membership concentrating on modern conventional cargo-carrying vessels engaged in bulk and general trades thereby maintaining the underlying philosophy of the early mutual Clubs.

The Swedish Club

The Swedish Club (Sveriges-Angfartygs Assurans Forening) – founded in 1872 – is a mutual association of shipowners providing hull and machinery, war risks and protection and indemnity cover.

The facilities of the Swedish Club are available to shipowners of all nationalities and hull and machinery cover is provided on any internationally recognized insurance form.

The Club operates a loss prevention programme and one of the features is regular teach-ins for masters, deck officers and engineers, the object of which is to discuss nautical and technical matters and to inform about insurance covers and costs.

The Transmarine Mutual Loss of Hire Association

The Association was formed in 1978 to provide cover for shipowners against reduction of earning capacity following a marine casualty. Cover is divided into the following two classes:
1. Class 1: Reduction of earning capacity caused by or in consequence of one of the perils enumerated in the ordinary form of English Marine Policy.
2. Class 2: Reduction of earning capacity resulting from loss or damage caused by or in consequence of one of the perils enumerated in the Institute War and Strike Clauses (Hulls).

The Association was the first of its kind in the world to offer loss of earnings/hire insurance on the mutual principle.

The Transmarine Mutual Strike Association

The Association was formed in 1974 to provide cover for ship-owners and charterers against delay to their ships due to strike. The rules of the Association define a strike as 'any form of industrial action taken by workers with the intention of preventing, restricting or otherwise interfering with the production of goods or the provision of services'. Covered under this definition are strikes of stevedores, longshoremen, tallymen, crane operators, lockgatesmen and all port workers including tug crews and lightermen. Also covered are strikes by road transport workers and railwaymen, and strikes in factories, mills or mines resulting in the non-availability of cargo for ships. Cover is divided into the following three classes:

1. Class 1 covers a delay to a vessel while a strike is in operation.
2. Class 2 covers delay caused by congestion resulting from a strike but after the strike has ended.
3. Class 3 covers delay caused by a strike of the officers or crew.

In the course of more than a hundred years, the P & I Clubs have established themselves as an integral part of worldwide marine insurance, and provide a service not readily available in any other market.

8.15 SALVAGE ASSOCIATION

The Association was founded in 1856 by a group of underwriting members of Lloyd's and representatives of marine insurance companies practising in London. It was quickly successful in bringing malefactors to justice and in 1867 it was incorporated by Royal Charter thus becoming a legal entity with corporate status. In October 1971, Her Majesty Queen Elizabeth the Second granted a new Charter under the name of the 'Salvage Association'. The Association is therefore now known by this name and not the lengthy title it previously held which was 'The Association for the Protection of Commercial Interests as respects Wrecked and Damaged Property', although this is still a thumbnail sketch of its activities.

Business activities of the Salvage Association are controlled from London. Overall policy is laid down by a committee of 23 people, 3 of whom are *ex-officio* members, namely the Chairman of Lloyd's, the Chairman of the Institute of London Underwriters and the Chairman of Lloyd's Underwriters' Association, 10 members representing Lloyd's, and 10 the insurance companies. The Chairman and Deputy Chairman of this committee are elected annually, usually serving for 2 years, and each position being held alternately by a representative of Lloyd's and the companies.

The main functions of the Association are to deal with damaged vessels and cargo and to investigate frauds. It provides expert knowledge, assistance and advice based on vast experience. The Association is a non-profit-making concern acting for whoever instructs it and charging fees for its services on a time and trouble basis. Although the members of the committee of the Association are all Underwriters' representatives the Association is not solely an underwriters' body. It is an independent organization and accepts instructions not only from Underwriters but also from shipowners, P & I Clubs, average adjusters, solicitors acting for interested parties, government departments, merchants and manufacturers, whether they be insured or not. Approximately 15 000 cases are handled annually.

When a vessel is in distress and requires towing the Association frequently assists by getting in touch with tugs and arranging towage terms. When a vessel is sunk or ashore a salvage officer may be appointed to advise on the best means to raise or refloat her and again the Association is able to advise on the availability of salvors and appropriate forms of contract.

Ship repairs are of great importance and form a large part of the Association's work. A Salvage Association ship surveyor not only notes the extent of damage and agrees the cost of repairs, but he also establishes the cause of damage, so that he can apportion it between accident and wear and tear. This often involves lengthy negotiation with owners' superintendents and repairers and always involves vigilance to ensure that repairs are correctly allocated between owners' and damage accounts.

In 1979 the Association purchased the long established loss adjusting firm of Rush Johnson and Associates Inc., located in Houston, Texas, with an office in London which provides a comprehensive adjusting and appraising service to the oil industry.

It also regularly serves as a consultant to insurance underwriters, assisting them in writing complicated high-risk insurance for oil fields and wells.

Association surveyors advise what should be done with damaged cargo and, where appropriate, they agree allowances for depreciation, they arrange for reconditioning on the spot or wherever better facilities are available or they arrange sale in the damaged condition locally or wherever they know of a better market. Like the ship surveyors they establish the cause of loss or damage so that underwriters can decide whether there is a claim under their policy.

Information obtained for the Hull underwriters is not made available to the cargo underwriters and vice versa and information received from the surveyor acting for the ship in the general interest is not made available to the other parties.

Where insurance contains warranties requiring the Salvage Association to approve preparations for particular voyages, the Association's hull and cargo surveyors by reason of their experience of damage, are particularly qualified in this field and are being called upon with increasing frequency to assess fitness for voyages of vessels or craft in tow, cargo stowage and securing and, in special circumstances, for specific voyages of vessels under own power.

Information concerning maritime casualties pours into the Association daily by cable and telex. Much of this is passed to the intelligence department at Lloyd's for display in the underwriting room for the information of the insurance market or for publication in *Lloyd's List*. The Association also provides a useful service in the London insurance market by giving advice and information based on knowledge and experience built up over the years. The information department of the Association keeps all kinds of interesting statistics, maintains records of the laws governing removal of wrecks in various parts of the world and records information about commodities with special reference to the hazards involved in their carriage. Not only does this department keep records concerning wrecks – but it also handles numerous queries from all over the world about wrecks from firms or individuals wishing to buy whatever may remain in known wrecks.

Finally, the Association's activities have been extended to the survey of such things as power stations, electrical plant, damaged wharves, locks, and underwater cables, when asked to do so.

8.16 BALTIC EXCHANGE

The Baltic Exchange is the only international shipping exchange in the world and a major earner of foreign currency for Britain.

Its origins can be traced to the seventeenth century, when shipowners and merchants met in London coffee houses. Foremost among these were the Jerusalem Coffee House and the Virginia and Maryland Coffee House (known from 1744 as the Virginia and Baltic as the cargoes dealt with came from the American colonies or from the countries on the Baltic Seaboard). The proprietors provided newspapers and commercial information for their customers as well as refreshments, and cargoes were auctioned there.

In 1810 larger premises were acquired at the Antwerp Tavern in Threadneedle Street which was renamed the Baltic. Membership of the 'Baltic Club' was limited to 300, and a committee set up to control its affairs in 1823. From this moment onwards the importance and membership of the Baltic increased.

In 1900 the Baltic amalgamated with the London Shipping Exchange and became the Baltic Mercantile and Shipping Exchange Limited. Shortly afterwards a site was purchased in St Mary Axe and in April 1903 the present building was in use. After the Second World War an adjoining bomb-site was acquired, and the foundation stone for a new wing was laid by Sir Winston Churchill on 2 March 1955.

This building was opened by Her Majesty The Queen on 21 November 1956. Today the membership of the Baltic includes over 600 companies on whose behalf about 2000 individual men and women are entitled to trade on the 'floor' of the Exchange. Foreign concerns may become members if they have offices in Britain. The Baltic Exchange as the title is today, is a private limited company, and on admission members are required to become shareholders in the Exchange.

The business carried out on the Baltic provides a vital service for world trade. According to leading shipping consultants in London, the total world seaborne trade in 1987 amounted to around 3500 million tonnes. Of this around 1400 million tonnes was dry bulk cargo with roughly 63% of this being accounted for by the five main dry bulk commodities: iron-ore, grain, coal, bauxite/alumina and phosphate rock. The remainder being attributed to cargoes such as sugar, forest products, ores and minerals, fertilizers, some manufactured commodities and various agricultural products. Many operators in these trades are themselves members of the Exchange, particularly international commodity traders in grain, oils, seeds and fats.

Servicing these trades on the Baltic are brokers, acting for those who require ships or for those who own or operate them. Many merchants and shipowners are members of the Exchange and have broking staff who act for them. Business is done verbally on the 'floor' where various markets are located. Foremost of these is the Freight market where cargoes are found for ships and ships for cargoes.

Shipping is the main activity of the Baltic Exchange, and it has been estimated that about three-quarters of all the world's tramp market bulk cargo movement is at some stage handled by members of the Baltic Exchange.

A number of member companies have Sale and Purchase departments, and some engage exclusively in this activity. It is estimated that about half the world's sale and purchase of ships is dealt with through firms represented on the Baltic.

Other important activities which take place on the 'floor' of the Exchange concern commodities and futures trading. Under the umbrella of the newly-formed Baltic Futures Exchange (BFE) futures trades are undertaken by members of BFE in Freight (BIFFEX Dry Bulk Cargo contract), grain (wheat and barley), potatoes ('main' and 'earlies'), soyabean meal and meat (pigmeat and beef).

BIFFEX (The Baltic International Freight Futures Market) was opened on 1 May 1985. A BIFFEX futures contract is traded against the *Baltic Freight Index (BFI)* published daily.

Each of these futures markets is conducted across a 'ring' during two trading sessions held daily, each session being opened and closed by the ringing of a bell. This 'open outcry' system means that contracts are made as a result of bids and offers across the ring so that all traders are aware of market prices and have an equal chance of doing business. In active sessions hundreds of contracts can be traded in a matter of minutes.

Airbroking is another of the activities of members of the Baltic. The air-charter business was developed after the Second World War with many small operators, and today there are aircraft operating companies from all parts of the world, both national and independent airlines, represented on the Exchange. The Baltic Air Charter Association (BACA) is the trade body of the airbrokers.

In August 1987 the London Corn Exchange moved to the Baltic floor where it holds its weekly market session on Mondays.

The importance of the Baltic Exchange is reflected in the achievement of its members as invisible export earners for Britain. Their net contribution is calculated to be in the region of £300 million annually at the present time.

8.17 BALTIC INTERNATIONAL FREIGHT FUTURES EXCHANGE (BIFFEX)

The Baltic International Freight Futures Exchange was opened in 1985 in London and provides a means by which the many elements of the international freight and shipping industry can protect themselves against adverse price movements. Overall, it provides an essential economic function of providing members of the international shipping and commodity trading communities with a viable, effective and consistent means of reducing the risk inherent in fluctuating freight rates. Trade participants buy and sell Baltic Freight Index Futures to offset their exposure of forward commitments, transferring the price risk to other trade participants with opposing viewpoints and to speculators who are willing to assume these risks in pursuit of profit.

Risk control using futures trading is called 'hedging'. Broadly defined it is taking a position in a futures market as a substitute for a forward cash transaction. For example, using BIFFEX, a charterer who has sold a commodity forward is concerned that freight rates will rise, eroding or eliminating his trading profit. To protect himself against this he buys BIFFEX Futures Contracts. If freight rates do rise the loss incurred in the 'cash' shipping market, when he actually secures a ship, will be offset by a profit on BIFFEX.

A shipowner's risk is the exact reverse of the charterer's risk, hence he sells BIFFEX Futures to protect himself against the market falling by the time he actually fixes his ship on a charter.

By using the BIFFEX futures market it is possible to secure a forward cost of freight at the level of the future prices that are being traded up to two years ahead. Traded futures prices are broadcast worldwide, second by second, through data vending companies and are also obtainable from the market floor brokers.

It operates on the basis the Baltic Exchange publishes each day, the *BFI*, which shows the weighted average freight rate level, on that day, of the dry bulk cargo shipping market.

The Index (BFI) is traded on BIFFEX for specified future settlement months (up to 2 years ahead) by open negotiation between a willing buyer and a willing seller on the 'ring' of the market. The price being quoted for each contract month will constantly change in line with supply and demand from the market – hence the prices will reflect the views of investors in the market as to what the settlement price for the futures contract position will be and, thereby, what the level of the physical shipping market will be at that time.

Table 8.2 The Baltic Freight Index (BFI)

Route No.	Cargo Size	Voyage	Weighting (%)
1.	55 000 Grain	US Gulf to North Continent	20.0
2.	52 000 Grain	US Gulf to South Japan	20.0
3.	52 000 Grain	US North Pacific to South Japan	15.0
4.	21 000 Grain	US Gulf to Venezuela	5.0
5.	35 000 Barley	Antwerp to Jeddah	5.0
6.	120 000 Coal	H. Roads/R. Bay to South Japan	5.0
7.	65 000 Coal	H. Roads to North Continent	5.0
8.	110 000 Coal	Queensland to Rotterdam	5.0
9.	55 000 Pet Coke	Vanc/San Diego to Rotterdam	5.0
10.	90 000 Iron Ore	Monrovia to Rotterdam	5.0
11.	25 000 Pig Iron	Vitoria to China	5.0
12.	13–20 000 Potash	Hamburg to West Coast India	2.5
13.	14 000 Phosrock	Aqaba to West Coast India	2.5
			100.0

Details of a contract specification are as follows:

Contract	Baltic Freight Index
Unit of Trading	Baltic Freight Index value at $10 per full Index point
Trading Months	January, April, July, October, 2 years forward
Settlement	Each trading month (four times a year)
Settlement Day	The business day after the last trading day of the settlement month
Last Trading Day	The last business day of the settlement month
Minimum price movement	0.5 index points ($5 per lot)
Settlement price	The average of the Index on the last trading day and the 4 previous working days of the settlement month

As it is not possible to deliver a freight rate, all contracts traded on the market are settled in cash, based on an average of the *Baltic Freight Index (BFI)* over the last 5 days of the settlement month. Cash settlement is by far the most convenient method of settling futures contracts and has been seen to operate successfully for many years.

Freight futures are of use to all those involved in the shipping markets and provide a management tool to be used in conjunction with traditional operations to control the financial risks inherent in ship chartering. Details of hedging examples are given below:

(a) Sell hedge

An Owner may have a number of his ships coming free over the next half-year or year but is unable to find suitable business on the freight market for those forward positions. The BIFFEX futures prices are being traded at a level which the owner considers to be a satisfactory relationship to the current BFI and he wishes to lock in this level of income. He calculates the amount of freight he wishes to cover (freight rate × cargo quantity) and divides it by the contract value (Index × $10.00) to give the number of lots to sell.

Subsequently, as his ships are actually fixed he then buys back the lots he had sold. If the freight market has fallen in comparison with the price at which he originally sold he will have reduced earnings on his ship but will have made a profit on his futures contract, and vice versa, i.e. his loss or profit on his physical ship transaction will be offset by his profit or loss on his futures transaction.

This method of hedging is completely flexible as if at any time the owner finds suitable contract or timecharter employment he can fix the business and buy back his sold futures contracts thus cancelling his futures position(s).

(b) Buy hedge

A shipper makes a sale on C. & F. terms for delivery north Europe from the US Gulf area of one cargo per quarter over one year. The shipper does not wish an exposure to the forward freight market.

To protect himself and to lock in his freight costs he should identify the forward prices on BIFFEX and relate them to the current freight market (the *BFI*) to see what premium or discount is being applied to the four Freight Futures positions that he wishes to trade. He calculates the amount of freight he wishes to cover and divides by the contract value to give the number of lots to buy (in exactly the same way as the Owner calculates the amount of cover needed to sell).

Subsequently, he sells the lots he bought (for each position) as he fixes a ship to carry each cargo. Any loss or gain in the physical ship market will be offset by a compensating gain or loss in his future contracts.

In addition to the price protection gained from the futures market, the shipper retains maximum logistical flexibility and is not constrained by specific cargo size or origin/destination.

A number of factors can affect freight rates and these are given below:

(a) Ship draught restrictions that are temporary in nature – seasonal or unusual weather conditions, siltation or obstructions – at major ports.

(b) Changes in the price of bunker fuel for ships.

(c) Changes in international currency values – the US dollar is the dominant currency for freight and changes in its relative value to other major currencies will affect the cost of running ships and operating them in International trades.

(d) Changes in the cost of port expenses and in major canal transits.

(e) War and acts of aggression may affect the level of

confidence in world economic conditions and cause shortages of raw materials and finished products. Disruptions in patterns of supply and demand can cause increases or decreases in the costs of transportation.

(f) Strikes and other disruptions in the supply of labour or services will affect the volume of cargo that can be handled and produce a temporary aberration in shipping markets.

(g) Severe weather conditions can cause reductions in the supply of material and in the amount of cargo a ship can carry.

(h) Seasonal variations in commodity demand and production – the world's grain harvests are seasonal and the demand for coal energy will be highest in winter months.

Significant or sharp changes, or the perception of likely changes, in freight rates can be expected to cause changes in the futures prices traded on BIFFEX.

The importance of BIFFEX as a means of facilitating the development of international trade and shipping cannot be overstressed.

8.18 FREIGHT TRANSPORT ASSOCIATION INCORPORATING THE BRITISH SHIPPERS' COUNCIL

The British Shippers' Council was founded in 1955 to further the interests of importers and exporters in the UK in all matters concerning the overseas transport of their goods, whether by sea or air. The Council was the first such national body to be formed but, under the stimulus of organizations such as the International Chambers of Commerce and UNCTAD, the movement has spread rapidly in the last twenty years and there are few significant trading countries which do not now possess one. Since the early 1960s, the movement has become particularly strong in Western Europe where there are now 14 national councils, many of whose activities are co-ordinated through an International Secretariat at the Hague.

The British Shippers' Council is an independent voluntary functional trade association whose membership comprises other trade associations, representing most of the major industries of the country (including the Confederation of British Industry and the Association of British Chambers of Commerce) as well as individual trading companies numbering some 150. It is widely recognized both in governmental and commercial circles as the representative national body of the users of international freight transport.

About 90% by value, and a much higher percentage of volume, of our overseas trade is still carried by sea. The remainder is carried by air. It is thus natural and inevitable that the main emphasis of the Council's work has been with the problems and costs of the sea carriage of our goods but, in recent years, much more attention has been given to the interests of the air shipper. It is fair to say also that the majority of our export trade is sold on CIF or similar terms, and even where goods are sold ex-works or FOB, it is frequently the case that the seller acts as agent for the buyer in arranging the shipment. Thus, no matter what the terms of sale, the exporter nearly always has a direct interest in the cost of the overseas movement of his goods and in the efficiency with which they are handled and carried, so that their delivered price may be competitive in overseas markets and commercial goodwill may be maintained by the assurance that deliveries arrive on time and in good condition. These considerations tend to place the main emphasis of the Council's work on our export trades, though there are aspects of it which also benefit importers.

Nowadays, the exporter has a wide variety of choice in the services available to him to carry his goods, whether by sea or air. Our entry into the European Community has resulted in a much larger proportionate growth in our trade with Western Europe than with other parts of the world. There is an abundance of ferry services from a wide range of ports to all parts of the Continent and, through the use of groupage and transport operators, goods can be transported quickly from the consignor's warehouse in the UK direct to the point of delivery in Europe without ever leaving their trailer. Strictly speaking, the Council is only concerned with the sea voyage part of this operation but inevitably the problems and cost of the whole movement come increasingly under scrutiny as the techniques and services are further developed. At present, the ferry operators consist of individual lines operating a range of routes in competition with each other. They tend to regard their main customers as the road haulage operators rather than the cargo owner himself. It is the latter, however, which the Council represents and the Council, in common with several other

Councils on the Continent, has recently been giving much greater attention to the ever rising costs of moving goods to and from the Continent.

The majority of British exports of manufactured goods to deep-sea destinations is carried by liner shipping operating within the conference system. Relationships with the shipping conferences have lain at the centre of the Council's work for many years and this has developed into a close and continuing process of consultation under a voluntary commercial Code of Practice negotiated within Europe in 1971. This code, which is distinct from that published by UNCTAD in 1974, has undoubtedly served a major purpose over the last seven to eight years in trying to get the interests of shippers and shipowners on a far better mutual understanding to the undoubted benefit of international trade. It is not a perfect instrument since there are several conferences who do not accept it owing, principally, to governmental regulations in varying degree at the far end of the trade routes. It is notable that relationships with these conferences are less constructive than they are in those trades where the code is fully accepted and implemented.

The premier role of the British Shippers' Council is, therefore, to act as a commercial counterbalance to the cartel structure and power, which is implicit in the conference system and which has, over many years, been the subject of criticism.

A most important role of the Council lies in the field of trade documentation and procedures. By bringing together shippers from many different organizations and backgrounds in committee, the Council is able to offer a body of experience unequalled in the country on these most complicated but vital matters. The Council has had the closest association with SITPRO and it is represented on many of the committees and working groups which that organization has set up. It is similarly represented on the consultative committees of HM Customs and Excise and it is thus able to exert a very powerful influence on official policy affecting trade documentation generally.

As the representative of the owners of cargo, the Council can claim to be one of the two chief interests in the operation of British ports, the other being the shipowners. The Council has sought to develop more consultative arrangements between port users and port managements so that the latter can make reasoned judge-ments about future developments and can be kept aware of the effects of their pricing and charge structure on the interests of users. Owing to the large number of British ports, consultative arrangements of a formal character tend to exist chiefly at the larger ports but the Council, through a series of regional committees, have established relationships with all the ports of significance to British shippers. Besides this, shippers have an abiding interest in Government policy towards the ports industry and the Council has played an influential part in recent years in influencing Government policy towards the industry.

Finally, the Council acts as the focus of the shippers' viewpoint in determining changes to international conventions and other legislation affecting the carriage of goods by sea and air.

In mid-1979, the Council was absorbed into the Freight Transport Association. It is the only UK trade association existing solely to safeguard the interests of and provide services for trade and industry as operators and users of all forms of freight transport. It is recognized as such by central and local Government and other public bodies, as well as in the Common Market and other countries abroad.

FTA membership ranges from small businesses operating only one or two small vans to the largest industrial concerns in the country, including the major nationalized industries. Hauliers, other transport providers, local authorities, statutory boards and indeed virtually anyone with an interest in freight transport and distribution are additionally to be found in the ranks of associate members.

The FTA is consulted by Government when new transport laws are under consideration. In addition, with the agreement of the CBI, it represents the UK on the important transport commission of UNICE, the organization covering the whole of industrial interests in the twelve Common Market countries. Additionally FTA has its own contacts with EEC officials responsible for transport and with similar bodies in all other eleven Common Market member states. It is currently involved in the 1992 Single European Market developments.

The FTA is a service-based organization offering a wide range of tangible services, including consultancy, engineering, cost and rates and wages, education and training, and information.

8.19   SIMPLER INTERNATIONAL TRADE PROCEDURES BOARD (SITPRO)

(a) Simplifying international trade

Trading between different countries, cultures and currencies worldwide is complex and absorbing, but it is made unnecessarily complex by the procedural and documentary obstacles which must be surmounted whenever goods are moved internationally to their delivery point and whenever money is moved in the opposite direction.

Such practical difficulties have traditionally been given a very low priority compared to financial and marketing issues, but of course they can severely hinder a marketing effort by building delay and uncertainty into deliveries. They also damage companies financially by absorbing unnecessarily high amounts of cash in administration and interest costs. SITPRO, the board in Britain negotiating and simplifying international trade procedures, is the largest of some 30 similar organizations worldwide, set up to do what its name suggests. It is a small organization partly funded by the British Government and partly earning its own keep, with a governing board made up of heads of industry and government representatives, backed by over 100 members of advisory groups. SITPRO aims to bring people together to negotiate solutions to the practical problems of international deliveries and payment, and develops tools by which they can be managed better, particularly using information technology and sound management techniques.

Efficiency in international trade paperwork

The inefficiency of the traditional paperwork system, even though it is just the tip of the iceberg, causes a lot of delay and uncertainty to international deliveries. Standard documentation and related systems developed from United Nations standards by SITPRO have helped over 4000 exporters in Britain to streamline their paperwork, cut their administration cost by up to half, and apply a range of systems solutions. These can be very simple. A starter kit for new exporters includes one-typing sets for exports by freight or by post which give a low-cost solution to companies who do not wish to get involved in unnecessary complexity when they would prefer to be making and marketing their products. Systems using ordinary photocopiers to produce documents from a single typed or computer-printed master have been extremely popular during the last 15 years, and have changed the face of British export documentation practice. Now the application of information technology has improved the situation still further. Powerful but inexpensive microcomputers enable export offices to handle their paperwork more efficiently than before, and techniques such as laser printing are combining the best features of microcomputer systems with the best features of photocopier systems to produce highly cost-effective and integrated methods. SITPRO's own software for export invoicing and paperwork, Spex, is by a long way the world leader in this field.

Information in the right place at the right time

Clearly, systems such as those described are an incomplete solution. There is little point in producing documents quickly if they are in the wrong place. The export office is the last place where they are needed, so the problem remains of getting the paperwork and/or the information to the correct place, at the correct time, and into the recipient's computer system. Standards and technology have now developed to the extent that it is possible to transmit structured 'messages' between computer systems, instead of backing-up documents. The technique is known as Electronic Data Interchange (EDI). The individual items of information found on a document or a set of documents are grouped together according to United Nations and ISO standards, and so can be transmitted through telecommunications networks between otherwise quite different computer systems. This technique has already become well established in a number of British, North American and European industries, particularly in High Street retailing and motor manufacturing, where it has had a remarkable impact on increasing the efficiency of just-in-time inventory control. It is estimated that the use of this EDI technique will increase exponentially. Sometimes it will replace documents altogether. On other occasions it will enable the overall door-to-door movement to take place quicker while still producing the documents either for convenience (something has to show the lorry driver where to go) or for legal reasons (such as documents required under international conventions, or in countries where non-paper evidence of contract is not permitted).

The United Nations, through its Economic Commission for Europe in Geneva, in an activity linked with UNCTAD, is the standards maker for documentation and EDI. SITPRO and its counterparts worldwide are active participants. The work links in as necessary other relevant organizations such as the International Chamber of Commerce (ICC) and International Organization for Standardization (ISO).

Single European market
The years to 1992 should see a major drive within the European Community towards a single integrated European market in goods and services. One of the main planks of this would be the removal of Customs frontier posts within the European Community. This will require radical changes not only in procedural and statistical matters but in highly political matters such as the harmonization of VAT rates. SITPRO is working as a priority on the mechanics of such arrangements to help clear the way for frontierless trading in what is already the biggest industrial community in the world. Already, the whole of western Europe and Scandinavia uses a single type of Customs document, the Single Administrative Document (SAD) for Customs control of its exports, imports, and transit across the territories.

Cash flow and security in payments
It is one thing to deliver goods to customers on time. It is quite another to get paid on time and without problems. Apart from commercial delays, there is a whole set of procedural difficulties, some of which are governmentally imposed, such as exchange control, but most of which arise from inappropriate management of the commercial systems available. Generally speaking, exporters' and importers' main financial concerns are cash flow and security. From an exporter's point of view, payment is sought as soon as possible after despatch of the goods, and with the highest possible degree of security. This often stands in the way of the commercial need to give customers open credit terms. SITPRO has looked at and supports the move in Britain towards an increasing range of bank and finance house schemes for short-term export finance. These generally give payment of most or all the export invoice value, at the time of exportation, and with a pretty good degree of security, at least fully credit-insured on the private or public sector

market. Such schemes are particularly useful for new exporters or those who do not wish their overdraft or working capital planning to be constrained by export cash flow or unsecured debtors problems.

However, on many occasions exporters will need to get payment in from abroad, and frequently this causes up to a month's delay, after the customer has paid the money over to his bank, but before it is credited to the exporter's account. Any international traders in goods or services can experience such problems, but a number of solutions exist which SITPRO has uncovered and on which it advises companies through its publications.

Likewise, much secured business under documentary letters of credit is not operated as efficiently as it could be. Shipping documents have to be presented to the bank by the exporter in good time, and scrupulously correct, to obtain payment. In over 50% of cases the paperwork is wrong or late, so the security and right to prompt payment are lost. Again, most of the causes for error can be put right by proper management control, and SITPRO advises on how this can be done.

Trading in and with developing countries
The international debt situation and the difficult economic conditions experienced in many countries, particularly those in the course of development, appear unlikely to improve substantially during the next few years. These conditions frequently lead to additional regulations, paperwork and controls which have to be applied somehow, but the way in which they are applied usually seems to worsen the situation. Although countries experiencing economic difficulties need to ensure that their exports increase, and that their indigenous manufacturing is improved by a regular supply of raw materials and components from abroad, the barriers put in the way by belt-tightening regulations can frustrate these aims. Part of the work of SITPRO-type organizations around the world is to help avoid this frustration by smoothing out the procedures at both ends of the transaction.

Sometimes this can be partly achieved by a greater integration and streamlining of the procedural system in the country concerned. Sometimes it is more than that and touches on some sensitive areas such as the price comparison procedures imposed by an increasing number of importing countries as part of their pre-shipment inspection controls. All the same, there is little point in computerizing only the export system of highly industralized countries in order to cut an hour or two off the time it takes to get goods out of those countries, when the unreformed systems of the importing countries hold up those same goods for a month or more before they are cleared and delivered.

SITPRO can provide further information on international moves to simplify trade practice. Enquirers should write to its office at Almack House, 26–28 King Street, London SW1Y 6QW, or telex to UK 919130. Some of its publications are:

Top Form (documentation and systems)
Customs Now (distance learning kit with video and audio)
Letter of Credit Management and Control
Export Finance Checklists
Cash by Express (quicker international money transfers)
Instant Export Payments (a review of short-term export finance schemes)
Export Documentation Starter Kit (for newer exporters)

The foregoing SITPRO entry is reproduced by kind permission of SITPRO.

CHAPTER 9

Passenger fares and freight rates

9.1 THEORY OF PASSENGER FARES

Passenger fares are normally dictated by the nature of the voyage, the class of ship and the accommodation offered. They are also influenced by demand and supply factors, and on international voyages can be subject to conference agreements, a subject which will be dealt with in the next chapter. The Italians have the largest deep-sea passenger fleet. The docking expenses of the passenger vessel on an international voyage involving the disembarkation of passengers is costly and many cruise operators rely on passenger tenders (launches) to convey passengers to and from the vessel situated in outer harbour. Shipboard operating costs are high, since food and service must be provided, and speed and regularity of sailings are of great importance. Product differentiation is an outstanding factor, since the service and comfort of different cruise lines and vessels by class of cabin accommodation vary greatly.

Generally speaking, the cruise shipowner will charge a fixed rate per day depending on the accommodation offered. The technique of market pricing has been introduced on some cruise markets, differing fares being charged according to demand; for example, during off-peak periods a lower tariff would be offered.

An interesting cruise market situation is operated by Chandris who provide a range of cruises in the Mediterranean and Caribbean. One can book on the 7-day cruise or opt for the 'cruise and stay' package whereby one can cruise for 7 days and reside in a resort hotel for a further 7 days. The option also exists to fly-cruise by flying to the nearest airport to join the cruise liner. Passenger tariffs are geared to the type of cabin, cruise itinerary and ports of call. The Caribbean cruise programme operates all the year round whereas the Mediterranean schedule exists from the early Spring to the Autumn. Passengers taking the Mediterranean programme are subject to a high season supplement in July/August/September. Tariff reductions are granted on groups of 20 persons or more; passengers who booked with Chandris the previous year, and old-age pensioners for the Mediterranean cruises.

A substantial volume of passengers and motorist business is found in the short sea trades involving vehicular ferries carrying passengers, accompanied cars, commercial road vehicles, etc. The pricing technique varies, but on those routes subject to peak summer demand some three bands of tariff exist: the off-peak tariff, the summer season fare and finally the most expensive, the peak weekend rate. The latter usually operates throughout the summer period of up to twelve weeks. Overall such tariffs are motorist and coach business orientated.

The demand for passenger accommodation on a liner route with business passengers tends to be inelastic, whilst the demand for pleasure cruising tends to be elastic. For the benefit of the student unfamiliar with the economic meaning of the term elasticity, elasticity of demand refers to the responsiveness of demand to changes in price. When a change in price produces a more than proportionate change in the quantity bought, the demand is said to be elastic. Conversely, when a change in price produces a less than proportionate change in the quantity demanded, demand is said to be inelastic. the main factor influencing the elasticity of demand is the availability of alternatives or substitutes.

9.2 SHORT SEA AND ESTUARIAL PASSENGER TRADES

Since the 1960s the passenger market in the short sea and estuarial trades has substantially increased in many countries. Much of this growth can be attributed to the accompanied car market as for example in the UK, Irish and Continental passenger trades. It is also found in many parts of the world including the Mediterranean and the Far East, markets including their short sea and estuarial trades carrying passengers and some cars. The voyage time varies greatly by route and can range from 10–45 minutes in estuarial services to 2½ to 36 hours in the short sea trades. In the main the bulk of the traffic in the short sea passenger trade moves in the voyage time band of 3 to 8 hours.

The fares strategy varies and depends on competitive circumstances by individual route. It must be remembered that particularly with the modern vessels – which are usually one or two class – the vessel is capable of carrying road haulage (TIR) vehicles, foot passengers and accompanied cars – with caravans sometimes. The short sea trade foot passenger market, i.e. those going by rail/sea are vulnerable to air competition, but this is not the case with the accompanied car market as air ferry services are of comparatively limited capacity.

The following factors are relevant in fare evaluation:

(a) voyage distance/speed and time;

(b) competition by sea and air;

(c) passenger, car, etc. port dues;

(d) fuel, crew and other expenses involved in voyage cost embracing direct and indirect charges;

(e) agreements with other operators;

(f) basically on many routes for the motorist three tariff bands exist: off peak which is the cheapest; the summer season period tariff, and finally the most expensive the summer season weekend tariff. On the longer voyage a cheaper rate may operate in the off-peak season on the day service, than on the night service;

(g) class of travel, adult or child and type of cabin – if any. Concessionary fares sometimes available to students, old age pensioners, or for special events. Some shipowners offer a fare inclusive of the cabin accommodation, whilst others embrace meal provision with the fare;

(h) party travel – concessionary fares usually available to parties in excess of ten. This is very much in evidence with rail/sea travel agency market offering inclusive holiday/tours;

(i) length of car and number of accompanying passengers;

(j) any government statutory control over rates;

(k) revenue accruing from catering, entertainment facilities on board ship, advertising, shop sales, i.e. tobacco/cigarettes/spirits/ gifts etc. and the bars.

The operator will prepare his tariffs to maximize his revenue production. In so doing he will have regard to ensure his regular clientele have preference in shipment over the optional traveller. For example the regular road haulier will have preference on deck space allocation to the optional accompanied motorist. Moreover, the shipowner will formulate his tariff to ensure capacity is utilized to the full, i.e. deck space, cabin accommodation, seats, etc. during the off-peak season, thereby maximizing profitability.

9.3   INCLUSIVE TOURS

As we progress into the 1990s the development of the inclusive tour market will grow. This applies both to the airline and shipping companies. It arises when a shipping company has an agreement with a hotelier to provide accommodation who earmarks all or a proportion of it to the shipping company to retail as a package or inclusive tour at an overall price. This may be retailed by the shipping company or more usually through agents in the travel trade.

The package would include hotel accommodation, travel arrangements, and optional excursions provided at the hotel destination. Travel arrangements will include either the motorist conveyance on the ferry or the passenger travelling by rail/ship/rail. Both the travel facilities and hotel accommodation are provided at a discount to the normal individual tariffs and the two elements merged to give a package to the client.

An example is found in a family of two adults and two children travelling in a car to a hotel offering bed and breakfast with evening meal. The family is provided with two double rooms. The overall cost for 2 weeks is £800 including £650 in the hotel and £150 on the ship. The package is sold through an agent or direct by the shipping company. If the family elected to travel and book the hotel independently the cost would be £950 involving £200 on the ship and £750 in the hotel. Further it is unlikely they would be offered any excursions at a discount which is often available with the package facility.

The package can be linked to a particular type of holiday or event. For example, it may include a golfing holiday or festival.

Such facilities are very evident in the passenger shipping market particularly the short sea trades. Such discounted tariffs has helped the market to expand particularly in the off-peak season. It enables the client to take a holiday without the obligation to arrange all the travel, hotel and possible excursion arrangements as all this is done for him in the package. Moreover, as the traffic is generated in volume, it enables the tariffs to be lower and thereby stimulates the market development.

The passenger may also travel by coach throughout including the transit on the ship and has a package arrangment with a hotel or series of hotels if a tour is involved.

It is likely the market will develop particularly in the off-peak season.

9.4 THEORY OF FREIGHT RATES AND EFFECT OF AIR COMPETITION ON CARGO TRAFFIC

Freight is the reward payable to the carrier for the carriage and arrival of goods in a mercantile or recognized condition, ready to be delivered to the merchant.

The pricing of cargo ships' services, like all pricing, is dependent on the forces of supply and demand, but the factors affecting both supply and demand are perhaps more complicated than in the case of most other industries and services. As with all forms of transport, the demand for shipping is derived from the demand for the commodities carried, and is, therefore, affected by the elasticity of demand for these commodities.

The demand for sea transport is affected both by direct competition between carriers and, because it is a derived demand, by the competition of substitutes or alternatives for the particular commodity carried. On any particular route, the shipowner is subject to competition from carriers on the same route, and also from carriers operating from alternative supply areas. The commodities carried by the latter may be competitive with the commodities from his own supply area and, to that extent, may affect the demand for his services. On some routes there is also competition from air transport, and in the coasting trade there is also competition from inland transport.

The elasticity of demand for shipping services varies from one commodity to another. In normal times, an important factor affecting elasticity of demand for sea transport services is the cost of transport in relation to the market price of the goods carried. Although it can be negligible, the cost of sea transport is often a considerable element in the final market price of many commodities. It may be between 8 and 15%.

The price eventually fixed depends largely on the relationship between buyers and sellers. Where both groups are numerous, and have equal bargaining power, and where demand is fairly elastic, conditions of relatively perfect competition prevail. Under these circumstances, prices are fixed by the 'haggling of the market' and are known as contract prices. The market for tramp charters operates under such conditions, and the contract is drawn up as an agreement known as a charter party. The tramp companies are usually medium-sized concerns and the merchants who deal in the commodities carried by them usually possess equal bargaining power.

The contract may be for a single voyage at so much per tonne of the commodity carried, or it may be for a period at a stipulated rate of hire, usually so much per tonne of the ship's deadweight carrying capacity. The charter rates are quoted on a competitive basis, in various exchanges throughout the world. Foodstuffs and raw materials in particular are traded in a highly competitive world market, and their movement is irregular, depending upon demand and supply conditions. It is quite usual for cargoes of these commodities to be loaded, and actually marketed during transit, the charterers instructing the ship to proceed to a certain range of ports and determining the port of discharge while the ship is en route. In the case of very long-term charters, tankers or ore carriers, the rate of hire is fixed to give the owner a reasonable return on his investment.

Under these conditions, the rate structure for tramps is a very simple product and emerges from competitive interplay of supply and demand. From the economist's point of view, rates made in this way represent the most efficient methods of pricing, for where price is determined under conditions of perfect competition, production is encouraged to follow consumers' wishes, and price itself does not deviate to any great extent from average total cost. In this way the customer is satisfied and production capacity most usefully employed. Detailed below are the factors influencing the formulation of a fixture rate:

(a) Ship specification which would also embrace the type of vessel, i.e. bulk carrier, containership, oil tanker.

(b) The types of traffic to be conveyed.

(c) General market conditions. This is a major factor and generally an abundance of available ships for charter tends to depress the rate particularly for voyage and short-term charters.

(d) The daily cost to be borne by the charterer. This basically depends on the charter-party terms. In a favourable shipowners' market situation the shipowner would endeavour to negotiate a rate to cover not only direct cost, which depending on the charter-party terms, embraces fuel, crew, etc. but also a contribution to indirect cost such as depreciation, mortgage repayments. In so doing the shipowner would strive to conclude a profitable fixture rate. Some shipowners under demise time charter terms insist on retaining their own master for a variety of reasons, and this cost is borne by the charterer. This could be extended to include chief engineer.

(e) The duration of the charter. Generally speaking the longer the charter, the less it is influenced by the market situation relative to the availability of ships and the demand for them.

(f) The terms of the charter. It must be remembered that the shipowner and charterer are free to conclude a charter party of any terms. Usually however, a charter party bearing one of the code names for a particular trade, i.e. Cemenco for cement, is used when practicable. It is frequently necessary in such circumstances to vary the terms of the charter party by the deletion or addition of clauses to meet individual needs.

(g) The identity of cost to be borne by the charterer and shipowner must be clearly established. For example it may be a gross form charter or FIO charter or net form (see p. 344).

(h) The survey cost responsibility of the vessel must be clearly defined as to whether it is for the charterer's or shipowner's account.

(i) The urgency of the charter. If a charterer requires a vessel almost immediately there tends to be less haggling on fixture rates and this favours the shipowner.

(j) The convenience of the charter to the shipowner. If the broker negotiates a charter which terminates and places the vessel in a maritime area where demand for tonnage is strong, it will tend possibly to depress the rate. In such cicumstances the shipowner will have a good chance to secure another fixture at a favourable rate with no long ballast voyage.

(k) The BIFFEX criteria (see pp. 192–6).

The importance of each of the foregoing points will vary by circumstances.

The tramp industry can be regarded as a pool of shipping, from which vessels move in accordance with world demand, to the employment in which they are most valued by the consumer.

Freight fixtures for tramp charters are recorded daily in such shipping publications as *Lloyd's List*, which students are recommended to study. The General Council of British Shipping publishes a quarterly issued *Tramp Time Charter Index* for 5 shipping size groups – group 1: 12 000–19 999 dwt; group 2: 20 000–34 999 dwt; group 3: 35 000–49 999 dwt; group 4: 50 000–84 999 dwt and group 5: over 85 000 dwt. Additionally there is a Combined Index Number for the Tramp Trip Charter Index. All the 6 indices are based in 1976 as 100. This is a good indication of the state of world tramp market. In January 1989, the Combined Index was 219.

In the liner trades, the shipowners control fairly large concerns, and although some of their shippers may be very large firms, the bulk of their traffic comes from the numerous small shippers. In these conditions, it is more convenient for the shipowner to estimate how much his customers are prepared to pay, and fix his own rate. Such prices are known as tariff prices, which the liner conference issues. As liner rates are relatively stable, merchants can quote prices (including freight) in advance of sailings.

Liner rates are based partly on cost, and partly on value. Many freight rates are quoted on a basis of weight or measurement at ship's option. This means that the rate quoted will be applied either per metric ton of 1000 kg (2205 lb) or per tonne of 1.133 m^3, whichever will produce the greater revenue. The reason for this method of charging is that heavy cargo will bring a vessel to her loadline before her space is full, while light cargo will fill her space without bringing her down to her maximum draught. To produce the highest revenue a vessel must be loaded to her full internal capacity, and immersed to her maximum permitted depth. Therefore, charging by weight or measurement is a cost question. In most trades, cargo measuring under 1.133 m^3 per tonne weight is charged on a weight basis, whilst cargo measuring 1.133 m^3 or more per ton is charged on a measurement basis. With the spread of the metric system, most freight rates are quoted per 1000 kg or m^3 (35.33 ft^3).

Liner tariffs quote rates for many commodities which move regularly. These rates are based on the stowage factor (rate of bulk to weight), on the value of the cargo and on the competitive situation. Many tariffs publish class rates for general cargo not otherwise specified. Some tariffs publish class rates whereby commodities are grouped for charging into several classes. On commodities of very high value *ad valorem* rates are charged at so much per cent of the declared value. When commodities move in large quantities, and are susceptible to tramp competition, tariffs often employ 'open rates', i.e. the rate is left open, so that the shipping line can quote whatever rate is appropriate.

In recent years there has been a tendency in an increasing number of liner cargo trades to impose a surcharge on the basic rate and examples are given below of the types which emerge:

(a) Bunkering or fuel surcharge. In an era when fuel costs now represent a substantial proportion of total direct voyage cost – a situation which has arisen from the very substantial increase in bunkering expenses from 1973 and 1979 – shipowners are not prepared to absorb the variation in fuel prices. They take the view that price variation of bunker fuel tends to be unpredictable bearing in mind it is usually based on the variable dollar rate of exchange and it is difficult to budget realistically for this cost to reflect it adequately in their rate formulation. Moreover, an increase in the bunkering price erodes the shipowner's voyage profitability. The fuel or bunkering surcharge is not so common today compared with the mid 1970s when inflation was more evident.

(b) Currency surcharge. This arises when the freight rate is related to a floating currency such as sterling. For example, if the rate was based on French or Belgian francs which both operate fixed rates of currency, the sterling rate of exchange in January would be probably different to the situation in the following July. For example when sterling is depressed, sterling would probably earn more French and Belgian francs per £1 sterling in January than in the following July. Accordingly a currency surcharge is imposed to minimize losses the shipowner would incur bearing in mind the shipowner would obtain less sterling equivalent in French or Belgian franc-rated traffic, whilst at the same time the port expenses in Belgium and France would be more expensive due to the depressed sterling rate of exchange.

An example of currency surcharge scale is given below. It involves the Anglo/French trade. The freight tariff is sterling based calculated in 11.50 French francs to £1 and the rate per tonne is £20 or 230 French francs.

When charges are to be paid in French francs French francs to £1.	Surcharge in French francs (%)
12.42 to 12.64	5
12.19 to 12.41	4
11.96 to 12.18	3
11.73 to 11.95	2
11.62 to 11.72	1

No surcharge 11.38 to 11.61 (void area) Nil (no surcharge)

When charges are to be paid in Sterling	Surcharge in French francs (%)
11.37 to 11.26	1
11.25 to 11.03	2
11.02 to 10.80	3
10.79 to 10.57	4
10.56 to 10.34	5

The percentage of surcharge will be determined each week by reference to the average rate as published in *Le Monde* and *The Financial Times* on Saturdays, i.e. Friday's closing prices.

(i) Payment in sterling – exchange rate
   10.90 French francs to £1   £
   10 tonnes merchandise at £20 per tonne   200
   3% surcharge based on exchange rate of
   10.90 French francs   6
                                   Total   £206

(ii) Payment in French francs – exchange rate 12.43ff to £1   £
    10 tonnes at 230 French francs per tonne   2300
    5% surcharge based on exchange rate of 12.43   115
              Total   French francs 2415

(c) Surcharges are usually raised for heavy lifts such as indivisible consignments and on excessive height or length of Ro/Ro rated traffic, together with any other traffic where special facilities are required.

For livestock and dangerous classified cargo special rates apply to reflect the additional facilities the shipowner must provide to convey such traffic. The dangerous cargo classified traffic normally attracts a 50% surcharge above the general rated traffic. Such traffic requires extensive prebooking arrangements and a declaration signed by the shipper of the cargo contents. This is extensively dealt with in Chapter 6 of my book *The Elements of Export Practice.*

It is important to note that a substantial volume of general merchandise cargo now moves under groupage or consolidation arrangements. This involves the freight forwarder who originates the traffic from a number of consignors to a number of consignees and despatches the compatible cargo in a container, train ferry wagon or international road haulage vehicle. The freight forwarder in consultation with another freight forwarder in the destination country operates on a reciprocal basis. The rate includes the collection and delivery charges, usually undertaken by road transport. The freight forwarders operate from a warehouse which may form part of some leased accommodation at a container base with inland clearance depot facilities. The latter will permit the cargo to move under bond to and from the port. The rates are based on a weight/measurement (W/M) basis whichever produces the greater revenue to the freight forwarder and described in detail on p. 212. A cargo manifest accompanies the consolidated consignment throughout the transit and the merits of groupage are described on p. 260. It is usual for the freight forwarder to prebook shipping space involving the container, train ferry wagon or road vehicle on specified sailings to thereby offer a regular assured service to the shipper.

With regard to train ferry wagon rates these are based on the origin and destination of the consignment and per wagon charge to encourage good loadability. Special rates exist for particular streams of traffic and between selective countries. A number of privately owned train ferry wagons exist and in such cases special rates apply.

Rate making is affected by such factors as susceptibility of the cargo to damage or pilferage, nature of packaging, competition, transit cost and convenience of handling. A properly compiled tariff should encourage the movement of all classes of cargo, to ensure the best balance between revenue production and the full utilization of vessels.

It is important to note than in liner trades cargo is received and delivered into transit sheds or on to the quay, so that loading and discharging expenses are met by the shipowner and covered by the rate of freight quoted. Therefore, the efficiency of ports and their labour and equipment has a direct influence on rate making.

As indicated elsewhere in this book, liner cargo trades are becoming containerized and, whilst the factors relating to rate making tend to remain virtually unchanged, it should be noted that the tariff is now being based on the container as a unit. It does of course vary by ownership, distance, route, size and type. Many containers are consigned on a through-rate basis from the inland point of despatch to the destination with the maritime transit intervening.

A market which has developed extensively in recent years is project forwarding. It involves the despatch/conveyance arrangements which stem from a contract award such as a power station project. The contract is usually awarded to a consortium and the freight forwarder undertakes all the despatch/conveyance arrangements. This involves the freight forwarder negotiating with the shipowner special rates for the merchandise conveyed and the associated prebooking and shipment arrangments. Often such shipments require special arrangements and purpose-built equipment being provided for which a comprehensive rate is given, usually on a cost plus profit basis.

Another market is antiques. It may be a valuable painting, collection of furniture, etc. Such goods require specialized packing undertaken by professional packers. Pre-shipment arrangements are extensive including security and documentation. Two types of antiques market exist: one as just described, the very valuable art treasure of national prestige, and the other involving the much larger market of antiques. The rates of the former market are negotiated with the shipowner and have regard to various provisions including security and the cost thereof. Much of such traffic travels by air freight. The latter market of less valuable antiques is usually containerized as found in the Anglo/North American trade. Standard rates for the range of antiques exist which are subject to strict conditions of shipment such as to be professionally packed.

An additional method of freight rate assessment is found in Ro/Ro services. It is based either on the square footage occupied by the vehicle on the ship's deck, or on a linear footage basis calculated at so much per foot depending on the overall length of the road vehicle. The rate usually remains unchanged irrespective of type of cargo shipped in the road vehicle. Rates vary in whether the vehicle/trailer is empty or loaded, accompanied or unaccompanied. Concessionary rates sometimes apply in certain trades when the vehicle uses the same route for the return load. Generally speaking, air competition has so far not made any serious inroads in cargo traffic – certainly not to the same extent as has been experienced in the passenger trade. Nevertheless, the tendency has been for certain types of traffic which have a relatively high value or demand a fast service, due to the nature of the cargo or urgency of the consignment, to be conveyed by air transport. Such competition has not been felt very much in tramping, but has had a more significant effect on liner cargo services. The liner operator is very conscious of such competition, and to help combat the situation, vessels of higher speeds have been introduced.

It must be recognized as mentioned earlier that many of the world's most important liner cargo routes are now containerized offering much faster services through the provision of faster ships and rationalization of ports of call. The rates are often from the inland terminal such as a Container Base, to a similar facility in the destination country. Many of the container shipments for the general cargo-covered type of container are mixed cargoes, each individually rated by commodity classification. The more specialized form of container has individual rates formulated by classified container type.

The escalation of fuel cost from 1973 to 1986 plus the continuous expansion of maritime containerization has adversely tempered the further growth of air freight. However, the world's airlines are beginning to devote more resources to develop increased air freight capacity through wide-bodied aircraft and increased marketing effort. Such developments will marginally abstract traffic from the consolidated ISO container market of high value and high cube in distance markets. Currently some 10% of the world's trade by value is conveyed by air transport.

In recent years the CABAF technique has been introduced which is the currency adjustment and bunkering adjustment factor. When shipping companies calculate their freight rates, they take account of the exchange rate level and fuel costs. In so doing they can use rates applicable at the time the freight rate is compiled or the market forecasts currency exchange rates level and bunker cost operative at the time the new freight rate is introduced on the service/trade. For example, if the shipowner is calculating their rate in deutschmarks, and an exporter is paying for freight in sterling, in the event of the deutschmark rate rising the shipowner will want more sterling for the freight and an adjustment factor will be added to the freight invoice. If the price of bunker fuel is also likely to vary similarly a surcharge is likely to be imposed relative to the increased cost. In some trades they are called simply currency and fuel surcharge and their application varies. The bunker surcharge is usually consolidated into the rate as soon as new rate levels are introduced which in many trades is every six or twelve months depending on the level of inflation operative.

9.5 RELATION BETWEEN LINER AND TRAMP RATES

In general, liner and tramp rates fluctuate in the same direction. But liner rates are more stable than tramp rates, which are particularly sensitive to short-term supply and demand conditions. Comparisons are not easy, however, since published data on liner rates are fragmentary, and no index of liner rates is available to set against the quarterly issued *Tramp Time Charter Index* (see p. 212). Nevertheless, although tramps provide liners with only limited competition, the world tramp fleet is a factor to be taken into account, and, in times of falling tramp rates, liner rates must inevitably be influenced in the same direction by fear of such competition. Conversely, when tramp rates rise, liner operators will feel able to follow in the same direction, particularly if costs are rising. Generally speaking, liner rates are less sensitive to changes in market demand and more sensitive to changes in cost than tramp rates. The student should note that the increasing specialization of liners may remove tramp competition from some commodities and routes, so that rates for such commodities may remain outside the influence of competition. During the past decade the correlation between liner and tramp rates has been less significant and this trend is likely to continue.

9.6 RELATION BETWEEN VOYAGE AND TIME CHARTER RATES

A voyage charter is a contract for specific voyage, while a time charter is a contract for a period of time which may cover several voyages. Therefore, the voyage charter rate is a short-term rate, while the time charter rate is often a long-term rate. When trade is buoyant and voyage rates are rising, charterers, in anticipation of further rises, tend to charter for longer periods to cover their commitments; when rates are expected to fall, they tend to contract for shorter periods. Therefore, the current time charter rate tends to reflect the expected trend of voyage rates in the future. If rates are expected to rise, it will tend to be above the current voyage rates; if they are expected to fall, it will tend to be below the current voyage rates. Generally speaking, the two rates move in the same direction but because time charter rates depend on market expectations, they tend to fluctuate more widely than voyage rates. When conditions are improving, long-term rates tend to rise more rapidly than voyage rates; when conditions are deteriorating, voyage rates tend to fall more rapidly.

9.7 TYPES OF FREIGHT

This study of freight rates would not be complete without an examination of the types available. The true test of the ship-owner's right to freight is whether the service in respect of which the freight was contracted to be paid has been substantially performed, or, if not, whether its performance has been prevented by any act of the cargo owner. Freight is normally payable 'ship lost or not lost'. Details of the various types are given below:

(a) *Advance freight* is payable in advance, before delivery of the actual goods. This is generally regarded as the most important type of freight, and is extensively used in the liner cargo trades and tramping. It must not be confused with 'advance of freight' which may be a payment on account of disbursements or an advance to the Master, in which case the charterer would be entitled to a return of the monies advanced. Such a payment is really in the nature of a loan.

(b) *Lump sum freight* is the amount payable for the use of the whole or portion of a ship. This form of freight is calculated on the actual cubic capacity of the ship offered, and has no direct relation to the cargo to be carried. Lump sum freight is payable irrespective of the actual quantity delivered.

(c) *Dead freight* is the name given to a damage claim for breach of contract by, for example, the charterer to furnish a full cargo to a ship. Such a situation would arise if the charterer undertook to provide 500 tonnes of cargo, but only supplied 400 tonnes. The shipowner would, under such circumstances, be entitled to claim dead freight for the unoccupied space. Alternatively, a shipper may fail to provide all the cargo promised and for which space has been reserved on a particular sailing, in which case the shipowner would again claim dead freight for the unoccupied space. The amount of deadfreight chargeable is the equivalent of the freight which would have been earned, less all charges which would have been incurred in the loading, carriage and discharge of the goods. It will therefore be seen that, as it is a form of compensation, the shipowner is not entitled to make more profit by deadfreight than he would by the actual carriage of the goods. He must make an allowance for all expenses which have not been incurred. There is no lien on deadfreight, but by express agreement in the contract a lien may be extended to other cargo for the payment of deadfreight.

(d) *Back freight* arises when goods have been despatched to a certain port, and on arrival are refused. The freight charged for the return of the goods constitutes back freight.

(e) *Pro-rata freight* arises when the cargo has been carried only part of the way and circumstances make it impossible to continue the voyage further. For example, ice formation may exist at the original port of delivery, and the owner may decide to accept delivery of the cargo at an intermediate port. The point then arises whether the freight calculated *pro rata* for the portion of the voyage actually accomplished becomes payable. It will only do so when there is a clear agreement by the cargo owner to pay.

(f) *Ad valorem freight* arises when a cargo is assessed for rate purposes on a percentage of its value. For example a 2% *ad valorem* rate on a consignment value at £100 would raise £2.

Additionally as described on pages 209–18 other forms of freight rates exist. These include Ro/Ro (pp. 216–17); Dangerous cargo (p. 303–13); livestock (p. 212); antiques (p. 216); project forwarding (p. 251); personal effects (p. 210); weight/measurement (W/M) ships option (p. 212); groupage/consolidated (p. 260); and commodity rates (p. 213).

9.8 MAIL CONTRACTS AND AGREEMENTS

A mail contract is a long-term contract between the Post Office and a liner company. The essentials of a mail contract are a regular and reliable shipping service with scheduled sailing and arrival dates and a relatively fast vessel suitably equipped to carry mails, with adequate and good stowage accommodation and appropriate security facilities.

Mail agreements concern the individual shipments. The Post Office Corporation and foreign postal authorities negotiate with the shipping conferences for mail as a commodity on a tonnage basis. For purposes of measuring the tonnage, sixteen bags of letter mail, or seven bags of parcels constitute one tonne (1.133 m^3). All British vessels have a statutory obligation to carry mails if they are so requested by the Post Office Corporation.

There is a considerable prestige value derived by operators who have secured mail contracts. The shipowner in undertaking to convey mails must keep to his scheduled sailings. This tends to attract to the service other high-rated traffic which requires reliable sailing and arrival dates.

9.9 MARKET PRICING

An increasing number of shipowners today are using the technique of market pricing. In so doing it aims to fulfil five main objectives: maximizing cash flow; attaining high load factors; countering competition; stimulating market development and improving profitability levels.

Basically, market pricing is the process of devising passenger and freight tariffs correlated to potential market demand and sensitivity, and optimum utilization of shipping capacity. Moreover, it provides a good stimulus to market development.

An example of market pricing is found in the full-load container market. Demand for containers in the eastbound direction may be very strong and therefore normal tariff levels would apply. However, in the westbound direction in the autumn and winter periods the demand is weak and many containers are shipped empty. To stimulate market demand a lower rate is quoted offering 40% off the normal tariff. This encourages new streams of traffic to be shipped. Hitherto, the rate in this period was too high to make it economic for the goods to be sold in the overseas westbound market. Such a policy generates additional revenue and redresses the imbalance of traffic flow.

A further example is found in the passenger trade in the short sea services. During the summer period traffic levels reach their peak and particularly at weekends. In the autumn, winter and spring periods traffic flow tends to be at a low level. To help stimulate market demand, the three tariff levels are imposed: the peak summer weekends, the summer period and the lowest tariff covering the autumn, winter and spring periods.

Features of market pricing are detailed below:

(a) It maximizes cash flow.

(b) Ship capacity utilization is maximized.

(c) It facilitates trade development and encourages balance of trade.

(d) Profitability is improved.

(e) It enables through-pricing policy to regulate to some extent market demand and so optimize shipping capacity utilization. This is an important area inasmuch that the more consistent the demand for the shipping capacity throughout the year, the more likely the financial results would be favourable. Excessive peak demands with little work for much of the fleet outside this period is usually very uneconomic to the shipping company.

(f) It helps to optimize the use of resources throughout the year and their associated infrastructure, such as port facilities, etc. Moreover, it avoids the need to recruit large numbers of seasonal staff.

(g) It improves the general competitiveness of the service.

Market-pricing technique is very much on the increase and is doing a lot to improve profitability levels in shipping companies. It must be formulated with discretion to ensure it maximizes revenue production overall. Market pricing should have regard to existing traffic levels, cost, competition, any agreement with other operators, market sensitivity etc. For example, it is no use offering a 40% 'off-season' discount for a particular market stream, if it is not sensitive to price mechanism. This may involve the present load factor rising to 35% but with a 40% discounted tariff, it will produce less revenue. It is better to allow the normal tariff to remain generating a 30% load factor. It is dealt with more fully in *Economics of Shipping Practice and Management,* Chapter 13.

CHAPTER 10

Liner conferences

10.1 LINER CONFERENCE SYSTEM

The liner conference is an organization whereby a number of shipowners offer their services on a given sea route on conditions agreed by the members. Conferences are semi-monopolistic associations of shipping lines formed for the purpose of restricting competition between their members and protecting them from outside competition. Conference agreements may also regulate sailings and ports of call, and in some cases arrangments are made for the pooling of net earnings. Conferences achieve their object by controlling prices and by limiting entry to the trade. Their chief policy is to establish a common tariff of freight rates and passenger fares for the trade involved, members being left free to compete for traffic by the quality and efficiency of their service. The organization of a conference varies from one trade to another. It may consist of informal and regular meetings of shipowners at which rates and other matters of policy are discussed, or it may involve a formal organization with a permanent secretariat and prescribed rules for membership, together with stipulated penalties for violations of agreement. Members are often required to deposit a cash bond to cover fines in respect of non-compliance with their obligations.

Conferences emerged as a result of the cut-throat competition between steamships which began about 1870, when their cargo capacity increased enormously. The first conference, the Calcutta Conference, was formed in 1875 and fixed equal rates from each of the ports from which vessels were despatched. A deferred rebate system was introduced whereby shippers were granted rebates for consistent patronage over a given period, but were not paid the rebates until they had shipped all their traffic by conference ships for a further period. Conferences spread rapidly to other trades until by 1939 practically every liner trade or route of any importance was governed by conference agreements. Membership of such conferences is international in character: for example, the Far East Freight Conference, which operates in the Far East/European trade, comprises British, French, Dutch, Italian, Swedish, Danish and Japanese lines. In 1939 there were twenty-one conferences in the Far Eastern trades to and from Europe. Shipping lines often belong to several conferences and there are several inter-conference agreements. In most cases conference policy is decided by the votes of the members. Conference rights have a market value when shipping lines are sold.

In some conferences there exists a pooling agreement whereby traffic or gross or net earnings in the trade are pooled, members receiving agreed percentages of the pool. Under the gross earnings arrangements, each shipowner bears all his operating/investment cost and pools all the gross revenue. With a net earnings situation each operator pools only his net earnings. Hence under the latter arrangement the more efficient low-cost shipowner operating within the pool is penalized by the more expensive and less efficient operator. It arises as each operator has no control on other operators' expenditure and this tends to favour the less efficient shipowner as there is no real incentive for him to contain his cost as indirectly it will be borne by other members of the pool. The object of such an arrangement is to guarantee to members a certain share of the trade, and to limit competition. It leads to the regulation of sailings and may in some circumstances enable the trade to be rationalized. Pools are becoming more common, where shipowners normally prefer to establish an agreed tariff and permit competition in quality of service. An excess of tonnage in a particular trade may very likely lead to an agreed reduction in the number of sailings and poolings of receipts. Often when the conferences perform special services, such as lifting unprofitable cargo or resorting to chartering to cover temporary shortages of tonnage, they pool the losses or profits on such operations.

A further example of a liner conference agreement is where each member agrees to operate a percentage of the sailings and thereby have an identical percentage of the total pooled income. Hence one may have four operators and two may each undertake 20% of the sailings and receive 20% of the pooled revenue. The other two may provide 30% of the sailings and likewise receive 30% of the pooled receipts. Each operator would be responsible for his cost.

The objects of the liner conference are to provide a service adequate to meet the trade requirements; to avoid wasteful competition among members by regulating loading; to organize themselves so that the conference can collectively combat outside competition; and to maintain a tariff by mutual agreement as stable as conditions will permit.

10.2 ADVANTAGES AND DISADVANTAGES

The main advantages claimed for the conference system are as follows:

1. Avoidance of wasteful competition.

2. The reasonable assurance that members have a good chance of realizing a profit; and no rate wars, as freight rates are determined by the conference.

3. Stability of rates which enables manufacturers and merchants to make forward contracts for goods and so diminishes undesirable risk and uncertainty in international trade.

4. Regular and frequent sailings which enable the shipper/ exporter to plan his supplies to overseas markets and avoid the need to carry large stocks with the risk of obsolescence and commodity deterioration, and the operator to maximize the use of his vessels.

5. Equality of treatment, i.e., the rate quoted applies to all shippers whether they are large or small.

6. Economies of service which enable operators to concentrate on providing faster and better ships.

The disadvantage from the shipper's point of view arises from the fact that, if he is tied to a particular conference, he cannot take advantage of tramp tonnage when rates are low. Moreover, if he is a large shipper he often cannot use his superior bargaining power to obtain lower rates. Carriers who are not members of a conference object to the system because it prevents their competing successfully with conference vessels.

The question of conferences was considered by the Royal Commission on shipping in 1909 and the Imperial Shipping Committee in 1920–23. Both these bodies came to the conclusion that where a regular organized service was required, the conference system, strengthened by some tying arrangement, was necessary. That is, if liner companies provide a regular service, available whether freights are plentiful or not, and if they are prepared to sail on advertised dates, whether full or not, then they must have some assurance that sporadic competition will not skim the cream off the traffic. The Imperial Shipping Committee recommended that shippers should be given a choice between the deferred rebate system and a form of contract (see below). It suggested further that shippers should combine to deal with conferences on a more equal footing.

During 1955 the British Shippers' Council was formed with the object 'to further the interests of exporters and importers in the UK in relation to the transportation of goods by sea and air'. This resulted in the emergence of a new era of joint consultation between the Shippers' Council and liner conferences. The Council participated in the formulation of the liner conference machinery of consultation between shipowners and shippers, to consider representations from a shipper or trade association which cannot be resolved by an individual shipowner.

In 1963 there was a major step forward when the European Shippers' Councils and European Shipowners' Associations (CENSA) agreed a 'note of understanding' to govern their consultation arrangements. It resulted in the setting up of a number of joint European committees and working groups to resolve matters of mutual concern and agree on recommendations to which shippers and shipowners comply. By 1974, 18 joint recommendations had been agreed, brief details of which are given below:

(a) period of notice to be given of increases in freight rates;
(b) procedure for introducing freight surcharges;
(c) standard rules for cargo measurement;
(d) declaration of dangerous goods;
(e) availability of conference tariffs and regulations;
(f) introduction of, and alterations in shippers' contracts and agreements.
(g) fibreboard containers and cartons – clausing of bills of lading;
(h) diversions – co-operation with cargo interests;
(i) heavy lifts of cargo;
(j) long lengths of cargo;

(k) pallet rules;
(l) currencies – methods of dealing with devaluation, revaluation, and rates of exchange;
(m) container standard sizes;
(n) prevention of malpractices;
(o) shippers' loyalty contracts with conferences;
(p) deferred rebate system;
(q) machinery for the resolution of disputes;
(r) simplification of conference tariff rules and conditions.

By 1974, fifteen European countries each had National Shippers' Councils and the movement had spread widely overseas.

The ESC/CENSA Code under which consultation proceeds with Liner Conferences serving Europe has not been universally accepted by all such Conferences.

The European Code has been adopted by 46 conferences and accepted by all European Shippers' Councils. Many other conferences have been unable to adopt it formally primarily because they contain non-European lines subject to some form of government ownership and direction.

Coincident with the development of the European Code, proposals were made by UNCTAD to introduce a world code and these were subsequently made in a general assembly resolution. It was substantially different from the European Code as it seeks to bind shipping conferences by convention and international law, and to involve governments in the consultative process. This is not generally favoured by the Western maritime nations who prefer the minimum of governmental interference in liner conference activity. Conversely the developing countries seek a system which gives their national shipping line rights of entry into conferences serving their country's trade and of a larger share of that trade. Moreover they favour some form of inter-governmental regulation of conference freight rates. Communist bloc countries express similar policies.

A significant factor of the UNCTAD Liner Conference code is that some 40% of the cargo will be reserved for each of the maritime countries participating in the trade with the residue of 20% to the established liner conference operator operating in the cross trade or other operators. The 40/40/20 conference code is strongly opposed by Western countries who have been established for many years as liner conference operators within such cross trades. They take the view that such a policy is one of trade protectionism thereby reserving a substantial volume of the trade (import and export) for their own maritime fleets irrespective of the commercial considerations involved. This situation is particularly relevant to third world developing countries who are anxious to sustain and in some cases inaugurate their own maritime fleets to save hard currency and develop their maritime fleets many of which are subsidized. Moreover, such developing countries wish to have a greater influence on liner tariffs and by operating their own fleets are able to control them more directly. A further point is that Western countries regard the UN code as non-commercial competition and prefer the voluntary commercial principles as found in the ESC/CENSA code.

To enable the UN code to become International now requires an International Convention. This involves ratification by 24 states representing 25% of world liner tonnage. By 1979 some 28 states representing some 5.71% of world liner tonnage had ratified the code. However, in June 1979 the UNCTAD V conference was held in Manila which discussed the UN Code of Conduct for liner conference involving the 40/40/20 rule. This involved the trading partner country having the right to carry 40% generated by their own trade. The remaining portion would be available for third flag carriers. The code actually allows considerable flexibility in reaching agreements on cargo shares.

The following points emerged from a UN Liner Code review conference held in Geneva, November 1988.

The scope of the Convention must be defined

(a)   The Code should apply only to Conference pier-to-pier services between contracting parties. The clause should relate only to liner services and should include:

the limitation of the Code to Conferences serving the liner trade between two or more contracting parties

application to all entities operating in a Codist Liner Conference trade irrespective of nationality.

(b)   National line membership rights in Conferences does not relate to membership of consortia.

(c)   The existing definition of 'Shipper' under the Code should be maintained.

(d) Care should be taken in case attempts are made to 'tighten up the Code'. This does not refer to attempts to remove ambiguities of language (which are acceptable) but to efforts to widen the areas of shipping to which the Code should relate (for example, an attempt to bring non-conference lines within the scope of the Code). These efforts should be opposed. Equally, there may be attempts to introduce a cargo reservation system for the bulk trade. This concept is currently being examined, but the immediate response should be that if the matter is raised at all, it is outside the scope of the Review Conference which relates strictly to the U.N. Liner Code.

Conferences must operate without government intervention

(a) Cargo reservation: The current Code limitation should be maintained with no derogation

(b) Sailing and loading rights: Implementation of trade participation agreements should be left to Conference member lines

(c) Day-to-day operation of Conferences: There should be no 'back door' regulation of Conferences using Article 47

(d) Fixing of freight rates: Governments should have no role in deciding the timing and level of changes in freight rates; and the fifteen month rule should be deleted, and periods of notice of freight rate changes left to commercial negotiation

(e) Consultation: The Joint Recommendation of CENSA and the European Shippers' Council should be used as the pattern for consultation. The essential points of the Recommendation are as follows:

There should be consultation between liner conferences and shippers' organizations on the following basis

Consultation in the country of export
Liner conferences should on request hold consultations with shippers' organizations in the country of export on:
changes in general ocean tariff conditions and related regulations
changes in the general level of ocean tariff rates
rates for major commodities (where these are not covered by consultations with commodity groups)
imposition of surcharges and related changes in their methods of application

contractual arrangements, their establishment or changes in their form and general conditions

port congestion in exporting ports

the amount and nature of cargo for shipment to be made available to the conference and indications of delivery schedules

Consultation in the country of import

Liner conferences should on request hold consultations with importers or their organizations in the country of import on:

changes in the general level of tariff rates and general terms and conditions and related regulations solely for long term contracts of carriage for specific major commodities purchased on FOB terms

problems related to receipt of cargo, including port congestion in importing ports

Consultation (general)

Liner conferences may, on request, hold consultations with shippers' organizations at both ends of the trade on the following subjects to the extent that they fall within the scope of activity of a conference and will have a market effect on a substantial volume of the cargo in the trade:

changes in the pattern of services

effects of the introduction of new technology

adequacy and quality of shipping service

Parties to the consultations are free to communicate on request the results of consultation at one end of the trade to organizations at the other end of the trade.

Where appropriate, shippers' organizations should be encouraged to establish close contacts with shippers' organizations at the other end of the trade to seek agreement for mutual adherence to these model procedures.

(f)   Admission of new members etc. *National Lines*: There should be no admission to Conference membership as a result of government directive.

Conferences must be subject only to fair competition

Any proposals for multilateral regulation of outsiders which preserve shares in the whole liner trade for national lines and regulate rates for commercially competing outsiders should be opposed.

The code was finally adopted in 1983. Overall it is a code for less competition rather than more.

10.3 DEFERRED REBATE AND CONTRACT SYSTEMS

Associated with liner conferences are the deferred rebate and contract systems.

The deferred rebate is a device to ensure that shippers will continue to support a conference. A shipper who ships exclusively by conference vessels can, at the end of a certain period (usually 6 months), claim a rebate, usually 10% of the freight money paid by him during the period. Hence the shipper has an inducement to remain loyal to the conference in so far as he stands to lose a rebate by a non-conference vessel. This system is described as the deferred rebate, and has tended to become less popular in some trades in recent years due to the high cost of clerical administration. Accordingly, it has been substituted – under the same code of loyalty conditions – by the immediate rebate system. This is a somewhat lower rebate – maybe 9½% – but granted at the time freight payment is made and not some 6 months later with the deferred rebate system. Such a lower deferred rate is termed a nett rate. The level of deferred rebate varies by individual conference.

A further way of retaining the shipper's patronage of a conference is by the contract or special contract agreement systems. The contract system is for a shipper who signs a contract to forward all his goods by conference line vessels either in the general course of business, or perhaps associated with a special project over a certain period. The particular contract concerned may be associated with a large hydroelectric scheme, for example, and the goods would then probably be special equipment. Under this system the shipper would be granted a cheaper freight rate than a non-contract shipper. In addition there are the special commodity agreements which are specially negotiated between the trade and conference to cover goods shipped in large quantities and often for short duration. The shipper may be forwarding a commodity such as copper, tea, rubber, foodstuffs or cotton, in considerable quantities.

The shippers' criticism of the deferred rebate system is that it enables conferences to build up monopolies tending to keep rates at a high level. Furthermore, the shipper is reluctant to use outside tonnage for fear of loss of rebate and the system thus restricts his freedom of action. Another point is that a record must be kept of all freight paid subject to rebate to enable claims to be made in due course. This involves clerical expenses, and moreover, the shipper contends that he is out of pocket to the extent of the interest on the rebate while it is in the carrier's hands. So far as the carrier is concerned, the retention of the rebate for the appropriate period has the added advantage of an automatic deterrent to shippers using non-conference vessels. In fact, it can be a very strong weapon, as the carrier is the sole arbitrator in deciding whether or not any shipper's rebate should be forfeited. The carrier also finds it easy to maintain rebate records in his manifest freight books and, by virtue of the amount of work involved, finds it convenient to have a small rebate department. He maintains that there is no compulsion on the shipper to remain with the conference, although of course if he chooses to ship outside it, the shipper will forfeit his rebate. A shipper who forfeits his rebate has, after all, had the benefits of conference shipment which later he discards for something he considers better.

The 1923 Report on the Imperial Shipping Committee was conclusive as to the necessity of a tie between shipper and carrier, if the advantages of regular, frequent and efficient services were to be maintained. This view was endorsed by the Government Committee on Industry and Trade in 1929. A Royal Commission also considered the possibility of legislation to control shipping conferences and reported that evidence was inadequate to justify this measure. They took the view that conferences were almost always exposed to one or other form of competition and, moreover, the members themselves enjoyed free competition with one another within limits.

Government inquiries have confirmed that the liner industry, as with other industries, requires a high degree of organization, otherwise a reversion to irregular services and unstable freight rates is unavoidable. If the shipowners are to maintain services in periods of recession as in more favourable times, they are entitled to expect a partial monopoly of the trade when conditions are good. Efficiency is improved with stable rates and services, and the assurance of continual support from shippers will be effective in preventing intermittent and irresponsible competition for berth cargo. The Rochdale Committee in 1970 endorsed the need for the retention of the Liner Conference system.

In countries where much of the trade overseas is carried in foreign ships there may be a suspicion upon the part of traders that conference organizations are operating to the detriment of the trade. This is illustrated in commercial thought in Australia and South Africa, but it is in the USA, with its long history of anti-trust legislation, that the conference is under attack.

Because of the overwhelming proportion of US exports carried by other countries at the outbreak of the war in 1914, as confirmed from the Alexander Committee report, the economy of the USA was adversely affected by the withdrawal of European vessels for wartime duties. An act was passed in 1916 by the USA to encourage their own flag shipping, and special regulations were included as to the operation of conferences. One of the provisions was that deferred rebates were prohibited. More recently, the 1961 Bonner Act gave the Federal Maritime Board greater power to intervene in the operation of conferences. This caused concern to many of the European maritime nations, who relied on the existing conference arrangements to maintain the efficiency and economy of their American trade.

However, in 1963, CENSA (whose role is explained in Chapter 8) was formed, its purpose being to endeavour to eliminate restrictions and interference by various governments in the free flow of commercial shipping and thereby safeguard its members' interest. It works in close liaison with the various National Shippers' Councils and has dealt with the US regulatory, protectionist and maritime policies.

The American companies who are members of the conferences are generally subsidized by the US Government, and it may well be that the anti-monopolist tendencies of the USA will be tempered by the desire of their authorities for their own shipping companies to operate with the security that only conference arrangements can give.

10.4 GOVERNMENT CONTROL OF FREIGHT RATES

In practice, Government control of shipping rates does not exist in the UK, except somewhat loosely in the coasting trade, as the UK has been a pioneer among the maritime nations in maintaining that freight charges on international sea routes should find their level from the free interplay of the freight markets. Today the deep-sea routes are free of control, and in the coastal trades there are sometimes conferences with State or board-controlled shipping organizations. Nevertheless in 1974 the Monopolies Commission report on the cross channel car ferry services was accepted by the Government insofar as its principal recommendations were concerned. These may be summarized as follows:

(a) The cross channel ferry operators covered by the reference should be required not to participate in any collective agreement of fares in respect of the services covered by the reference such as that now operated by the Cross Channel Study Group.

(b) The cross channel ferry operators concerned should be required not to become parties to any extension of any exisiting pooling agreement covering the reference services which would have the effect of providing for any greater degree of pooling.

(c) No further pooling agreements covering the reference services should be entered into without Government approval.

(d) Unless and until discontinuance of supervision is justified by a substantial change in the competitive situation, fare increases should be subject to the Government's approval, and the possibility of improving the fare structure should be considered.

It will be interesting to follow the impact and application of these recommendations on British registered tonnage engaged in the cross channel ferry operators' business.

Tramp rates in the coastal trade are governed by a General Council of British Shipping schedule of charges, agreed between owners and the trades concerned. There is no legal basis for this schedule, however, and foreign vessels are able to offer cut rates if they wish.

The immediate post-war period saw an era of rate control inasmuch as freight rates were approved by the Ministry of Transport, in co-operation with the Government departments concerned, e.g. Ministry of Food, Ministry of Supply. But with the gradual release of voyage controls, the market was considered to be the best assessment of rates according to supply and demand of ships and cargoes. During 1934 and 1936, when a form of subsidy was granted to British shipping, this was linked with a scheme whereby owners agreed to accept a minimum rates schedule as a condition of subsidy, but, again, this was only an indirect form of rate fixing, necessitated by the need for uniform rates as a basis for even subsidy distribution.

Foreign powers have attempted to enforce fixed freight rates, particularly in their home trades where this can be done by the threat of cabotage (the restriction of home trades to the national flag). But, in general, the international nature of deep-sea trading makes any form of rate control difficult, and usually impolitic to enforce. The inter-coastal trade of the USA has rates approved by the body approving rail and road rates.

The UK takes the view that generally to impose control on sea freights is not in the best interest of free trading, and is likely to give rise to retaliatory measures, especially where there is flag discrimination. Experience has shown that attempts to fix arbitrary freight rates for specified traffic are likely to unbalance the whole structure of international trade, and may create artificial demands and shortages, unrelated to the needs of world trade.

Attempts have been made here and there, where a national line has been operating, to introduce a control of freight rates which is virtually a subsidy in itself. In practice these ventures have not been sustained, and, generally speaking, it can be said that a trade which cannot support a well-managed fleet of ships is incapable of development.

In liner trades, shipping rates, as has been seen, are largely regulated by Liner Conferences. Certain governments, including South Africa and Australia, insist on consultation and approval before permitting any rate increases. This provides an effective brake on attempts to raise rates unreasonably, as all increases must be justified to the satisfaction of the government concerned.

A feature of the European Code is that the shipping conferences must justify their need of periodic increases in the general level of freight rates by disclosing an analysis of their costs and revenue. Moreover, the European Code also embraces a system for the adjustment of freight rates to take account of changes in international exchange rates. This is particularly important when a currency is floating and the code aims to ensure neither the shipper nor shipowner suffers as a result of a variation in the exchange rate, and the shipowner receives the true value for his services as set out in his freight tariff.

There have been extensive changes in many liner cargo trades during the past decade through the development of containerization. These include particularly the North Atlantic, Australasia, South Africa and the Far East. They have involved the inauguration of a container company consortium who have been confronted with many problems such as what to do with cargo that can never be containerized because of its shape and size. Shippers' Councils have worked closely with such container consortia to overcome this and many other problems inherent in such a change.

As we progress through the 1990s the Geneva and Manila Conferences will have a profound effect on the liner conference system. Third World countries will feature more than hitherto whilst the cross trade operator will become less dominant. The time scale of the change will depend on the Third World countries' resources to fund the requisite tonnage and develop the expertise to manage and operate the fleet. Moreover, the Eastern bloc countries will become more involved in liner trades as detailed on p. 457.

10.5 HARMONIZATION CONFERENCES

A development in recent years has been the formulation of harmonization conferences amongst liner cargo operators, some of which may be members of a number of different conferences.

The situation may emerge in a particular trade whereby the bulk of the cargo operators are anxious to avoid rate wars and keen to concentrate on providing a quality service at a reasonable competitive tariff. The services are likely to be indirectly in competition with each other, operating from different ports and each having a varying voyage time and distance. The individual rates would be different.

The object of the harmonization conference is to move in harmony with any rate increases and agree on the level of rebate and its code of application. Other matters of mutual concern are similarly discussed such as documentation, the basis of the constituents of the freight rate, currency/fuel surcharges etc.

Such harmonization conferences are entirely voluntary and often involve shipowners of differing nationality. This type of conference is likely to increase in its application.

10.6 THE FUTURE OF LINER CONFERENCES

Since the inception of the liner conference system it has been the subject of constant examination and enquiry in many countries. It has established that international quality shipping services require an adequate secretariat organization to support them. Moreover, it facilitates the provision of an economic shipping service requisite to the market/shipper's need and offering reasonable levels of rates thereby ensuring the shipowner can fund quality tonnage. Furthermore, there is no doubt that the liner conference system has served international trade well and there is no apparent realistic substitute for it offering the same benefits to shippers and shipowners.

The UNCTAD V conference decisions will have a profound effect on the liner conference system. It will be recalled that it adopted the 40/40/20 code involving 40% of the cargo being reserved for each of the maritime countries participating in the trade with the residue to the established liner conference members operating in the cross trade, or other operators. This policy is in process of adoption. It particularly favours the developing countries who will demand a bigger share of the business up to their 40% limit. This can be only achieved – in a period of modest growth – at the expense of another conference member. Moreover the developing-country fleet could be state-owned. Thus one may have a conference which has been working well through the co-operation of all its members of the UNCTAD V conference code application. This could produce ultimately political interference, jealousy and ill feeling.

The development in the next decade in the liner conference is at the moment difficult to foresee. There is no doubt that state involvement in shipping will tend to increase both by developed and developing countries each for different reasons. Moreover, as the development of the 40/40/20 code unfolds, the traditional cross-trade operators who have featured in such trades for decades will diminish. This is particularly true of Western fleets especially of the UK and Scandinavia. The situation will be aggravated by the Eastern bloc countries' development.

The time-scale of such developments will depend on many factors particularly the availability of funds and credit to provide the requisite tonnage. A further significant factor is the availability of experienced competent crew and professional ship management personnel. Some countries will have to embark on extensive training for both ship- and shore-based personnel.

A further factor is the trade situation and prospects. In a period of expansion it is easier to adjust to change than in a period of trade stagnation.

The development of containerization, especially those operating round-the-world services such as the Evergreen Line, have tended not to favour the liner conference system. Such new operators tend to ignore the liner conference criteria but prefer to operate on a free market basis. The implications of the 1988 Geneva conference may prove profound as we progress through the 1990s.

Despite such changes there is no doubt the liner conference system will survive albeit in a different form and probably less efficient in some trades particularly in the early years. State intervention, over tonnaging and subsidized fleets could be a feature in some trades. Meanwhile, under the 1992 EC Single Market Entity, the liner conference system between EC states will cease, as will the reservation of coastal trades to national carriers; the latter, expressed in the Merchant Shipping Act 1988, introduces licensing in the UK coastal trades. The reader is particularly urged to study Chapter 15 of *Economics of Shipping Practice and Management* which deals with the political aspects of international trade and shipping.

CHAPTER 11

Ship operation

11.1 FACTORS TO CONSIDER IN PLANNING SAILING SCHEDULES

In planning a vessel's sailing schedule it is of the utmost importance that she should be fully employed while she is available. She earns no money for the shipowner when laid up – whether for survey, general maintenance or due to lack of traffic – and such periods must be kept to an absolute minimum.

This is particularly important in shipping, because of the large amount of capital invested in a ship which itself has heavy annual depreciation charges. Furthermore, a ship has only a limited life, and when she is ultimately withdrawn from service it may fairly be asked what profit she has earned. It is obvious that the owner who has secured full employment for the vessel is more likely to realize a larger profit than one who has been content to operate the vessel only during peak periods, and made no effort to find additional employment at other times. In this latter case, where the vessel might be involved in a few months' uneconomic service a year, it might be worth while reducing the size of the fleet to give the owner a more reasonable opportunity for improved utilization.

There comes a time, however, when the cost of increasing the size of the fleet exceeds the additional revenue thereby gained, and so the operator sustains a loss. If such is the case, the project should be abandoned unless there are compelling reasons, e.g. social, political, or even commercial, to the contrary. The optimum size of fleet is that where the minimum number of vessels is earning the maximum revenue. It should also be remembered that the owner is not normally able to have a standby vessel available, as the amount of capital tied up in any one vessel is considerable.

Today an increasing number of vessels are multi-purpose in their design and accordingly permit flexibility of operation which is particularly advantageous in times of international trade depression. It enables the vessel to switch from one trade to another, or carry a variety of cargoes as distinct from one specialized cargo. Examples are found in the multi-purpose container ship capable of carrying containers and vehicles; the Ro/Ro vessel capable of shipping all types of vehicular traffic; the OBO ship able to convey oil or ore, and the very versatile multi-purpose dry cargo carriers found in the SD-14 and Freedom-type tramp tonnage. Such tonnage is better able to combat economically unequal trading.

There are basically two types of service: the regular and those operated according to a particular demand. The first type of vessel is primarily associated with liner cargo trades, whilst the latter is mostly confined to tramps.

Liner cargo vessels may be cellular container ships, dual purpose vessels having accommodation for both container and conventional cargo, Ro/Ro vessels, and conventional break bulk ships. The tramp vessel may vary from the Freedom-type vessel to modern bulk carrier of 90 000 tonnes. Additionally there exists a significant volume of world trade which is moved by specialized – often purpose-built – bulk cargo tonnage owned or on charter to industrial companies conveying their raw material for industrial processing. Such services are often scheduled to meet an industrial production programme and operate from specialized purpose-built berths.

The number of passenger vessels engaged in deep-sea schedules today is very few. In the main they are engaged in all-the-year cruising which remains a buoyant market. The cruise vessel operates on a sailing schedule prepared many months in advance on a particular itinerary. A number are linked to the fly-cruise concept whereby the passenger is flown to the port to join the passenger cruise liner.

A substantial volume of trade is now found in the short sea trade such as UK/Europe involving multi-purpose vessels. These vessels of up to 10 000 GRT are capable of conveying passengers, coaches, accompanied cars, and Ro/Ro vehicles. A recent tendency is for such vessels to be primarily designed for the Ro/Ro market. Such schedules are fully integrated with the port operating arrangements and a dominant feature is the quick port turnround of such tonnage. These vessels primarily convey Ro/Ro vehicles and operate a year-round schedule with little variation. Such services carry substantial quantities of passengers, coaches, accompanied cars and tend to vary their sailings to meet varying market demands with the sailings being greatly increased in the peak summer months.

Similar conditions apply to multi-purpose vessels carrying road haulage vehicles, passengers and accompanied cars except the schedules are usually fully integrated into the port operating arrangements.

With the cargo liner, the frequency of sailings is predetermined months in advance, and agreed within the Conference. Cargo traffic attracted to a liner service covers a wide variety of commodities, including machinery, steel rails, foodstuffs, motor vehicles, and so on. At certain times and in various trades, there is, of course, a need for increased sailings to cater for seasonable traffic variations, and these are sometimes obtained by chartering additional tonnage. This has the advantage of ensuring that the additional tonnage required is available only in peak periods, and not throughout the year when traffic considerations could not justify it. Surveys and overhauls are again undertaken when practicable outside peak periods. In many container liner trades, vessels are on continuous survey to ensure the frequency and time spent in dry dock is kept to a minimum. This also applies to modern specialized bulk carriers.

A variety of specialized bulk carrier tonnage has emerged in the international shipping scene particularly since the 1960s. These now include the mammoth oil tankers and ore carriers, very large crude carriers, liquefied natural gas carriers and so on. Such tonnage often under charter requires extensive planning of schedules which are designed to maximize ship utilization. They have to be integrated with production areas at the point of cargo despatch port of supply, and dove-tailed in with the industrial processes and/or storage capacity at the destination port. Many of the terminals are situated off shore to meet the excessive draught of such vessels which can exceed 65 m. The schedules and type of ship usually permit cargo to be conveyed in only one direction, with the return voyage in ballast and frequently at slightly faster speed. The development of unidirectional cargo shipments has been partially overcome by the oil bulk ore (OBO) carrier which also allows such tonnage to be switched from one trade to another when market demands so dictate. This is a very flexible situation operationally.

The tramp operator has no regular sailing schedule, but plies between ports throughout the world, where cargo is offering. As was established earlier in the book, the extent of advanced sailing schedules varies from weeks, days or, in extreme cases, a matter of hours, to many months, depending on market and trading conditions.

So far we have reviewed the background against which schedules are compiled. Given below are the various factors influencing the formulation of sailing schedules:

1. The overall number of ships and their availability.

2. The volume, type, and any special characteristics of the traffic.

3. Traffic fluctuations such as peak demands.

4. Maintenance of time margins where services connect. For instance, a passenger vessel may be served by a connecting rail service.

5. Availability of crew.

6. Arrangements for relief measure which may arise in cases of emergency.

7. Climatic conditions. Some ports are ice-bound throughout certain periods of the year, which prevents any shipping calling at these particular ports.

8. Competition. This arises when conference and non-conference tonnage, for example, operate schedules alongside each other and compete in the same marketplace.

9. Time necessary for terminal duties at the port. This will embrace loading and/or discharging, Customs procedure, bunkering, victualling etc.

10. Voyage time.

11. The actual types of ship available and in particular their size, incorporating the length, beam, and draught, together with any special characteristics. For instance, some may be suitable for cruising. Other vessels, by virtue of their size, can only operate between ports that have deep-water berth facility. Hence, a large fleet of small vessels has more operating flexibility than a small fleet of large vessels which are restricted to a limited number of ports having adequate facilities to accommodate them. Another

vessel may require special equipment for loading and discharging her cargo.

12. Any hostile activities taking place or envisaged in any particular waters.

13. Location of canals such as the Suez and Panama, as alternative routes.

14. Actual estimated voyage cost and expected traffic receipts.

15. Political actions such as flag discrimination, bilateral trade agreements causing unbalanced trading conditions.

16. General availability of port facilities and dock labour, and any tidal restrictions affecting times of access and departure.

17. Plying limits of individual ships, and for liner tonnage, any condition imposed by Liner Conference agreements.

18. With multi-purpose vessels conveying road haulage vehicles, passengers and accompanied cars, the number of cars and road haulage vehicles shipped can vary according to the time of year and/or period of the day.

The schedule ultimately devised in liner cargo trades should facilitate the operator increasing his market share of the trade and have particular regard to the need to operate a profitable service. Such variations in demand are accommodated by the use of vehicle decks controlled by means of hydraulically operated ramps. Thus the vessel which for one sailing may accommodate 50 cars and 30 large road haulage vehicles can on another occasion carry as many as 300 cars exclusively.   ·

Thus it is apparent that sailing schedules are based primarily on commercial considerations with political, economic, operating and, to some extent, the technical capabilities of the ship all playing their role as contributory factors.

11.2 PROBLEMS PRESENTED TO SHIPOWNERS BY FLUCTUATIONS IN TRADE AND UNEQUAL BALANCE OF TRADE

The problem of unused capacity in ocean transport is largely caused by secular or long-term fluctuations in world trade. It is chiefly a problem of joint supply involving an outward and home journey. Two or more commodities are often produced together in the sense that one of them cannot be produced without the other.

Mutton and wool are examples. The position is further aggravated by the fact that shipping capacity, in common with all forms of transport, cannot be stored and is consumed immediately it is produced.

An unequal balance and fluctuation in trade is common to all forms of transport, and particularly difficult to overcome satisfactorily in shipping. It is caused by economic, social or political factors. In all, there are nine main sets of circumstances in which unbalanced trading arises in shipping:

1. One of the largest streams of unbalanced trading is found in the shipment of the world's oil. Tankers convey the oil outwards from the port serving the oilfield, whilst the return voyage is in ballast.

2. An abnormal amount of cargo in a particular area can give rise to unequal trading. Such a glut tends to attract vessels to the area for freight, the majority of which often arrives in ballast. The situation may arise due to an abnormally heavy harvest. Conversely, a country may be in a state of famine or short of a particular commodity or foodstuff. This tends to attract fully-loaded vessels inward to the area whilst on the outward voyage the ship is in ballast.

3. Government restrictions might be imposed on the import and/or export of certain goods. This may be necessary to protect home industries, restricting certain imports to help maintain full employment. Additionally, this restriction may be introduced due to an adverse balance of trade caused by a persistent excess of imports over exports. Such restrictions may be short term or permanent, depending on the circumstances in which they were introduced.

4. Climatic conditions such as ice formation restrict the safe navigation of rivers, canals and ports to certain periods of the year.

5. The passenger trades are, of course, subject to seasonal fluctuations, which present to the shipowner the problem of filling the unused capacity during the off-peak season.

6. Political influence can also cause unequal balance of trade. This can be achieved by flag discrimination which in effect is pressure exerted by governments, designed to divert cargoes to ships of the national flag, regardless of commercial considerations normally governing the routing of cargo. Flag discrimination can

be exercised in a number of ways, including bilateral trade treaties, import licences and exchange control. Bilateral trade treaties include shipping clauses reserving either the whole of the trade between the two countries, or as much of it as possible to the ships of the two flags. Brazil, Chile, and India have all used the granting of import licences to ensure carriage of cargoes in ships of the national flag. Exchange control also offers endless means of making shipment in national vessels either obligatory or so commercially attractive that it has the same effect. Brazil, Colombia, Czechoslovakia, Poland and Turkey have all indulged in this method of control in the interest of their national fleets.

7. The fast-growing Eastern bloc mercantile fleet – particularly of Soviet operators – is penetrating more and more major liner trades and in so doing creating unequal balance of trade. Such developments are adversely affecting long established liner cargo operators in the 'cross-trade' market. The Eastern bloc operators charge rates up to 30% below established liner cargo operators, and are operating under a much reduced cost compared with Western free-enterprise countries operating maritime liner cargo fleets. For example the Eastern bloc mercantile fleet insurance risks are borne by the State, and crew wages are low.

8. The practice of trade protectionism in many parts of the world is much on the increase. It finds itself in the UN Liner Conference cargo code with the 40/40/20 cargo-sharing formula. Under such conditions the two countries participating in the trade convey in their national maritime fleets some 40% each of the cargo, with the residue of 20% being shipped by cross-trade established liner cargo operators. Subsequently the UNCTAD VI Conference resolution 144 (vi) directed the shipping committee to work towards a number of objectives. This included establishing an equitable basis for the participation of developing countries in the carriage of bulk cargoes. The implication of the Geneva Conference 1988 needs to be reconciled.

9. Another example of trade protectionism is found in the US government policy. It takes the view that government super-vision and control is in the interest of the public and US com-merce. Conversely European liner cargo operators involved in the North American trade consider that generally the best results are achieved by self-regulation, competition, and the minimum amount of government involvement. The US government is keen

to impose policies which would assume a certain percentage of various trades are shipped in US cargo vessels. For example, the Jones Act provides that only US vessels may engage in the US coastal trades; and 50% of all government-generated cargo must be carried on US flag ships to the extent of their availability.

To counteract unequal trading, it is necessary for the liner and tramp operators to take measures to obtain the maximum loaded capacity of the vessel and reduce ballast runs to an absolute minimum. The development of OBO type of tonnage has partially countered the problem of unequal trading in modern bulk carrier tonnage. Moreover, there is the growing tendency to develop multi-purpose vessels to permit their operating flexibility and counter trade imbalance in liner trades. Of the two types of operator, the tramp owner is better fitted successfully to combat unequal trading as he has no scheduled advertised sailings and thereby becomes more flexible.

The larger the fleet the more flexible it is to combat unequal trading problems. The operator of a large fleet is generally in a number of different trades and is thus able to switch his vessels to the trades where the demand is greatest. Hence in particular trade 'A', due to seasonal variations, demand for shipping may be light, whilst in another trade 'B' the demand may be exceptionally heavy. The prudent operator would accordingly arrange to transfer some of his vessels from trade 'A' to 'B'.

Cargo liners are more vulnerable to unequal trading inasmuch as normally they must stick to the berth and not jump from one trade into another, as in tramp operating. To combat this, a liner may return for instance from the Pacific coast of North America as a tramp vessel. This necessarily involves a short ballast haul to link up with one of the tramp trades. Alternatively, the liner can change her berth. This system, which is very satisfactory, operates where a liner goes out on one berth and then at some time changes to another berth within another trade, possibly within a group of companies. Hence the vessel may operate independently for one company but co-ordinate with other companies within the group; thereby ensuring that the maximum use is made of the vessel in various parts of the world. Such a system is very flexible.

A further method of combating unequal trading is to have dual-purpose vessels. Thus a ship may be equipped to carry either oil or ore. Another example is a vessel which can convey either refrigerated or general cargo. Ships of this type, which are more expensive to build, are flexible to operate as the shipowner can vary the trades in which they ply.

The tramp operator obtains much of this trade through a ship-broker on the Baltic Exchange. His vessel is chartered by the shipper, who is responsible for providing the cargo, on a voyage or time-charter basis. When the charter has been fixed, the prudent operator will endeavour to obtain a further fixture. By adopting these tactics, coupled with the most favourable rate offered, the operator will plan the movement of his vessels as far in advance as possible and reduce ballast hauls to a minimum.

Since the 1960s, modern technology has developed various schemes which have permitted the seasonal nature of international bulk food stuff distribution in certain trades to be spread over a longer period – in particular modern processing and storage plant. This has helped counter the problem of unequal trading by extending the period over which such shipments are made.

On the passenger side the problem of unused capacity during off-seasons is largely solved by the organization of cruises but in many markets such an opportunity does not exist. Cruising is now confined to purpose-built tonnage operating in all the year round schedules.

11.3 THE RELATIVE IMPORTANCE OF SPEED, FREQUENCY, RELIABILITY, COST AND QUALITY OF SEA TRANSPORT

There are five factors that influence the nature of a shipping service: speed, frequency, reliability, cost and quality.

Speed is important to the shipper who desires to market his goods against an accurate arrival date and to eliminate banking charges for opening credits. This can be achieved by selecting the fastest service available and thereby obtaining the minimum interval between the time the goods are ordered and the date of delivery at their destination. Speed is particularly important to manufacturers of consumer goods as it avoids expense and the risk of obsolescence to the retailer carrying large stocks. In the case of certain commodities, and especially fresh fruit and semi-frozen products and fashionable goods, a regular and fast delivery is vital to successful trading. The need for speed is perhaps most felt in the long-distance trades where voyage times may be appreciably reduced and the shipper given the benefit of an early delivery and frequent stock replenishment. These various needs are fully recognized by the liner operator, to whom speed is expensive both in terms of initial expenditure on the marine engines and the actual fuel cost. His aim is to obtain the optimum and provide a vessel with the maximum speed at the minimum cost which will fulfil the requirements of the shipper. These aspects have partially precipitated the development of container services in liner cargo trades offering faster transits.

Speed is not so important in the world tramp trades where generally lower-value cargoes are being carried and where many trades are moving under programmed stock-piled arrangments. In this category are included coal, mineral ores, timber, bulk grain and other cargoes which normally move in shiploads and have a relatively low value: these demand a low transport cost.

Frequency of service is most important when goods can only be sold in small quantities at frequent intervals. Here the liner operator will phase his sailings to meet shippers' requirements, whilst the vessels must be suitable in size, speed and equipment for the cargoes offering. The shipper of perishable fruit and vegetables also relies on frequent, as well as fast, ships to obtain maximum benefit from the season's crop. Fashionable goods and replacement spare stock also benefit from frequent service.

To the tramp charterer, frequency of sailings is not of paramount importance. He must not, of course, allow his stocks to run down too far, but he will have a margin within which he can safely operate and will come in to buy and ship when conditions suit him.

Reliability is an essential requirement to the shipper engaged in the liner service, whose goods are sold against expiry dates on letters of credit and import licences. Furthermore, the liner shipper relies upon the operator to deliver his traffic in good condition. To the shipper, therefore, reliability infers that the vessel will sail and arrive at the advertised time; the shipowner will look after the cargo during pre-shipment, throughout the voyage and after discharge; and, finally, the operator can be relied upon to give adequate facilities at the docks and at his offices to enable the appropriate documents and other formalities to be satisfactorily completed. In short, prestige in the liner trade goes with the reliance which the shipper can place on any particular owner.

The tramp shipper marketing goods of relatively low value must seek the lowest possible transport charge, as the freight percentage of the total value may have a direct bearing on the saleability of the commodity. He has thus a prime interest in the availability of tramp shipping space at any particular time by reason of the fact that freight and chartering rates will vary reflections of the economic forces of supply and demand. In a market situation where there are plenty of vessels the shipper will be able to charter at a rate which will be only marginally above the operating costs of the vessel. In the opposite situation he will be forced to pay more but there is a limiting factor in the price of the commodity at the point of sale to the rate which the shipowner may receive. In these conditions the premium returns are earned by the operators of the most efficient ships. In weak market conditions their relative efficiency ensures a small profit while others just break even. Where the market is strong the proven reliability shown before will ensure that the services of such vessels will be sought out before opportunities are taken up.

In the liner trades the freight costs are more stable and controlled; the shipowner is able to hold the rate at a fair level to show a profit margin, but he must be careful not to hold his rates so high that they price the goods out of the market; at this point there is need for joint consultation between shipper and carrier. It can be argued that the liner shipper should pay a higher transport charge to compensate for the liner service which in itself is expensive.

Quality of service is especially important in the competitive world of shipping and international trade today. The service provided must be customer-oriented with emphasis being placed on providing a reliable service and handling the goods and documentation in an efficient way.

11.4 VOYAGE ESTIMATES

The shipping industry is more cost-conscious today than ever before. Although voyage estimates have been a very long-standing management tool in the tramp field, they are equally common in the liner trade as new types of services are introduced – particularly container/cellular ships – involving different types of tonnage.

Voyage estimates enable a shipowner to broadly determine the cost of providing a ship for a particular voyage, for example Southampton/New York. Included in the voyage estimate would not only be the indirect cost, such as depreciation, maintenance/ survey, administration etc., but also direct cost, such as fuel, crew, port cost, agency charges etc.

Table 11.1 Analysis of a voyage estimate

Item	Percentage of Total Costs
Fuel oil	25.6
Lubricating oil	0.9
Engine maintenance	1.2
Hull maintenance	4.0
Crew cost	25.0
General administration	0.4
Insurance	8.0
Capital cost (depreciation/ interest charges etc).	30.2

The subject of voyage estimates relevant to shipbroking practice is dealt with on pages 368–72 but given above is an analysis of the significant constituents of a voyage estimate of a typical 60 000 dwt modern bulk carrier with a 16-knot service speed.

It will be appreciated that each vessel will vary according to specification, age, and crew commitment. The economics of ship operation is an important aspect of shipping today and the reader is recommended to study Chapter 7 of *Economics of Shipping Practice and Management*.

11.5 INDIVISIBLE LOADS

A market which has grown in recent years is the movement of the indivisible load. It may be a transformer or engineering plant with a total weight of up to 250 tonnes.

Such a product requires special arrangements and the freight forwarder specializing in such work usually has a project forwarding department to handle such transits. The following points are relevant in the movement internationally of the indivisible load.

(a)   The ports of departure, destination and any transhipment areas require to be checked out to ensure they can handle such a shipment especially the availability of heavy lift equipment.

(b)   The shipowner requires to have a plan and specification of the shipment to evaluate the stowage and handling arrangments. Also to identify the weight distribution.

(c)   The transportation of the indivisible load to and from the ports requires pre-planning in regard to route and time scale. Usually such goods may only move at night under police escort and subject to police and/or transport department permission.

(d)   The rates are usually assessed on a cost plus profit basis. The cost can be very extensive in any heavy lift equipment and special arrangements to transport the goods overland to and from the ports. Freight forwarders tend to work closely with the correspondent agent in the destination country. Transhipment cost can be much reduced if a MAFI type 6-axle trailer is used as in the Ro/Ro tonnage.

The advantages of the indivisible load shipment to the shipper/ buyer/importer include lower overall transportation cost, quicker transit; much reduced site assembly cost; less risk of damage in transit; lower insurance premium; less technical aid – staff resources – required by the buyer as no extensive site assembly work; equipment tested and fully tested operationally in the factory before despatch; no costly site assembly work; less risk of malfunctioning equipment arising; earlier commissioning of the equipment which in turn results in the quicker productive use of the equipment with profitable benefits to the buyer overall.

CHAPTER 12

Bills of lading

When a shipowner, or another authorized person, for example an agent, agrees to carry goods by water, or agrees to furnish a ship for the purpose of carrying goods in return for a sum of money to be paid to him, such a contract is a contract of affreightment and the sum to be paid is called freight. Shipment of the goods is usually evidenced in a document called a bill of lading.

The bill of lading has been defined as a receipt for goods shipped on board a ship, signed by the person (or his agent) who contracts to carry them, and stating the terms on which the goods were delivered to and received by the ship. It is not the actual contract, which is inferred from the action of the shipper or shipowner in delivering or receiving the cargo, but forms excellent evidence of the terms of the contract.

Before examining the salient points, function and types of bills of lading, we will first of all consider two Acts which have played an important role in the development of this document, namely the Bills of Lading Act 1855 and the Carriage of Goods by Sea Act 1924.

12.1 BILLS OF LADING ACT 1855

The Bills of Lading Act 1855 has established the following, relating to the bill of lading document.

1. It preserved the right of the original shipper to 'stoppage *in transitu*' (in transit). Moreover, not only did it give the right of conditional endorsement and of reserving the '*jus disponendi*' (law of disposal) but also the unpaid seller could resume possession of the goods by exercising the right of 'stoppage *in transitu*'.

2. It established the principle of transferability, permitting the transfer of a bill of lading, from the holder to a person to whom the property in the goods passes, together with any rights and liabilities incorporated in the document.

3. It provided that, once the bill of lading has been issued, it is *prima facie* evidence that the goods have been shipped.

12.2 CARRIAGE OF GOODS BY SEA ACTS 1924 AND 1971

Before the Carriage of Goods by Sea Act 1924 had reached the Statute Book, it had been the practice of shipowners to include as many exception clauses as they wished in a bill of lading, thereby reducing their liability. Furthermore, the rights and liabilities had been differently defined in various countries, with consequent embarrassment to overseas trade, and the holder of a bill of lading had to scrutinize it carefully in order to ascertain the extent of his rights. It was therefore considered necessary to introduce this Act with the aim of standardizing the rights of the holder of every bill of lading against the shipowner.

In September 1921, a meeting of the International Law Association was held at The Hague, with the object of securing the adoption by the countries represented of a set of rules, later known as the Hague Rules, which were embodied in the Act relating to bills of lading, so that the rights and liabilities of the cargo owners and shipowners respectively might be subject to rules of general application.

These rules were agreed at an international convention at Brussels on 25 August 1924 and give effect in the UK to the Carriage of Goods by Sea Act (COGSA) 1924. They are officially known as 'the International Convention for the Unification of Certain rules relating to Bills of Lading and govern liability for loss or damage to goods carried under a Bill of Lading'.

The main effect of the Act was that it radically changed the legal status of the shipowner by imposing on him a precise liability and giving precisely defined rights and remedies in place of the previous freedom.

The rules apply to all outward (export) shipments from any nation which ratified the rules. They apply almost universally wherever they have not been superseded by the Hague–Visby rules. A summary of the main features of the Hague rules are given below:

(a) It lays down minimum terms under which a carrier may

offer for the carriage of all goods, other than live animals, non-commercial goods (such as personal and household effects) experimental shipments and goods carried on deck where the bill of lading is claused to indicate such carriage.

(b) The carrier (shipowner) has to exercise due diligence to provide a seaworthy vessel. The basic principle is that the carrier is only liable for loss or damage caused by his own negligence or that of his servants, agents or sub-contractors. However, the carrier is still protected in three cases where the loss or damage has been caused by negligence. Negligence in navigation; negligence in the management of the vessel (as opposed to the care of the cargo); and fire, unless by the actual fault or privity of the carrier.

(c) Liability is limited to the following per package:

Australia A$200	Japan Y100,000
Canada C$500	USA $500
West Germany DM 1250	USSR R250
Greece DR 8000	UK £100

Bills of lading may also be issued under a charter party. The 1924 Act applies from the time a third party (e.g. the shipper or consignee) becomes a holder of the bill of lading. This implies that the charterer and the shipowners may agree on any terms they like irrespective of the provisions of the Act, but if a third party becomes interested in the goods, the provisions must be complied with. In actual fact, many charter parties indicate that bills of lading incorporating the Hague Rules be issued.

In 1967 a further international conference adopted some revisions to the Hague Rules – principally affecting their limitation. The amended rules are officially known as the Brussels Protocol signed on 23 February 1968 and known as the Hague–Visby rules and contained in the UK by the Carriage of Goods by Sea Act 1971. The Special Drawing Rights Protocol was adopted in February 1984 which placed all the contracting states' carriers under a liability per package/weight of SDR 2 per kg or SDR 666.67 per package or unit whichever is the greater. This embraces (autumn 1987) Belgium, Denmark, Finland, Italy, Netherlands, Norway, Poland, Spain, Sweden and UK.

The 1968 Convention came into effect on 23 June 1977 and the contracting states applying the Hague–Visby rules (autumn 1987) include Belgium, Denmark, Ecuador, Egypt, Finland, France, German Democratic Republic, Italy, Lebanon, Holland, Norway, Poland, Singapore, Spain, Sri Lanka, Sweden, Switzerland, Syria, Tonga, UK and West Germany. The Visby amendment applies to all bills of lading in the following circumstances:

(a)   The port of shipment is in a ratifying nation, or the place of issue of the bill of lading is in a ratifying nation.

(b)   The bill of lading applies Hague–Visby rules contractually.

In March 1978 at a further international conference in Hamburg, a new set of rules termed the Hamburg rules was adopted. If adopted the Hamburg rules will radically alter the liability which shipowners have to bear for loss or damage to goods. The main differences between the new Rules and the old Hague-Visby rules are given below:

(a)   The carrier will be liable for loss, damage or delay to the goods occurring in his charge unless he proves that 'he, his servants, or agents took all measures that could reasonably be required to avoid the occurrence and its consequences'.

(b)   The carrier is liable for delay in delivery if, 'the goods have not been delivered at the port of discharge provided for under the Contract of Carriage within the time agreed expressly upon or, in the absence of such agreement, within the time which it could be reasonable to require of a diligent Carrier having regard to the circumstances of the case'.

(c)   The dual system for calculating the limit of liability either by reference to package or weight as set out in the Hague–Visby rules has been readopted but the amounts have been increased by about 25% to SDR 835 per package and SDR 2.5 per kg.

(d)   The Hamburg rules cover all contracts for the carriage by sea other than charter parties.

(e)   They cover live animals and deck cargo.

(f)   They apply to both imports and exports.

The rules will come into effect one year after ratification or accession by twenty nations and by autumn 1987 eleven nations have acceded including Barbados, Chile, Egypt, Hungary, Lebanon, Morocco, Romania, Senegal, Tanzania, Tunisia and Uganda.

12.3 SALIENT POINTS OF A BILL OF LADING

The salient points incorporated in a bill of lading can be conveniently listed as follows:

1. the name of the shipper;
2. ship's name;
3. full description of the cargo (provided it is not bulk cargo) including any shipping marks, individual package numbers in consignment, contents, cubic measurement, gross weight, etc;
4. port of shipment;
5. port of discharge;
6. details of freight, including when and where it is to be paid – whether freight paid or payable at destination;
7. name of consignee or, if the shipper is anxious to withold the consignee's name, 'shipper's order' or 'order';
8. number of bills of lading signed on behalf of the Master or his agent acknowledging receipt of the goods;
9. terms of the contract of carriage;
10. the name and address of the notified party (the person to be notified on arrival of the shipment, usually the buyer);
11. the date the goods were received for shipment and/or loaded on the vessel;
12. actual date of the Master's or his agent's signature.

12.4 TYPES OF BILLS OF LADING

There are several forms of bills of lading and these include the following:

(a) Shipped bill of lading.

Under the Carriage of Goods by Sea Act 1924, the shipper can demand that the shipowner supplies bills of lading proving that the goods have been actually shipped. For this reason most bill of lading forms are already printed as shipped bills and commence with the wording: 'Shipped in apparent good order and condition.' It confirms the goods are actually on board the vessel. This is the most satisfactory type of receipt, and the shipper prefers such a bill as there is no doubt about the goods being on board and consequent dispute on this point will not arise with the bankers or consignee, thereby facilitating earliest financial settlement of the export sale.

Code Name: "COMBICONBILL"

Combined Transport BILL OF LADING
N e g o t i a b l e

Shipper

B/L No.

Reference No.

Consigned to order of

Notify address

Place of receipt		
Ocean vessel	Port of loading	
Port of discharge	Place of delivery	Freight payable at	Number of original Bs/L
Marks and Nos.	Quantity and description of goods		Gross weight, kg	Measurement, m³

Particulars above declared by Shipper

Freight and charges

RECEIVED the goods in apparent good order and condition and, as far as ascertained by reasonable means of checking, as specified above unless otherwise stated.

The Carrier, in accordance with the provisions contained in this document,

a) undertakes to perform or to procure the performance of the entire transport from the place at which the goods are taken in charge to the place designated for delivery in this document, and

b) assumes liability as prescribed in this document for such transport.

One of the Bs/L must be surrendered duly endorsed in exchange for the goods or delivery order.

IN WITNESS whereof TWO (2) original Bs/L have been signed, if not otherwise stated above, one of which being accomplished the other(s) to be void.

Place and date of issue

Signed for the Carrier

Note:
The Merchant's attention is called to the fact that according to Clauses 11 to 13 of this B/L, the liability of the Carrier is, in most cases, limited in respect of loss of or damage to the goods and delay.

Printed and sold by
Fr. G. Knudtzon Ltd., 55, Toldbodgade, Copenhagen,
thority of The Baltic and International Maritime Conference.
Copenhagen. Copyright.

56-0

As agent(s) only   p.t.o.

Fig. 12.1 Combined transport bill of lading. (Reproduced by kind permission of BIMCO).

COMBINED TRANSPORT BILL OF LADING

Adopted by The Baltic and International Maritime Conference in January, 1971
Code Name: "COMBICONBILL"

I. GENERAL PROVISIONS

1. **Applicability.** Notwithstanding the heading "Combined Transport Bill of Lading", the provisions set out and referred to in this document shall also apply, if the transport as described on the face of the B/L is performed by one mode of transport only.

2. **Definitions.** "Carrier" means the party on whose behalf this B/L has been signed. "Merchant" includes the Shipper, the Receiver, the Consignor, the Consignee, the Holder of this B/L and the Owner of the Goods.

3. **Carrier's Tariff.** The terms of the Carrier's applicable Tariff at the date of shipment are incorporated herein. Copies of the relevant provisions of the applicable Tariff are available from the Carrier upon request. In the case of inconsistency between this B/L and the applicable Tariff, this B/L shall prevail.

4. **Time Bar.** All liability whatsoever of the Carrier shall cease unless suit is brought within 11 months after delivery of the goods or the date when the goods should have been delivered.

5. **Law and Jurisdiction.** Disputes arising under this B/L shall be determined at the option of the Claimant by the courts and subject to Clause 12 of this B/L in accordance with the law at

(a) the place where the Carrier has his habitual residence or his principal place of business or the branch or agency through which the contract of combined transport was made, or

(b) the place where the goods were taken in charge by the Carrier or the place designated for delivery.

No proceedings may be brought before other courts unless the parties expressly agree on both the choice of another court or arbitration tribunal and the law to be then applicable.

II. PERFORMANCE OF THE CONTRACT

6. **Sub-contracting.**

(1) The Carrier shall be entitled to sub-contract on any terms the whole or any part of the carriage, loading, unloading, storing, warehousing, handling and any and all duties whatsoever undertaken by the Carrier in relation to the goods.

(2) For the purposes of this contract and subject to the provisions in this B/L, the Carrier shall be responsible for the acts and omissions of any person of whose services he makes use for the performance of the contract of carriage evidenced by this document.

7. **Methods and Routes of Transportation.**

(1) The Carrier is entitled to perform the transport in any reasonable manner and by any reasonable means, methods and routes.

(2) In accordance herewith, for instance, in the event of carriage by sea, vessels may sail with or without pilots, undergo repairs, adjust equipment, drydock and tow vessels in all situations.

8. **Optional Stowage.**

(1) Goods may be stowed by the Carrier by means of containers, trailers, transportable tanks, flats, pallets, or similar articles of transport used to consolidate goods.

(2) Containers, trailers and transportable tanks, whether stowed by the Carrier or received by him in a stowed condition from the Merchant, may be carried on or under deck without notice to the Merchant.

9. **Hindrances etc. Affecting Performance.**

(1) The Carrier shall use reasonable endeavours to complete the transport and to deliver the goods at the place designated for delivery.

(2) If at any time the performance of the contract as evidenced by this B/L is or will be affected by any hindrance, risk, delay, difficulty or disadvantage of whatsoever kind, and if by virtue of sub-clause (1) the Carrier has no duty to complete the performance of the contract, the Carrier (whether or not the transport is commenced) may elect to

(a) treat the performance of this contract as terminated and place the goods at the Merchant's disposal at any place which the Carrier shall deem safe and convenient; or

(b) deliver the goods at the place designated for delivery.

In any event the Carrier shall be entitled to full freight for goods received for transportation and additional compensation for extra costs resulting from the circumstances referred to above.

III. CARRIER'S LIABILITY

10. **Basic Liability.**

(1) The Carrier shall be liable for loss of or damage to the goods occurring between the time when he receives the goods into his charge and the time of delivery.

(2) The Carrier shall, however, be relieved of liability for any loss or damage if such loss or damage arose or resulted from:

(a) The wrongful act or neglect of the Merchant.

(b) Compliance with the instructions of the person entitled to give them.

(c) The lack of, or defective conditions of packing in the case of goods which, by their nature, are liable to wastage or to be damaged when not packed or when not properly packed.

(d) Handling, loading, stowage or unloading of the goods by or on behalf of the Merchant.

(e) Inherent vice of the goods.

(f) Insufficiency or inadequacy of marks or numbers on the goods, covering, or unit loads.

(g) Strikes or lock-outs or stoppage or restraints of labour from whatever cause whether partial or general.

(h) Any cause or event which the Carrier could not avoid and the consequence whereof he could not prevent by the exercise of reasonable diligence.

(3) Where under sub-clause (2) the Carrier is not under any liability in respect of some of the factors causing the loss or damage, he shall only be liable to the extent that those factors for which he is liable under this clause have contributed to the loss or damage.

(4) The burden of proving that the loss or damage was due to one or more of the causes, or events, specified in (a), (b) and (h) of sub-clause (2) shall rest upon the Carrier.

When the Carrier establishes that in the circumstances of the case, the loss or damage could be attributed to one or more of the causes, or events, specified in (c) to (g) of sub-clause (2), it shall be presumed that it was so caused. The Merchant shall, however, be entitled to prove that the loss or damage was not, in fact, caused either wholly or partly by one or more of the causes or events.

11. **The Amount of Compensation.**

(1) When the Carrier is liable for compensation in respect of loss of or damage to the goods, such compensation shall be calculated by reference to the value of such goods at the place and time they are delivered to the Merchant in accordance with the contract or should have been so delivered.

(2) The value of the goods shall be fixed according to the commodity exchange price or, if there be no such price, according to the current market price or, if there be no commodity exchange price or current market price, by reference to the normal value of goods of the same kind and quality.

(3) Compensation shall not, however, exceed 30 Francs per kilo of gross weight of the goods lost or damaged. A Franc means a unit consisting of 65.5 milligrammes of gold of millesimal fineness 900'.

(4) Higher compensation may be claimed only when, with the consent of the Carrier, the value for the goods declared by the consignor which exceeds the limits laid down in this clause has been stated in this B/L. In that case the amount of the declared value shall be substituted for that limit.

12. **Special Provisions.**

(1) Notwithstanding anything provided for in clauses 10 and 11 of this B/L, if it can be proved where the loss or damage occurred the Carrier and/or the Merchant shall, as to the liability of the Carrier, be entitled to require such liability to be determined by the provisions contained in any international convention or national law, which provisions

(a) cannot be departed from by private contract, to the detriment of the Claimant, and

(b) would have applied if the Merchant had made a separate and direct contract with the Carrier in respect of the particular stage of transport where the loss or damage occurred and received as evidence thereof any particular document which must be issued if such international convention or national law shall apply.

(2) Insofar as the Hague Rules contained in the International Convention for the Unification of Certain Rules relating to Bills of Lading, dated 25th August, 1924, do not apply to carriage by sea by virtue of the foregoing provisions of this clause, the liability of the Carrier in respect of any carriage by sea shall be determined by that Convention. The Hague Rules shall also determine the liability of the Carrier in respect of carriage by inland waterways as if such carriage were carriage by sea. Furthermore, they shall apply to all goods, whether carried on deck or under deck.

13. **Delay, Consequential Loss, etc.** If the Carrier is held liable in respect of delay, consequential loss or damage other than loss of or damage to the goods, the liability of the Carrier shall be limited to the freight for the transport covered by this B/L, or to the value of the goods as determined in Clause 11, whichever is least.

14. **Notice of Loss.** Unless notice of loss of or damage to the goods and the general nature of it be given in writing to the Carrier at the place of delivery before or at the time of the removal of the goods into the custody of the person entitled to delivery thereof under this B/L, or if the loss or damage be not apparent, within six consecutive days thereafter, such removal shall be *prima facie* evidence of the delivery by the Carrier of the goods as described in this B/L.

15. **Defences and Limits for the Carrier.**

(1) The defences and limits of liability provided for in this B/L shall apply in any action against the Carrier for loss or damage to the goods whether the action be founded in contract or in tort.

(2) The Carrier shall not be entitled to the benefit of the limitation of liability provided for in Clause 11 sub-clause (3), if it is proved that the loss or damage resulted from an act or omission of the Carrier done with intent to cause damage or recklessly and with knowledge that damage would probably result.

16. **Defences and Limits for Servants, etc.**

(1) If an action for loss or damage to the goods is brought against a servant, agent or independent contractor, such person shall be entitled to avail himself of the defences and limits of liability which the Carrier is entitled to invoke under this contract.

(2) However, if it is proved that the loss or damage resulted from an act or omission of this person, done with intent to cause damage or recklessly and with knowledge that damage would probably result, such person shall not be entitled to the benefit of limitation of liability provided for in Clause 11 sub-clause (3).

(3) Subject to the provisions of Clause 11 sub-clause (3), of Clause 15 sub-clause (2) and of sub-clause (2) of this clause, the aggregate of the amounts recoverable from the Carrier and his servants, agents or independent contractors shall in no case exceed the limits provided for in this document.

IV. DESCRIPTION OF GOODS

17. **Carrier's Responsibility.**

This B/L shall be *prima facie* evidence of the receipt by the Carrier of the goods as herein described in respect of the particulars which he had reasonable means of checking. In respect of such particulars, proof to the contrary shall not be admissible, when this document has been transferred to a third party acting in good faith.

18. **Shipper's Responsibility.** The Shipper shall be deemed to have guaranteed to the Carrier the accuracy, at the time the goods were taken in charge by the Carrier, of the description of the goods, marks, number, quantity and weight, as furnished by him, and the Shipper shall indemnify the Carrier against all loss, damage and expenses arising or resulting from inaccuracies in or inadequacy of such particulars. The right of the Carrier to such indemnity shall in no way limit his responsibility and liability under this B/L to any person other than the Shipper.

V. FREIGHT AND LIEN

19. **Freight.**

(1) Freight shall be deemed earned on receipt of the goods by the Carrier and shall be paid in any event.

(2) The Merchant's attention is drawn to the stipulations concerning currency in which the freight and charges are to be paid, rate of exchange, devaluation and other contingencies relative to freight and charges in the relevant tariff conditions. If no such stipulation as to devaluation exists or is applicable the following clause to apply:

If the currency in which freight and charges are quoted is devalued between the date of the freight agreement and the date when the freight and charges are paid, then all freight and charges shall be automatically and immediately increased in proportion to the extent of the devaluation of the said currency.

(3) For the purpose of verifying the freight basis, the Carrier reserves the right to have the contents of containers, trailers or similar articles of transport inspected in order to ascertain the weight, measurement, value, or nature of the goods.

20. **Lien.** The Carrier shall have a lien on the goods for any amount due under this contract and for the costs of recovering the same, and may enforce such lien in any reasonable manner.

VI. MISCELLANEOUS PROVISIONS

21. **General Average.**

(1) General Average to be adjusted at any port or place at the Carrier's option, and to be settled according to the York-Antwerp Rules 1974, this covering all goods, whether carried on or under deck. The Amended Jason Clause as approved by BIMCO to be considered as incorporated herein.

(2) Such security including a cash deposit as the Carrier may deem sufficient to cover the estimated contribution of the goods and any salvage and special charges thereon, shall, if required, be submitted to the Carrier prior to delivery of the goods.

22. **Dangerous Goods.**

(1) When the Merchant hands goods of a dangerous nature to the Carrier, he shall inform him in writing of the exact nature of the danger and indicate, if necessary, the precautions to be taken.

(2) Goods of a dangerous nature which the Carrier did not know were dangerous, may, at any time or place, be unloaded, destroyed, or rendered harmless, without compensation; further the Merchant shall be liable for all expenses, loss or damage arising out of their handing over for carriage or of their carriage.

(3) If any goods shipped with the knowledge of the Carrier as to their dangerous nature shall become a danger to the ship or cargo, they may in like manner be landed at any place or destroyed or rendered innocuous by the Carrier without liability on the part of the Carrier except to General Average, if any.

23. **Both-to-Blame Collision Clause.**

The Both-to-Blame Collision Clause as adopted by BIMCO to be considered incorporated herein.

24. **Shipper-packed Containers, etc.**

(1) If a container has not been filled, packed or stowed by the Carrier, the Carrier shall not be liable for any loss of or damage to its contents and the Merchant shall cover any loss or expense incurred by the Carrier, if such loss, damage or expense has been caused by

(a) negligent filling, packing or stowing of the container;

(b) the contents being unsuitable for carriage in container; or

(c) the unsuitability or defective condition of the container unless the container has been supplied by the Carrier and the unsuitability or defective condition would not have been apparent upon reasonable inspection at or prior to the time when the container was filled, packed or stowed.

(2) The provisions of paragraph (1) of this clause also apply with respect to trailers, transportable tanks, flats and pallets which have not been filled, packed or stowed by the Carrier.

(b) Received bill of lading
This arises where the word 'shipped' does not appear on the bill of
lading. It merely confirms that the goods have been handed over to
the shipowner and are in his custody. The cargo may be in his dock
warehouse/transit shed or even inland. The bill has therefore not
the same meaning as a 'shipped' bill and the buyer under a CIF
contract need not accept such a bill for ultimate financial
settlement unless provision has been made in the contract.
Forwarding agents will invariably avoid handling 'received bills'
for their clients unless special circumstances obtain. (It is often
termed Received for shipment bill of lading.)

(c) Through bills of lading
In many cases it is necessary to employ two or more carriers to get
the goods to their final destination. The on-carriage may be either
by a second vessel or by a different form of transport (e.g. to
destinations in the interior of Canada). In such cases it would be
very complicated and more expensive if the shipper had to arrange
on-carriage himself by employing an agent at the point of
transhipment. The carrier who issues the through bill of lading/
through transport document acts as a principal only during the
carriage of his own vessel(s) and as an agent only at all other times.
Hence the liabilities and responsibilities are spread over several
carriers and the Merchant is in contract with different carriers
under different conditions at different stages of carriage. Shipping
companies therefore issue bills of lading which cover the whole
transit and the shipper deals only with the first carrier. This type of
bill enables a through rate to be quoted and is growing in
popularity with the development of containerization. Special bills
of lading have to be prepared for such through-consigned cargo.

(d) Stale bills of lading
It is important that the bill of lading is available at the port of
destination before the goods arrive, or failing this, at the same
time. Bills presented to the consignee or his bank after the goods
are due at the port are said to be stale. A cargo cannot normally be
delivered by the shipowner without the bill of lading, and the late
arrival of this all-important document may have undesirable
consequences such as warehouse rent, etc.

(e) Groupage bill of lading
Forwarding agents are permitted to 'group' together particular

compatible consignments from individual consignors to various consignees, situated usually in the same destination country/area, and despatch them as one consignment. The shipowner will issue a groupage bill of lading, whilst the forwarding agent, who cannot hand to his principals the shipowners' bill of lading, will issue to the individual shippers a Certificate of Shipment often called 'house bills of lading'. At the destination, another agent working in close liaison with the agent forwarding the cargo will break bulk the consignment and distribute the goods to the various con-signees. This practice is on the increase, usually involving the use of containers and particularly evident in the continental trade and deep-sea container services. It will doubtless increase with containerization development and is ideal to the shipper who has small quantities of goods available for export. Advantages of groupage include less packing; lower insurance premiums; usually quicker transits; less risk of damage and pilferage; and lower rates when compared with such cargo being despatched as an individual parcel/consignment.

(f) Transhipment bill of lading
This type is issued usually by shipping companies when there is no direct service between two ports, but when the shipowner is prepared to tranship the cargo at an intermediate port at his expense.

(g) Clean bills of lading
Each bill of lading states 'in apparent good order and condition', which of course refers to the cargo. If this statement is not modified by the shipowner, the bill of lading is regarded as 'clean' or 'unclaused'. By issuing clean bills of lading the shipowner admits his full liability of the cargo described in the bill under the law and his contract. This type is much favoured by banks for financial settlement purposes.

(h) Claused bills of lading
If the shipowner does not agree with any of the statements made in the bill of lading he will add a clause to this effect, thereby causing the bill of lading to be termed as 'unclean', 'foul', 'dirty' or 'claused'. There are many recurring types of such clauses including inadequate packaging; unprotected machinery; second-hand cases;

wet or stained cartons; damaged crates; two cartons missing, etc. The clause 'shipped on deck at owner's risk' may thus be considered to be a clause under this heading. This type of bill of lading is usually unacceptable to a bank.

(i) Negotiable bills of lading
If the words 'or his or their assigns' are contained in the bill of lading, it is negotiable. There are, however, variations in this terminology, for example the word 'bearer' may be inserted, or another party stated in the preamble to the phrase 'Bills of lading may be negotiable by endorsement of transfer'.

(j) Non-negotiable bills of lading
When the words 'or his or their assigns' are deleted from the bills of lading, the bill is regarded as non-negotiable. The effect of this deletion is that the consignee (or other named party) cannot transfer the property or goods by transfer of the bills. This particular type is seldom found and will normally apply when goods are shipped on a non-commercial basis, such as household effects.

(k) Container bills of lading
Containers are now playing an increasing role in international shipping and the container bill of lading – the combined transport document – is becoming more common in use. They cover the goods from port to port or from inland point of departure to inland points of destination. It may be an inland clearance depot or container base. Undoubtedly, to the shipper, the most useful type of bill of lading is the clean, negotiable 'through bill', as it enables the goods to be forwarded to the point of destination under one document, although much international trade is based on free-on-board (FOB) or cost, insurance, freight (CIF) contracts. With regard to the latter, the seller has no further interest in the movement of the goods once they reach their port of destination.

(l) Straight bill of lading
This is an American term used to describe the sea waybill.

(m) Combined transport bill of lading
This is a bill of lading issued by a combined transport operator that

covers the multimodal transport on a door to door basis in one contract of carriage. The combined transport operator undertakes to perform in his own name the performance of the combined transport. Hence it is issued by a carrier who contracts as a principal with the merchant to effect a combined transport. It is ideal for container movements. An example of a combined transport bill of lading negotiable is found on page 257 (see Fig. 12.1).

A development in recent years emerging from combined transport operation is the non vessel operating carrier (NVOC) or non vessel operating common carrier (NVOCC). It may arise in a container (FCL or LCL) movement or trailer transit. In such a situation the carrier issues Bills of Lading for the carriage of goods on ships which he neither owns nor operates. It is usually a freight forwarder issuing a 'house' bill of lading for a container or trailer movement, or if the trailer movement is in UK/Continental trade a CMR consignment note. A carrier defined by maritime law is one offering an international cargo transport service.

12.5 FUNCTION OF THE BILL OF LADING

From our study of the bill of lading, it will be appropriate to record the four functions of this document. Broadly it is receipt for the goods shipped, a transferable document of title to the goods thereby enabling the holder to demand the cargo, evidence of the terms of the contract of affreightment but not the actual contract, and a quasi-negotiable instrument.

Once the shipper or his agent becomes aware of the sailing schedules of a particular trade, through the medium of sailing cards or some form of advertisement, he communicates with the shipowner with a view to booking cargo space on the vessel or container. Provided satisfactory arrangements have been concluded, the shipper forwards the cargo. At this stage, it is important to note that the shipper always makes the offer by forwarding the consignment, whilst the shipowner either accepts or refuses it. Furthermore, it is the shipper's duty, or that of his agent, to supply details of the consignment; normally this is done by completing the shipping company's form of bill of lading, and the shipping company then signs the number of copies requested.

The goods are signed for by the vessel's chief officer or ship's agent, and in some trades this receipt is exchanged for the bill of lading. If the cargo is in good condition and everything is in order, no endorsement will be made on the document, and it can be termed a clean bill of lading. Conversely, if the goods are damaged or a portion of the consignment is missing, the document will be suitably endorsed by the Master or his agent, and the bill of lading will be considered 'claused' or 'unclean'.

Bills of lading are made out in sets, and the number varies according to the trade. Generally it is three or four – one of which will probably be forwarded immediately, and another by a later mail in case the first is lost or delayed. In some trades, coloured bills of lading are used, to distinguish the original (signed) bills from the copies which are purely for record purposes.

Where the shipper had sold the goods on letter of credit terms established through a bank, or when he wishes to obtain payment of his invoice before the consignee obtains the goods, he will pass the full set of original bills to his bank, who will in due course arrange presentation to the consignee against payment.

The shipowner or his agent at the port of destination will require one original bill of lading to be presented to him before the goods are handed over. Furthermore, he will normally require payment of any freight due, should this not have been paid at the port of shipment. When one of a set of bills of lading has been presented to the shipping company, the other bills in the set lose their value.

In the event of the bill of lading being lost or delayed in transit, the shipping company will allow delivery of the goods to the person claiming to be the consignee, if he gives a letter of indemnity; this is normally countersigned by a bank, and relieves the shipping company of any liability should another person eventually come along with the actual bill of lading.

The following items are common discrepancies found in bills of lading when being processed and should be avoided:

(a) Document not presented in full sets when requested.

(b) Alterations not authenticated by an official of the shipping company or their agents.

(c) The bill of lading is not clean when presented in as much that it is endorsed regarding damaged condition of the specified cargo or inadequate packing thereby making it unacceptable to a bank for financial settlement purposes.

(d) The document is not endorsed 'on board' when so required.

(e) The 'on-board' endorsement is not signed or initialled by the carrier or agent and likewise not dated.

(f) The bill of lading is not 'blank' endorsed if drawn to order.

(g) The document fails to indicate whether 'freight prepaid' as stipulated in the credit arrangements, i.e. C and F or CIF contracts.

(h) The bill of lading is not marked 'freight prepaid' when freight charges are included in the invoice.

(i) The bill of lading is made out 'to order' when the letter of credit stipulates 'direct to consignee' or vice versa.

(j) The document is dated later than the latest shipping date specified in the credit.

(k) It is not presented within 21 days after date of shipment or such lesser time as prescribed in the letter of credit.

(l) The bill of lading details merchandise other than that prescribed.

(m) The rate at which freight is calculated, and the total amount is not shown when credit requires such data to be given.

(n) Cargo has been shipped 'on deck' and not placed in the ship's hold. Basically 'on-deck' claused bills of lading are not acceptable when clean on-board bills of lading are required.

(o) Shipment made from a port or to a destination contrary to that stipulated.

(p) Other types of bills of lading presented although not specifically authorized. For example, charter party to forwarding agents bills of lading are not accepted unless expressly allowed in the letter of credit.

It is appropriate to record that Buyers (importers) who normally call for a Shipped on Board Bill of Lading may consider it more advantageous to consider whether they need to include in their instructions the usual 'Shipped on Board Bill of Lading' wording, or whether it might be more appropriate to call for a Combined Transport Bill of Lading and omit all reference to 'On Board'. This would in no way prejudice their interest, and would enable the necessary documents to be issued more quickly as there would be no delay awaiting confirmation of shipment on board.

12.6 INTERNATIONAL CONVENTION CONCERNING THE CARRIAGE OF GOODS BY RAIL (CIM)

Our study of bills of lading would not be complete without examining the CIM and CMR documentation – the latter being dealt with in the next section.

The International Convention concerning the Carriage of Goods by Rail (CIM) has existed in some form since 1893. It permits the carriage of goods by rail under one document – consignment note (not negotiable) under a common code of conditions applicable to 34 countries mainly situated in Europe and Mediterranean areas. It embraces the maritime portion of the transit subject to it being conveyed on shipping lines as listed under the Convention. Advantages of the system embrace through-rates under common code of conditions; simplified documentation/accountancy; flexibility of freight payment; no intermediate handling usually or customs examination in transit countries; through transits; and minimum documentation.

The Convention is revised from time to time to reflect modern needs and the current one is the COTIF/CIM Convention of 10th May 1985, which contains a revised version of the CIM uniform rules of the international carriage of goods by rail.

12.7 CONVENTION ON THE CONTRACT FOR THE INTERNATIONAL CARRIAGE OF GOODS BY ROAD (CMR)

The International Convention concerning the Carriage of Goods by Road (CMR) came into force in the UK in October 1967. It permits the carriage of goods by road under one consignment note under a common code of conditions applicable to 26 countries. These include Austria, Belgium, Bulgaria, Czechoslovakia, Denmark, Finland, France, the Federal Republic of Germany, Greece, Hungary, Italy, Luxembourg, the Netherlands, Norway, Poland, Portugal, Romania, Spain, Sweden, Switzerland, the United Kingdom, West Germany and Yugoslavia. Additionally, by order in Council, the convention has been extended to cover the Isle of Man, the Isle of Guernsey and Gibraltar. It applies to all international carriage of goods by road for reward to or from a contracting party. It does not apply to traffic between the UK and the Republic of Ireland.

This convention which has established the carrier's liability to SDR 8.33 per kg and the documentation to be used in respect of goods to be carried by road vehicles between two countries has facilitated the development of Ro/Ro UK/Europe traffic. The statutory provisions are embodied in the Carriage of Goods by Road Act 1965 as amended by the Carriage by Air and Road Act 1979.

12.8 COMBINED TRANSPORT

In the 1970s an attempt was made to draft a convention to cover loss or damage to goods carried under a Combined Transport Document. It was known variously at different stages as the Tokyo–Rome rules, the Tokyo rules, and the TCM convention. Regretfully it failed to gain adequate support and subsequently the International Chamber of Commerce revised particular elements of it, with the result the final draft was published as the 'ICC rules for a Combined Transport Document'.

However, UNCTAD was unhappy with this situation and decided to intervene with an international convention to govern Combined Transport. It was finally adopted at an international conference in Geneva in May 1980 as the 'United Nations Convention on International Multi-modal Transport of Goods' or as more commonly known 'UNCTAD MMO convention'.

Like the Hamburg Rules, if introduced, it is likely to increase the carrier insurance costs which will probably result in increased freight rates without any corresponding reduction in cargo insurance premiums. Some thirty countries need to ratify it before acceptance and by the autumn of 1987 it had the support of only four countries.

12.9 COMMON SHORT FORM BILL OF LADING AND COMMON SHORT FORM SEA WAYBILL

The use of a negotiable bill of lading which has to be surrendered to the carrier at destination in order to obtain delivery of the goods is traditional – but not without disadvantages. The document has to follow the goods, and often for commercial or financial reasons

1 'Received for carriage as above in apparent good order and condition,
2 unless otherwise stated hereon, the goods described in the above
3 particulars.

4 The contract evidenced by this Short Form Bill of Lading is subject to
5 the exceptions, limitations, conditions and liberties (including those
6 relating to pre-carriage and on-carriage) set out in the Carrier's
7 Standard Conditions applicable to the voyage covered by this Short
8 Form Bill of Lading and operative on its date of issue.

9 If the carriage is one where the provisions of the Hague Rules
10 contained in the International Convention for unification of certain
11 rules relating to Bills of Lading dated Brussels on 25 August 1924,
12 as amended by the protocol signed at Brussels on 23 February 1968,
13 (the Hague Visby Rules) are compulsorily applicable under Article X,
14 the said Standard Conditions contain or shall be deemed to contain a
15 Clause giving effect to the Hague Visby Rules. Otherwise, except as
16 provided below, the said Standard Conditions contain or shall be
17 deemed to contain a Clause giving effect to the provisions of the
18 Hague Rules.

19 The Carrier hereby agrees that to the extent of any inconsistency the
20 said Clause shall prevail over the exceptions, limitations, conditions
21 and liberties set out in the Standard Conditions in respect of any
22 period to which the Hague Rules or the Hague Visby Rules by their
23 terms apply unless the Standard Conditions expressly provide otherwise
24 neither the Hague Rules nor the Hague Visby Rules shall apply to this
25 contract where the goods carried hereunder consist of live animals or cargo
26 which by this contract is stated as being carried on deck and is so carried.

27 Notwithstanding anything contained in the said Standard Conditions, the
28 term Carrier in this Short Form Bill of Lading shall mean the Carrier
29 named on the front thereof.

30 A copy of the Carrier's said Standard Conditions applicable hereto may
31 be inspected or will be supplied on request at the office of the
32 Carrier or the Carrier's Principal Agents.

33 In witness whereof the number of original Bills of Lading stated below
34 have been signed, all of this tenor and date one of which being accomplished,
35 the other to stand void'.

Fig. 12.2 Incorporation clause for the common short form bill of lading
and common short form sea waybill.

passes through a variety of hands, resulting in the goods being held
up at destination pending arrival of the document, and thereby
expenses and additional risks are incurred and customer goodwill
is possibly lost.

In 1979 the common short form bill of lading was introduced and replaced the traditional shipping company 'long form' bills. It is identical in legal and practical terms to the traditional bills, but is more simple and can be used with any shipping line.

The document covers shipper/forwarder and provides bills from port to port and through-transport including container bills of lading. It does not cover combined transport bills of lading which are almost always completed by computer by the combined transport operator.

The common short form bill of lading is fully negotiable and the normal bill of lading lodgement and presentation procedures remain unchanged. However, instead of the mass of small print on the reverse, there is an approved 'short form' clause on the face which incorporates carriers' standard conditions with full legal effect.

The common short form bill of lading has the following salient features:

(a) It is approved by SITPRO, GCBS, HM Customs and Excise, insurance underwriters, ECGD and IBAP. It may be used by shippers and freight forwarders and presented for signature to the carrier or his authorized agents, after a perusal and acceptance of the carriers' standard terms and conditions to which the incorporation clause in the short form bill of lading refers.

(b) It is suitable for outward shipments from the UK involving 'through' transit, or 'port-to-port' carriage of cargo for both 'break bulk' and 'unit loads' of all types traditionally covered by 'long form' bills of lading.

(c) It is based upon an internationally accepted layout adopted by the United Nations. Such widespread acceptance of its format facilitates fast and accurate recording, processing, transmission and receipt of data relating to the movement of cargo.

(d) As confirmed by the ICC it is acceptable within the 'uniform customs and practice for documentary credits'. (ICC Brochure No 290; article 19(b) refers.)

(e) It is a document recommended by GCBS for use of all outward shipments from the UK and particularly by all UK shipper/carriers and their conference associates.

(f) It is a document of title under which the contracting carrier undertakes to deliver the subject goods against surrender of an original document.

(g) It is a 'received-for-carriage' bill with provision for endorsement evidencing goods shipped on board when so required.

(h) It is suitable for conventional and through-liner services irrespective of whether the vessel is chartered or owned by the contracting carrier. (Use of the form is not currently available for goods carried by combined transport operators.)

(i) It is described as a 'short form' document because of the use of an abridged standard clause on the face of the document which incorporates the conditions of carriage of the contracting carrier (see Fig. 12.2). The change eliminates the mass of small print on the reverse side of bills of lading without affecting the status of the document or rights and obligations of any interested party.

(j) It is a document fully aligned to the SITPRO 'master' with the opportunity to complete the bill of lading from such a document without any additional typing.

(k) It is an aid to achieve lower stationery costs through a reduced need to hold a variety of stocks of long form bills of lading and with its individual carrier's name and conditions plus the elimination of the risk of using obsolescent forms together with attendant complications.

A specimen of a common short form bill of lading is found in Fig. 12.3.

The General Council of British Shipping with the co-operation of SITPRO has also developed the concept of a non-negotiable type of transport document – termed a common short form sea waybill – in place of the negotiable traditional bill of lading. Its basic feature is that it provides for delivery to the consignee named in it without surrender of the transport document.

The common short form sea waybill has the following salient features which are similar in many ways to the common short form bill of lading:

(a) It is a common document upon which the shipper adds the name of the contracting carrier to be used.

(b) It is a non-negotiable document consigned to a named consignee and not requiring production to obtain possession of the goods at destination – a salient advantage thereby obviating delay of release of goods at destination.

Shipper		COMMON SHORT FORM BILL OF LADING	UK Customs Assigned No.	B/L No.

Shipper's Reference

F/Agent's Reference

Consignee (if 'Order' state Notify Party and Address)

Name of Carrier

The contract evidenced by this Short Form Bill of Lading is subject to the exceptions, limitations, conditions and liberties (including those relating to pre-carriage and on-carriage) set out in the Carrier's Standard Conditions applicable to the voyage covered by this Short Form Bill of Lading and operative on its date of issue.

If the carriage is one where the provisions of the Hague Rules contained in the International Convention for unification of certain rules relating to Bills of Lading dated Brussels on 25th August 1924 as amended by the Protocol signed at Brussels on 23rd February 1968 (the Hague Visby Rules) are compulsorily applicable under Article X, the said Standard Conditions contain or shall be deemed to contain a Clause giving effect to the Hague Visby Rules. Otherwise except as provided below, the said Standard Conditions contain or shall be deemed to contain a Clause giving effect to the provisions of the Hague Rules.

The Carrier hereby agrees that to the extent of any inconsistency the said Clause shall prevail over the exceptions limitations conditions and liberties set out in the Standard Conditions in respect of any period to which the Hague Rules or the Hague Visby Rules by their terms apply. Unless the Standard Conditions expressly provide otherwise neither the Hague Rules nor the Hague Visby Rules shall apply to this contract where the goods carried hereunder consist of live animals or cargo which by this contract is stated as being carried on deck and is so carried.

Notwithstanding anything contained in the said Standard Conditions the term Carrier in this Short Form Bill of Lading shall mean the Carrier named on the front thereof.

A copy of the Carrier's said Standard Conditions applicable hereto may be inspected or will be supplied on request at the office of the Carrier or the Carrier's Principal Agents.

Notify Party and Address (leave blank if stated above)

Pre-Carriage by*	Place of Receipt by Pre-Carrier*

Vessel	Port of Loading

Port of Discharge	Place of Delivery by On-Carrier*

Marks and Nos.	Container No.	Number and kind of packages: Description of Goods	Gross Weight	Measurement

*Applicable only when document used as a Through Bill of Lading

Particulars declared by Shipper

Freight Details: Charges etc.

RECEIVED FOR CARRIAGE as above in apparent good order and condition, unless otherwise stated hereon, the goods described in the above particulars.

IN WITNESS whereof the number of original Bills of Lading stated below have been signed, all of this tenor and date, one of which being accomplished the others to stand void.

Ocean Freight Payable at

Place and Date of Issue

Number of Original BsL

Signature for Carrier; Carrier's Principal Place of Business

GCBS
CSF
BL
1979

710

Printed by Systemforms Ltd 01-505 6125-6
Authorised and Licensed by the
General Council of British Shipping © 1979

Fig. 12.3 Common short form bill of lading.

(c) It is a received-for-shipment document, with an option for use as a shipped document.

(d) It is an aid to achieve lower stationery costs through a reduced need to hold stocks of individual carriers bills, and with its individual carrier's name and conditions plus the elimination of the risk of using obsolescent forms together with attendant complications.

(e) It is a document fully aligned to the SITPRO 'master' with the opportunity to complete the sea waybill from such a document without any additional typing.

(f) It is described as a 'short form' document because of the use of an abridged standard clause on the face of the document which incorporates the conditions of carriage of the contracting carrier (see Fig 12.2). The change eliminates the need to reprint documents to accommodate changes and conditions.

(g) It facilitates earlier release of the goods – if received for shipment – and thereby reduces delays associated with negotiability. Moreover, it helps the speedier flow of goods to the consignee. One must bear in mind the named consignee is not required to produce the sea waybill to obtain possession of the goods at destination.

(h) It is approved by SITPRO, GCBS, HM Customs and Excise, insurance underwriters, ECGD, and IBAP. It may be used by shippers and freight forwarders and presented for signature to the carrier or his authorized agents, after a perusal and acceptance of the carrier's standard terms and conditions to which the incorporation clause in the sea waybill refers.

(i) It is suitable for outward shipments from the UK involving 'through' transit, or 'port-to-port' carriage of cargo for both 'break bulk' and 'unit loads' of all types. Moreover, it is suitable for conventional and through-liner services, irrespective of whether the vessel is chartered or owned by the carrier.

(j) It is based upon an internationally accepted layout adopted by the United Nations. Such widespread acceptance of its format facilitates fast and accurate recording, processing, transmission and receipt of data relating to the movement of cargo.

(k) It is not a document of title. Hence the shipper retains his waybill as a receipt for the goods and delivery is made to the nominated consignee at destination upon proof of identity.

(l) It is evidence of the contract with the shipper only so that he remains in control and can vary instructions to the carrier all the time that the goods are in transit, unless he waives this control with a 'NODISP' (no disposal) clause on the face of the waybill.

The commercial and financial feasibility of using the waybill clearly rests with the shipper/consignee and is dependent upon the type of trade transaction involved. The waybill is ideal for use in the following circumstances:

(a) House-to-house shipments such as shipments between associated companies or branches of multinational companies where no documentary credit transaction is involved.

(b) Open account sales which arise where goods are shipped to an agent for sale at destination on an account sale basis.

(c) Transactions between companies where the security of a documentary credit transaction is not required perhaps because of trust stemming from a long trading relationship or an alternative basis of payment being arranged.

The point at which sea waybills are released will depend upon whether the document is 'received for shipment' or 'shipped on board'. In signing waybills, the carrier or his agent is required to insert the carrier's cable address within the signature or date stamp.

If a received-for-shipment document was issued and cargo was subsequently short-shipped or a carrier's clause required (for example, to indicate that damage was sustained whilst the goods were on the quay) then a qualification report should be issued to the shipper, consignee and those concerned within the carrier's organization; information concerning such reports should also be made available to insurers on request. Use of the 'shipped' option would, however, obviate the need for a qualification report, and, in such circumstances the normal bill of lading procedures would apply.

If a 'shipped-on-board' document was issued, then the provision of the 'shipped' option should be in a manner which if the document was to be presented under a documentary credit, will satisfy 'Uniform Customs and Practice for Documentary Credits' 1983 revision. This refers to a procedure whereby waybills can be endorsed to specify that the goods mentioned have been loaded on board a named vessel or shipped on a named vessel, the loading-on-board date being specified.

The specific requirement to be met is that of Article 20(b) of the Uniform Customs and Practice for Documentary Credits, i.e. 'loading on board a named vessel or shipment on a named vessel, may be evidenced either by a Bill of Lading bearing wording indicating loading on board a named vessel or shipment on a named vessel, or by means of a notation to that effect on the bill of lading signed or initialled and dated by the carrier or his agent, and the date of this notation shall be regarded as the date of loading on board the named vessel or shipment on the named vessel'.

Once released by the carrier, and returned to the shipper forwarding agent, the waybill should simply be retained. However, certain carriers may recommend that the waybill be presented to the carrier's agent at the port of delivery as a record that the transaction has been completed.

The consignee and notify party should receive an arrival notice (which can be a copy of the waybill) giving instructions for the collection of cargo and indicates that no bill of lading has been issued.

The cargo should be released by the carrier on surrender of the arrival notice or some other means of identification, subject to normal arrangements as to the payment of freight and charges (whether prepaid or collect).

In America a waybill is referred to as straight bill of lading and shows a nominated consignee and is marked 'non (or not) negotiable'.

12.10 STANDARD SHIPPING NOTE

In 1975 a Standard Shipping Note (SSN) was introduced in the UK. It is available for use for the delivery of FCL and LCL goods to the CFS or CB or for uncontainerable items direct to the terminals. It is a six-part document and fully aligned to the SITPRO master.

It is used when delivering cargo to any British port, container base or other freight terminal. It must accompany the goods to the receiving berth/dock or container base etc., or be lodged at the receiving authority's designated office before arrival of the goods for shipment according to local port practice. Only goods for shipment to one port of discharge on one sailing and sometimes relating to only one bill of lading may be grouped on one shipping note.

The SSN contains the following information:

(a) name and address of the exporter/shipper;
(b) vehicle booking refence, when relevant, as issued by the receiving authority;
(c)   (i) Customs' reference;
       (ii) exporter's reference;
       (iii) forwarding agent's reference;
(d) shipping company's booking reference where issued;
(e) details of company responsible for FOB/receiving authority's export charges;
(f) name of shipping line or combined transport operator;
(g) name and address of forwarding agent or merchant;
(h)   (i) ship's receiving date(s);
       (ii) berth and dock/container base etc;
(i) ship's name and port of loading;
(j) port of discharge and, for less than container loads, final destination depot;
(k) name of receiving authority, e.g. port authority, shipping company, container base, to whom the shipping note is addressed;
(l) port scale of charges;
(m)   (i) marks and numbers of packages in full. With regard to container shipments details of container owner's marks, serial numbers, and seal number to be given;
       (ii) number and kind of packages;
       (iii) description of goods;
       (iv) package dimensions in centimetres;
(n)   (i) gross weight in metric units for each item;
       (ii) total gross weight;
(o)   (i) cubic measurement of packages in cubic metres;
       (ii) total cubic measurement;
(p) Indication of cargo status, i.e.
       (i) HM Customs free status;
       (ii) pre-entry (bonding or drawback formalities etc.);
       (iii) hazardous or other special stowage cargo;
(q)   (i) name of company/telephone number;
       (ii) name and status of person preparing the note;
       (iii) Place and date of issue.

Overall the use of the SSN may vary according to individual port practices. The reader is also recommended to study Chapter

12 of *The Elements of Export Practice* which deals with export documentation.

12.11 GOLD CLAUSE AGREEMENT

The Gold clause agreement is an agreement between British shipowners and British and foreign insurers and cargo interest designed to preclude the need to test the Gold clause in the Hague rules as enacted in the Carriage of Goods by Sea Act 1924.

It was drafted because the limitation of liability in the Hague rules had devalued due to inflation. It provided an agreed basis of operation between the signatories on limitation of liability to preclude litigation on the interpretation of £100 as in the UK Act: sterling or gold? It was originally drafted between British insurers and cargo owners' associations but subsequently whilst few non-British shipowners have become parties to the agreement, many foreign insurers and merchants have signed it.

It was signed in 1950 by the drafters, the P & I clubs signing to signify approval and support but signifying that members' commitment was a prerequisite, so that shipowners were free to take up or reject the agreement severally.

The original provisions embraced the following:

(a) Shipowners would agree to automatic extensions of time from one to two years provided (i) no undue delay in prosecuting claim (ii) notice of claim with best particulars given within 12 months.

(b) Shipowners further agreed to interpret the limitation to parties to the agreement as £200 per package or unit which was revised to £400 from 1 July 1977.

(c) Shipowners also agreed on qualifying voyages to apply the Hague rules whether contractually incorporated into the bill of lading or not, and in return insurers/merchants agreed that they would use best endeavours to preclude claims against shipowners in foreign jurisdictions.

Despite the inauguration of the Hague–Visby rules, the Gold clause agreement continues to operate particularly because of the importance to both parties relative to items (a) and the latter part of (c). It is applicable only to claims arising during the sea transit under the Hague rules.

12.12 LIABILITY OF THE CARRIER

The liability of the carrier under any of the sea carriage conventions examined in this chapter are subject to the overriding application of the provisions of the Merchant Shipping Acts relating to the limitation of liability. The current Act is the Merchant Shipping Act 1979 which implemented the 1976 International Convention on limitation of liability for Maritime claims with effect from 1 December, 1986. This new convention involves the following increased levels of limitation:

(a) In respect of loss of life or personal injury (other than passengers)

      (i) 330 000 units of account (SDRs) for a vessel with a tonnage not exceeding 500 tonnes,

      (ii) For a vessel with a tonnage in excess thereof, in addition:

for each tonne from 501 to 3000	500 SDRs
for each tonne from 3001 to 30 000	333 SDRs
for each tonne from 30 001 to 70 000	250 SDRs
for each tonne in excess of 70 000	167 SDRs

(b) In respect of any other claims:

      (i) 167 000 SDRs for a vessel not exceeding 500 tonnes

      (ii) For a ship with a tonnage in excess thereof, in addition:

for each tonne from 501 to 30 000	167 SDRs
for each tonne from 30 001 to 70 000	125 SDRs
for each tonne in excess of 70 000	83 SDRs

By the autumn of 1987 the 1976 convention had been ratified by the following Nations: Bahamas, Benin, Denmark, Finland, France, Japan, Liberia, Norway, Poland, Spain, Sweden, UK and the Yemen Arab Republic.

CHAPTER 13

Cargoes

13.1 CARGO STOWAGE/PACKING OVERVIEW

Cargo stowage is the process of accommodating an item of merchandise in a transport unit with a view to its arrival in a mercantile condition and has regard to the nature of the transit, any likely hazards and the most economic conveyance of the cargo.

As we progress through the 1990s the significance of cargo stowage and packing will grow in international trade. It is an area where cost effective cargo stowage can aid overseas market development through lower distribution cost. Factors influencing such developments are given below and reflect the changing pattern of international trade distribution.

(a)   The development of the LCL and NVOCC transport mode requires more skill in stowage of compatible cargo.

(b)   New technology involving computers and packing techniques will add a new dimension to cargo stowage.

(c)   More pressure is being placed on shippers to reduce their distribution unit cost. This can be realized through more productive stowage techniques and more sophisticated skills to devise in formulating the stowage plan.

(d)   The transport unit especially in the area of combined transport operation is tending to become of greater capacity as found in the trailer and container. This will provide more skills for effective stowage.

(e)   As world trade develops especially in the growth market of consumer goods, it will intensify the competition in the market place to have/receive quality goods in an undamaged condition. This requires more advanced stowage/packing techniques.

(f)   Technology is developing rapidly in international destinations. New equipment is constantly being introduced and existing equipment improved. Moreover, new regulations are being adopted continuously. Furthermore the range of equipment is being so designed to reduce packing specification/cost and thereby lower distribution cost. For example the range of container types introduced in the past ten years have all striven towards improved quality international distribution. For example the purpose-built ISO container has encouraged bulk shipment thereby eliminating packing needs as found in cement, fertilizers, and so on.

(g) The development of combined transport operation has encouraged the door to door transit with no transhipment. Again, packing cost/needs are much reduced.

(h) The producer should ideally design the product with regard to making transportation relatively easy and so capable of being lifted and secured safely, clear factory doors and entrances, and not exceeding the weight or size restriction of transit.

The foregoing must be reconciled when examining cargo stowage and packing in the 1990s. Future needs will involve better co-operation/consultation by all interested parties in the transit with the principal carrier and buyer taking the leads. The exporter must ensure the production process/packing specification is so designed to make the best use possible of the transport unit capacity available both in cubic and weight terms.

13.2 STOWAGE OF CARGO

The ultimate responsibility for the stowage of cargo rests with the Master. In practice, whilst the Master retains overall responsibility, the supervision of stowage of cargo normally is delegated to the chief officer. His task is to see that neither the ship nor her cargo is damaged. Furthermore, he is responsible for safe handling, loading, stowage and carriage, including custody of the cargo throughout the voyage. Above all, he must ensure that the safety of the ship is not imperilled by the carriage of goods. His aim must be to have the cargo evenly distributed throughout the ship, to ensure her general stability. In regard to container ships computers are used to formulate the stowage plan. In practice, it is usual for the ship to be loaded a little deeper aft, to improve the vessel's movement through the water. This is called 'trimmed by the stern', the term 'trim' referring to the difference in draught between the stem and stern. A vessel trimmed by the bow refers to the difference in draught between the stern and bow. It is regarded as an unseaworthy vessel. A ship with a centre of gravity too low will be stiff and consequently apt to strain heavily in rough weather. Conversely, a ship with a centre of gravity too high will be tender and inclined to roll, thereby creating an unstable vessel.

Basically, there are two types of cargo; bulk and general cargo. Bulk cargoes present little difficulty in stowage, as they tend to be conveyed in specialized vessels between two ports, and are often loaded and discharged by modern technology. Cargoes such as grain, coal, copra and similar cargoes, are usually carried in bulk, and must be adequately ventilated during the voyage, as they are liable to spontaneous combustion.

With general cargo, the problem is more difficult, and calls for much greater skill when shipped in a loose condition and conveyed in cargo liners, provided with numerous decks, including 'tween decks, which act as pigeon holds to facilitate stowage. Most liner cargoes are conveyed in containers, often in consolidated consignments, whilst in the UK/European trade, a substantial volume of traffic is conveyed by international road haulage – again usually under consolidated arrangements of a throughout road trailer movement. The position is made more difficult with 'tween deck tonnage by the variety of cargoes conveyed, each with their own characteristics such as fragility, tainting, sweating, etc. Hence such vessels are relatively few in number and have been replaced by container ships. This causes many problems to the stevedore in charge of the discharging and loading, and responsible to the Master. Nevertheless, he is assisted by a stowage plan, i.e. an outline plan of the ship upon which is entered the stowed position of all cargo. It is desirable that this plan should be in the hands of the stevedore at the discharging port before the ship commences to unload, or preferably before arrival, so that discharge and shed stowage arrangements (bedding out) can be made in advance.

In regard to container tonnage it involves a mammoth task of extensive pre-planning to ensure up to 3500 TEUs are unloaded and loaded from the vessel operating on a quick port turn-round time. Some containers would be locally customs cleared through the port whilst an increasing number would travel by rail or road to an ICD or CFS outside the port or in an industrial centre (see p. 105). It involves co-ordination with customs, port authorities, rail/road/lighterage operators, stevedoring personnel, agents and so on. Computers play a major role in the planning and operation of such a task in a modern port and shipping company.

A similar criterion applies to the consolidated consignment conveyed under international road haulage arrangements.

There are four main factors to consider in the stowage of cargo:

1. The best possible use should be made of the ship's deadweight and cubic capacity. Hence, broken stowage, which is space wasted in the ship by cargo of irregular-shaped packages, or irregularity of cargo spaces, should be kept to a minimum consistent with the general stability of the ship. Generally 10 to 15% of the total cubic capacity is allowed for broken stowage. Thus, as far as practicable, full use should be made of the cubic capacity of the vessel, with a view to ensuring that the ship is down to her marks when she sails. If there is not an even distribution of cargo when the ship sails, with no compensating ballast, hogging or sagging may arise. Hogging arises when most of the cargo's weight has been stowed in the forward and after holds of the vessel, causing the two ends of the ship to drop lower than the amidship portion. Conversely, if most of the cargo is stowed amidships, the two ends of the vessel tend to be higher than the amidship portion. This is called sagging. Both hogging and sagging have an adverse effect on the hull, and impair the general stability of the vessel. It can largely be overcome by ballasting the portion of the ship empty of cargo.

2. Associated (to some extent) with the previous factor, is the need to prevent damage to the ship. Not only must there be a proper distribution of cargo to ensure adequate stability and trim, but also it must be properly secured to prevent shifting. If there is a movement of the cargo during the voyage it will tend to cause the ship to list. Furthermore, the position can be seriously aggravated if the cargoes involved are dangerous, where spontaneous combustion for example could cause a fire or explosion. Shifting of cargo applies primarily to bulk cargoes such as grain, small coal, flint stone or iron ores, and is not usually associated with liner cargo shipments. To reduce movement of cargo, dunnage is provided. This is in the form of foam rubber, polystyrene, inflatable bags, timber boards or mats, which are placed between the cargo to prevent movement during the voyage.

3. Similarly, cargo which is fragile, taints very easily, is liable to leakage, scratches easily, has strong odours, or is liable to sweat, requires proper segregation; otherwise the shipowner will be faced with heavy claims and possible loss of much goodwill amongst

shippers. Obviously, a crate of oranges with a penetrating odour cannot be stowed adjacent to a consignment of tea, which taints easily, and steel rails cannot be placed on top of a crate of eggs. 4. Finally, a proper segregation of stowage of different consignments for various ports must be made, to prevent delay in discharging and avoid double handling, which is not only costly and increases the risk of cargo damage and pilferage, but also increases turn-round time. The stevedore is helped considerably by the stowage plan in realizing this objective. This applies equally to container vessels which call at fewer ports compared to the 'tween deck tonnage they displaced. The 'stowage plan' is completed after the cargo is loaded. A stevedore superintendent may have an outline of intention which may have to be amended in the course of loading the ship. To the reader wishing to know about the technique of stowing consignments within the container, this is fully explained in Chapter 6 of my book *The Elements of Export Practice*.

13.3 TYPES AND CHARACTERISTICS OF CARGO

The following is a broad selection of the main cargoes carried, together with their characteristics, including stowage factors where appropriate. The stowage factor is the space occupied in cubic metres in the ship's hold by one metric tonne of cargo (1000 kg). Heavy cargoes, such as those with a low stowage factor, occupy the smallest space, and are most suitable for single deck type of ships. Those cargoes of a higher stowage factor, such as wool, are lighter, occupy more space, and are best suited to 'tween-deck or shelter-deck vessels. In considering the following cargoes one must bear in mind most cargoes are now containerized and the sender must reconcile the container type required (see pp. 394–403) with the merchandise available for shipment.

Apples are packed in cases, boxes, cartons or pallet boxes and stowed at a temperature of about 1°C. If the temperature is too high, the fruit becomes sticky and soft. Apples breathe after being picked, and are individually wrapped in chemically treated paper to help absorb carbon dioxide. Their stowage factor is about 2.266, and they are mainly shipped in fruit carriers; cargo liners with suitable accommodation; or containers. Shipments originate in Canada, South Africa and Australasia in containers. The latter involves the Scoresby tray pack carton of either pulp or polystyrene trays which are accommodated in cartons. Each 20-ft (6.1-m) covered container has a 518-carton capacity. The fruit is packed diagonally allowing more and larger fruit to be packed per layer in the non-pressure tray pack design.

Butter is packed in cases, cartons, boxes or kegs, with a stowage factor varying from 1.558 to 1.699. It is normally conveyed in cargo liners with refrigerated space; in specialized refrigerated vessels; or in containers. Main shipments originate in Australasia (in refrigerated containers) and a number of European countries, such as Denmark and Holland. New Zealand is one of the most important sources of imported butter.

Cement may be shipped in five- or six-ply paper bags, containers, or conveyed in bulk. With a stowage factor varying from 1.0 to 1.133, it is most suitable for single-deck vessels. It must be stowed flat and tightly wedged from side to side, to avoid movement and subsequent splitting of the bags. The holds must be absolutely dry and the cargo stowed clear of the ship's sides, so that any condensation will run free down the plates. If a vessel is not provided with cargo battens (wooden planks fitted down the sides of the hold) a considerable amount of dunnage will be needed to stow cargo properly. Main shipments originate in the UK, Sweden, Poland, Western Germany, Yugoslavia and Holland. Most of the world's cement is now distributed in purpose-built cement bulk carriers and on liner containerized cargo routes in specialized containers.

Coal constitutes a dangerous cargo. It is liable to spontaneous combustion, especially on long voyages, and therefore, it is undesirable for it to be shipped with acids or chemicals. The stowage factor varies from 1.0 to 1.416, according to the grade of cargo. Coal (especially small coal) is liable to shift on a long voyage. It therefore must be well trimmed into the sides and ends of the holds if a full cargo is to be loaded, to maintain the ship's stability. The cargo loses its value if broken into small pieces or dust during loading and discharge. Main shipments originate in the UK, Poland, Western Germany, Holland, Belgium, Australia, South Africa, Canada and the USA. The volume of coal shipments has increased marginally following the rise in the price of oil in the 1970s. A particular example is the shipment of coal from Hampton-Roads to Japan employing vast quantities of bulk tonnage. Coal is generally conveyed in tramps or coastwise colliers, vessels with a single deck, large hatches and self-trimming holds being most suitable.

Coffee is packed in hessian bags. It must be kept dry and taints very easily. With a stowage factor of 1.699, it is normally shipped in cargo liners with 'tween decks or ventilated containers (see p. 399). Main shipments originate in Brazil, Colombia, and West and East Africa.

Confectionery is shipped in many forms of packing, the most common of which are cartons. Shipments originate in many parts of the world and are shipped on most liner services much of it being containerized. It has a somewhat high stowage factor, and must be given cool stowage and not, for instance, stowed adjacent to the engine room. The cargo must be kept dry, and shipped in shelter-deck vessels. It is particularly suitable for FCL container shipments.

Copra is usually shipped in bulk, but small shipments may be carried in second hand (S/H) bags. It has a stowage factor varying from 2.125 to 2.266. This commodity gives off oily odours, and should therefore never be shipped with such commodities as tea or sugar. It is liable to heat, and good ventilation is essential. This cargo must not come in contact with the sides of the ship, or it will be affected by the condensation. Copra is liable to spontaneous combustion. It is most suitable for shelter-deck vessels. Main shipments originate in East Africa, Sri Lanka, East Indies and Malaya.

Cotton is shipped in pressed bales, and has a stowage factor varying, according to the quality of the cargo, from 1.416 to 2.833. It is highly inflammable, and liable to spontaneous combustion if shipped damp or greasy. Cotton should be kept dry and must not come into contact with the ironwork of the ship, or it will be damaged by rust. Main shipments originate in Pakistan, Egypt, India and the United States in Combi carriers or liner tonnage (containers).

Eggs are conveyed in crates or cases. Raw eggs taint very easily, and can be refrigerated down to about 2°C, but must not be frozen. Cooked shelled eggs are shipped in a frozen condition in tins. The stowage factor is somewhat high and varies according to the type of packing. Vessels with refrigerated accommodation are most suitable. Main shipments originate in Holland, Denmark, Poland, Sweden and Canada. The bulk of the shipments are containerized.

Esparto grass is shipped in bales both under deck and on deck. It is liable to spontaneous combustion, and this cargo must be well ventilated. It has a low stowage factor varying from 2.833 to 4.249. Main shipments originate in Tunisia and Algeria. Shelter-deck vessels are the most suitable.

Fertilizers are shipped in bulk or bags, and should be kept dry. Their stowage factor varies according to the variety. Main shipments originate in Western Europe, Morocco and the USA. Single-deck vessels are most suitable when fertilizers are conveyed in bulk, and 'tween-deck ships when despatched in bags. A large volume of the world's fertilizer shipments is now distributed in purpose-built fertilizer bulk carriers and in containers.

Flour is generally shipped in bags, and must be kept dry. It taints very easily, and is subject to weevil damage. It has a stowage factor of 1.416. Main shipments originate in the UK, the USA, Australia and Canada. Containers are the most suitable.

Grain is usually conveyed in bulk, although a small proportion of it may be shipped in bags to improve the general stability of the vessel. The IMO convention on Safety of Life at Sea includes grain regulations. Precautions must be taken to stop the cargo shifting, and in many countries statutory provisions stipulate that shifting boards must be fitted. Shifting boards consist of a wooden centre-line – in the centre line of the ship, running fore and aft – fitted in the hold of the vessel. The boards extend one-third of the depth of the hold, with a minimum of 2.45 m measured from the top of the hold, and actually separate the hold into divisions. They prevent the grain from shifting in heavy weather and consequently the vessel from developing a dangerous list. The dangers arise due to settling of the grain after loading. In the 'tween- and shelter-deck type of vessel a feeder must be provided. This built of timber around the square of the hatch in the 'tween or shelter deck, and is open to the hold below. The feeder must have a capacity of at least

2½% of the quantity of cargo in the hold below. The object of the feeder is to keep the lower hold full of bulk grain. During the voyage, the grain in the lower hold settles and leaves a space at the top where the grain might shift and cause the vessel to have a list. The space is kept filled with grain from the feeder. Another method of preventing movement of the cargo is to provide bags layered or tiered into the holds, which results in a general stiffening of the cargo. Grain must be kept dry and requires good ventilation, as it is liable to heat and ferment. Its stowage factor varies according to the type of grain and whether it is shipped in bulk or bags. The heavy grains such as wheat, maize and rye have a stowage factor of approximately 1.416, whilst with the lighter grains, which include barley, oats and linseed, it is about 1.558 to 2.408. If the cargo is shipped in bags, these figures need to be increased by 10%. Grain is most suitably conveyed in single deck vessels with self-trimming holds, and it forms one of the major tramp cargoes. Main shipments originate in Australia, Canada, the USA, Russia, Romania, Bulgaria and the Argentine.

Jute is usually shipped in bales by liner tonnage, and is liable to spontaneous combustion. It has a stowage factor of 1.699 and shipments originate in India and Pakistan.

Meat is shipped frozen in refrigerated holds, at a temperature of −10°C or is chilled at −3°C. Main shipments originate in Australasia and the Argentine. It is usually shipped in liner tonnage in containers.

Motor vehicles are frequently shipped unpacked to reduce freight. Each vehicle must be individually secured and stowed on a firm level floor. Space must be left round each vehicle to avoid damage by scratching or rubbing. Cars cannot be over-stowed, and space is lost if other cargo cannot be built-up under vehicle stowage. More recently, an increasing number of ships have been adapted by incorporating skeleton decks built into the holds to which the vehicles are secured thus in effect increasing the number of 'tween decks. This has permitted bulk shipments of motor vehicles in vessels called auto-carriers. The decks can be removed either wholly or partly for the return voyage, thus allowing cargoes of a different nature to be carried. In some cases, the vehicles are transhipped by means of a ramp. Cars are also shipped in collapsible crates. Some cargo liners have been constructed with a centre-castle or extended bridge to give additional space. Nowadays, the distribution of motor vehicles – frequently termed as trade cars – is very much a growth sector of international trade development. To meet this expansion, purpose-built vessels with up to thirteen decks and capable of conveying 3500 cars are now operational, with 'drive on/drive off' facilities at the ports. Main shipments originate in the UK, Sweden, Japan, USA, France, Italy and Western Germany (see p. 57).

Oil cakes are conveyed in bulk or bags. They are liable to sweat damage and spontaneous combustion. Their stowage factor is 1.558. Main shipments originate in India and Nigeria. Oil cakes are most suitable for single-deck vessels when carried in bulk, and 'tween-deck ships when despatched in bags.

Oil and petroleum are conveyed in specialized vessels, called tankers, and are dangerous cargoes. Oil, being a liquid, will follow all movement of the ship, and thus have a large free surface, unless some method is employed in breaking up this surface. This is done by the use of longitudinal bulk heads, which divide the vessel into either three or four longitudinal sections. Other bulk heads athwartships divide the longitudinal sections into tanks. The number of tanks depends on the design of the tanker. During the voyage the tanks are never filled to capacity, i.e. there is always a free surface in the tanks of a tanker. Cofferdams are found fore and aft of the tank space as a protection against the serious fire risk inherent with this cargo. Oil is classified as clean or dirty, according to type, and it is usual for vessels to carry the same type on consecutive voyages, as the cost of tank-cleaning is high. Dirty oils include fuel oil, and crude oil, whereas clean oil covers refined petroleum, lubricating oil, diesel oil and so on. Shipments of oil are mainly from the Persian Gulf, the West Indies, the USA, Black Sea, Nigeria, Libya, Venezuela and the East Indies.

Oranges are shipped in boxes (though these are not fully enclosed) and cartons. They should not be stowed anywhere near cargo liable to taint. Main shipments originate in Spain, Israel and South Africa. They are usually shipped in 'tween-deck vessels, containers or from Spain in road trailers or railway wagons, and have a stowage factor of about 1.841 to 2.125.

Ores There is a great variety of ores, including chrome, manganese, copper, bauxite, iron, zinc and barytes. Ores are essentially bulk cargoes, often conveyed in specialized single-deck ore carriers and depending on the type of cargo, have a stowage factor varying from 0.340 to 0.850. They are therefore very heavy cargoes, and, although the vessel may be fully loaded down to her marks, very little of the actual space in the vessel is utilized. Consequently, the whole weight of the cargo is concentrated in the bottom of the vessel, which tends to make the vessel 'stiff' and causes her to roll heavily in bad weather, with consequent stress and strain. There is very little risk of most types of ores shifting, and in order to raise the height of the cargo so that the ship will ride more easily, the cargo is heaped up in the middle of the holds, and not trimmed into the wings (the sides of the holds). Some ores are, however, shipped wet, and set in stowage to reduce the possibility of the cargo shifting. Ores form one of the major tramp cargoes, and specialized ore carriers are used. Main shipments of iron ore originate in Newfoundland, Brazil, Spain and North Africa; copper ore from Chile, Spain and East Africa; chrome ore from Turkey and South Africa; bauxite from Malaysia and British Guiana; zinc ore from Chile, Newfoundland and Spain; barytes from Nova Scotia; and manganese ore from Ghana, Sierra Leone and India.

Rice is shipped in bags, and is liable to heat and sweat. Rice bran is generally shipped as a tramp or liner filler cargo. Rice generally is stowed by itself although there can be consignments of polished and brown rice in the same stow. Ironwork in the holds must be covered to prevent condensation, and good ventilation is essential. The stowage factor is 1.416, and main shipments originate in Burma, Italy, Thailand, Egypt and Brazil. Shipments are usually made in 'tween-deck vessels.

Rubber is conveyed in bags, bales or cases. Its stowage factor varies from 1.481 to 2.125, and main shipments originate in Malaysia, Indonesia and West Africa. This cargo is conveyed in liners operating in these trades, and latex is also often shipped in deep tanks.

Salt is shipped in bulk or bags, and must be kept dry as it absorbs moisture very rapidly. Excessive ventilation results in loss of weight in very dry weather. It has a stowage factor of 1.000, and is best shipped in single-deck vessels. Main shipments originate in Egypt, Spain and the West Indies.

Steel rails are shipped loose or in bundles in single-deck vessels when conveyed in bulk; small consignments may be carried by cargo liners. Steel rails must not be placed on top of other cargoes. Their stowage factor is 0.340, and main shipments originate in the USA and Western Europe.

Sugar is usually shipped in bulk (raw), or bags (raw or refined). If it is overheated it sets hard, and if too cold the sugar content diminishes. Sugar must be kept dry, and is liable to taint. When shipped in bulk, it is conveyed in single-deck sugar carriers. Its stowage factor varies from 1.133 to 1.416, and main shipments originate in Australia, Brazil, Cuba, Jamaica, Philippines, Java and San Domingo. There is an increasing tendency for sugar to be shipped in bulk or in containers or Combi carriers.

Tea is shipped in lined cases, and loses its aroma and value if not kept dry. It taints very easily, and has a low stowage factor of about 1.481. Main shipments originate in India, Sri Lanka and China. Tea is shipped in liner tonnage in containers or Combi carriers.

Timber is carried both under deck and on deck. The stowage of timber varies considerably, according to the type of timber carried. Hardwoods, such as teak and mahogany, have a stowage factor of about 0.708 to 0.850, pitprops about 1.699 and DBB (deals, battens and boards) about 2.550. Hardwoods are carried on a metric tonne basis, whilst props and DBB are conveyed on a fathom and standard basis respectively. A large quantity of timber is moved under the Nubaltwood charter party terms which provides the following definitions in regard to the method of shipment.

(a) Battens to be considered 44 mm × 100 mm and up to 75 mm × 175 mm.

(b) Slattings to be considered 25 mm and under in thickness, and 75 mm and under in width.

(c) Packaged goods will have a single length and size in each package except that where the residue is insufficient for complete package lengths they may be combined provided that one end of each package is squared off.

(d) Truck bundled goods involves goods bundled in mixed lengths of one size provided that one end of each bundle is squared off.

(e) Pre-slung goods involves the owner providing slings to place around the cargo before loading onto vessel and for these to remain during the voyage until the cargo has been discharged.

The most suitable vessel for bulk shipments is the single-deck three-island type with well decks and a broad beam, which make for easier stowage and a good deck cargo. Considerable quantities of soft woods are also conveyed in tramps, whilst hardwoods are usually shipped in liner tonnage, either in logs or cut. Shipments of soft woods originate in the Baltic and the White Sea, and North and South America, whilst hardwoods emanate from Southern Europe, Japan and numerous tropical countries. Today, to facilitate speedy transhipment, package timber is shipped.

Tobacco is packed in hogsheads, bales or cases. Moisture causes mildew, and excessive ventilation reduces the flavour. It is a cargo that taints very easily. Main shipments originate in the USA and South Africa. This cargo is conveyed in liner cargo tonnage in containers or Combi carriers.

Wines are shipped in drums or barrels. A small amount of leakage is almost unavoidable. More recently it has been shipped in bulk in glass-lined tanks, which have overcome this problem. It is usually shipped in cargo liners, but in the European trades small tank vessels are employed. Main shipments originate in South Africa, USA, Australia, France and Spain.

Wool is shipped in pressed bales or large bags. It is an inflammable cargo, and needs to be kept dry. This cargo should be stowed clear of the ship's sides to avoid sweat and rust damage. Its stowage factor varies from 5.099 to 7.932, according to the quality. Main shipments originate in Australasia, South Africa and the Argentine. Wool is shipped in shelter-deck vessels.

As the shipping industry progresses through the next decade, many of the aforementioned cargoes quoted as suitable for shelter-deck or 'tween-deck ships will in some cargo liner trades be despatched in container tonnage or Combi-carriers.

13.4 CARGO-HANDLING EQUIPMENT

The form of cargo-handling equipment employed is basically determined by the nature of the actual cargo and the type of packing used.

The subject of handling facilities raises the important question of mechanization. Bulk cargoes such as grain, sugar, coal, ore and oil lend themselves to mechanical handling, and, provided the equipment is well utilized to cover capital charges and interest, it cheapens and speeds output. Such equipment is normally situated at a special berth and reflects modern technology.

So far as bulk cargoes are concerned, handling facilities may be in the form of power-propelled conveyor belts, usually fed at the landward end by a hopper (a very large container on legs) or grabs, which may be magnetic for handling ores, fixed to a high capacity travelling crane or travelling gantries. These gantries move not only parallel to the quay, but also run back for considerable distances, thus covering a large stacking area, as well as being able to plumb the ship's hold. These two types of equipment are suitable for handling coal and ores. In the case of bulk sugar, for which the grab is also used, the sugar would be discharged into a hopper, feeding by gravity a railway wagon or road vehicle below.

Elevators are normally associated with grain. They may be bucket elevators, or operated by pneumatic suction which sucks the grain out of the ship's hold. The Port of London (Tilbury) grain terminal uses both bucket and pneumatic suction. Faster operation is with the plastic buckets although the other type is preferred once the hold is near empty. This latter type is growing in popularity, and is designed to weigh the grain at the same time. Elevators may be situated on the quayside or be of a floating type, involving the provision of special pipes. The elevators are connected to the granaries (bulk grain storage warehouse) by power-operated conveyor belts.

The movement of bulk petrol and oils from the tanker is undertaken by means of pipelines connected to the shore-based storage tanks. Pumping equipment is provided in the tanker storage plant or refinery ashore, but not on the quayside. In view of the dangerous nature of such cargo, it is the practice to build the special berths some distance from the main dock system on the seaward side.

With regard to general merchandise, the long-term tendency in many liner cargo trades is to containerize such cargo. This transformation to containerization has taken many years to gain predominance in all trades. Meanwhile the system of dockers handling cargo will continue, particularly in the third-world countries where dock labour costs are more moderate, but doubtless every effort will be made to expand the already extensive use of mechanized cargo-handling equipment. Nevertheless, it must be recognized that containerization by the early 1990s will be very firmly established in the distribution of international trade under liner cargo arrangements, and that very few maritime countries will not be served by a container service. Moreover, it should be noted that not every liner cargo trade will be containerized, completely or partially, as circumstances will dictate otherwise.

When the cargo consists of a heterogeneous collection of packages of different sizes, weight and shapes, its loading and unloading, as compared with the handling of bulk shipments, presents a very different problem, particularly in regard to the use of mechanized equipment.

General loose non-containerized cargo is handled by cranes on the quay, floating cranes or by the ship's own derricks. Attached to such lifting gear is a U-shaped shackle (see Fig. 13.1) which links the crane or derricks with the form of cargo-handling equipment being used. The shackle is joined at its open end by means of a loose pin to form a link. For most lifts a hook is used. It will be appreciated that the volume of loose cargo using 'tween-deck tonnage is much diminished following the emergence of containerization, the Combi carrier, Ro/Ro, and the change in the general pattern of world trade. Hence much of the equipment found in Figs 13.1 and 13.2 and described in the following paragraph is primarily used in less developed countries and have been displaced elsewhere by the fork lift truck and other modern methods of cargo handling equipment/techniques.

There are numerous types of cargo-handling equipment that can be attached to the lifting gear, many of which are illustrated in Figs 13.1 and 13.2. They include the sling or strop, which is probably the most common form of cargo-handling gear. Such equipment, generally made of rope, is ideal for hoisting strong packages, such as wooden cases or bagged cargo, which is not likely to sag or damage when raised. Similarly, snotters or canvas slings are suitable for bagged cargo. Chain slings, however, are used for heavy slender cargoes, such as timber or steel rails. Can or barrel hooks are suitable for hoisting barrels or drums. Cargo nets are suitable for mail bags and similar cargoes that are not liable to be crushed when hoisted. Heavy lifting beams are suitable for heavy and long articles such as locomotives, boilers or railway passenger coaches. Vehicle-lifting gear, consisting of four steel wire legs (with spreaders) attached to one lifting ring, are suitable for hoisting motor vehicles. Cargo trays and pallets, the latter being wooden or of steel construction, are ideal for cargo of moderate dimensions, which can be conveniently stacked, such as cartons, bags, or small wooden crates or cases. Additionally, dog or case hooks, and case and plate clamps are suitable for transhipping cargo to railway wagons or road vehicles, but not to or from the ship, except to facilitate transhipping the cargo in the hold to enable suitable cargo-handling gear to be attached. Dog hooks are not suitable for frail cases and should only be used to enable slings to be placed. Case clamps are used to strike cargo from vehicles etc. but should not be used for loading vehicles or vessels with casework. Plate clamps are used for lifting metal plates.

Dockers working in the ship's hold also use pinch -or crowbars for heavy packages, and hand hooks for manoeuvring packages into position.

Much equipment is provided to facilitate movement of the cargo to and from the ship's side and the transit shed, warehouse, barge, railway wagon or road vehicle. These include two-wheeled hand barrows and four-wheeled trucks either manually or mechanically propelled, and mechanically or electrically propelled tractors for hauling four-wheeled trailers. There are also conveyor belts mechanically or electrically operated, or rollers, all perhaps extending from the quayside to the transit shed, warehouse, railway wagon or road vehicle. Mechanically powered straddle carriers are designed to straddle their load or set, pick it up and convey it to a convenient point on the quayside, transit shed, or elsewhere in the dock area. In appearance they are similar to a farm tractor with a raised chassis, below which are clamps to raise and carry the cargo underneath the 'belly' of the tractor. They are suitable for timber, pipes and long cases. The larger straddle carriers distribute the ISO containers on the quay and stand over 12 m high giving an appearance of inverted 'U'-shaped structure.

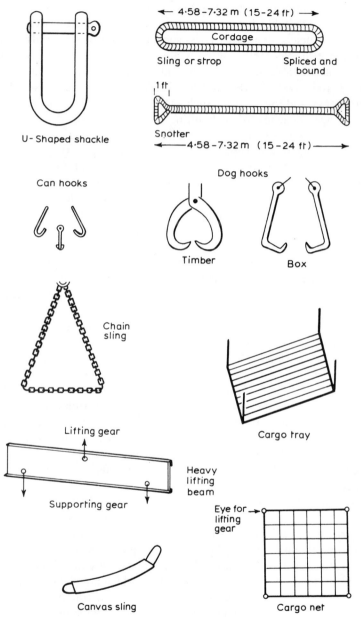

U-Shaped shackle

4·58–7·32 m (15–24 ft)

Cordage

Sling or strop

Spliced and bound

1 ft

Snotter

4·58–7·32 m (15–24 ft)

Can hooks

Dog hooks

Timber

Box

Chain sling

Cargo tray

Lifting gear

Supporting gear

Heavy lifting beam

Eye for lifting gear

Canvas sling

Cargo net

Fig. 13.1 Cargo-handling equipment.

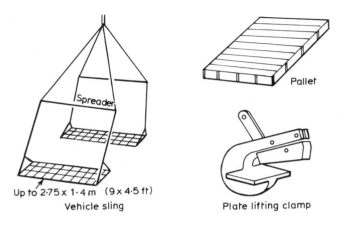

Up to 2·75 x 1·4 m   (9 x 4·5 ft)
Vehicle sling

Pallet

Plate lifting clamp

Fig. 13.1 *Contd*. Cargo-handling equipment.

Mechanical shunters are designed to propel or draw up to six railway wagons on the quayside and environs, thereby avoiding the need for a locomotive or capstan.

A wide range of cargo-handling equipment exists. The handling method used should be the one which gives the greatest efficiency with economy and which makes full use of any existing facilities and equipment.

Fork-lift trucks are battery, electric or gas operated and fitted in front with a platform in the shape of two prongs of a fork or other device. The prongs lift and carry the pallet either by penetrating through specially made apertures, or passing under it. The platform, affixed to a form of mast, can be raised and tilted, and the truck can travel with its load at any height up to its maximum. It is very manoeuvrable, and can stack cargo up to a height of 5 m. The lifting capacity varies from 1000 to 3000 kg, when the trucks are called freight lifters. The majority of trucks in use are limited to 1000 kg lifting capacity.

Details are given below of the types of fork-lift trucks available:

(a) *Side shift mechanism.* It enables the forks to move laterally either side of centre and thus considerably reduces the necessity to manoeuvre the fork-lift truck in the container or confined space.

(b) *Extension forks.* Ideal for handling awkward loads and to obtain extra reach. Subject to the fork truck being of sufficient capacity for clearing a space equivalent to the depth of two pallets on each side of a trailer-mounted container thus providing easy operation of the pallet. Numerous other examples of its use exist.

(c) *Boom.* Ideal for carpets, pipes, etc.

(d) *Crane jib.* Converts the fork-lift truck into a mobile crane.

(e) *Squeeze clamps.* Suitable for handling unit loads and individual items without the aid of pallets.

(f) *Drum handler.* Handles one or two drums at a time.

(g) *Barrel handler.* Not only does it clamp the barrel with two sets of upper and lower arms, but it also revolves so that the barrel can be picked up and handled on the roll or in the upright position.

(h) *Push–pull attachment.* It is specifically designed for use with slip sheets on containers.

(i) *Lift truck satellite.* A form of powered pallet truck which can be attached to a fork-lift truck carriage and used both to load/ unload and also to transport pallet loads down the length of containers under remote control from the fork-lift truck which remains on the ground outside the container. A selection of fork-lift trucks is found in Fig. 13.2.

The pallet transporter/truck may be battery, electric or manually operated. It is very manoeuvrable and efficient in transporting and positioning loads into and within the container, railway wagon or trailer. The manually operated pallet truck has a capacity of 1 tonne and the powered type 1½ tonnes.

The portable hydraulic roller has a capacity of 2 tonnes. It is capable of loading/unloading any size or weight up to the maximum dimensions and weight capacity of the container. Parallel lines of channel track connected together are laid on the container floor and the requisite number of roller sections placed into them. The load suitably fitted with a flat base or cross bearers, is positioned on the roller sections by crane, large capacity fork truck or other equipment.

The roller sections are then raised by the hydraulic units which are always exposed beyond the load and pushed into the container with the load which is now lowered into prefixed bearers by operating the hydraulic units. The channels and rollers are then withdrawn.

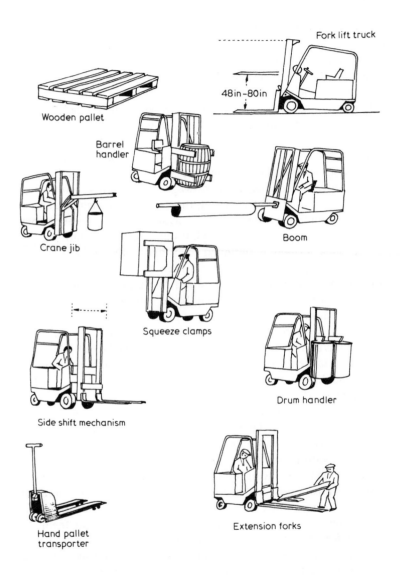

Wooden pallet

Fork lift truck

48in–80in

Barrel handler

Crane jib

Boom

Squeeze clamps

Drum handler

Side shift mechanism

Hand pallet transporter

Extension forks

Fig. 13.2 Fork-lift trucks.

The portable pneumatic roller unit, unlike the hydraulic unit which has separate channels, is integral and consists of a channel, an air hose and roller conveyor. Units to give any desired length run are connected up in parallel lines and the load placed upon them. The air bags are inflated from an air supply thus raising the roller conveyor and enabling the load to be moved into the container. By releasing the air the load is lowered onto prefixed bearers and the units withdrawn.

For handling small packages the conveyor belt is ideal. A wide variety of powered mobile or static conveyors exist. The conveyor can be of a flexible type which can be extended and retracted, and which has a boom controlled by the operator, adjustable in the lateral and vertical planes. It may operate from a loading bank or ground level involving final stowage in a trailer, container, warehouse, or simply discharging the cargo from such situations.

Cargo-handling equipment is also available in the form of dock levellers, mobile ramps, bridge plates and elevating platforms.

The dock leveller is designed to bridge both the vertical and horizontal gap. For example between a loading bank and a trailer-mounted container. There are two types primarily: those positioned exterior to the loading bank and those made integral with the bank.

The mobile ramp obviates the need for a loading bank. It is ideal for stuffing/unloading a trailer or container affixed to a trailer. The ramp is attached securely to the rear of the container or trailer unit. The height of the operation from ground to the trailer/container is adjustable.

Bridge plates simply bridge the gap either from a loading bank or at ground level. They are portable and can be moved to different positions as required.

The elevating platform can be either static or mobile and thereby obviate the need for a loading bank. The mobile type can easily be positioned at the doors of a trailer-mounted container adjacent to any vehicle, or any other situation. The platform raises the mechanical handling equipment, load and operator from the ground, for example, to the level of the container floor onto which it is driven by means of an integral bridge plate. They are powered usually by electro/mechanical or electro/hydraulic packs.

The fork-lift truck, and such equipment as the pallet and pallet truck, operate on the basis that goods at first handling are placed on boards, skids or pallets. The fork-lift truck inserts its fork through or under the pallet, situated in the railway wagon, transit shed or on the quayside, raises the load and carries it to the ship's side. The pallet is then used as a sling and hoisted direct into the ship's hold where the contents are stowed. The fork-lift truck can also be used to tier cargo in a shed or on the quay. This system is called palletization, and has been introduced on a large scale during the past decade. It has to some extent changed methods of cargo handling in many liner ports. Both the fork-lift truck and to a lesser extent the pallet truck are used in stuffing and discharging containers.

With the containerized shipment, particularly the full load, despatched by one shipper, as distinct from the consolidated break bulk consignment, the total consignment is sometimes fully palletized. In such circumstances it facilitates container-contents stowage and permits quicker loading/discharging of the contents. The pallet forms an integral part of the packaging and remains with the cargo until it reaches its final destination which may be a lengthy rail or road journey from the importer distribution depot.

A further development in cargo-handling is the introduction of containers (see Chapter 16 and Fig. 16.1 p. 395) for liner trade cargo, which greatly reduces the labour needed for handling cargo. The containers have a capacity up to 30 tonnes and most are built to ISO (International Standards Organization) standards with an 8 ft module (8 ft wide × 8 ft high) and a length of 20 ft (6.10 m) or 40 ft (12.20 m) (see p. 396). Various types of container exist: tanks for liquid and powder; covered for general merchandise etc; insulated for perishable traffic; car carriers for trade cars; Lancashire flats for steel plates, etc. and tilt containers capable of being affixed to road vehicles for powdered cargoes. Such containers are used worldwide in almost every cargo liner trade and are usually conveyed to and from the port by road or rail, thereby affording a door-to-door service.

The advantages and disadvantages of containerization are fully explained on pages 403–6. The container may be provided by one of several people: the shipowner; a forwarding agent or container operator, an individual shipper often of a large industrial concern despatching regular shipments, or finally a container consortium such as Associated Container Transportation Group. Moreover, there is an increasing tendency for the shipowner to market the container and consolidate the consignments through the container base (CFS/ICD) involving both FCL and LCL shipments and not rely on the freight forwarder to canvass and sponsor the container movement.

Container terminals are purpose-built and are equipped on the quay face with giant portainer cranes capable of lifting containers – sometimes two at a time – in and off the container vessels. A feature of the cranes is the lifting or spreader frame which automatically connects with the top corner castings of each of two containers to lift them. The system is so designed that it can compensate for slight malpositioning of containers in the stack, or on a land vehicle, and for slight variations from the vertical of the cell guide rails in the ship. Gantry cranes of 45 000 kg (45 tonnes) capacity are used to handle the container stack. A typical container terminal would be a 8.5-hectare site designed to handle 3000 containers on and off a ship within 72 hours, and at the same time deal with road and/or rail transport carrying import and export containers. Stacking area would be of 1800 general cargo and 400 insulated containers – the latter being housed in a specially cladded stack connected to a refrigeration plant. This area is much increased where double stack container trains serve the container berth as found, for example, in some parts of the west coast of North America.

Cargo carried in containers includes most consumer goods, such as furniture, bicycles, light machinery, meat, steel, liquids, confectionery, and fruit and vegetables.

To sum up, cargo in cases, crates, boxes, sacks, bags, etc. should be handled by slings or pallets. Hooks should be used for barrels and drums, and lifting gear for motor cars and lorries. No hooks should be used with bagged cargo. Bulk cargoes are loaded and discharged by grabs or by special equipment such as grain elevators, pipes, conveyor belts and coal hoists.

The efficiency of the dock labour force is a vital factor in cargo handling. The dockers' attitude towards mechanization and containerization is very important, because such equipment must be used intelligently if it is to be of value in speeding and cheapening cost and reducing port turn-round time. A vessel of increasing popularity is the Combi carrier (see pp. 51, 64) and undoubtedly this will help to speed up the handling of cargo using the container, MAFI trailer, fork-lift truck etc.

With the development of the multi-purpose vessel conveying road haulage vehicles and trailers – some of the latter being unaccompanied – the tug master has emerged as an essential part of port equipment. The tug master is a motorized unit which can be attached to the unaccompanied trailer enabling it to be driven on or off the vessel.

13.5 TYPES OF PACKING

The method of packing depends primarily on the nature of the goods themselves and the method of transit for the anticipated voyage. Further subsidiary factors include the use to which the packing may be put when the goods reach their destination, the value of the goods (low value goods have less packing than those of high value); any Customs or statutory requirements that must be complied with; ease of handling (awkward-shaped cargo suitably packed in cartons or cases can facilitate handling); marketing requirements; general fragility; variation in temperature during the voyage; the size of the cargo and its weight, and, in particular, whether elaborate packing is likely to increase the freight to the extent that it might price the goods out of the market; facilities available at the ports (in some ports they may not have highly mechanized cargo-handling equipment or elaborate storage accommodation); type and size of container; and lastly, the desirability of affixing to the packing any suitable advertisement. Overall the export product price will include packing cost which will have particular regard to transit, packaging design and its cost.

Packing, therefore, is not only designed as a form of protection to reduce the risk of the goods being damaged in transit, but also to prevent pilferage. It is, of course, essential to see not only that the right type of packing is provided, but also that the correct quality and form of container is used. There are numerous types of packing and a description of the more important ones follows.

Many goods have little or no form of packing whatsoever, and are carried loose. These include iron and steel plates, iron rods, railway sleepers and steel rails. Such cargoes are generally weight cargoes, with a low stowage factor. Heavy vehicles, locomotives and buses are also carried loose, because of the impracticability and high cost of packing.

Baling is a form of packing consisting of a canvas cover often cross-looped by metal or rope binding. It is most suitable for paper, wool, cotton, carpets and rope.

Bags made of jute, cotton, plastic or paper, are a cheap form of container. They are suitable for cement, coffee, fertilizers, flour and oil cakes. Their prime disadvantage is that they are subject to damage by water, sweat, hooks or, in the case of paper bags, breakage.

A recent development in packaging technique has emerged with the liquid rubber containers. It is called a bulk liquid bag or container, and can store various kinds of liquid cargo. When not in use the bag can be folded to 2% of its volume. Other cargoes can be conveyed in the unit on the return trip. The fold-up facility eliminates waste of space of the rigid tank containers and steel drums which cannot carry dry goods on the return journeys. Moreover, in cost terms the bulk liquid bag is one sixth of the price of a steel drum and one fourth of a tank container. Each bulk liquid bag can carry a volume of liquid cargo equivalent to 210 large capacity steel drums.

Cartons are a very common form of packing, and may be constructed of cardboard, strawboard or fibreboard. This form of packing is very much on the increase, as it lends itself to ease of handling, particularly by palletization. The principal disadvantage is its susceptibility to crushing and pilfering. It is a very flexible form of packing and therefore prevents the breakages which may occur if rigid containers are used. A wide range of consumer goods use this inexpensive form of packing, and it is ideal for container cargo. Polystyrene now features more and more as a packing aid in cartons. The triwall in common with the carton may be palletized with provision for fork lift handling.

Crates, or skeleton cases, are a form of container, half-way between a bale and a case. They are of wooden construction. Lightweight goods of larger cubic capacity, such as light machinery, domestic appliances like refrigerators, cycles, and certain foodstuffs, for instance oranges, are suitable for this form of packing.

Carboys, or glass containers, enclosed in metal baskets have a limited use, and are primarily employed for the carriage of acids and other dangerous liquids transported in small quantities.

Boxes, cases and metal-lined cases are also used extensively. Wooden in construction, they vary in size and capacity, and may be strengthened by the provision of battens and metal binding. Many of them, such as tea chests, are lined to create airtight packing, so as to overcome the difficulties that arise when passing through zones of variable temperature. Much machinery and other items of expensive equipment, including cars and parts, are packed in this form.

Barrels, hogsheads and drums are used for the conveyance of liquid or greasy cargoes. The main problem associated with this form of packing is the likelihood of leakage if the unit is not properly sealed, and the possibility of the drums becoming rusty during transit. Acids can also be carried in plastic drums and bottles. The drum is usually of 45 gallons or 205 litres capacity and may also convey liquid (oil, chemicals) or powder shipments. They are usually stowed in a cradle to facilitate mechanical handling stowage and stacking.

Shrink wrapping is a relatively new technique in packing and has arisen through the need to reduce packaging cost particularly in the area of wooden cases and similar relatively high-cost material. It is undertaken by placing the goods to be covered on a base – usually a pallet for ease of handling – and covering it with a film of plastic which is shrunk to enclose the items by the use of hot-air blowers (thermo-guns). It is a relatively cheap form of packing particularly in relation to timber and fibreboard cartons. Moreover, it gives a rigid protection and security to the cargo and its configuration follows the outline of the goods.

Shrink wrapping is also used extensively with palletized consignments to secure the goods to the pallet unit. This ensures a more rigid unit and improves the security of the goods throughout the transit. It can facilitate handling of the palletized unit and stacking of the goods in the warehouse. The palletized goods maybe in a trailer movement, container (LCL or FCL) or break bulk shipment as for example in 'tween-deck tonnage, lighterage and so on. Colour films are available to protect light-sensitive cargo, and to provide a degree of protection against pilferage.

A further packaging resource is the metal envelope which is used in the movement of steel shipments and encapsulates the consignment thereby making it more secure.

It is apparent that, as containerization develops, packing needs for shipped cargo will change, as containerization requires less packing. Undoubtedly, packing will become less robust.

Fig. 13.3 Recognized international marking symbols.

Associated with the types of packing is the marking of cargo. When goods are packed, they are marked on the outside in a manner which will remain legible for the whole of the voyage. First of all, there is some mark of identification, and then immediately underneath this, the port mark is shown. For example, the merchant may be J. Brown Ltd, and the goods are being shipped in the s.s. *Amsterdam* to Rotterdam, in which case the marks will be as follows:

J.B. LTD. No. 2
2.5 m x 1.8 m x 1.3 m
Rotterdam

Fig. 13.4 Example of the marking of cargo.

These simple markings are adequate for identification, and are entered on the bill of lading. In the event of there being several cases in one shipment, the number of the case is also entered, in this case No. 2. It is essential all goods are marked on at least two sides clearly with a shipping mark, which includes the name of the destination Port/Depot, and making sure that the marks on the shipping documents correspond exactly with those on the goods. The figures below the number are the dimensions of the case in metres, and may be used in assessing the freight. An internationally recognized code sign may also be stencilled on the case to facilitate handling, and indicate the nature of the cargo. Such code signs would indicate 'sling here', 'fragile goods', 'keep dry' (as illustrated above), 'do not drop', etc. A selection of the labels used in the international cargo-handling code is found in Fig. 13.3.

13.6 DANGEROUS CARGO

Dangerous goods may be defined as those substances so classified in any acts, rules, or bye-laws or having any similar properties or hazards. The handling, and carriage of dangerous goods must be carried out in full compliance with all relevant legislation which covers inland transport, stowage in the container, trailer, and on the ship, and includes those of the ports of loading, discharge and transit.

The movement internationally of dangerous cargo is very much on the increase and a strict code of acceptance is laid down for all forms of transport relative to the acceptance of this cargo, particularly packing, documentation and marking specification. For the exporter who is unfamiliar with the situation and wishes to have adequate advice on a consignment, it is wise to consult a freight forwarder, container operator or shipowner. Failure to comply with such regulations, particularly in documentation declaration and stowage, can lead to severe penalties.

The regulations relating to the movement of dangerous cargo by sea are defined in the UK by the Department of Trade and Industry. They conform to the code. Details of the classification are given below:

Class I: Explosives.
Class II: Gases – compressed, liquefied or dissolved under pressure.
Class III: Inflammable liquids.
Class IV: Inflammable solids and substances spontaneously combustible, or substances emitting inflammable gases when wet.
Class V: Oxidizing substances and organic peroxides.
    (a) Oxidizing substances.
    (b) Organic peroxides.
Class VI: Poisonous (toxic) and infectious substances.
    (a) Poisons.
Class VII: Radioactive substances.
Class VIII: Corrosives.
Class IX: Miscellaneous dangerous substances.

The Merchant Shipping (Dangerous Goods) Regulations 1981 has the following provisions regarding the packaging of the goods:

(a) Classified and declared by the shipper to the Master.
(b) Packaged in a manner to withstand the ordinary risks of handling and transport by sea having regard to their properties.
(c) Marked with the correct technical name and indication of the danger.
(d) Properly stowed and effectively segregated from other cargoes which may dangerously interact.

(e)   Listed on a manifest or stowage plan giving stowage details. This must be aboard the ship.

Three types of packaging groups exist: maximum, intermediate and low-level hazards.

By 1988 a major revision was under way relative to Class I – explosives; Class III – inflammable liquids; and Class VII – radioactive materials and segregation of radioactive cargoes.

The shipowner will only handle such dangerous cargo by prior written arrangement and with the express condition the shipper provides a very full and adequate description of the cargo. If accepted, a special stowage order will be issued which will indicate to the Master that the cargo conforms to the prescribed code of acceptance laid down by the shipowner. It cannot be stressed too strongly that shipment will not take place until a special stowage order has been issued by the shipowner, which is the authority to shipment. Moreover, the shipper must fully describe the cargo and ensure it is correctly packed, marked and labelled. This he can do through a freight forwarder, which is often the practice.

It must be borne in mind that ships carrying general liner cargo usually only accept a limited quantity of dangerous classified cargo and as such require it to be stowed in a specified portion of the vessel for safety reasons.

To amplify the code of procedure regarding the movement of dangerous cargo internationally, it would be appropriate to examine shipment in ISO maritime covered containers which now follows.

In the main, the container is ideal for the shipment of dangerous cargo particularly as it avoids multiple handling, protects the goods from interference by unauthorized persons and eliminates the risk of damage from the use of inappropriate methods of slinging. The following information is required at the time of booking the container:

1.   Name of vessel.
2.   Port of loading.
3.   Port of discharge.
4.   Correct technical name of the substance.
5.   Quantity – gross and net weight in kilos.
6.   Description of packing (with inner if valid).
7.   Classification of substance (IMO code).

LABELS

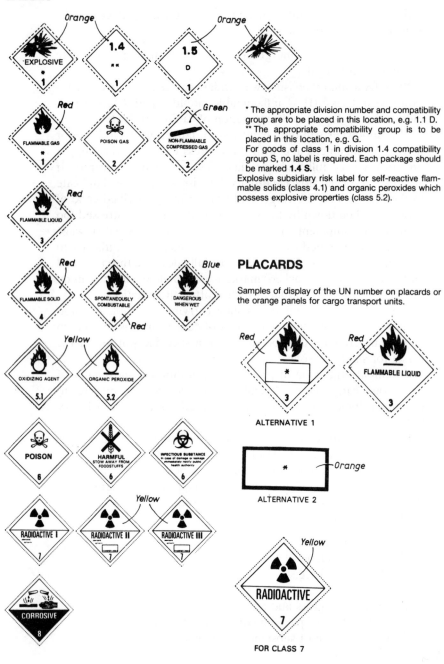

* The appropriate division number and compatibility group are to be placed in this location, e.g. 1.1 D.
** The appropriate compatibility group is to be placed in this location, e.g. G.
For goods of class 1 in division 1.4 compatibility group S, no label is required. Each package should be marked **1.4 S.**
Explosive subsidiary risk label for self-reactive flammable solids (class 4.1) and organic peroxides which possess explosive properties (class 5.2).

PLACARDS

Samples of display of the UN number on placards or the orange panels for cargo transport units.

ALTERNATIVE 1

ALTERNATIVE 2

FOR CLASS 7

Solas Convention

According to regulation 4 (marking, labelling and placarding) of part A of chapter VII of the 1974 SOLAS Convention, as amended, packages containing dangerous goods shall be durably marked with the correct technical name and be provided with distinctive labels or stencils of the labels, or placards, as appropriate.

IMDG Code

Labels and placards are assigned to each class of dangerous goods in the IMDG Code other than class 9, and denote the hazards involved by means of colours and symbols. Colours and symbols should be illustrated except that symbols and texts on green, red and blue labels and placards may be white.

The class number should appear in the bottom corner of the label or placard. The use of the texts shown on the illustrations and of further descriptive texts is optional. However, for class 7 the text should always appear on the labels and the special placard. If texts are used for the other classes, the texts shown on the specimens are recommended for the purpose of uniformity.

Dangerous goods which possess subsidiary dangerous properties must also bear subsidiary risk labels or placards denoting these hazards. Subsidiary risk labels and placards should not bear the class number in the bottom corner.

Labels for packages should not be less than 100 mm × 100 mm except in the case of packages which, because of their size, can only bear small labels. Placards for cargo transport units should not be less than 250 mm × 250 mm, should correspond with respect to colour and symbols to the labels and should display the number of the class in digits not less than 25 mm high.

Some consignments of dangerous goods should have the UN number of the goods displayed in black digits not less than 65 mm high either against a white background in the lower half of the placard or on a rectangular orange panel not less than 120 mm high and 300 mm wide, with a 10 mm black border, to be placed immediately adjacent to the placard.

The detailed requirements regarding marking, labelling and placarding are contained in the IMDG Code.

Fig. 13.5 IMO dangerous goods labels and placards. It must be noted that dangerous goods conveyed internationally by road are governed by the ADR regulations, and by rail and train ferry by the RID. When undertaking the maritime element of their transit, the road vehicle or railway wagon must comply with the IMDG code. (Reproduced by kind permission of IMO).

8. Properties of substance.
9. Flash point, if any.
10. UN number.
11. Ems (if NOS).

With 'tween-deck or bulk-cargo shipments, the loading of the ship is undertaken by stevedores, but with containerization this is done by container packers who are usually container operators or freight forwarders. Accordingly, with regard to the latter, a 'packing certificate' must be completed which certifies the following:

1. The container was clean, dry and fit to receive the cargo.
2. No cargo known to be incompatible has been stowed therein.
3. All packages have been inspected for damage, and only dry and sound packages loaded.
4. All packages have been properly stowed and secured and suitable materials used.

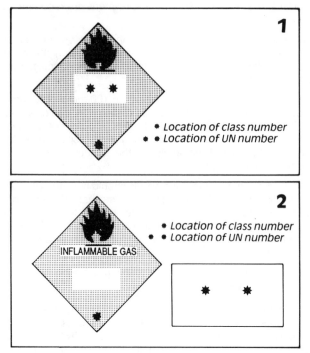

Fig. 13.6 Typical IMO dangerous goods placards. (Reproduced by kind permission of IMO).

5. The container and goods have been properly marked and labelled.

6. A dangerous goods declaration has been received/completed for each dangerous consignment packed in the container.

It is essential the shipowner checks out the acceptance of the contents and size of the container at the port of departure, transhipment port and destination port. In some ports in the subcontinent, Far East, and South America, dangerous cargo is loaded/unloaded overside.

Basically, the code of 'one class–one container' must be observed unless the container operator has expressly agreed to a relaxation. Substances which fall into the same class but are incompatible must also be stowed in different containers, for example, peroxides and permanganates (both oxidizing substances).

Dangerous goods may be incompatible with certain non-dangerous substances. Examples are poisons and foodstuffs, or those which react in contact with harmless organic materials such as nitrates, chlorates, etc.

A container in transit is subjected to acceleration and deceleration forces in a longitudinal and to some degree, a lateral direction when travelling overland, and in a vertical and lateral direction at sea. At all times it is subjected to some degree of vibration. Hence, the contents must be firmly stowed and secured against movement and chafing. Particular care with dangerous cargoes must be taken to ensure that the contents will not fall outwards when the doors are opened. Dangerous cargoes forming only part of the load must be stowed in the door area of the container for ease of access and inspection. In the case of non-dangerous goods, damage arising from poor stowage is usually confined to the container concerned, but in the case of dangerous goods the effects could be widespread.

It is relevant to note that obnoxious/irritant substances are classified as non-hazardous, but must be stowed and treated as dangerous cargo. Hence, any cargo having such substances must be clearly labelled prior to shipment and the carrier notified.

Dangerous goods containers are required to be marked with placards in accordance with the following criteria:

(a) All containers must display the dangerous goods placard (IMO class label not less than 25 cm × 25 cm) each side and ends.

When applicable secondary and tertiary hazard placards (i.e. placards without the class number) also on each side and ends.

(b) In regard to full container loads of a single commodity (except class 1) additionally the UN Number of the commodity must be shown with each placard in numbers of at least 65 mm height. This may be shown in either of two ways: on a white patch on the placard, or an orange label alongside the placard.

(c) In regard to less than container loads or mixed loads, the IMDG code no longer recommends exact identification of goods when mixed loads are packed in the container. Hence only the four class placards need to be shown for each class in the container together with secondary or tertiary hazard placards are required.

(d) After unpacking and when the container can be considered non-hazardous, the labels must be removed or masked.

The International Maritime Dangerous Goods Code produced by the International Maritime Organization (IMO) is now universally accepted as the basis for international movement of Dangerous Goods by sea.

The requirements of the Merchant Shipping (Dangerous Goods) Regulation 1981 as referred to above will have been deemed to have been complied with if shipments are carried out in accordance with the recommendations of the IMDG Code.

If the dangerous goods to be shipped is one of the very few which are covered in the recommendations of 'The Carriage of Dangerous Goods in Ships' – *The British Blue Book*, then this will take precedence over the IMDG Code.

If the shipper wishes to forward a commodity under conditions different from those specified in the above codes, then the onus will be on the shipper to demonstrate that such conditions are achieving at least an equivalent standard of safety.

The universal adoption of the International Maritime Dangerous Goods Code (IMDG) has greatly facilitated movement of dangerous goods between countries. Accordingly, a dangerous goods labelling code for maritime consignments exists and some codes are given in Fig. 13.6.

The 'dangerous' cargo rates tend to be higher than the conventional cargoes, and usually involve a surcharge of some 25–50%.

New legislation was introduced in 1987 under the Dangerous Substances in Harbour Areas which provided a comprehensive framework of controls over the carriage, loading, unloading, and storage of dangerous substances in harbours and harbour areas. Main features of the regulations included every person handling a dangerous substance in a harbour or harbour area must do so safely; vessels carrying certain dangerous substances must show a red flag or light; freight containers and portable tanks must be suitable for the purpose and properly packed and labelled; each harbour must prepare an emergency plan; and anyone wishing to handle explosives must have a Health and Safety Executive licence.

CHAPTER 14

The shipping company

14.1 SIZE AND SCOPE OF THE UNDERTAKING

Sea transport provides a fairly wide range of different services. There are, in fact, not one but several markets for its products. The demand for passenger services is very different from the demand for cargo space, although the two services may be provided in the same vessel. Tanker tonnage is highly specialized and can only serve the demand for the carriage of bulk liquid cargoes. Much refrigerated tonnage is very specific, and, although refrigerated ships can and do carry general cargo in refrigeration spaces, the demand and supply of refrigerated tonnage form separate markets.

Not so obvious is the fact that in a large part of their operations, liners and tramps form two broad divisions serving two different types of markets, each with its own conditions of supply and demand, and indeed there is some overlap between the two markets. For example, when tramp rates are low, liner conference companies often charter ships to take certain of their sailings, rather than invest in new tonnage to replace vessels that have ended their economic life. Similarly, a new liner service is commenced with chartered vessels by an organization wishing to establish itself in a trade already covered by existing liner companies.

The size of the shipping undertaking, its organization and cost structure, and the pricing of sea transport services are influenced largely by the type of service which is operated, and particularly by the difference between liner and tramp operation.

Hence there is a great variation in size among shipping undertakings, which range from the single ship company, to the giant groups. From an economic standpoint, the entrepreneur will try to maximize his profits and therefore expand his output, so long as the increase in his total costs is less than the increase in his total revenue. He will therefore continue to expand to the point where his marginal additional cost is equal to his marginal additional revenue.

Increased profits generally arise from lower cost due to operating on a larger scale, or from the ability to control the price of the product. There are certain economies which occur in a large-scale operation. The large firm may be able to specialize and to use elaborate mahinery, the cost of which can be spread over a large number of units of output.

The tendency in recent years, both with liner and tramp shipping companies, is to merge. The reasons are numerous and include economies realized on administration cost; improved prospects of raising more capital for new tonnage; rationalization of facilities, for example port agents, departments, overseas offices etc; the long-term consideration of likely improvement on tonnage utilization and productivity, with possible limited rationalization of the fleet; a larger customer portfolio; a larger trading company with improved competitive ability and the long-term possibility of a more economical service at lower cost with consequently improved tariffs; and finally the larger the company, generally speaking, the better it will be able to combat the challenges of the 1990s, in particular new investment, which will be vast, and competition, which will intensify.

14.2 LINER ORGANIZATION

The production unit in the liner trade is the fleet, and the operator must plan and think in terms of a service rather than a number of self-contained voyages. The liner service implies the operation of a fleet of vessels which provides a fixed service at regular advertised intervals between named ports; the owners offer space to cargo or accommodation to passengers destined for the named ports and delivered to the ship by the advertised date. The liner company, unlike the tramp operator, must seek its own cargo, which originates mainly in relatively small consignments from a multitude of shippers. This involves an expensive organization ashore at all ports which its sailing schedule covers.

The liner company – which may contain an element of tonnage on charter or available for charter – tends to have a diverse organization reflecting the complex nature of its business and extent of its trades involving numerous countries/ports.

The shipping company is managed by a general manager, who is responsible to a board of directors, and normally on the board. He is responsible for carrying out the board's directions dealing with all major issues of policy, including finance, senior executive appointments, the introduction of new services, and major items of capital expenditure including new tonnage, etc. In some companies to facilitate a more prompt decision-making process and streamline administration the general manager post has been abolished and the day-to-day control and management of the company vested in the managing director. Each board director is usually responsible for certain aspects of the business, such as finance, marketing, passenger, cargo, staff and administration, etc.

The organization may be functional or departmental. The functional system involves direct responsibility for a particular activity of the company business, such as trade or service manager for a particular route, who would be responsible for its ultimate performance and control embracing operating/commercial/marketing/financial, etc. The advantage of such a system is that it produces better financial discipline. The departmental system involves the splitting up of all the company activities into various departments, i.e. commercial/operating/technical etc. Both types of organization have merit and one must decide which suits the situation best. Generally the larger the company, the greater the advantages of a functional organization which encourages better financial control.

It will be appreciated that the organizational structure of a shipping company engaged in the liner business will vary according to a number of factors which are detailed:

(a) Fleet size and overall financial turnover.
(b) The trade(s) in which the company is engaged.
(c) The scale of the business involved. For example, the company may rely on agents to develop the business in terms of canvassing for traffic and thereby have only a few salesmen in the field. Additionally, all new tonnage design may be entrusted to a consultant naval architect, and thereby avoid the need to have a full-time naval architect employed in the company with an intermittent workload. Another example is that the company may have a shipbroker's department to diversify the company business.

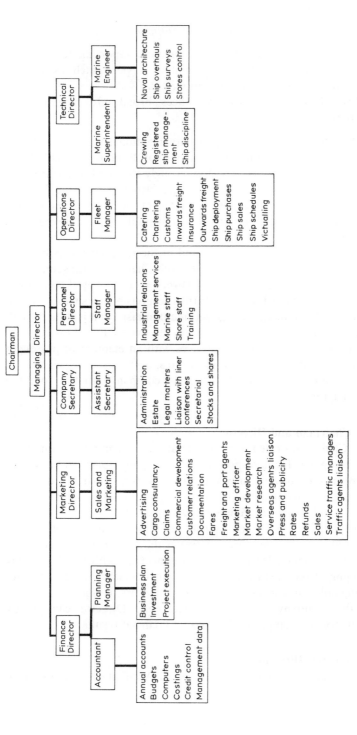

Fig. 14.1 A liner company organization.

(d) It may be a subsidiary company reporting to a parent company which may have common services such as a legal department, planning organization, etc.

(e) The company may have offices abroad, rely on agencies, or be part of a consortium.

A possible shipping company organizational structure is found in Fig. 14.1 and a commentary on each of the departments follows. Again it cannot be stressed too strongly the need to ensure each company devises its organizational structure to suit best its business needs etc. and this should be reviewed from time to time to reflect changed situations. It is essential each employee has a job specification.

In the company structure found in the diagram the policy and control of the company is vested in the Chairman with some seven directors including a Managing Director. This overall constitutes the company board which in turn is responsible to shareholders if it is a public company or a government minister if it is state owned.

It is assumed the company has some twenty-five ships engaged in six deep-sea liner cargo services with an element of passenger business in two short sea trade routes.

A commentary now follows on the company structure found in the diagram.

(a) Chairman and Directors

The Chairman's role is one of ultimate control and management of the company. He is responsible for company policy and development of the business in collaboration with his board of directors who overall form the most senior management team. He works very closely with the Managing Director.

The Managing Director's role tends to be the liaison link in general management terms between the Board of Directors and senior managers. He is essentially concerned with the day-to-day running of the business, particularly its development, and formulating policy in consultation with his directors. It is a very key post in the company and a good Managing Director can greatly influence the company's favourable financial results.

(b) Finance Director

The Finance Director would have an Accountant responsible to him. The Accountant's department is responsible for the annual accounts; budgets embracing revenue, expenditure, investment and cash flow forecasts; credit control involving the billing of customers/shippers and payment of accounts; preparation of management data which may embrace every month's traffic carryings, revenue and expenditure results against budget; costing data such as voyage costs, economics of individual traffic flows; and computers involving their use and development such as stores control, payment of wages, customer billing, market data analysis, etc. It is likely that the Accountant's department would be so organized to have an individual officer responsible for each function such as Budgets Officer, Costing Officer, Credit Controller, Computer Officer, etc. All would have supporting staff and be responsible to the Accountant and liaise with other departments.

The Planning Manager features only in a large shipping company. He is under the Finance Director's control in this particular company. This department is particularly concerned with developing company policy and strategy over a wide range of activities. It embraces the development and implementation of capital projects, formulation of a 5- to 10-year business plan, liaison with government and other national and international organizations relative to general matters appertaining to shipping. The planning department works in very close liaison with other departments and officers within the company.

(c) Operations Director
The Operations Director has the responsibility of producing the optimum performance from the fleet. In so doing it requires a reconciliation of traffic needs with ship capacity availability and other aspects to ensure the most viable service is devised taking into account both short- and long-term needs. It may also involve reconciling the sailing schedules with obligations of a joint service or liner conference whereby each operator may be allocated a certain percentage of the sailings. The Operations Director's policy must be to ensure as far as practicable that such sailings are profitable. Basically the success of a shipping line depends on the efficient operation of its ships under a budgetary control system.

The operations department is under the control of the Fleet Manager who is responsible to the Operations Director. The Fleet Manager covers ship schedules, ship deployment, Customs formalities (including the entering and clearance of ships), chartering, insurance, victualling, ship sale and purchase, inwards freight and outwards freight departments.

Ship schedules may be entrusted to the Operations Officer, which includes Customs formalities (including the entering in and clearance of ships), and port operation. The Operations Officer would work closely with the Marine Superintendent on a ship manning/crew cost having regard to the required schedules. He would liaise and appoint port agents/loading brokers, etc. Additionally he is likely to become involved in negotiating with port authorities, the provision of berthing/quay facilities and related equipment/handling equipment, etc. A qualified shipbroker would look after chartering, insurance and ship sale and purchase. In such circumstances the chartering department would fix additional tonnage, and secure fixtures for the company's own vessels when offered on the market. In some cases he may act in his own capacity of a shipbroker.

The inwards freight department deals with the Customs clearance of imports and their delivery to consignees. It also deals with the transhipment of such cargo, if necessary. Likewise the outwards freight department is to process export cargo and related documentation, and to supervise the provision of shipping space for cargo bookings. The processing of the international consignment is an important function and is more fully explained in Chapter 17. It involves close liaison with the ports. Pre-booking of cargo shipping space – with the development of containerization – is now computerized and this extends to the billing of customers, preparation of Bills of Lading, etc.

(d) Personnel Director

The Personnel Director's responsibilities cover all aspects of staff and embrace those both ashore and afloat. The Staff Manager is responsible to the Personnel Director. This post covers training/ education/recruitment/career development/appointments/redundancy/shore discipline/wages and salaries negotiation/industrial relations/service conditions etc. Management services provide a consultancy service within the company. The Staff Manager's department would work in close liaison with other departments and the extent of the management services role will much depend on the company policy of employing such a specialist or engaging outside consultants for specified projects such as reorganization, recruitment of senior managers, etc.

(e) Technical Director
The Marine Engineer and Marine Superintendent are under the Technical Director. The Marine Engineer department embraces marine engineering, electrical engineering, naval architecture, ship contracts for new building and surveys. It provides technical advice and service, etc. on new construction design; negotiation and monitoring of shipbuilding contracts, fleet maintenance/ surveys to required statutory/classification society obligations. The annual survey programme of the fleet would be undertaken in this department in consultation with the Fleet Manager's organization to reflect ship availability and traffic needs. The Naval Architect is responsible for ship design and providing data on ship stability etc. In smaller companies a consultant is engaged on ship design when new tonnage is required. The marine workshop and stores control is part of the Marine Engineer's department together with bunkering arrangements. All these three activities may be co-ordinated under a Marine Services Officer, responsible to the Marine Engineer.

Also responsible to the Technical Director is the Marine Superintendent who is the Registered Manager. This latter task devolves on the Marine Superintendent who is legally responsible for the maintenance and operation of the registered fleet in accordance with the relevant merchant shipping legislation. It could be equally undertaken by the Fleet Manager but it is usual to entrust the responsibility with someone who is of wide nautical experience and of high professional calibre. The Marine Superintendent within the organizational structure of this particular company is also responsible for crewing involving the level of manning and appointments of ship officers. Additionally the Marine Superintendent is very closely involved in ship safety, relevant navigational matters and ship discipline. The Marine Superintendent is very closely concerned in the acceptance and conveyance of dangerous cargo and the related procedures/ conditions.

(f) Marketing Director
The Marketing Director's responsibilities are extensive and

primarily involve the development of the company business within the freight and passenger markets. In this particular organization the Sales and Marketing Manager is the departmental head but depending on the size of the business, the job could be split between the Marketing, Passenger and Freight Managers. The marketing function in the liner shipping company today is an important one.

The Marketing and Sales Manager would have a number of officers under him to facilitate the smooth running of the department to aid quick decision making and maximize market impact within the commercial policy of the Board as processed through the Marketing Director.

The Marketing Manager would be responsible for the sales and marketing plan devised annually. His job includes selling responsibilities including a field sales force, advertising – particularly promotions – publicity material including public relations.

(g) Public relations

Additionally it could include development of the market/business in both the passenger and freight sectors liaising with the Passenger and Freight Managers. This would include market research. The Marketing Manager would also be responsible for the appointment of the advertising agency.

The Freight Manager's task includes freight rates; freight and customs documentation; liaison with trade associations, chambers of commerce, shippers' councils; liner conferences and cargo claims. Some companies have a cargo consultancy organization to advise on the most ideal methods of transit involving the transport distribution analysis technique. The Freight Manager would be responsible for the appointment and liaison with port agents and freight forwarders.

The Passenger Manager would cover fares, refunds, baggage, appointment and liaison with travel agents, passenger complaints and liaison with passenger associations and liner conferences.

It cannot be stressed too strongly the need of the Passenger, Freight and Marketing Managers to liaise closely to realize the best results.

Some companies have a Service, Sector or Route Manager who is responsible for the traffic management of the route(s), embracing fares, rates, service pattern and so on. Overall, it is a profit centre and subject to strict budgetary control techniques. Such a company structure ensures the optimization of resources on the route(s) compatible with market demand. It comes under the control of the Marketing Manager but requires close liaison with the Freight and Passenger Managers and other departments including the Fleet Manager.

(h) Company Secretary
The Company Secretary is responsible for convening Board meetings, preparation and circulation of Board minutes, and looking after the shipping company statutory affairs. In this particular company, the Assistant Secretary takes charge of the department and responds to the Company Secretary. The department is likely to be small compared with the Marketing Manager's organization. It will include maintaining records of stocks and shares; processing estate matters such as land and property sale and purchase; general administration of the company affairs; and dealing with legal matters. The larger company would employ a solicitor whilst the smaller company would merely engage a solicitor as required.

The department is the organization responsible for liaising with liner conferences but this could be equally undertaken by the Marketing Manager. The Assistant Secretary's department would be responsible for the retention of any company agreements such as a revenue pooling agreement with four other operators on a particular service. Negotiations for renewal of any such agreements or evolvement of other similar agreements would involve this department in consultation with other parts of the organization particularly the Fleet and Marketing Managers.

To conclude our examination of the organization structure, one must stress that each shipping company must devise its organization to suit best its needs and thereby maximize its profitability and long-term future.

The size of each department, and in fact its actual existence, does depend on the size of the company and trades in which it operates. The larger the company the greater is the tendency to have a large number of departments. Overall there is much merit to review the adequacy of an organization in the light of market considerations every 2 years.

The duties of many of the departments outlined may well be

performed by individual firms. Inward freight, stevedoring and forwarding may be dealt with by local port agents. Loading brokers can obtain and document cargo. Technical services given by independent consultants – the Protection and Indemnity Clubs and insurance brokers settle all claims – leave to the shipowner only the major decisions and the working out of the financial results of his acitivities. More recently some companies have entrusted the appointment and recruitment of their crews to specialist agencies.

The shipping companies conduct their business abroad by means of branch offices or agents; they act as the owners' local representatives in the clearance and discharge of the owners' vessels, and they secure cargo for shipment. At head office, the departmental managers specialize in the particular duties performed by their departments; but the manager of a branch or agency has a much wider range of duties, and is usually responsible for all aspects of the shipping work of his office.

As we progress through the 1990s numerous shipping companies, especially those in Western countries, will develop diversified business interests. Such a policy is largely determined by the need to lessen the impact of trade recessions and low profitability levels, and an adequate profitable cash flow situation. Some may be related to shipping business which provide other financial and competitive advantages whilst offers are entirely divorced. Examples are given below:

(a) shipbroking;
(b) freight forwarding including international road haulage operation as found in Ferrymasters operated by 'P & O' Containers;
(c) off-shore oil drilling and related activities;
(d) merchant banking;
(e) real estate involving office blocks, land investment, etc;
(f) container operation;
(g) hotels;
(h) travel agents;
(i) ship management services;
(j) ports;
(k) transportation.

Such activities together with others mentioned on p. 360 can be operated under a holding company arrangement (see also *Economics of Shipping Practice and Management*, Chapter 10).

14.3 TRAMP ORGANIZATION

Tramp companies do not have the many specialized departments found in liner companies. The function of the tramp operator is to provide ships for hire or charter. Therefore he must keep in close touch with the market for tramp ships. The other main departments will be those dealing with operation, maintenance and victualling.

The board of management concerned with tramp ships is similar to that of the liner organizations.

The tendency for specialized functions to be undertaken by independent contractors is even greater in the case of tramp companies.

An increasing number of family-owned tramp shipping companies are experiencing extreme difficulty to raise funds to embark on new tonnage provision. With profitability being at a low ebb for many years and high inflation in shipbuilding cost the tramp shipping company is resorting more to the sale and lease concept (see p. 330) of new tonnage provision. Alternatively they are merging with other shipping companies to help raise capital and reduce cost especially in administration, technical resources etc. Hence in the future the number of family-owned tramp companies worldwide will decline.

14.4 HOLDING COMPANIES AND SUBSIDIARIES INCLUDING ANCILLARY ACTIVITIES OF SHIPPING UNDERTAKINGS

In the liner trade, with its greater financial requirements, there has been considerable growth, and several large groups of associated and subsidiary companies have been formed. In some cases two companies competing on the same route have found it advantageous to arrange a merger or amalgamation.

In other cases, the companies have arranged to retain their individual identities, but have made provision for exchange of shares and common directorships. Sometimes successful companies have bought out unsuccessful companies, often with a view to securing their goodwill and loading rights in a particular trade.

Many of these groups are controlled by means of holding companies. The term 'holding company' was originally used to describe a company formed with the object of taking shares in two or more operating concerns. But more recently the term has come to include companies which, besides having a controlling interest in others, carry on business themselves. Generally, the associated and subsidiary companies in these groups are run as individual concerns with separate identities, organizations, and ships.

With the expansion of containerization in recent years it has stimulated the development of the consortium concept. An example in the 1970s of such a development is the containerized service UK/Europe/South Africa which involved an investment of £520 million. It emphasizes such capital outlay can only be undertaken realistically on a consortium basis.

The merits of the consortium concept are given below:

(a) It is impracticable for a sole shipowner to raise capital and bear the risk involved of such an assignment.

(b) A consortium facilitates good development/relationships with governments/countries involved through the shipping company resident in the country.

(c) A consortium is best able to counter Eastern bloc infiltration through concerted action through their governments. A sole operator would not be so effective in dealing with such a situation.

(d) A consortium which is broadly based strengthens the economic ties amongst the countries involved which in turn helps to influence trade to such a service and counter trade depression.

(e) A consortium normally reflects the shipping corporation formally associated with the 'tween-deck tonnage which in turn reflects much experience of the trade. A sole operator could not achieve such expertise/commercial intelligence and, long-term, attract quality management.

(f) A consortium produces economies of scale particularly in terms of agents and encourages the use of common services.

(g) A consortium involving individual shipping companies of varying nationalities tends to permit the maritime countries involved to make, if available, any contribution to subsidize new building terms.

The shipping undertaking, besides being responsible for the provision and operation of the fleet, also frequently engages in certain ancillary services. Included in such services are stevedoring, lighterage, warehousing, wharfingering, bunkering, shipbroking, road haulage, ship agencies, merchanting, ship repairing, ship management, forwarding agents, aircraft operating and container operation.

14.5 SHIP MANAGEMENT COMPANIES

Ship management companies are now becoming more common today and their expansion in recent years can be attributed to the gradual change from the traditional shipping company to two new shipping groups: the developing nation bloc and the large bulk shippers who are seeking greater involvement in shipping operation. Additionally, for many years a number of multinational companies have tended to rely on ship management companies.

Ship management companies primarily become involved in the efficient manning, chartering and maintenance of a vessel for an owner. Other areas of ship management include the recruitment, training, and appointment of both ship- and shore-based personnel; advice on the most suitable type of vessel, method of financing and source of ship supply; advice on the options available of ship registration, manning, trading and maintenance – this situation tends to emerge with the developing nation who is required by law for their ships to be manned by nationals, whilst the management company has the flexibility to register the vessel elsewhere yet use her as a training ship for national crews for subsequent additions to the fleet. A further area is the ability of the management company to obtain cheaper insurance by inclusion of the vessel(s) on the main owner-fleet cover to take the advantages of sharing in bulk buying of spares, stores etc. overall. To be really effective the shipowner must seek a manager who relects this philosophy.

The ship management company has long been recognized by the major oil companies who operate on an owner/time chartered/spot chartered mix of vessels. Accordingly the management company provides the ideal method for ensuring that the daily operation and maintenance of the vessels is correctly superintended rather than indulging in the expense of setting up their own operations department. It also has the advantage of terminating the agreement when the market can no longer support the chartered tonnage.

The basic criterium of the ship management service is to provide the owner, for a management fee, with vessels attaining quality service standards at reasonable competitive cost.

During the past decade some multinational companies have built up their own fleets to carry their raw materials or manufactured products to overseas markets. It offers many benefits to the multinational company. This includes complete control of the transport distribution system which can be fully integrated into the manufacturer's distributor's programme; it aids competitiveness of the product as the goods are conveyed at relatively low cost and not at the normal market public tariffs found on liner cargo services; it permits flexibility of operation inasmuch as when trade is buoyant additional tonnage can be chartered; and finally it enables the multinational company to exploit the economics of scale by permitting various countries to specialize in particular products thereby avoiding duplication of investment plant. This latter arrangement can be very advantageous in free trade areas. More recently the tendency of multinational companies is to charter tonnage or rely on existing liner cargo services, rather than develop their own fleets. This trend will continue as the pattern of world trade changes.

The ship management company may be a subsidiary of an established liner company and thus is able to draw on the expertise available within the parent shipowning group. In so doing a package deal can be concluded of a most comprehensive nature. Long-term, the role and popularity of the ship management company could decline as the pattern of world trade changes and similarly the changing pattern of shipownership of individual nations.

14.6 OWNERSHIP OF VESSELS

The Merchant Shipping Act 1988 incorporates the following relative to the registration of British ships:

1. the exclusion of Commonwealth citizens and companies from those persons qualified to be owners of British ships;

2. the replacement of the present obligation to register a British ship by an entitlement to register;

3. the introduction of a requirement to appoint a representative person when a company qualified to own a British ship wishes to register it in the UK, but has its principal place of business outside the UK;

4. The Secretary of State to have the power to refuse or terminate the registration of a ship; and

5. powers to restrict the size and types of ships registered in the British Dependent Territories (with the exception of Hong Kong).

The above represent Part I of the Merchant Shipping Act 1988: Part II deals with the registration of British fishing vessels.

British vessels have to be registered (through the Customs at their local port) with the 'General Register and Record Office of Shipping and Seamen', a section of the Department of Trade.

14.7 CAPITALIZATION AND FINANCE OF SHIPPING UNDERTAKINGS

Most British shipping companies grew up during the nineteenth century on the retention of profits earned, short-term finance for expansion being obtained by security on the fleet. The shares of the larger companies were normally quoted on the Stock Exchanges, but large-scale public subscriptions to form new undertakings were rare, as shipping has always been considered a risky undertaking.

Since 1945 the only public subscriptions have been in the form of loan capital, but with the increase in the number of long-term charters for 12 or even 15 years (practically the whole of the life of a tanker), mortgages can be obtained from many international finance houses, insurance companies and similar organizations. Thus, anyone with some knowledge of ship management can get a long-term charter from an oil company or iron and steel organization, and borrow money to have the vessel built. The charter hire is pledged against interest and repayments of the mortgage.

Resulting from the vulnerability of freight rates, profits and depreciation funds have been barely sufficient to allow shipowners to renew their fleets at current shipbuilding prices. To stimulate shipbuilding and ship operation, many governments have adopted a policy of cheap loans for the shipping industry, and give operating subsidies, particularly for new independent countries with maritime fleets. The USA practises both building and operating subsidies extensively.

Today many shipowners finance their new tonnage from three sources: loan capital obtained on the open market including a bank mortgage or provided by Government on very favourable low interest terms; money provided by the shipping company through liquidation of reserve capital, and finally Government grants, which are usually conditional. Very few shipping companies today are able to finance their new tonnage from within their own financial resources. This is due to the low level of profitability and return on capital, often between 2% and 3%; depressed trading conditions; and the failure in many trades for rates to keep pace with rising cost.

A further method of financing new tonnage is through a leasing arrangement with a finance company. This enables the maximum benefit to be taken of any available tax advantage, and the quarterly or half-yearly leasing payments will reflect this. With these sort of agreements, though, it is not normal for legal ownership of the vessel to pass to the shipping company even after the leasing period expires. Usually there is provision for a peppercorn rental to be paid until it is desired to dispose of the vessel, when the shipping company would take all but a tiny percentage of the sale value realized. With the development of the oil resources of the Arab countries with their consequential industrial expansion, the situation has emerged whereby such oil producers have taken over the distribution of the product. Such countries have now their own oil tanker fleets.

As we progress through the 1990s the funding of new tonnage and the financial structure of shipping companies could change. Traditional shipping nations such as the UK are tending to diversify their company structure to offset any trade recession experienced in their shipping activities. A number of them are tending to invest in real estate such as office blocks whilst others have financial interest and/or activity in oil exploration/development. Other shipping companies are merely entering industries with no direct relationship with shipping such as computers, publishing, etc. An example of a progressive modern shipping company is found in the Maersk Company Limited, London which was formed in 1951. Today it is one of the leading European ship-owners but has also in recent years diversified into other activities.

The Maersk fleet includes crude oil tankers, product carriers, chemical tankers, Ro/Ro ferries, multipurpose support vessels, anchorhandlers, oil rig supply vessels, a diving support vessel and a maintenance vessel. The group currently operates a fleet of 29 vessels, fully owned or on long-term charter, with a total dead-weight of 372,450 tons.

The second main activity is door-to-door transportation. The Norfolk Line Group with seven companies in the UK, the Netherlands, Germany, Belgium and representation in Denmark is a fully owned subsidiary of Maersk UK. Nearly 2000 Norfolk Line trailers are constantly on the road over most of Europe and the Norfolk Group operates three ferry services from the UK to Holland, to Belgium and to Denmark.

The third main activity is industrial and engineering services. The Scottish-based Salamis Group operates in a number of indus-trial fields; engineering, marine-servicing, offshore and onshore maintenance, coating, insulation, scaffolding and grit sales. With joint-venture partners, Salamis is active in the Far East and also owns Europe's most advanced tubular maintenance factory, situated at Peterhead in Scotland.

The Maersk UK Group also provides a range of services in ship management, chartering, bunker-broking, liner-agencies and travel-agencies. Such developments have emerged for a variety of reasons but the prime one is the low profitability of shipping and potentially improved overall financial results when companies diversify their industrial activity. Furthermore a large number of shipowners have 'flagged out' to reduce crew cost by engaging foreign crews. A similar policy has been adopted by the US, Japan, Greece, Western Germany and Norway. Overall the UK fleet has dramatically declined from 1614 vessels in 1975 represent-ing 50 million dwt – 8.9% of the world fleet to 43 vessels in 1988 representing 8.7 nm dwt – 1.4% of the world fleet.

A further factor to bear in mind is that an increasing number of countries is now subsidizing in one way or other their fleets. This may be a building or operating subsidy. Alternatively some other financial contribution may be provided such as subsidized bunker fuel, state aid for social contribution for crew personnel etc.

Overall such practices tend to be found in Eastern bloc fleets and those fleets emerging from developing countries.

Overall this subject is fully dealt with in *Economics of Shipping Practice and Management*, Chapter 4.

14.8 INCOME AND EXPENDITURE

This will vary according to the type of operations conducted by the shipping organization.

With a liner company conveying passengers and cargo, there are many items of income and expenditure. Items of income would include revenue from passengers, cargo, catering, postal parcels, letter mails and perhaps chartering. This last item would arise if a liner company releases a vessel on charter to another undertaking. Expenditure items would include crew cost, maintenance of ships, fuel, lubricants, port disbursements (including dues and cargo-handling cost), depreciation, publicity expenses, administration cost, insurance commission to agents, passenger and cargo claims, interest on capital, compensation for accidents in collisions, and any chartering expenses involving the hire of additional vessels to augment the fleet.

In the case of the tramp undertaking, there is of course only one main source of income and this accrues from chartering. The items of expenditure, however, do vary according to the type of charter party. With a 'demise' charter, there are very few items of expenditure, and these broadly include ship depreciation, interest on capital and administration cost. The number of expenditure items is, however, increased with non-demise 'time' and 'voyage' charters, and embrace crew cost, ship maintenance, depreciation, insurance, interest on capital, compensation for accidents in collisions and administration cost. The administration cost forms a very small portion of the expenditure of a tramp undertaking compared with the liner company.

In view of the large payments incurred when new vessels are purchased, shipping companies as far as possible maintain reserves in easily redeemable securities.

14.9 STATISTICS

Statistics play an important role in the successful management of shipping and the shipowner must keep under constant review the performance of his ships, items of earnings and costs. A careful and detailed analysis must thus be made of the revenue and expenditure accounts of each voyage.

Important operational statistics include, for example, voyage distances, fuel consumption, load factors and fleet utilization. The shipowner will particularly require to know the voyage distances in relation to the fuel consumed per nautical mile. This will give an indication of engine performance. Passengers and/or cargo conveyed have to be recorded and related on a voyage basis to the available capacity. This will give the ship's load factor on a percentage basis, indicating how much of the available revenue earning capacity on a particular voyage has been filled. For example, if a ship with a passenger certificate of 1000 conveyed 750 passengers, it would have a load factor of 75%. It will also be necessary to record the number of days a vessel is at sea and the time spent in port loading and/or discharging or alternatively undergoing survey and overhaul. Turn-round time in port will be influenced by the cargo handled and port resources, and will necessitate the compilation of statistics showing average tons loaded or discharged per day in various ports which the ship visits. The aim should be, of course, to keep turn-round time to an absolute minimum, as it represents idle time to the shipowner, and earns no revenue. Similarly, time spent on surveys and overhauls should be kept to a minimum, and if possible undertaken outside times of peak traffic. How successful the shipowner is in achieving these objectives can only be established if proper statistics are maintained. These will enable him to relate the days a vessel spends at sea with the time spent either in port or in a shipyard.

The victualling department of passenger-carrying lines will require such statistics as meals served and cost per meal and profitability per day or per head. Such data, when related to the number of passengers carried, will help to establish the general popularity and profitability of the meals, and enable the victualling results on one ship to be compared with another.

Traffic analysis is also important, and statistics must be kept of various commodity movements and average freight earnings. Bills of lading and charter parties must be carefully analyzed and data abstracted regarding commodities, ports of loading and discharge, weight and stowage factor, and other features of interest, such as damage or pilferage to cargo. When properly analyzed, this data will enable the shipowner to estimate in advance his future tonnage requirements throughout the year, and provide valuable information which will influence the design of future ships.

In the shipping industry, statistics have become more important, particularly in recent years, because greater emphasis has been placed on improved efficiency, and there is an ever-increasing cost consciousness involving the development of profit centres in a trade or particular area basis. Statistics are one of the most reliable means of measuring the performance and efficiency of the individual ship and the fleet, but the subject has tended to become very specialized and many of the large shipowners therefore have qualified statisticians. The provision of statistics can be very costly, and the volume of data should be kept under constant review. Most major shipping companies today use computers to provide essential management information to run their business. This embraces traffic analysis, voyage cost, load factors etc. Such data are produced maybe weekly or monthly and related to budget predictions.

14.10   COMPUTERIZATION

As we progress through the 1990s the use of computers within the shipping business will expand and in so doing aid more efficient management of the shipping company. It will greatly facilitate the optimum use of available resources and overall should improve profitability levels within the industry.

Given below are details of the various items in which computers feature:

(a) *Stores control.* Details of stores in stock, their value and consumption are recorded on the computer for inventory management purposes. At regular intervals, such as weekly or monthly, a statement can be produced detailing the stores consumed during the period, and an inventory of those on hand together with their value. This helps to keep stores consumption and inventory levels down to an economic minimum and facilitates replacement planning.

(b) *Pay bills.* The staff salaries including national insurance, overtime, pension contributions, tax deductions can be processed through the computer on a weekly or other prescribed period basis.

(c) *Reservations.* Operators in the passenger business and motorist market tend to insist on prebooking of vehicle deck space, cabin or rest chairs. This is usually undertaken on a computer to control the traffic volume accepted at particularly busy summer periods and avoid outshipments. It is essential with overnight cabin accommodation on short sea trade services, and also in the cruise market. Computers undertake such reservation work through a central reservation unit.

(d) *Ship design/specification.* Most classification societies offer the facility to provide a basic ship specification/profile on receipt of a parameter of traffic data such as capacity, length, beam, draught, speed etc. Computers feature strongly in such developments.

(e) *Speed/navigation aids.* Modern ships are provided with a computer facility which regulates their optimum speed and fuel consumption. It results in the engine room being controlled from the bridge outside normal working hours. Computer navigation aids are also available.

(f) *Management information.* An increasing volume of statistical data is now computerized. This includes traffic statistics, staff numbers, number of sailings, etc. It enables the data to be produced regularly and accurately together with relevant financial data.

(g) *Billing of customers.* Large shipowners now bill their customers on a periodic basis with the aid of a computer. It ensures prompt despatch and provides a useful reminder service to late payers, thereby aiding credit control.

(h) *Schedules.* Some major operators are now using the computer as an aid to schedule formulation and particularly with regard to traffic potential and optimum ship use.

(i) *Documentation.* The transmission and design of shipping documents has been transformed in recent years. A more recent development has been the use of computers to transmit the relevant cargo shipment details found on the shipping documents involving the electronic data processing technique to the destination port, etc. to facilitate the speedy clearance and payment settlement arrangements.

(j) *Containers.* The development of deep-sea container services has involved closely the use of computers particularly in their control, stowage and overall shipment arrangements. It has greatly facilitated the optimum use of the container unit together with its infrastructure. Moreover, it also provides a booking facility reserving container unit space on a specified sailing and associated rail services to and from the port. The facility enables the shipowner to record the progress/location of the container from the time it is made available to the shipper for stuffing until the goods are discharged in the importer's warehouse.

(k) *Ship maintenance.* The development of ship maintenance techniques has been facilitated through the use of the computer. It has facilitated the formulation on an individual ship basis the maintenance programme, particularly survey requirements.

(l) *Customs clearance.* Computers now feature strongly in the customs clearance techniques as, for example, with the Direct Trader Input System operative in the UK.

(m) *Marketing.* All statistical data and associated documentation are now computerized in most major shipping companies. It includes customer portfolios, market intelligence data, market analysis, etc.

The development of computers in shipping will doubtless continue particularly in terms of optimizing use of ship capacity and controlling expenditure providing financial data to enable the Company to plan ahead in the light of market opportunities. It features very strongly in budgetary control (financial/statistical) techniques.

14.11 CREDIT CONTROL

At a time of increasing financial discipline in shipping today, it is appropriate to examine briefly the role of credit control. Basically it is a technique whereby a vigilant eye is kept on clients who enjoy credit facilities with the shipping company to ensure their accounts are paid regularly and the period of credit afforded to them is not abused. Moreover, any disputed accounts are quickly settled and where a large disputed amount is involved a partial settlement is made 'without prejudice' pending agreement on the account.

In large companies the bills are computer compiled and despatched usually weekly. The computer will send out a reminder to clients failing to pay within the prescribed period. Moreover such a system enables the credit controller to have a readily up-to-date statement on each individual account. This also aids in the detection of the firm which through sluggish payment of bills is in financial difficulties. In such circumstances immediate measures must be taken to review the credit facility and agree with the client programmed payments over a period of the outstanding amount. In more serious cases discussions also involve the firm's bankers and in extreme situations the appointment of a receiver. With regard to the latter, all trading with the firm ceases unless it is through the receiver or his appointed agent.

Advantages of a credit control system are given below:

(a) It facilitates prompt payment of accounts.

(b) It improves cash flow which is monitored against the budget.

(c) It keeps the shipping company's working capital level down to a minimum.

(d) It facilitates improved profitability.

(e) The risk of bad debt is minimized and the prospect of their partial recovery is enhanced.

(f) Credit facilities are usually granted to those clients who fulfil a stringent code of enquiry regarding their creditability and usually involves the use of bank references. In some cases particularly in the travel trade bonds are required. This lessens the risk of bad debts.

(g) The credit controller usually responsible directly to the treasurer and/or sales manager enables the system to be centralized and close liaison maintained with the various departments. This is particularly relevant when a bad debt situation arises and the client is also owed money by the shipping company for a particular transaction. In such circumstances no monies would be paid until the client's creditability had been resolved.

(h) Variation in exchange rate levels is particularly important to ensure appropriate measures are taken to contain such adverse effect and full use is made of international currency settlement techniques.

To conclude, credit control is an important activity today in shipping practice.

14.12 FREIGHT FORWARDER

Our study of the shipping industry would not be complete without examining the important function and role of the shipping and forwarding agent, now termed the freight forwarder.

The freight forwarder is concerned with the transport arrangements of all kinds of goods across international frontiers. In reality he is responsible for the co-ordination of the various forms of transport, and related ancillary activities embracing documentation, customs clearance, booking cargo space, packing, etc. for any particular international consignment.

The freight forwarder's knowledge must therefore be very extensive, as he is responsible for the consignment from the time he has secured it through his canvassing, to the point it is delivered to the consignee at the final destination. He must be in a position to advise his principal as to the most suitable service available which may be train ferry, road transport throughout, air freight, high capacity container, etc; the most suitable packing; compliance with any maritime and other statutory obligations; customs procedure clearance, including related documentation needs; rates and insurance premiums for individual services, including related conditions of liability; schedule and transit times of the various forms of transport service available; the most satisfactory method of concluding the international financial arrangments for the cargo; all technical aspects of international forwarding; marking of cargo; and any particular circumstances/obligations obtaining in the country of destination with which the exporter must comply. In short, the freight forwarder must have a good knowledge of commerce, the finance of international trade, forwarding practice including customs, commercial geography, cargo insurance, the law of carriage and the economics of international trade distribution.

In more recent years, the freight forwarder has entered such specialized but ancillary fields to international forwarding as packing, warehousing and the actual carriage of goods generally involving road transport to/from the Continent. Moreover, this trend is growing with a much larger share of the UK/Continent trade being conveyed by road under the freight forwarder sponsorship involving break-bulk cargoes. Similar situations have emerged in other trades where Ro/Ro services are provided. Additionally, an increasing number of freight forwarders own ISO containers for use in international services and operate on a similar basis. It is called non-vessel operating carrier (see p. 262).

Freight forwarders tend to specialize in the international trades they serve and the products they deal in. Such specialisms includes project forwarding involving the despatch of all the merchandise for a major contract such as a power station, hospital, bridge, telecommunications network; antiques involving priceless paintings; bloodstock involving racehorses; dangerous classified cargoes; groupage/consolidated goods which may be in a trailer or LCL container for specific trades; indivisible loads involving heavy lifts such as transformers; household removals overseas; livestock; exhibitions and trade fairs; and so on.

There is no doubt that the freight forwarder has an important role in developing traffic for liner cargo services, and as such has made, and will continue to make, an important contribution to the UK balance of payments by using his expertise to foster international traffic. Indeed the freight forwarder, by developing groupage traffic (involving a groupage bill of lading as described in Chapter 12), has helped the development of trade for the small emerging inexperienced exporter who often uses the agent's transport throughout.

In common with other sections in shipping, the agents are tending to merge to raise capital, often for ISO container investment. The agents operate under their trading conditions, dated 1984, and, to facilitate international trade development, operate in conjunction with another freight forwarder in the destination country. Freight forwarders originating cargo for individual liner cargo services receive a commission which varies according to the tonnage forwarded.

14.13 CHARTERED SHIPBROKER

The basic function of the shipbroker is to bring together the two parties concerned involving the ship and cargo owners. In so doing following negotiations between them, a charter party is ultimately concluded. The broker's income is derived from the commission payable by the shipowner on completion and fulfilment of the contract.

A further role of the shipbroker – other than fixing vessels – is acting as agent for the shipowner. As such he is responsible for everything which may concern the vessel whilst she is in port. This embraces Customs formalities; matters concerning the crew; loading/discharge of vessels; bunkering/victualling and so on.

Duties of the shipbroker can be summarized as follows:

(a)　Chartering agent whereby he acts for the cargo merchant seeking a suitable vessel in which to carry the merchandise.

(b)　Sale and Purchase broker acting on behalf of the buyer or seller of ships and bringing the two parties together.

(c)　Owner's broker whereby he acts for the actual shipowner in finding cargo for the vessel.

- (d)　Tanker broker dealing with oil tanker tonnage.

(e)　Coasting broker involving vessels operating around the British coast and/or in the short sea trade, e.g. UK/Continent. Additionally he can at the same time act for the cargo merchant in this trade should circumstances so dictate. The deep-sea broker, however, will act for the shipowner or cargo merchant – not both at the same time.

(f)　Cabling agent involving the broker communicating with other international markets.

There is no doubt the shipbroker is a man of many parts. In reality he is the middle man between the two principals concerned in a charter party.

14.14　SHIP'S AGENT

An agent is a person who acts for, or on behalf of another (the principal) in such a manner that the principal is legally responsible for all acts carried out under such agency.

Basically, the ship's agent represents the shipowner/Master at a particular seaport, either on a permanent or temporary basis. This includes notification of arrival and departure of vessel; acceptance of vessel for loading, discharge, repairs, storing and victualling; arranging berths, tugs, harbour pilots, launches; ordering stevedores, cranes, equipment etc. and so on. 'In port' requirements include requirements of the Master, embracing bunkers, stores, provisions, crew mail and wages, cash, laundry, engine and deck repairs, and crew repatriation; completion of customs, immigration and port health formalities; hatch and cargo surveys; collection of freight; collection and issuing of bills of lading; completion of manifests; notorial and consular protests and so on.

BIMCO has formulated the criteria under which the ship's agents should function. These include protection of the vessel's interests at all times – especially with regard to the quickest turnround of the ship; attendance to time-chartered vessels; attendance as agents appointed by the charterers; agency fees and ship disbursements.

Given below is an outline of an agreement between a Jordanian ship agency and a UK shipowner involving services in Aqaba and European ports.

Agency agreement

An agency agreement made between shipowners (EF–Steamship Co.) Party A and shipping agents (AC–Agent) Party B on following points:

Preamble – description of parties to the agreement.

1. Owners to provide regular line from Europe to Red Sea ports on monthly basis, of two trips per month.

2. The agents will provide:

(a) Traffic volume (marketing), i.e. backload to Europe on the same basis as company freight rate. Volume to be agreed regularly.

(b) Agent will be offered 10% on return cargo booked through shipowner's office and 5% of total cargo freight received and delivered.

(c) Service frequency to be determined by shipowner whilst facilities such administration offices, advertising provisions, back-up services, crew services and documentation to be provided by ship agency.

(d) Agent will obtain traffic right to the port within a certain time limit.

(e) Ship owners to delegate a qualified representative of their company to avoid freight collection problems with customers, i.e. to act as a consultant.

(f) Shipowner to respect rules and laws of the receivers destination he is dealing with.

(g) Owners to respect and abide by the schedule of sailings and keep the agents duly notified of vessel's arrival – 72 hours in advance.

(h) The owners to instruct loading agents to despatch shipping documents 3 days prior to ship's arrival enabling agents to make necessary arrangements.

(i) Agent not to handle any competitive vessels from any other shipping line on the same route.

(j) All freight charges paid at port of this destination must be collected by the agent and transferred to the shipowner account.

(k) Agent to provide handling facilities for loading and unloading operation.

(l) Agent to submit report of the ship's position at the port every 15 days.

(m) Shipowner to arrange transfer of regular despatch accounts, for later settlement, prior to vessel's arrival.

(n) This agreement is valid for 5 years with 3 months notice in case of any conflicts.

(o) Owners to comply with rules and regulations such as boycott articles.

(p) Unity of language i.e English on basis of which all correspondence to be exchanged.

(q) Owners to provide modern vessels with all regular operational facilities.

(r) Both parties agree upon the financial settlement on monthly basis – settled by the end of the next month only in US dollars by telex transfer.

(s) Arbitration clause.

(t) Agreement subject at Jordanian law.

Signed by directors of each company/shipowner/ship's agency.

CHAPTER 15

Charter parties

A very large proportion of the world's trade is carried in tramp vessels. It is quite common to find one cargo will fill the whole ship, and, in these circumstances, one cargo owner or one charterer will enter into a special contract with the shipowner for the hire of his ship – such a contract is known as a charter party. It is not always a full ship-load, although this is usually the case.

A charter party is a contract whereby a shipowner agrees to place his ship, or part of it, at the disposal of a merchant or other person (known as the charterer), for the carriage of goods from one port to another port on being paid freight, or to let his ship for a specified period, his remuneration being known as hire money. The terms, conditions and exceptions under which the goods are carried are set out in the charter party.

15.1 DEMISE AND NON-DEMISE CHARTER PARTIES

There are basically two types of charter parties: demise and non-demise.

A demise or 'bareboat' charter party arises when the charterer is responsible for providing the cargo and crew, whilst the shipowner merely provides the vessel. In consequence, the charterer appoints the crew, thus taking over full responsibility for the operation of the vessel, and pays all expenses incurred. However, in some situations it is the practice for the chief engineer to be the shipowner's representative and thereby provide experience of the shipboard maintenance needs of the vessel's machinery. A demise charter party is for a period of time which may vary from a few weeks to several years.

A non-demise charter arises when the shipowner provides the vessel and her crew, whilst the charterer merely supplies the cargo. It may be a voyage charter for a particular voyage, in which the shipowner agrees to carry cargo between specified ports for a pre-arranged freight. The majority of tramp cargo shipments are made on a voyage charter basis. Alternatively, it may be a time charter for a stated period or voyage for a remuneration known as hire money. The shipowner continues to manage his own vessel, both under non-demise voyage or time charter parties under the charterer's instructions. With a time charter, it is usual for the charterer to pay port dues and fuel costs, and overtime payments incurred in an endeavour to obtain faster turnrounds. It is quite common for liner companies to supplement their services by taking tramp ships on time charter, but this practice may lessen as containerization develops.

There are several types of non-demise voyage charter and these are given below. It will be seen that they all deal with the carriage of goods from a certain port or ports to another port or ports, and the differences between them arise mainly out of payment for the cost of loading and discharging, and to port expenses.

1. *Gross terms form of charter.* This is probably the most common form of charter used by tramp ships today. In this form, the shipowner pays all the expenses incurred in loading and discharging and also all port charges plus of course voyage cost. It can be varied by having gross terms at the loading port and nett terms at the discharging port in which case it is called gross load, free discharge.

2. *FIO charter.* Under this charter, the charterer pays for the cost of loading and discharging the cargo, hence the expression of FIO (meaning 'free in and out'). The shipowner is still responsible for the payment of all port charges. It can be described as nett terms.

3. *Lump sum charter.* In this case, the charterer pays a lump sum of money for the use of the ship and the shipowner guarantees that a certain amount of space (i.e. bale cubic metres) will be available for cargo, along with the maximum weight of cargo that the vessel will be able to carry. A lump sum charter may be on either a gross basis or an FIO basis. Such a charter is very useful when the charterer wishes to load a mixed cargo – the shipowner guarantees that a certain amount of space and weight will be available and it is up to the charterer to use that space to his best advantage.

The above forms of charter are all quite common today, and in each case the shipowner pays the port charges.

4. *Liner terms*. An inclusive freight rate more usually found on cargo liner services which embraces not only the sea freight, but also loading and discharging cost for a particular consignment. Under a voyage charter the shipowner is paid freight which includes the cost of loading, stowing and discharging the cargo. It is particularly evident in the short sea area of tramp shipping. It is desirable the shipowner agrees with the shipper or receiver the appointment of the stevedores.

5. *Berth terms*. Under this term the shipowner agrees to his vessel's loading or discharging operation begin subject to the custom of the port where the cargo handling is taking place, or he may be agreeing that the vessel will load or discharge as fast as can or under customary despatch or any or all of this type of term. Hence the shipowner is responsible to pay for loading and discharging cost and only indefinite laytime exists.

There are, of course, numerous variations that may be made to the above broad divisions and this is a matter for negotiation when the vessel is being 'worked' for future business. For example, the gross and FIO charters may be modified to an FOB charter (free on board) meaning that the charterer pays for the cost of loading and the shipowner pays for the cost of discharge, or alternatively the charter may be arranged on the basis of free discharge, i.e. the charterer pays for the cost of discharging.

The same general terms of contract are found in all the above types of charter.

A significant proportion of the charters in this country are negotiated through a shipbroker on the Baltic Exchange situated in London. The role of this Exchange has been explained in Chapter 8.

The following items would be included when formulating a remit to a shipbroker to obtain a general cargo vessel on charter.

(a) vessel capacity;
(b) vessel speed;
(c) actual trade/ports of call including cargo specification and volume;
(d) duration of charter;
(e) type of charter, i.e. demise or non-demise, voyage or time;

(f) date of charter commencement and duration – the latter with any options for extensions;
(g) overall dimensions of vessel, draught, length and beam;
(h) any constraints likely to be imposed, e.g. carriage of dangerous cargo;
(i) classification of vessel and any trading limits;
(j) possible band of fixture rate likely to be viable;
(k) any shipboard cargo-handling equipment needs.

The extent to which the foregoing items would need to be included would depend on circumstances. Moreover, the urgency of the need of the tonnage would be significant and whether the market fixture rates were falling or rising. Given time, the charterer could examine the market in greater depth and have the benefit of securing a more suitable vessel which may not be immediately available.

The negotiations are carried out by word of mouth in the Exchange, not by letter, and when the contract has been concluded the vessel is said to be 'fixed'. Factors influencing the ultimate fixture rate are described on pages 10–12. The charter party is then prepared and signed by the two parties or their agents. In addition to the trade to and from this country, a large number of cross voyages, i.e. from one foreign country to another, are fixed on the London market, quite often to a vessel owned in yet another foreign country. There is no compulsion to conduct negotiations through a shipbroker on the Baltic Exchange. Many negotiations are conducted direct between charterer and ship-owner. It is a matter for the shipowner's judgement whether he engages a shipbroker to conduct his negotiations direct with the charterer. Obviously, when the shipbroker is negotiating a series of voyage charters for his principal, the shipowner will endeavour to reduce to an absolute minimum the number of ballast voyages. These arise between termination of one voyage charter, for example at Rotterdam, and commencement of the next voyage charter, for example at Southampton, involving a ballast voyage Rotterdam–Southampton.

The report of a vessel's fixture is recorded in the shipping press. Extracts of two fixtures in grain and two time-charter fixtures are given below:

**(a) Interpretation of two fixtures in grain
and two time-charter fixtures**

(i) Chicago–Belfast: *Sugar Crystal*, 14 000 HSS $27.50, Option Glasgow/Leith $28.00, 3 days/3000, 2–14 May (Peabody). Loading Chicago, discharging Belfast: MV *Sugar Crystal*; cargo 14 000 tonnes heavy grains, sorghums or soyabeans at a freight rate of US $27.50 per tonne, with the charterer's option to discharge instead at Glasgow or Leith at the freight rate of US $28.00; 3 days allowed for loading; 3000 tonnes rate per day allowed for discharging. Vessel to present ready to load between laydays 2 May and the cancelling date of 14 May, charterers being Messrs Peabody.

(ii) US Gulf–Constanza: *Myron,* 19 000/19 800 min/max SBM, $31.50, FIO, 3000/1000, option 4000 load at $31.25, 26 May – 15 June (Coprasol). Loading at a port in the US Gulf, discharging Constanza: MV *Myron*; cargo minimum 19 000 tonnes/maximum 19 800 tonnes soyabean meal, at a freight rate of US $31.50 per tonne; cargo to be loaded and discharged free of expense to the owner (FIO). 3000 tonne rate per day for loading, 1000 tonnes rate per day for discharging, with charterer's option to increase the speed of loading to 4000 tonnes per day, in turn paying a reduced freight rate of US $31.25 per tonne. Vessel to present ready to load between laydays 26 May and the cancelling date of 15 June, charterers being Messrs Coprasol.

(iii) *Acropolis* (Fortune type): Greek, built 1978, $5350 daily. Delivery Casablanca trip, redelivery Le Havre. 20–25 April (Dreyfus). MV *Acropolis* (a Japanese Fortune type of vessel), Greek flag. Built 1978, $5350 daily hire. Delivery to charterers at Casablanca for a time charter trip, redelivery to owners at Le Havre. Delivery not earlier than 20 April, not later than 25 April charterers being Messrs Dreyfus.

(iv) *Camara*, 25 689 dwt, 1.2 m ft³, Danish, built 1979, 15 knots on 37 tonnes, 1500 s. 5 × 15 tonne cranes. $6250 daily. Delivery Antwerp, trip via North France and Bulgaria, redelivery Gibraltar. Spot (Philipp Bros.). MV *Camara*, 25 689 summer deadweight 1 200 000 ft³ capacity, Danish flag, built 1979. 15 knots on 37 tonnes (CS 180) F/O, 5 × 15 tonne cranes, US $6250 daily hire. Delivery on time charter at Antwerp for a time charter trip via North France and Bulgaria with redelivery to owners upon vessel passing Gibraltar. Vessel available immediately at Antwerp (spot), charterers being Messrs Philipp Bros.

15.2 VOYAGE AND TIME CHARTER PARTIES

Basically, there are no statutory clauses required to be incorporated in a charter party. The terms and conditions found in a charter party represent the wishes of the two parties to the contract. In extreme cases it has been known for a charter party contract to be completed on the back of a stamp. Nevertheless, there are certain essential clauses necessary to some charter parties, whilst other clauses are of an optional nature. For example, an ice clause would be essential if the vessel were trading in the White or Baltic Seas but would not be necessary if the ship was operating in the Tropics. Given below are the desirable essential clauses found in a voyage charter party but it is stressed they are not always found in all charters.

1. *The preamble.* The contracting parties; description of the vessel; position of vessel and expected readiness date to load.

2. *Description of the cargo.* The quantity of cargo is usually stated as a full and complete cargo, with a minimum and a maximum quantity. This means that the ship guarantees to load at least the minimum and the ship may call for any quantity up to the maximum, which the charterer must supply; in other words, the quantity of cargo loaded is any quantity between the minimum and the maximum in the shipowner's option. The normal margin is 5 to 10% more or less than a stated quantity. If the cargo is liable to occupy a lot of space (or cubic) it is advisable to have the stowage factor stated in the charter. The word 'stemmed' means that the cargo (or bunkers) for the ship have been booked, or reserved.

3. *Loading date and cancelling date.* This is the period of time (anything from a few days to a few weeks) given in the charter during which the vessel may present herself for loading, and is sometimes rather loosely referred to as her laydays, although this is not the correct meaning of laydays. The charterer is not bound to load the vessel before her loading date, even though the vessel may be ready. If the vessel is not ready to load on or before the cancelling date, the charterer shall have the option of cancelling the charter with a right of damages against shipowners. Even if it is quite obvious that the vessel will miss her cancelling date, she is

still legally bound to present for loading, even if it means a long
ballast voyage, and it only then that the charterers need declare
whether they will cancel or maintain the vessel. In practice, if the
vessel looks like being late the shipowner will approach the
charterer to get an extension of the cancelling date or else a
definite cancellation before the vessel proceeds to the loading
port.

4. *Loading port or place.* The loading port or place is always
stated in a voyage charter. Sometimes it is just a single named
port, or one out of a range of picked ports (i.e. several good
named ports) or a port to be nominated along a certain stretch of
coastline (e.g. 'A/H Range' which means a port between Antwerp
and Hamburg inclusive). If the loading port is named, the vessel is
under an obligation to get to that port, and if a particular berth or
dock in that port is named in the charter, then the vessel is under
an obligation to get to that dock or berth. In other words, when
fixing his vessel to load at a named port it is up to the owner to
make sure that the vessel can both enter and leave the port safely.
These remarks also apply if the vessel is to load at one or more
named ports out of a selection. If they are named in the charter
then the shipowner undertakes to get there, and is excused only if
he is frustrated from so doing. Quite often a vessel is fixed to load
at any port in the charterer's option out of a range (i.e. a particular
stretch of coastline) in which case the charterer could order the
vessel to any port in that range. The shipowner, to protect his
interest, should stipulate, when fixing, for a *safe port*. The
charterer can then order the vessel only to one which the owner
and the master consider safe for the vessel. A safe port means a
port which a vessel may go to and leave safely, without danger
from physical or political causes. The port must not only be safe
when the vessel is ordered to it, but also safe when the vessel
arrives at the port. If, in the meantime, the port has become
unsafe the shipowner may refuse to send his ship there, and
request the charterer to nominate another port.

5. *Discharging port or place.* The above remarks apply to the
discharging port. As soon as a discharging port is ordered (out of
say a range of ports) then that port becomes the contract terminus
of the voyage.

6. *Alternative ports of discharge; seaworthy trim between ports;
geographical rotation.* When there is more than one port of

discharge, the shipowner should stipulate that the ports are in geographical rotation, i.e. in regular order along the coast, either north to south, east to west, or vice versa, and not jumping about from one to another, backwards and forwards in a haphazard manner.

7. *Payment of freight.* Unless there is a condition to the contrary (e.g. special terms of contract as to 'advance freight' etc.) freight is construed in the ordinary commercial meaning, i.e. the reward payable to the carrier on arrival of the goods, ready to be delivered to the consignee. The true test of the right of freight is whether the service in respect of which freight was contracted has been substantially performed. The following circumstances are relevant.

(a) Ships to deliver cargo on being paid freight. This establishes that freight is payable as the cargo is discharged, i.e. concurrent with discharge. Literally it means that as each ton is discharged freight is payable. In practice, freight is paid so much on account at various stages of the discharge, e.g. day by day on out-turn.

(b) On right and true delivery of the cargo. In this case freight is earned only after delivery of the cargo, but is paid for day by day on out-turn and adjusted on final delivery.

(c) On signing bills of lading. Freight is payable when the ship is loaded and the bills of lading have been signed. This is usually followed by the words 'dis-countless and non-returnable, ship and/or cargo lost or not lost', i.e. once the shipowner receives his freight he retains it. Payment in this manner is known as advance freight and the bill of lading is endorsed 'freight paid'. (The above is not to be confused with advance of freight which may be issued to the shipowner to cover his disbursements at the loading port. This advance of freight should really be considered as a loan, and the charterer who gives the shipowner this facility usually makes a small charge of, say 10%).

(d) The insurance of freight. Irrespective of how the freight is paid, both parties to the contract incur certain expenses in preparation for the voyage, and in the event of the ship being lost do not wish to lose the freight as well, and it is therefore insured. If freight is payable on delivery the shipowner will insure the freight in case the vessel is lost. If freight is paid in advance, then the charterer will insure the freight, because if the ship is lost he will not receive any refund from the shipowner.

8. *Laydays*. This is the rate of discharge per weather working day. Laydays are the number of days permitted in a charter party for loading and discharging the vessel. Alternatively, it may be either applied for loading or discharging a vessel in calculating the implications when the layday period prescribed has been exceeded. In such a situation demurrage arises the terms of which arise in the following clause. Conversely, despatch arises when the loading and/or discharge is completed sooner than prescribed. Various types of laydays exist, as detailed below:

(a) Running or consecutive days concern consecutive calendar days (midnight to midnight) including Sundays and holidays when laydays count. Hence once laydays commence this runs continuously unless any holidays arise which specifically excludes laydays.

(b) Reversible laydays confirming all time saved or lost on loading vessel may be added or deducted from the time allowed for discharge.

(c) Weather working days indicate that laydays do not count when adverse weather conditions prevail thereby preventing loading or discharging to take place.

(d) Surf days arise when a heavy swell or surf prevents loading or discharging at ports which are usually roadsteads. Surf days do not count as laydays.

(e) Working days are days when work is normally perfomed. These exclude Sundays (when recognized) and holidays officially recognized. The number of working daily hours depend on the custom of the port.

9. *Demurrage and despatch.* If a ship loads and/or discharges in less than the prescribed time, the owners pay a despatch money as a reward for time saved; if, on the other hand, the prescribed time is exceeded, then demurrage is payable at an agreed rate to the owner as compensation for delay of the ship.

10. *Cessor or limitation of liability clause.* Charterer's liability shall cease on the loading of cargo and qualified payment of freight, dead freight and demurrage. Hence when the charterer

has loaded the cargo and paid the charges incurred, his liability ceases.

11. *Lien clause.* This gives the shipowners the right to hold cargo against payment of freight or hire.

12. *Loading and discharging expenses.*

13. *Appointment of agents and stevedores.*

14. *Lighterage.*

15. *Deviation and salvage clause.* This permits or refuses to allow permission for the vessel to deviate in order to save life or property and also for the purpose of salvage.

16. *Bills of lading clause.*

17. *Exemptions from liability clause.* This clause includes many occurrences from which shipowners claim exemption and includes barratry – any wilful wrong doing of the Master and/or the crew without the connivance of the owners; capture and seizure – acts of taking the ship by an enemy or belligerent, or the forcible taking of the ship; Queen's enemies – opposing forces of the Crown; restraints of princes, and perils of the sea.

18. *General average.*

19. *Arbitration.*

20. *Ice clause.*

21. *Strikes and stoppages.*

22. *Overtime.*

23. *Sailing telegram.*

24. *Sub-letting.* This gives or refuses to allow permission of the ship to be sub-let, or sub-chartered under the charter party.

25. *Address commission.* A percentage of commission sometimes specified due to charterers based on the amount of freight.

26. *Brokerage.* Indicates the rate of brokerage that shall be paid.

27. *Penalty for non-performance.*

28. *War clause.*

29. *New Jason clause.*

30. *Both to blame clause.*

31. *Clause paramount.*

A time charter, as earlier indicated, is defined as a contract of affreightment under which a charterer agrees to hire, and the shipowner agrees to let, his vessel for a mutually agreed period of time or a specified voyage, the remuneration being known as hire. There are certain advantages and disadvantages both to the shipowner and the charterer in placing a vessel on time charter as compared with ordinary voyage charter trading.

From the shipowner's standpoint, the ship is employed for a definite period of time, with a regular income to the shipowner and the minimum of risk. Time charter provides the shipowner with a 'good cover' against a decline in freight rates. The shipowner does not have to worry about the day-to-day trading of the vessel so far as bunkers, port charges and cargo expenses are concerned; moreover the vessel will remain on hire even if delayed through port labour troubles. The disadvantages to the shipowner are that to a certain extent he loses control of his vessel, although he still appoints the Master and crew, but subject to the charter limitations he does not control the cargo loaded in the vessel or the voyage. If the freight market should rise the shipowner is unable to take advantage of it, and the charterer gets the benefit instead. The vessel may not be in a convenient position for the owner to perform maintenance work on his vessel, although the disadvantage would apply only in the case of a long-term charter.

In contrast, from the charterer's viewpoint there is the advantage of being able to trade the vessel almost as if it were his own, subject only to the charter party limitations. He can hire the vessel on a long- or short-term basis (generally the longer the period the cheaper the rate at which he can secure tonnage), and it provides him with a good cover if the freight markets show any signs of rising. The liner companies can take tonnage on time charter and so supplement their own sailing if the volume of trade is such as to warrant additional tonnage. The disadvantages to the charterer are that he is committed to the payment of hire over a period of time and, should trade diminish, he may have to face a loss. The charterer, by the terms of the charter, may be limited in his range of trading, but this is a point he should take into consideration when negotiating the charter. The charterer is responsible for the ship's bunker supply, port charges and cargo-handling expenses.

There is an increasing tendency for modern bulk purpose-built carriers, including tankers, to be on time charters of 7 years duration or longer. Special provision can be made in the charter party for the fixture rate to be reviewed, which at the time of the initial fixture negotiation broadly reflects a modest return to the shipowner on his capital investment throughout the duration of the charter.

When fixing a vessel on time charter, the shipowner should

Original drawn up and held by

1. Preamble

(a) *Subject of Contract.* – It is hereby agreed between the Owners and the Charterers that the Vessel shall be presented at the loading port or so near thereunto as she may safely get and lie always afloat, and there – being in every respect fitted for carriage of the agreed cargo – shall load the cargo, which the Charterers bind themselves to supply, and carry it with all possible despatch (unless economic speed to conserve fuel expressly agreed) to the port of discharge or so near thereunto as she may safely get and lie always afloat, and deliver it there. Carriage under this Charter shall be performed against payment of freight and in accordance with the terms contained herein.

(b) *Identity of Parties.* – Parties described in Cl. 2 as Owners or (Time-)Chartered Owners or Disponent Owners or Disponents (hereinafter called 'Owners') and in Cl. 3 as Charterers – shall each be deemed to be a Party to this Charter, and no evidence shall be admissible to show that they have contracted merely as agents.

(c) *Construction of the Charter.* – This charter consists of PART I and PART II. Typewritten provisions of PART I (and of the Rider, if any) shall prevail over printed provisions of this Preamble and of PART II to the extent of any conflict between them.

2. Owners	tlx No.
3. Charterers	tlx No.

4. Vessel name   flag
GRT-NRT   DWAT★/DWCC★   built   now
UMS: GT-NT

further particulars

cargo battens: not required★/required★

5. Cargo full★/part★ cargo of

% more/less at Owner's option, exact quantity being declarable *(when)*

of which   may be carried on d e c k

completion cargo: allowed★/not allowed★

6. Laydays not to commence before   CANCELLING DATE

7. Loading (a) port(s)/berth(s)

(b) Vsl's max draught loaded   sw★/bw★/fw★
(c) daily rate★/total laytime★   SHINC★/SHEX★
(d) shore winch/cranemen for   account   (e) dunnage for   account
(f) Shippers

(g) cost load

8. Discharge (a) Port(s)/berth(s)   (f) cost discharge

(b) Vsl's max arrival draught   sw★/bw★/fw★
(c) daily rate★/total laytime★   SHINC★/SHEX★
(e) Consignees   (d) shore winch/cranemen   account

Otherwise see PART II Cl. No.

18
22
19
43(c)
19(b)
-/39
-/32
27
29(c)/23
-/21
24/32
27
-/29(c)

★ delete the inapplicable

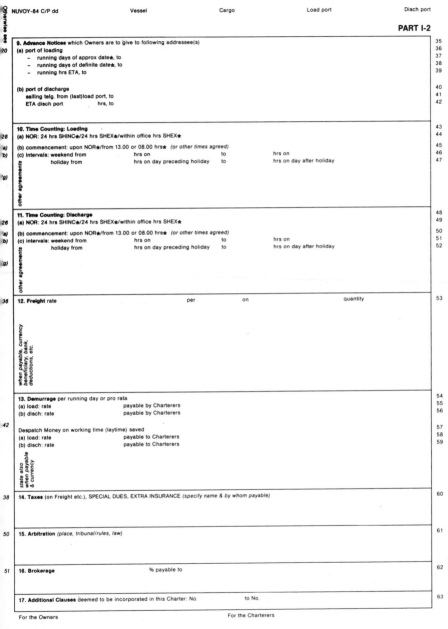

Fig. 15.1 Universal voyage charter party 1984. (Reproduced by kind permission of BIMCO).

Remark

Actual agreements that are at variance with the printed text of PART II – to be entered by typing in PART I or in the Rider (**not** in the printed text of PART II). Sub-clauses marked with an asterisk (⋆) are optional alternatives. The heading of the Sub-clause actually agreed – to be entered by typing in the relevant Clause of PART I, whereby all other alternatives in PART II shal become inapplicable.

DISCHARGE   146

25. **Cost** (always subject to Cl. 33: Overtime)   147

⋆ (a) *Free out (or: Free discharge).* – Charterers shall discharge the cargo 148
from Vessel's holds, including shovel-cleaning, free of expense to Owners. 149
⋆ (b) *Gross terms.* – Owners shall discharge the cargo from Vessel's holds, 150
and place it unhooked and unslung, or dumped by grab, alongside the Ves- 151
sel at their expense, and Charterers shall take the cargo from there at their 152
expense. 153

VESSEL and CARGO   64

18. **Vessel** 65

(a) *Prerequisites.* – Owners shall ensure that: 66
(aa) (class) the Vessel be classed Lloyd's Register 100 A1 or equivalent, 67
and Owners shall exercise due diligence to maintain that class throughout 68
the performance of this Charter, 69
(ab) (technical requirements) the Vessel be equipped to meet the techni- 70
cal requirements as specified in Cl. 4, 71
(ac) (compliance with regulations etc.) the Vessel and her Master and 72
crew will comply with all safety, health and other statutory rules, regulations 73
and internationally recognized requirements as are necessary to secure 74
safe and unhindered loading, performance of the voyage and discharge of 75
the cargo. 76
(b) *Substitution.* - If in Cl. 4 Owners have expressly been given liberty to pro- 77
vide a substitute vessel, such substitute shall be in all respects equivalent to 78
the Vessel named in this Charter. 79

19. **Cargo** 80

(a) *Warranty.* Charterers warrant that – unless otherwise specified in Part I – 81
the cargo referred to in Cl. 5 is non-dangerous for carriage according to ap- 82
plicable safety regulations including IMO Code(s). 83
(b) *Completion.* – If in Cl. 5 Owners have been given an option of completing 84
with other cargo, the latter must in no way be detrimental to cargo under this 85
Charter and is to be effectively separated therefrom at Owners' expense. 86

LOADING   87

20. **Advance notices** 88

(a) *Approximate date.* – Shippers are to receive from Owners a written notice 89
stating the approximate date of Vessel's readiness to load, containing also 90
Vessel's name and the approximate quantity of cargo required. 91
(b) *Definite date.* – Shippers are to receive from Owners a written notice of 92
the definite date of Vessel's readiness to load, containing also Vessel's 93
name and the approximate quantity of cargo required. 94
The definite date of Vessel's readiness to load shall not be earlier than the 95
approximate date. 96
In the event of Owners giving too short notice of the definite loading 97
date, commencement of the laytime shall be postponed by the number of 98
days by which the notice has fallen short of the period agreed in Cl. 9. 99
See also Cl. 27 'd' (Earlier commencement). 100
(c) *ETA.* – The Master shall despatch to Shippers an E(xpected) T(ime of) 101
A(rrival) message as per Cl. 9, or – if Vessel lying at the port of loading – 102
shall give to Shippers a 48-hours notice of Vessel's expected readiness to 103
load the cargo under this Charter. 104
(d) *Alteration in readiness.* – Shippers are to be kept advised of any altera- 105
tion in Vessel's expected readiness to load. 106

21. **Cost** (always subject to Cl. 33: Overtime) 107

⋆ (a) *Free in and stowed/trimmed.* – Charterers shall load and stow/trim the 108
cargo on board the Vessel free of expense to Owners. 109
Stowage includes the lashing and/or securing of the cargo. 110
⋆ (b) *Free in and spout/grab trimmed.* – Charterers shall load/dump the cargo 111
into Vessel's holds and trim it mechanically with shore spout, or (at Charte- 112
rers' option) with shore grabs, at their expense. Any extra trimming and/or 113
levelling as required by Master shall be for Owners' account and time so 114
used not to count as laytime or demurrage. 115
⋆ (c) *Gross terms.* – Charterers shall bring the cargo alongside the Vessel un- 116
der hook unslung, or under grab, at their expense, and Owners shall sling, 117
hook up, load and stow/trim the cargo at their expense. 118

22. **Cargo battens** 119

⋆ (a) *Required.* – Before tendering Master's notice of readiness, the Vessel to 120
have cargo battens fitted. 121
⋆ (b) *Not required.* – Before tendering Master's notice of readiness, the Vessel 122
to have cargo battens removed, failing which Charterers or their agents 123
shall not be held responsible for any damage to battens during loading/dis- 124
charge. 125

23. **Dunnage** 126

⋆ (a) *For Charterers' account.* Charterers shall provide and lay all dunnage 127
material as required by Master for proper stowage and protection of the car- 128
go, Owners allowing the use of all dunnage available on board. Dunnage 129
shall be laid in accordance with Master's instructions. 130
In the absence of disposal instructions from Charterers, Master shall 131
have liberty to dispose of the dunnage upon discharge. Any proved cost in- 132
curred thereby to be refunded by Charterers. 133
⋆ (b) *For Owners' account.* – Owners shall provide and lay all dunnage mate- 134
rial required for proper stowage and protection of the cargo. 135

24. **Separation** (see also Cl. 40 'b': Bs/L – Separate delivery) 136

Charterers have the right to ship parcels of different description and/or for 137
different Consignees in separate compartments within Vessel's natural se- 138
gregation provided that such stowage, carriage and discharge are compati- 139
ble with Vessel's seaworthiness, and provided that such separation does 140
not affect Owners' right to receive the quantity of cargo as per Cl. 5. 141
Charterers shall provide and lay all material as required by Master for 142
proper separation of various parcels within Vessel's compartments, Own- 143
ers allowing the use of all separation material available on board. Separa- 144
tion shall be laid in accordance with Master's instructions. 145

LOADING and DISCHARGE   154

26. **Notice of readiness (NOR)** 155

(a) *In port.* – When the Vessel – on arrival at the port – is in all respects ready 156
(whether in loading/discharging berth or not) to load/discharge the cargo 157
under this Charter, at each port of loading/discharge the Master shall ten- 158
der to Shippers/Consignees a written notice of Vessel's readiness to load/ 159
discharge, stating at loading port(s) the quantity of cargo required. 160
Such notice to be tendered: 161
⋆ (aa) *24 hrs SHINC:* at any time, day or night, Sundays (or their local equi- 162
valents) and holidays included, 163
⋆ (ab) *24 hrs SHEX:* at any time, day or night, Sundays (or their local equiva- 164
lents) and holidays excepted, 165
⋆ (ac) *within office hrs SHEX:* within ordinary office hours, Sundays (or their 166
local equivalents) and holidays excepted. 167
(b) *Off port* (not applicable in 'berth' charters). – If – on Vessel's arrival off 168
the port of loading/discharge – Charterers or their agents have not indica- 169
ted a ready accessible loading/discharging berth, the Master shall be enti- 170
tled to tender a written notice of readiness (as per 'a' hereabove) from such 171
place of arrival, whether cleared at customs or not, whether in free pratique 172
or not. 173
However, if at that time the Vessel should be prevented from entering the 174
port by reason of Vessel's inefficiency or of other hindrances which consti- 175
tute Owners' usual hazards – notice of readiness may not be tendered until 176
such hindrances have ceased to exist. 177

27. **Time counting** 178

(a) *Commencement.* – Laytime for loading/discharge shall commence to 179
count: 180
⋆ (aa) *upon NOR:* on tendering Master's notice of readiness to Shippers/ 181
Consignees or their agents 182
⋆ (ab) *from 13.00 or 08.00 hrs:* at 13.00 hrs if Master's notice of readiness 183
tendered to Shippers/Consignees or their agents before noon, or at 08.00 184
hrs next working day if notice tendered within office hours after noon. 185
Such notice time not to apply to second/subsequent port(s) of loading/ 186
discharge, where laytime always to count upon tendering Master's notice of 187
readiness. 188
Unless with Charterers' consent, laytime at loading port not to commence 189
counting earlier than on the day of the definite loading date given as per Cl. 190
20 'b'. 191
(b) *Excepted periods* (not applicable if SHINC terms agreed). – Sundays (or 192
their local equivalents) and legal holidays to be excepted unless used, in 193
which event actual time used shall count. 194
Periods indicated in Cl. 10 'c' (Loading: intervals) and in Cl. 11 'c' (Dis- 195
charge: intervals) to be treated as Sunday or holiday time. 196
(c) *Weather hindrances.* – Laytime shall not count when the loading/dis- 197
charge of cargo into/from the Vessel under this Charter is actually preven- 198
ted by adverse weather conditions. 199
(d) *Earlier commencement.* – Notwithstanding provisions of Cl. 20 'b' (Defini- 200
te date) and of Cl. 27 'a', if the loading/discharge has started before the 201
commencement of laytime, actual time used shall count in this period. 202
(e) *Waiting off port.* – If the notice of readiness as per Cl. 26 'b' (Off port) has 203
been tendered while the Vessel was off the port, the laytime shall com- 204
mence counting and shall count as if she were in berth. 205
The time of shifting to the loading/discharging berth or to a waiting berth 206
in port shall not count. 207
After berthing, the actual time lost until the Vessel is in fact ready in all re- 208
spects to load/discharge (incl. customs clearance, and free pratique if ap- 209
plicable) shall not count as laytime or time on demurrage. 210
(f) *Termination.* – Laytime/demurrage shall cease counting on completion of 211
loading (incl. trimming/stowage/lashing/securing) respectively discharge 212
(incl. shovel-cleaning and/or discharge of Charterers' dunnage), or draught 213
survey, or repairs of stevedore damage as per Cl. 34 'c' – whichever may be 214
later. 215
(g) *Inefficiency etc.* – Time lost due to inefficiency or any other cause attri- 216
butable to the Vessel, her Master, her crew or the Owners, which affects the 217
working of the Vessel – shall not count as laytime or as time on demurrage. 218

28. **Hatches** – opening/closing 219

At each port of loading/discharge, the first opening and the last closing of 220
hatches, including removal and replacement of beams, shall be effected at 221
Owners' expense and time shall not count, while 222
– (if free in and/or free out terms agreed) any other opening/closing as re- 223
quired by Master shall be effected by shore labour at Charterers' expense 224
and time to count, or 225
– (if gross terms loading and/or discharge agreed) any other opening/clo- 226
sing shall be effected at Owners' expense and time not to count. 227

29. **Vessel's cargo gear** (not applicable if Cl. 4 Vessel described as gearless) 228

(a) *Cargo handling gear.* – Owners shall always give free use, throughout the 229
duration of loading/discharge, of all Vessel's cargo handling gear and of 230
sufficient motive power to operate all cargo handling gear simultaneously. 231
(b) *Breakdowns.* – All such equipment to be in good working order up to the 232
sted capacity. Unless caused by negligence of Charterers' stevedores, time 233
lost by breakdown of Vessel's cargo handling gear – pro rata the total num- 234
ber of cranes/winches required at that time for loading/discharge (pro rata 235
under this Charter – shall not count as laytime or as time on demurrage. 236
(c) *Cranemen/winchmen.* – Owners shall provide free of charge cranemen/ 237
winchmen from crew unless local regulations prohibit this, in which latter 238
event shore labourers shall be for account of the party indicated in Cl. 7 239
(Loading) and Cl. 8 (Discharge). 240
Shore cranemen/winchmen shall always work under supervision of the 241
Master. 242

46. Strike etc.   424

(a) *General principle.* – Neither Charterers nor Owners shall be responsible 425
for the consequences of strike or lock-out preventing or delaying the fulfil- 426
ment of any obligation under this contract. 427
(b) *Loading port.* – In the event of strike or lock-out affecting the loading of 428
cargo, or any part of it, when the Vessel is ready to proceed from her last 429
port or at any time during the voyage to the port or ports of loading or after 430
her arrival there, Owners may ask Charterers to declare that they agree to 431
count the laytime as if there were no such hindrance. Unless Charterers ha- 432
ve given such declaration in writing (by telegram, if necessary) within 24 433
hours, Owners shall have the option of cancelling this Charter. If part cargo 434
has already been loaded, the Vessel must carry it to the port of discharge 435
(freight payable on loaded quantity only) having liberty to complete with 436
other cargo on the way for Owners' own account. 437
(c) *Anticipated strike etc.* – In the event of strike or lock-out which can rea- 438
sonably be expected – before the loading has commenced – to affect the 439
discharge of cargo, Owners are at liberty to cancel this Charter unless 440
Charterers declare (within 24 hours of receipt of Owners' notification of in- 441
tended. cancellation) that they agree to count the laytime at port of dis- 442
charge as if there were no such hindrance, without prejudice to the Consig- 443
nees' right of ordering the Vessel to a substitute port of discharge in accor- 444
dance with Sub-clause (d). In the said 24 hours time for loading does not 445
count. 446
(d) *Discharging port.* – In the event of strike or lock-out affecting the dis- 447
charge of cargo on or after Vessel's arrival at or off the port of discharge, 448
Consignees shall have the option of keeping the Vessel waiting until such 449
strike or lock-out is at an end against paying half demurrage after expiration 450
of the time provided for discharging, or of ordering the Vessel to a safe port 451
where she can safely discharge without risk of being detained by strike or 452
lock-out. Such orders to be given within 48 hours after Owners have given 453
notice to Consignees of Vessel's readiness to discharge or of Owners' re- 454
quest for orders. All conditions of this Charter and of the Bill of Lading is- 455
sued hereunder shall apply to the delivery of cargo at such substitute port, 456
and Owners shall receive the same freight as if the cargo had been dis- 457
charged at the original port of destination, except that if the distance of the 458
substitute port exceeds 100 nautical miles, freight on the cargo delivered at 459
the substitute port to be increased in proportion. 460
(e) *Notification.* – The party who first learns about the occurrence of strike or 461
lock-out shall immediately notify thereof the other party. 462

47. Ice   463

Loading Port   464
(a) *Before Vessel's arrival.* – If the Vessel cannot reach the loading port by 465
reason of ice when she is ready to proceed from her last port, or at any time 466
during the voyage, or on her arrival, or if frost sets in after her arrival, the 467
Master – for fear of Vessel being frozen in – is at liberty to leave without 468
cargo; in such cases this Charter shall be null and void. 469
(b) *During loading.* – If during loading the Master – for fear of Vessel being 470
frozen in – deems it advisable to leave, he has liberty to do so with what 471
cargo he has on board and to proceed to any other port with option of com- 472
pleting cargo for Owners' own account to any port or ports including the port 473
of discharge. Any part cargo thus loaded under this Charter to be forwarded 474
to destination at Vessel's expense against payment of the agreed freight, 475
provided that no extra expenses be thereby caused to Consignees, freight 476
being paid on quantity delivered (in proportion if lump sum), all other condi- 477
tions as per Charter. 478
(c) *Loading at more than one port.* – In case of more than one loading port, 479
and if one or more of the ports are closed by ice, the Master or Owners to be 480
at liberty either to load a part cargo at the open port and fill up elsewhere for 481
Owners' own account as under Sub-clause (b) or to declare the Charter null 482
and void unless Charterers agree to load full cargo at the open port. 483

Voyage and Discharging Port   484
(d) *Before Vessel's arrival.* – Should ice prevent the Vessel from reaching 485
the port of discharge, Consignees shall have the option of keeping the Ves- 486
sel waiting until the reopening of navigation and paying demurrage, or of or- 487
dering the Vessel to a safe and immediately accessible port where she can 488
safely discharge without risk of detention by ice. Such orders to be given 489
within 48 hours after Owners or Master have given notice to Charterers of 490
impossibility of reaching port of destination. 491
(e) *During discharging.* – If during discharging the Master – for fear of Vessel 492
being frozen in – deems it advisable to leave, he has liberty to do so with 493
what cargo he has on board and to proceed to the nearest safe and acces- 494
sible port. Such port to be nominated by Charterers/Consignees as soon as 495
possible, but not later than 24 running hours, Sundays and holidays exclud- 496
ed, of receipt of Owners' request for nomination of a substitute discharging 497
port, failing which the Master himself choose such port. 498
(f) *Discharge at substitute port.* – On delivery of the cargo at such port, all 499
conditions of the Bill of Lading shall apply and Owners shall receive the 500
same freight as if the Vessel had discharged at the original port of destina- 501
tion except that if the distance to the substitute port exceeds 100 nautical 502
miles, freight on the cargo delivered at that port to be increased in propor- 503
tion. 504

48. War risks ('Voywar 1950')   505

(1) In these Clauses "war risks" shall include any blockade or any action 506
which is announced as a blockade by any Government or by any belligerent 507
or by any organized body, sabotage, piracy, and any actual or threatened 508
war, hostilities, warlike operations, civil war, civil commotion, or revolution. 509
(2) If at any time before the Vessel commences loading, it appears that per- 510
formance of the contract will subject the Vessel or her Master and crew or 511
her cargo to war risks at any stage of the adventure, the Owners shall be en- 512
titled by letter or telegram despatched to the Charterers, to cancel this 513
Charter. 514
(3) The Master shall not be required to load cargo or to continue loading or 515
to proceed on or to sign Bill(s) of Lading for any adventure on which or any 516
port at which it appears that the Vessel, her Master and crew or her cargo 517
will be subjected to war risks. In the event of the exercise by the Master of 518
his right under this Clause after part or full cargo has been loaded, the Mas- 519
ter shall be at liberty either to discharge such cargo at the loading port or to 520
proceed therewith. In the latter case the Vessel shall have liberty to carry 521
other cargo for Owners' benefit and accordingly to proceed to and load or 522
discharge such other cargo at any other port or ports whatsoever, back- 523

wards or forwards, although in a contrary direction to or out of or beyond the 524
ordinary route. In the event of the Master electing to proceed with part cargo 525
under this Clause freight shall in any case be payable on the quantity deli- 526
vered. 527
(4) If at the time the Master elects to proceed with part or full cargo under 528
Clause 3, or after the Vessel has left the loading port, or the last of the load- 529
ing ports if more than one, it appears that further performance of the con- 530
tract will subject the Vessel, her Master and crew or her cargo, to war risks, 531
the cargo shall be discharged, or if the discharge has been commenced 532
shall be completed, at any safe port in vicinity of the port of discharge as 533
may be ordered by the Charterers. If no such orders shall be received from 534
the Charterers within 48 hours after the Owners have despatched a request 535
by telegram to the Charterers for the nomination of a substitute discharging 536
port, the Owners shall be at liberty to discharge the cargo at any safe port 537
which they may, in their discretion, decide on and such discharge shall be 538
deemed to be due fulfilment of the contract of affreightment. In the event of 539
cargo being discharged at any other port, the Owners shall be entitled 540
to freight as if the discharge had been effected at the port or ports named in 541
the Bill(s) of Lading, or to which the Vessel may have been ordered pursuant 542
thereto. 543
(5) (a) The Vessel shall have liberty to comply with any directions or re- 544
commendations as to loading, departure, arrival, routes, ports of call, stop- 545
pages, destination, zones, waters, discharges,delivery or in any other wise 546
whatsoever (including any direction or recommendation not to go to the port 547
of destination or to delay proceeding thereto or to proceed to some other 548
port) given by any Government or by any belligerent or by any organized bo- 549
dy engaged in civil war, hostilities or warlike operations or by any person or 550
body acting or purporting to act as or with the authority of any Government 551
or belligerent or of any such organized body or by any committee or person 552
having under the terms of the war risks insurance on the Vessel, the right to 553
give any such directions or recommendations. If, by reason of or in compli- 554
ance with any such direction or recommendation, anything is done or is not 555
done, such shall not be deemed a deviation. 556
(b) If, by reason of or in compliance with any such directions or recommen- 557
dations, the Vessel does not proceed to the port or ports named in the Bill(s) 558
of Lading or to which she may have been ordered pursuant thereto, the Ves- 559
sel may proceed to any port as directed or recommended or to any safe port 560
which the Owners in their discretion may decide on and there discharge the 561
cargo. Such discharge shall be deemed to be due fulfilment of the contract 562
of affreightment and the Owners shall be entitled to freight as if discharge 563
had been effected at the port or ports named in the Bill(s) of Lading or to 564
which the Vessel may have been ordered pursuant thereto. 565
(6) All extra expenses (including insurance costs) involved in discharging 566
cargo at the loading port or in reaching or discharging the cargo at any port 567
as provided in Clauses 4 and 5) hereof shall be paid by the Charterers 568
and/or cargo owners, and the Owners shall have a lien on the cargo for all 569
moneys due under these Clauses. 570

49. General average, New Jason and Both-to-Blame Collision Clauses   571

General average shall be adjusted in accordance with the York- Antwerp 572
Rules 1974, or any subsequent modification thereof, and as to matters not 573
provided for by these Rules – in accordance with the law and practice pre- 574
vailing at the place where the adjustment is drawn up. 575
Owners shall have the right to decide the place where the adjustment will 576
be drawn up and to appoint the average adjuster. 577
If the adjustment of the General Average or the liability for any collision in 578
which the vessel is involved while performing the voyage under this Charter 579
Party falls to be determined in accordance with the law and practice of the 580
United States of America, the following clauses shall apply: 581

New Jason Clause   582
In the event of accident, danger, damage or disaster before or after the com- 583
mencement of the voyage, resulting from any cause whatsoever, whether 584
due to negligence or not, for which, or for the consequence of which, the 585
Carrier is not responsible, by statute, contract or otherwise, the goods, 586
Shippers, Consignees or owners of the goods shall contribute with the Car- 587
rier in general average to the payment of any sacrifices, losses or expenses 588
of a general average nature that may be made or incurred and shall pay 589
salvage and special charges incurred in respect of the goods. 590
If a saving ship is owned or operated by the Carrier, salvage shall be paid 591
for as fully as if the said saving ship or ships belonged to strangers. Such 592
deposit as the Carrier or his agents may deem sufficient to cover the esti- 593
mated contribution of the goods and any salvage and special charges 594
thereon shall, if required, be made by the goods, Shippers, Consignees or 595
owners of the goods to the Carrier before delivery. 596

Both-to-Blame Collision Clause   597
If the Vessel comes into collision with another ship as a result of the negli- 598
gence of the other ship and any act, neglect or default of the Master, Mariner, 599
Pilot or the servants of the Carrier in the navigation or in the management of 600
the Vessel, the owners of the cargo carried hereunder will indemnify the 601
Carrier against all loss or liability to the other or non-carrying ship or her 602
Owners in so far as such loss or loss liability represents loss of, or damage to, or 603
any claim whatsoever of the owners of said cargo, paid or payable by the 604
other or non-carrying ship or her Owners to the owners of said cargo and 605
set-off, recouped or recovered by the other or non-carrying ship or her 606
Owners as part of their claim against the carrying Vessel or Carrier. The fo- 607
regoing provisions shall also apply where the Owners, operators or those in 608
charge of any ship or ships or objects other than, or in addition to, the collid- 609
ing ships or objects are at fault in respect of a collision or contact. 610

50. Arbitration   611

Any dispute arising under this Charter shall be referred to arbitration at the 612
place and before the arbitration tribunal indicated in Cl. 15 in accordance 613
with the procedure and (unless otherwise agreed) with the substantive law 614
prevailing there. 615

51. Brokerage   616

Brokerage upon the freight and deadfreight shall be paid by Owners and 617
shall be deemed to be earned by Brokers upon shipment of cargo. 618

consider the trading limits, or the areas where the vessel will be
trading, and also the type of trade in which the vessel will engage.
Many charters stipulate that the vessel shall trade within
Institute Warranty Limits (i.e. the districts considered safe by the
insurance authorities). If the vessel is to break these warranty
limits the question of who is to pay the extra insurance must be
decided. The owner must also consider what trade his vessel is to
be employed in. For example, regular employment in the ore trade
is likely to cause heavy wear and tear of the vessel; moreover,
loading and discharging of ore is usually very quick and the vessel
has little time in port in which to carry out maintenance on the
engine.

The clauses that go to make up a time charter are rather
different from those found in voyage charters, by reason of the
different nature of the trade. A number of clauses are common to
both types of charter and in these cases nothing more will be added
to what has already been said. There are a number of new clauses
and others that are adapted for use in a time charter are contained
in the NUVOY-84 specimen found on pp. 354–8. This is a universal voyage charter party and contains 51 clauses commencing
with the preamble and finishing with the brokerage involving 618
line entries.

15.3 APPROVED FORMS OF CHARTER PARTIES
AND RELATED BILLS OF LADING USED

It will be appreciated that the terms and conditions of a charter
party will vary according to the wishes of the parties to the
contract. Nevertheless the General Council of British Shipping
(formerly the Chamber of Shipping of the UK) and/or the Baltic
and International Maritime Conference (BIMCO) have approved
or recommended a number of charter parties – about fifty – for
certain commodities in specified trades. Most of these charter
parties have been negotiated with organizations representative of
charterers. Owners and charterers are recommended to use the
printed texts but there is no power of sanction and amendments
are made to suit the requirements of individual fixtures. A
selection of the more popular forms is found on pp. 360–4.

Table 15.1 Examples of standard charter parties approved by GCBS and/ or BIMCO

Commodity	Descriptions of Charter Parties	Code Name – (if any)
Bareboat	The Baltic and International Maritime Conference Standard Bareboat Charter	BARECON A
	The Baltic and International Maritime Conference Standard Bareboat Charter to be used for Newbuilding Vessels Financed by Mortgage	BARECON B
	Barecon 'A' Japanese terms	–
	Barecon 'B' Japanese terms	–
Cement	Chamber of Shipping Cement Charter Party, 1922	CEMENCO
Coal (including coke and patent fuel)	Chamber of Shipping East Coast Coal Charter Party, 1922	MEDCON
	Chamber of Shipping Coasting Coal Charter Party, 1920	COASTCON
	The Baltic and White Sea Conference Coal Charter, 1921	BALTCON
	The Baltic and International Maritime Conference Coal Voyage Charter 1971 (Revised 1976)	POLCOALVOY
	'Polcoalvoy' Slip-1986 Loading and Demurrage Scales	–
	'Polcoalvoy–ATIC' Terms for Shipments of Coal to France (Revised 1976)	–
	'Polcoalvoy' Rider for use with the 'Polcoalvoy' Charter	–
	The Baltic and International Maritime Conference German Coal Charter 1957 (Amend. 1975)	GERMANCON-NORTH
	Soviet Coal Charter 1962 (Amended 1971, 1981 and 1987). For Coal, Coke and Coaltarpitch from the USSR (Layout 1971)	SOVCOAL
	'Sovcoal-ATIC' Terms for Shipments of Coal to France	–

Table 15.1 continued

Commodity	Descriptions of Charter Parties	Code Name – (if any)
	The Japan Shipping Exchange, Inc., Coal Charter Party	NIPPONCOAL
Fertilizers	Chamber of Shipping Fertilizers Charter, 1942	FERTICON
	North American Fertilizer Charter Party 1978 (Ammended 1988)	FERTIVOY 88
Gas	Gas Voyage Charter Party to be used for Liquid Gas except LNG	GASVOY
	The Baltic and International Maritime Conference Uniform Time Charter Party for Vessels Carrying Liquid Gas	GASTIME
General	The Baltic and International Maritime Conference Uniform General Charter (as revised 1922 and 1976)	GENCON
	The Baltic and International Maritime Conference Uniform General Charter (Spanish Edition) (as revised 1922 and 1976)	GENCON
	Chamber of Shipping General Home Trade Charter, 1928	BRITCONT
	The Baltic and International Maritime Conference Scandinavian Voyage Charter 1956, amended 1962	SCANCON
	Universal Voyage Charter Party 1984 (revised Voyage Charter Party 1964) published by Polish Chamber of Foreign Trade, Gdynia	NUVOY-84
	The World Food Programme Voyage Charter Party	WORLDFOOD
Grain	Continent Grain Charter Party	SYNACOMEX
	North American Grain Charterparty 1973, issued by the Association of Ship Brokers and Agents (USA) Inc.	NORGRAIN

Table 15.1 continued

Commodity	Descriptions of Charter Parties	Code Name – (if any)
	Grain Voyage Charter Party 1966 (Revised and recommended 1974)	GRAINVOY
Nitrate	Hydrocharter Voyage Charter Party (amended 1975)	HYDROCHARTER
Ore	Soviet Ore Charter Party for Ores and Ore Concentrates from USSR Ports (amended 1987)	SOVORECON
	Apatite Charter Party for Shipments of Apatite Ore and Apatite Concentrate from Murmansk (amended 1987)	MURMAPATIT
	The Japan Shipping Exchange, Inc., Iron Ore Charter Party	NIPPONORE
	The Baltic and International Maritime Conference Standard Ore Charter Party	OREVOY
Stone	Chamber of Shipping Stone Charter-Party, 1920	PANSTONE
Tank	International Association of Independent Tanker Owners Voyage Charter Party	INTERTANKVOY 87
	International Association of Independent Tanker Owners Tanker Consecutive Voyage Clauses	INTERCONSEC 76
	The Baltic and International Maritime Council Standard Voyage Charter Party for Vegetable/Animals Oils and Fats	BISCOILVOY 86
	The Baltic and International Maritime Conference Standard Voyage Charter Party for the Transportation of Chemicals in Tank Vessels	BIMCHEMVOY
	International Association of Independent Tanker Owners Tanker Time Charter Party	INTERTANKTIME 80

Table 15.1 continued

Commodity	Descriptions of Charter Parties	Code Name – (if any)
	International Association of Independent Tanker Owners Tanker Contract of Affreightment	INTERCOA 80
	The Baltic and International Maritime Conference Uniform Time Charter Party for Vessels Carrying Chemicals in Bulk	BIMCHEMTIME
Time	The Baltic and International Maritime Conference Uniform Time-Charter (Box Layout 1974)	Baltime 1939
	The Baltic and International Maritime Conference Uniform Time-Charter (Traditional Layout)	Baltime 1939
	The Baltic and International Maritime Conference Uniform Time-Charter (French Edition)	Baltime 1939
	The Baltic and International Maritime Conference Uniform Time-Charter (Italian edition)	Baltime 1939
	The Baltic and International Maritime Conference Uniform Time Charter (Spanish edition)	Baltime 1939
	The Baltic and International Maritime Conference Deep Sea Time Charter (box layout 1974)	Linertime
	The Baltic and International Maritime Conference Deep Sea Time–Charter (traditional layout)	Linertime
	The Baltic and International Maritime Conference Uniform Time Charter Party for Offshore Service Vessels	Supplytime
	Chamber of Shipping Coasting and Short Sea Daily Hire Charter Party, 1954	Coasthire
	The Baltic and International	–

Table 15.1 continued

Commodity	Descriptions of Charter Parties	Code Name – (if any)
	Maritime Conference Uniform Time Charter Party for Vessels Carrying Liquefied Gas, Code Name: GASTIME	
	International Association of Independent Tanker Owners Tanker Time Charter Party, Code Name: INTERTANKTIME 80	–
	The Baltic and International Maritime Conference Uniform Time Charter Party for Vessels Carrying Chemicals in Bulk, Code Name: BIMCHEMTIME	–
Wood (including pitwood, props, pulpwood, roundwood and logs)	Black Sea Timber Charter Party for Timber from USSR and Romanian Black Sea and Danube Ports	Blackseawood
	Chamber of Shipping Baltic Wood Charter Party 1973	Nubaltwood
	Soviet Wood Charter Party 1961	Sovietwood
	'Sovietwood' Temporary Metrication Clause, 1970	–
	The Baltic and International Maritime Conference Soviet Roundwood Charter Party for Pulpwood, Pitwood, Roundwood and Logs from Baltic and White Sea Ports of the USSR.	Sovconround
	The Japan Shipping Exchange, Inc. Charter Party for Logs 1967	Nanyozai 1967

Associated with the charter parties listed above there exist a number of bills of lading with specific code names for use with such charter parties. Their use is purely optional and details of the bills of lading and sundry other forms are given below:

Table 15.2 Bills of lading

Code Names – (used in association with selected charter parties)	
Combined Transport Bill of Lading 1971	COMBICONBILL
Uniform Bill of Lading Clauses 1946 (to be used when no charter party is signed)	CONBILL
Bill of Lading to be used with Charter-Parties (edition 1978)	CONGENBILL
Liner Bill of Lading (liner terms approved by The Baltic and International Maritime Conference) (edition 1978)	CONLINEBILL
Liner Bill of Lading (French edition) (edition 1978)	CONLINEBILL
Liner Bill of Lading (German edition) (edition 1978)	CONLINEBILL
Liner Bill of Lading (Spanish edition) (edition 1978)	CONLINEBILL
Liner Bill of Lading (liner terms approved by The Baltic and International Maritime Conference) to be used in Trades where Hague-Visby Rules are compulsory	VISCONBILL
Liner Bill of Lading (French edition)	VISCONBILL
Liner Bill of Lading (German edition)	VISCONBILL
Liner Bill of Lading (Spanish edition)	VISCONBILL
BIMCO Blank Back Form of Liner Bill of Lading	–
For Shipments on the Chamber of Shipping General Home Trade Charter 1928	BRITCON
For shipments on the 'Nuvoy-84' Charter	NUVOYBILL–84
For shipments on the 'Scancon' Charter	SCANCONBILL
For shipments on the 'Germancon-North' Charter	GERMANCON-NORTH
For shipments on the 'Polcoalvoy' Charter (edition 1985)	POLCOALBILL
For shipments on the 'Sovcoal' Charter	SOVCOALBILL

Table 15.2 continued

For shipments on the 'Murmapatit' Charter	MURMAPATITBILL
For shipments on the 'Sovorecon' Charter	SOVORECONBILL
For shipments on the 'Blackseawood' Charter	BLACKSEAWOODBILL
For shipments on the 'Nubaltwood' Charter	NUBALTWOOD
For shipments on the 'Sovconround' Charter	SOVCONROUNDBILL
For shipments on the 'Norgrain' Charter Party: the North American Grain Bill of Lading Form	–
For shipments on the 'Grainvoy' Charter	GRAINVOYBILL
For shipments on the 'Biscoilvoy' Charter	BISCOILVOYBILL
For shipments on the 'Hydrocharter': Norsk Hydro a.s. Bill of Lading Form	–
For shipments on the 'Bimchemvoy' Charter	BIMCHEMVOYBILL
For shipments on Tanker Voyage Charter Party: the 'Intankbill 78' Bill of Lading	INTANKBILL 78
For shipments on the 'Orevoy' Charter	OREVOYBILL
For shipments on the 'Heavycon' Contract	HEAVYCONBILL

Sundry other forms

Liner booking note to be used with 'Conlinebill' Liner Bill of Lading	CONLINEBOOKING
Liner booking note to be used with 'Visconbill' Liner Bill of Lading	VISCONBOOKING
BIMCO blank back form of liner booking note	–
Memorandum of Agreement (revised 1983 and 1986)	SALEFORM 1987
Standard Statement of Facts (Short Form)	–
Standard Statement of Facts (Long Form)	–
Standard Time Sheet (Short Form)	–
Standard Time Sheet (Long Form)	–

Table 15.2 continued

Standard Statement of Facts (Oil and Chemical Tank Vessels) (Short Form)	–
Standard Statement of Facts (Oil and Chemical Tank Vessels) (Long Form)	–
Standard Disbursements Account	–
Combined Transport Document (edition 1 July 1977) Issued Subject to ICC Rules	COMBIDOC
Combined Transport Document (Edition 1 July 1977) (French edition)	COMBIDOC
Recommended Standard Bill of Sale	BIMCOSALE
BIMCO Blank Back Form of Non-Negotiable Liner Waybill	–
International Association of Independent Tanker Owners Tanker Contract of Affreightment, Code Name: 'INTERCOA 80'	–
International Association of Independent Tanker Owners Non-Negotiable Tanker Waybill	TANKWAYBILL 81
Standard Volume Contract of Affreightment for the Transportation of Bulk Dry Cargoes	VOLCOA
'Volcoa' Japanese terms	–
The Baltic and International Maritime Conference Dangerous Goods Declaration	–
The Baltic and International Maritime Conference Dangerous Goods Container/Trailer Packing Certificate	–
International Ocean Towage Agreement (daily hire)	TOWHIRE
International Ocean Towage Agreement (lump sum)	TOWCON
Non-Negotiable Chemical Tank Waybill	CHEMTANKWAYBILL 85
Non-Negotiable Cargo Receipt to be used with 'Worldfood' Charter	WORLDFOODRECEIPT
The Baltic and International Maritime Council Standard Transportation Contract for Heavy and Voluminous Cargoes	HEAVYCON
Non-Negotiable Cargo Receipt to be used with 'Heavycon' contract	HEAVYCONRECEIPT

Table 15.2 continued

Non-Negotiable General Sea Waybill for Use in Short-Sea Dry Cargo Trade	GENWAYBILL
Standard Contract for the Sale of Vessels for Demolition	SALESCRAP 87
Non-Negotiable Gas Tank Waybill for use in the LPG Trade	GASTANKWAYBILL
Standard Ship Management Agreement	SHIPMAN

15.4 VOYAGE ESTIMATES

Our study of chartering would not be complete without a review of the voyage estimate.

The aim of a voyage estimate is simply to provide the shipowner (or charterer) with an estimate of the probable financial return that can be expected from a prospective voyage. Provided with this information, the owner will be able to compare several possible alternatives and decide upon the most profitable and suitable venture. Although every estimator should aim to be as accurate as is reasonably possible, in modern shipbroking it will inevitably be found that time often does not permit a series of detailed estimates to be undertaken for each and every 'open' vessel. In practice, a 'rough' estimate is usually performed for each alternative, and only when two or three desirable voyages are thus identified does the more 'exact' estimating become necessary, along with the results of which must be borne in mind the owner's preferred direction of voyage, etc.

Needless to say, the final objective is for the estimate to compare favourably with the eventual voyage result, and normally reasonable comparisons can be made with experience of both the vessel and her trade, despite the vagaries of wind and tide, and, of course, the usual quota of man-made difficulties.

Voyage estimating is, however, an art, and an estimator – in order to succeed at his task – should aim to understand all the many complexities of ship operating and trading, together with the various methods of chartering and analyzing voyage returns, in order to perform his duties efficiently.

The example shown in this chapter is a basic, straightforward example, which provides only an idea of what an estimate sets out to achieve.

MV *Trader*
Open Seville
26 500 tonnes summer deadweight
15 knots (about) on 32 tonnes per day if IF C/S fuel oil and 1½
tonnes marine diesel oil at sea. 1½ tonnes MDO in port.
Running Costs: US $4000 per day.

Cargo Estimate: Sailing Philadelphia

Summer deadweight			26 500 tonnes
less			
1. Bunkers ROB	1000		
2. Constant weights	500		1 500
		Estimated cargo:	25 000 tonnes

s.s. *Trader*
Full cargo grain – Philadelphia/Bremen – US $16.50 per tonne –
Fiot – 4 days L/5000 MT D – per WWDAY – Shex Bends – 2.5%
A/C Chartcon – vessel open Seville

Freight (less commissions)
25 000 metric tonnes at $16.50 = $412 500
less 2.5% commission = $402 187 nett freight

Days		Ports	Disbursements		
					Agency Fees
			Port		Despatch
Steaming	Lay		Charges	Cargo	Sundries
9		Seville/Philadelphia			
	6	Philadelphia	$20 000	$–	$1500
11		Philadelphia/Bremen	$15 000	$–	$1500
—	7	Bremen			
20	13				

Fuel consumption:

At sea:	20 days at 32 tonnes p d	= 640 tonnes	F/O
In port:	13 days at – tonnes p d	– tonnes	F/O
		640 tonnes	

1. Agents Johan Smitzen Bremen	STANDARD TIME SHEET (SHORT FORM) RECOMMENDED BY THE BALTIC AND INTERNATIONAL MARITIME CONFERENCE (BIMCO) AND THE FEDERATION OF NATIONAL ASSOCIATIONS OF SHIP BROKERS AND AGENTS (FONASBA)		

2. Vessel's name m.v. Trader	3. Port Bremen	
4. Owners Disponent Owners Trader Shipping Enterprises Monrovia	5. Vessel berthed Thursday 14th June 0600 hrs	
	6. Loading commenced –	7. Loading completed –
8. Cargo 25000 Mtons Grain	9. Discharging commenced 14 June 1300	10. Discharging completed 22 June 1000
	11. Cargo documents on board –	12. Vessel sailed 22 June 1210
13. Charter Party * Norgrain 1st May 19	14. Working hours/meal hours of the port * 0800/1200) 1300/1700) Monday/Friday 1800/2200)	
15. Bill of Lading weight/quantity 25000 MT	16. Outturn weight/quantity 24995 MT	
17. Vessel arrived on roads 13 June 17.00 (Weser Pilot)	18. Time to count from 1st Working Period next working day following acceptance Nor	
19. Notice of readiness tendered 14 June 0900	20. Rate of demurrage ₤ 5000 pd.	21. Rate of despatch money ₤ 2500 pd.
22. Next tide available 13 June 2330	23.	
24. Laytime allowed for loading	25. Laytime allowed for discharging 5 WW Days	26.

LAYTIME COMPUTATION *

Date	Day	Time worked		Laytime used			Time saved on demurrage			Remarks *
		From	to	days	hours	minutes	days	hours	minutes	
14 June	Thursday	–	–	–	–	–				(NOR tendered and (accepted 0900 hrs
15	Friday				16					Laytime commenced 0800 hrs
16	Saturday	0800	1200		2					Overtime
17	Sunday									Holiday
18	Monday				16					Laytime recommenced 0800 hrs
19	Tuesday	1300	1500	–	2					(Rain 0300/1300
				–	1	30				(" 1500/2230
20	Wednesday			1	0	0				
21	Thursday			1	0	0				
22	Friday				10					Completed discharge 1000 hrs
							1	0	30	
				3	23	30	1	0	30	

General remarks *

Place and date Bremen 23/6/-	Signature *
Signature *	Signature *

* See Explanatory Notes overleaf for filling in the boxes

Printed and sold by Fr. G. Knudtzon Ltd., 55 Toldbodgade, Copenhagen, by authority of BIMCO

85-0

Published by The Baltic and International Maritime Conference (BIMCO), Copenhagen

Fig. 15.2 Standard time sheet (short form).

At sea: 20 days at 1.5 tonnes p d   = 30 tonnes D/O
In port: 13 days at 1.5 tonnes p d   = 20 tonnes D/O

               50 tonnes

Bunker oil:
On board: 640 tonnes F/O at $135 = $86 400
           50 tonnes D/O at $215= $10 750

               Total bunker cost: $ 97 150
            plus voyage expenses: $ 38 000

           Total voyage expenses: $135 150

Nett freight	$402 187
less	
Total voyage expenses	$135 150
Gross profit	$267 037

Gross profit: $267 037 ÷ 33 days voyage duration = gross daily profit $8092

Gross daily profit: $8092 less daily running cost $4000 per day = $4092 nett daily profit

An example of a time sheet and a statement of facts are given in Figs 15.2 and 15.4, based on the following charter party terms.

1. Discharge rate. 5000 metre tonnes per weather working day of 24 consecutive hours.

2. Sundays and holidays excepted, unless used, when half time actually used in excepted period to count as laytime.

3. Notice of readiness to be tendered in office hours Monday/ Friday 0900/1700 h.

4. Time to count from first working period on first working day following acceptance of notice of readiness to discharge.

5. Time not to count between midnight Friday (or day preceding a holiday) until commencement of first working period Monday (or day following a holiday).

6. Despatch on working time saved.

The time sheets and laytime calculations are based on the MV *Trader* voyage estimate for discharge at Bremen.

Laytime Calculation:

Laytime allowed	5 days 0 h 0 min
Laytime used	3 days 23 h 30 min
Laytime saved	1 day 0 h 30 min

1 day 0 h 30 min = 1.02 days

1.02 days at $2500 per day = $2550 despatch money

15.5 SALE AND PURCHASE OF SHIPS

The sale and purchase of vessels is a very specialized activity and is undertaken by a sale and purchase broker. He normally acts either for the buyer or seller of a ship, and occasionally acts between buyer's broker and seller's broker, each of which may be situated in different countries dealing with a foreign ship. The market is international and the ship may be sold for scrap or operational purposes. In the latter case the new owner must change the ship's name and usually is forbidden to operate in trades competitive to her former owner.

Details are given below of the information circulated of a possible ship sale:

(a) Classification society.

(b) Ship's deadweight, dimensions and draught; year of build, place, shipbuilder; cubic capacities, deck arrangements, water ballast capacities, number of holds and hatches; machinery details and builders, horse power, speed and consumption; bunker capacity, special and classification survey position.

(c) The purpose-built tonnage details of special facilities, i.e. refrigeration plant, tanker capacity, container capacity, passenger accommodation; derricks, car decks, etc.

(d) Light displacement including propeller details, i.e. bronze or iron, and if spare tail shaft on board. Such data only given in event of ship being sold as scrap.

(e) Ship price and position for inspection and delivery.

The brokers' function is not to express an opinion of the vessel's condition, unless there exists a serious defect, but to leave this assessment to the buyer's superintendent or consulting surveyor. On this aspect the ship classification records are critical. The ship

MEMORANDUM OF AGREEMENT

Dated:

Norwegian Shipbrokers' Association's Memorandum of Agreement for sale and purchase of ships. Adopted by The Baltic and International Maritime Conference (BIMCO)
Code name

SALEFORM 1983
Adopted 1956   Revised 1983

hereinafter called the Sellers, have today sold, and   1

hereinafter called the Buyers, have today bought   2

Classification: 3
Built: by: 4
Flag: Place of Registration: 5
Call sign: Register tonnage: 6
Register number: 7
on the following conditions: 8

1. Price   9
   Price: 10

2. Deposit   11
   As a security for the correct fulfillment of this contract, the Buyers shall pay a deposit of 10 % —   12
ten per cent — of the Purchase Money within   banking days from the date of this   13
agreement. This amount shall be deposited with   14

and held by them in a joint account for the Sellers and the Buyers. Interest, if any, to be credited the   15
Buyers. Any fee charged for holding said deposit shall be borne equally by the Sellers and the Buyers.   16

3. Payment   17
   The said Purchase Money shall be paid free of bank charges to   18

on delivery of the vessel, but not later than three banking days after the vessel is ready for delivery   19
and written or telexed notice thereof has been given to the Buyers by the Sellers.   20

4. Inspections   21
   The Buyers shall have the right to inspect the vessel's classification records and declare whether   22
same is accepted or not within   23
   The Sellers shall provide for inspection of the vessel at/in   24

   The Buyers shall undertake the inspection without undue delay to the vessel. Should the Buyers   25
cause such delay, they shall compensate the Sellers for the losses thereby incurred.   26
   The Buyers shall inspect the vessel afloat without opening up and without cost to the Sellers. During the inspection, the vessel's log books for engine and deck shall be made available for the Buyers'   27 / 28
examination. If the vessel is accepted after such afloat inspection, the purchase shall become definite   29

Fig. 15.3 Memorandum of agreement of sale form 1983. (Reproduced by kind permission of BIMCO).

— except for other possible subjects in this contract — provided the Sellers receive written or telexed 30
notice from the Buyers within 48 hours after completion of such afloat inspection. Should notice of 31
acceptance of the vessel's classification records and of the vessel not be received by the Sellers as 32
aforesaid, the deposit shall immediately be released, whereafter this contract shall be considered null 33
and void. 34

5. Place and time of delivery 35
The vessel shall be delivered and taken over at/in 36

Time of delivery/date of cancelling: 37

The Sellers shall keep the Buyers well posted about the vessel's itinerary and estimated time and 38
place of drydocking. 39
Should the vessel become a total or constructive total loss before delivery the deposit shall immedi- 40
ately be released to the Buyers and the contract thereafter considered null and void. 41

6. Drydocking 42
In connection with the delivery the Sellers shall place the vessel in drydock at the port of delivery 43
for inspection by the Classification Society of the bottom and other underwater parts below the Sum- 44
mer Load Line. If the rudder, propeller, bottom or other underwater parts below the Summer Load 45
Line be found broken, damaged or defective, so as to affect the vessel's clean certificate of class, such 46
defects shall be made good at the Sellers' expense to*) 47

satisfaction without qualification on such underwater parts.**) 48
Whilst the vessel is in drydock, and if required by the Buyers or the representative of the Classifi- 49
cation Society, the Sellers shall arrange to have the tail-end shaft drawn. Should same be condemned 50
or found defective so as to affect the vessel's clean certificate of class, it shall be renewed or made 51
good at the Sellers' expense to the Classification Society's satisfaction without qualification. 52
The expenses of drawing and replacing the tail-end shaft shall be borne by the Buyers unless the 53
Classification Society requires the tail-end shaft to be drawn (whether damaged or not), renewed or 54
made good in which event the Sellers shall pay these expenses. 55
The expenses in connection with putting the vessel in and taking her out of drydock, including dry- 56
dock dues and the Classification Surveyor's fees shall be paid by the Sellers if the rudder, propeller, 57
bottom, other underwater parts below the Summer Load Line or the tail-end shaft be found broken, 58
damaged or defective as aforesaid or if the Classification Society requires the tail-end shaft to be 59
drawn (whether damaged or not). In all other cases the Buyers shall pay the aforesaid expenses, dues 60
and fees. 61
During the above mentioned inspections by the Classification Society the Buyers' representative 62
shall have the right to be present in the drydock but without interfering with the Classification Surve- 63
yor's decisions. 64
The Sellers shall bring the vessel to the drydock and from the drydock to the place of delivery at 65
their own expense. 66

7. Spares/bunkers etc. 67
The Sellers shall deliver the vessel to the Buyers with everything belonging to her on board and on 68
shore. All spare parts and spare equipment including spare tail-end shaft(s) and/or spare propeller(s), 69
if any, belonging to the vessel at the time of inspection, used or unused, whether on board or not shall 70
become the Buyers' property, but spares on order to be excluded. Forwarding charges, if any, shall be 71
for the Buyers' account. The Sellers are not required to replace spare parts including spare tail-end 72
shaft(s) and spare propeller(s) which are taken out of spare and used as replacement prior to delivery, 73
but the replaced items shall be the property of the Buyers. The radio installation and navigational 74
equipment shall be included in the sale without extra payment, if same is the property of the Sellers. 75
The Sellers have the right to take ashore crockery, plate, cutlery, linen and other articles bearing 76

the Sellers' flag or name, provided they replace same with similar unmarked items. Library, forms, 77
etc., exclusively for use in the Sellers' vessels, shall be excluded without compensation. Captain's, 78
Officers' and Crew's personal belongings including slop chest to be excluded from the sale, as well as 79
the following additional items: 80

The Buyers shall take over remaining bunkers, unused lubricating oils and unused stores and pro- 81
visions and pay the current market price at the port and date of delivery of the vessel. 82

Payment under this clause shall be made at the same time and place and in the same currency as 83
the Purchase Money. 84

8. Documentation 85

In exchange for payment of the Purchase Money the Sellers shall furnish the Buyers with legal Bill 86
of Sale of the said vessel free from all encumbrances and maritime liens or any other debts whatsoe- 87
ver, duly notarially attested and legalised by the   consul toget- 88
her with a certificate stating that the vessel is free from registered encumbrances. On delivery of the 89
vessel the Sellers shall provide for the deletion of the vessel from the Registry of Vessels and deliver a 90
certificate of deletion to the Buyers. The deposit shall be placed at the disposal of the Sellers as well as 91
the balance of the Purchase Money, which shall be paid as agreed together with payment for items 92
mentioned in clause 7 above. 93

The Sellers shall, at the time of delivery, hand to the Buyers all classification certificates as well as 94
all plans etc. which are onboard the vessel. Other technical documentation which may be in the Sel- 95
lers' possession shall promptly upon the Buyers' instructions be forwarded to be Buyers. The Sellers 96
may keep the log books, but the Buyers to have the right to take copies of same. 97

9. Encumbrances 98

The Sellers warrant that the vessel, at the time of delivery, is free from all encumbrances and ma- 99
ritime liens or any other debts whatsoever. Should any claims which have been incurred prior to the 100
time of delivery be made against the vessel, the Sellers hereby undertake to indemnify the Buyers 101
against all consequences of such claims. 102

10. Taxes etc. 103

Any taxes, fees and expenses connected with the purchase and registration under the Buyers' flag 104
shall be for the Buyers' account, whereas similar charges connected with the closing of the Sellers' re- 105
gister shall be for the Sellers' account. 106

11. Condition on delivery 107

The vessel with everything belonging to her shall be at the Sellers' risk and expense until she is de- 108
livered to the Buyers, but subject to the conditions of this contract, she shall be delivered and taken 109
over as she is at the time of inspection, fair wear and tear excepted. 110

However, the vessel shall be delivered with present class free of recommendations. The Sellers 111
shall notify the Classification Society of any matters coming to their knowledge prior to delivery 112
which upon being reported to the Classification Society would lead to the withdrawal of the vessel's 113
class or to the imposition of a recommendation relating to her class. 114

12. Name/markings 115

Upon delivery the Buyers undertake to change the name of the vessel and alter funnel markings. 116

*) The name of the Classification Society to be inserted.
**) Notes, if any, in the Surveyor's report which are accepted by the Classification Society without
qualification are not to be taken into account.

13. Buyers' default 117

Should the deposit not be paid as aforesaid, the Sellers have the right to cancel this contract, and 118

they shall be entitled to claim compensation for their losses and for all expenses incurred together 119
with interest at the rate of 12% per annum. 120

Should the Purchase Money not be paid as aforesaid, the Sellers have the right to cancel this con- 121
tract, in which case the amount deposited together with interest earned, if any, shall be forfeited to 122
the Sellers. If the deposit does not cover the Sellers' losses, they shall be entitled to claim further com- 123
pensation for their losses and for all expenses together with interest at the rate of 12% per annum. 124

14. Sellers' default   125

If the Sellers fail to execute a legal transfer or to deliver the vessel with everything belonging to her 126
in the manner and within the time herein specified, the Buyers shall have the right to cancel this con- 127
tract in which case the deposit in full shall be returned to the Buyers together with interest at the rate 128
of 12% per annum. The Sellers shall make due compensation for the losses caused to the Buyers by 129
failure to execute a legal transfer or to deliver the vessel in the manner and within the time herein 130
specified, if such are due to the proven negligence of the Sellers. 131

15. Arbitration   132

If any dispute should arise in connection with the interpretation and fulfilment of this contract, 133
same shall be decided by arbitration in the city of*) 134
and shall be referred to a single Arbitrator to be appointed by the parties hereto. If the parties cannot 135
agree upon the appointment of the single Arbitrator, the dispute shall be settled by three Arbitrators, 136
each party appointing one Arbitrator, the third being appointed by**) 137
138

If either of the appointed Arbitrators refuses or is incapable of acting, the party who appointed 139
him, shall appoint a new Arbitrator in his place. 140

If one of the parties fails to appoint an Arbitrator — either originally or by way of substitution — 141
for two weeks after the other party having appointed his Arbitrator has sent the party making default 142
notice by mail, cable or telex to make the appointment, the party appointing the third Arbitrator 143
shall, after application from the party having appointed his Arbitrator, also appoint an Arbitrator on 144
behalf of the party making default. 145

The award rendered by the Arbitration Court shall be final and binding upon the parties and may 146
if necessary be enforced by the Court or any other competent authority in the same manner as a 147
judgement in the Court of Justice. 148

This contract shall be subject to the law of the country agreed as place of arbitration. 149

Copyright: Norwegian Shipbrokers' Association, Oslo.
Sole distributor in England: Messrs. S. Straker & Sons Ltd. London
Printed and sold by Halvorsen & Larsen A.s. Oslo.

*) The place of arbitration to be inserted. If this line is not filled in, it is understood that arbitration
will take place in London in accordance with English law.
**) If this line is not filled in it is understood that the third Arbitrator shall be appointed by the Lon-
don Maritime Arbitrators' Association in London.

inspection may take place prior to sale negotiations commencing, or be a condition of the sale offer. A dry dock inspection is usually not necessary. However, if conducted, it is the seller's responsibility and cost to bring the vessel to the dry dock and subsequently from the dry dock to the berth or place of delivery. The buyer bears the expense of putting in and taking out of dry dock the vessel plus the dry dock dues. The seller, however, would meet this expense if the rudder, propeller, bottom, or other underwater part(s) or tailend shaft were defective.

The buyer will make his offer for delivery at a specified port or time, with the option to cancel if the vessel is not delivered by the latest specified date. Moreover, the vessel's classification must not lapse. Additional payment to the seller is involved on delivery for on-board ship stores and bunkers. The vessel's trading certificates must be valid at the time of delivery.

On conclusion of the haggling over the price and conditions of sale, the seller's broker draws up a memorandum of agreement, which operates under the code name 'Saleform 1983'. A specimen is found on pp. 373–6 which contains 15 clauses ranging from the price to arbitration involving 149 lines.

On the occasion of a ship sale for scrap, this is a simpler procedure and carried out by the execution and delivery of a Bill of Sale under seal, a specimen of which is found on p. 380. The bill of sale is handed over against a letter releasing the deposit and a bankers draft for the balance of the price. Payment, if any, for bunkers and stores is dealt with at the same time.

The broker arranges to have provided for the vessel sold for operational purposes, the following documents which must be attached to any insurance cover and handed over at the time of delivery:

   (i) Certificate of registry.
   (ii) Load line certificate.
   (iii) Factories Act book.
   (iv) Deratting certificate.
   (v) Safety construction certificate.
   (vi) Safety radio certificate.
  (vii) Safety equipment certificate.
 (viii) Classification certificates.
   (ix) Plans.

1. Agents Johan Smitzen	STANDARD STATEMENT OF FACTS (SHORT FORM) RECOMMENDED BY THE BALTIC AND INTERNATIONAL MARITIME CONFERENCE (BIMCO) AND THE FEDERATION OF NATIONAL ASSOCIATIONS OF SHIP BROKERS AND AGENTS (FONASBA)

2. Vessel's name m.v. Trader	3. Port Bremen	
4. Owners Disponent Owners Trader Shipping Enterprises Monrovia	5. Vessel berthed Thursday 14th June 0600 hrs	
	6. Loading commenced —	7. Loading completed —
8. Cargo 25000 Mtons grain	9. Discharging commenced 14/6/— 1300	10. Discharging completed 22/6/— 1000
	11. Cargo documents on board —	12. Vessel sailed 22/6/— 1210
13. Charter Party* Norgrain 1st May 19	14. Working hours meal hours of the port*	
15. Bill of Lading weight quantity 25000 MT	16. Outturn weight quantity 24995 MT	0800/1200) 1300/1700) Monday/Friday 1800/2200)
17. Vessel arrived on roads 13 June 1700 (Weser Pilot)	18.	
19. Notice of readiness tendered 14 June 0900	20.	
21. Next tide available 13 June 2330	22.	

DETAILS OF DAILY WORKING*

Date	Day	Hours worked		Hours stopped		No. of gangs	Quantity load. disch.	Remarks*
		From	to	From	to			
14 June	Thursday	1300	1700	1700	1800	Two	1800 MT	Commenced
		1800	2200	2200	2400	Two	1698	discharge
15 June	Friday			0001	0800			
		0800	1200	1300	1300	Two	1727	
		1300	1700	1700	1800	Two	1715	
		1800	2200	2200	2400	Two	1720	
16 June	Saturday			0001	0800			
		0800	1200	1200	2400	Two	1637	Overtime
17 June	Sunday			0001	2400			
18 June	Monday			0001	0800			
		0800	1200	1200	1300	Two	1401	
		1300	1700	1700	1800	Two	1224	
		1800	2200	2200	2400	Two	1330	
19 June	Tuesday			0001	1300			) Rain
		1300	1500	1500	2400	Two	601	)
20 June	Wednesday			0001	0800			
		0800	1200	1200	1300	Two	1426	
		1300	1700	1700	1800	Two	1630	
		1800	2200	2200	2400	Two	1558	
21 June	Thursday			0001	0800			
		0800	1200	1200	1300	Two	1550	
		1300	1700	1700	1800	Two	1597	
General remarks*		1800	2200	2200	2400	Two	1525	
22 June	Friday			0001	0800			
		0800	1000			Two	856	Completed discharge
							24995 MT	

Place and date Bremen 23/6/—	Name and signature (Master)*
Name and signature Agents*	Name and signature (for the Charterers Shippers Receivers)*

* See Explanatory Notes overleaf for filling in the boxes

Published by The Baltic and International Maritime Conference (BIMCO), Copenhagen

83-0

Printed and sold by Fr. G. Knudtzon Ltd., 55, Toldbodgade, Copenhagen, by authority of BIMCO

Fig. 15.4 Standard statement of facts (short form).

(x) Passenger certificate – if applicable.

In the event of the broker requiring to register the vessel in the new owner's name, he presents the following documents to the registrar:

(a) Bill of sale.
(b) Declaration of ownership.
(c) Appointment of managing owner or ship's husband.
(d) Articles of association.
(e) Certificates of incorporation.
(f) Appointment of public officer.

The latter three items are only presented if the buyer has not previously owned a ship. With regard to foreign buyers, usually the bill of sale must be signed before a Notary Public and bear the visa of the Buyers Consul. The Certificate of British Registry is returned to the registrar at the port of registry. The foreign buyer for his own registration purposes will require a transcript of the cancelled British registry available from the registrar after the ship sale.

Frequently vessels are sold under extended terms of payment in which case a security for the unpaid portion of the purchase price is through a banker's guarantee otherwise a mortgage has to be given.

Details of vessels available for sale are recorded in the shipping press and an example of a bulk carrier and container ship is given below. Additionally a 'sold' tanker is likewise indicated.

(a) Interpretation of a bulkcarrier and a containership for sale

Bulkcarrier

MV *Federal Mackenzie* – 19 088 tonnes summer deadweight on 9.19 m draught, saltwater. Built 1969. Classed Lloyd's Register of Shipping with Hull Special Survey passed in June 1978 and with Machinery Special Survey due in June 1979. 22 848 m^3 grain capacity; 22 443 m^3 bale capacity. 4 holds/4 hatches. Burmaistar and Wain main engine giving 9400 brake horse power and 14.5 knots on a consumption of 30 tonnes fuel oil per day of 1000 second viscosity (Redwood No 1 at 100°F). 4 × 30 tonnes each derrick. Owners: Far East Shipping Ltd of Liberia. Delivery to

BILL OF SALE

RECOMMENDED STANDARD BILL OF SALE – CODE NAME: "BIMCOSALE"

1. Seller(s) (state full name, description and address)	2. Buyer(s) (state full name, description and address)

3. Name of Vessel	4. Type of Vessel	5. Port of Registry	6. Call Signs
7. Gross Register Tonnage	8. Net Register Tonnage	9. Date of Memorandum of Agreement	

10. Purchase Sum (in figures and in letters)

11. Details of subsisting or outstanding Mortgage(s) or other encumbrances, if any; also state other details, if any, relevant to the sale and transfer of the Vessel

The Seller(s), named in Box 1, who is (are) the Owner(s) of the Vessel described in Boxes 3 to 8, both inclusive, hereby confirm(s) having sold and handed over the said Vessel with everything belonging to her to the Buyer(s), named in Box 2, for the Purchase Sum, as stated in Box 10.
Unless otherwise stated in Box 11, the Seller(s) warrant(s) that the Vessel is free from encumbrances, debts and maritime liens of any kind whatsoever and confirm(s) that the sale and transfer of the Vessel is effected in accordance with Memorandum of Agreement dated as indicated in Box 9.
In consideration of the said Purchase Sum, paid to the Seller(s) by the Buyer(s), the Seller(s) hereby transfer(s) the Vessel to the Buyer(s) so that the Vessel shall hereinafter become his (their) legal property.
IN WITNESS whereof this Bill of Sale has been issued and signed at the place and on the date stated in Box 12 in the presence of the Witness(es) as indicated in Box 13 whose signature(s) has (have) been certified (if required) by the person indicated in Box 14.

(* Space for translation of text)

12. Place and date and signature of Seller(s)

13. The undersigned Witness(es) hereby certifies(y) the correctness of the Seller(s)' signature(s) to this Bill of Sale and the date hereof (state full name, title and address of Witness(es))

14. The undersigned Consul (General) hereby certifies the correctness of the Witness(es)' signature(s) as stated in Box 13

Published by The Baltic and International Maritime Conference (BIMCO), Copenhagen

Printed and sold by Fr. G. Knudtzon Ltd., 55, Toldbodgade, Copenhagen, by authority of The Baltic and International Maritime Conference (BIMCO), Copenhagen

Fig. 15.5 Bill of sale. (Reproduced by kind permission of BIMCO).

new owners can be arranged in Japan in mid-1979 with the entire Special Survey passed at the price of over US $3 500 000.

Containership

MV *Frontier* – 6533 tonnes summer deadweight. Built 1972. Lloyd's Register of Shipping. 166 20-ft unit container capacity. 3 holds, 9 hatches. Deutz main engine giving 4000 brake horse power, and 13.5 knots on 11 tonnes fuel consumption per day. Gearless (i.e. without derricks or cranes). Owner: Manchester Lines (Freighting) Ltd., U.K. Price £850 000 with delivery to new owners in May 1979.

(b) Interpretation of vessels sold

(a) Tankers

SS *Eagle Charger* and SS *Eagle Leader* – 38 414 summer deadweight each on 11.17 m. Built 1969. Classification society American Bureau of Shipping. 15 tanks, 53 232 m³. General Electric turbine giving 15 000 shaft horsepower and 16 knots. Sold by Eagle Terminal Tankers Inc., United States (United Maritime Corporation), to Ogden Marine Inc., United States, for US $15 500 000 each vessel, through the intervention of sale and purchase brokers A.L. Burbank. The reader is recommended to study Chapter 7 of *Economics of Shipping Practice and Management*.

CHAPTER 16

Containerization

Containerization is a method of distributing merchandise in a unitized form thereby permitting an intermodal transport system to be evolved providing a possible combination of rail, road, canal and maritime transport. The system is long established and was in being at the turn of the century in a somewhat less sophisticated form. It came more into use in the North American coastal trade in the 1930s when the vessels were called Van ships. Today we have seen the evolution of the fourth generation of container ships as the benefits of containerization become more attractive on a worldwide scale thereby aiding rising living standards and facilitating trade expansion.

16.1 CONTAINER SHIPS – TERMINALS – TRADES

Examples of modern container ships are found in Figs. 3.5 (p. 36) and 4.2 (p. 46). Both such vessels have been designed with flexibility of operation as paramount. There does exist especially with the larger tonnage the cellular vessel. Each hold is fitted with a series of vertical angle guides adequately cross braced to accept the container. Such holds are completely dedicated to either the 20- or 40-ft container and ensures that each succeeding container in a stack rests securely on the weight-bearing corner castings of the one below. The guides also facilitate discharging and loading by guiding spreader frames of container cranes onto the corner castings of containers without any need for the crane driver to make any fine adjustments to line up the lifting frame. Many of the non-cellular type ships are conversions and some are in the short sea trade. The modern cellular vessel found in the deep-sea trades is free of open deck obstructions – including derricks – to facilitate unimpeded container handling.

Third generation cellular tonnage which emerged in the late 1970s has 3000 TEUs capacity with a draught of 18.30 m. The fourth generation of container vessels encourages greater rationalization in ports of call and relies on smaller container tonnage or surface (rail) transport to act as distributors/feeders. An example is the fleet of nine Maersk vessels of 4700 TEUs capacity and speed of 27 knots which operate round the world container service. It has resulted in high capacity berths to cater for such tonnage, more pre-planning of port operation, rationalization of ports of call and greater reliance of feeder service by sea and overland. Such tonnage reduces the unit cost of container shipment.

Evergreen provided their round the world container service in 1984 and introduced a new dimension in container distribution. In 1989 the service was operated by twelve vessels. The G type has 1728 TEUs capacity and the GX type 3428 TEUs. In 1988 Evergreen introduced from Europe the US West coast and extra Japanese ports of Nagoya and Shimizu to their schedule.

Examples of extracts from the Maersk (see pp. 385–6) sailing schedules container southbound from UK to North America, Far East and West Africa are given in Table 16.1 (valid 1988).

Details of transit times offered by Maersk container services for imported products both worldwide and North America are given in Table 16.2(a,b).

In recent years a number of the deep-sea container vessels have been modified to become multi-purpose ships. In so doing the aft portion has been provided with deck accommodation to convey vehicular traffic transhipped via a ramp. It improves the versatility of the multi-purpose container ship.

An analysis of the P & O Containers Ltd fleet of 21 container ships indicated their service speed ranged from 17.5 knots to 23 knots. The faster vessels tended to have the higher capacity. Overall the capacity range was from 1138 TEUs to 2968 TEUs. All the vessels were marine diesel powered except one which was a steam turbine. The largest vessels were of 2968 TEUs, length overall 289.5 m, 50 880 BHP Marine Diesel and service speed of 21 knots.

The organization necessary to feed/distribute vessels of 2000/3000 TEUs at a specialized berth requires much pre-planning. Computers are provided to assist in the container control/distribution task. Rail has become more prominent in many countries in the feeder/distribution arrangements serving the container berth especially in western Europe, USA, and the trans-Siberian rail link.

Container berths are either purpose-built for exclusive container use, or multi-purpose in which container and other types of cargo vessels are handled. The purpose-built container berth is usually the

Table 16.1 Extracts from Maersk Line sailing schedule in 1988

Exports, North America – Maersk Line

Vessel	Lica Maersk	Dragoer Maersk	L-123 Maersk	Laust Maersk	Louis Maersk	Leise Maersk	Lars Maersk	Laura Maersk	Regina Maersk	Lexe Maersk
Voyage No.	8807	8803	8803	8807	8807	8809	8809	8809	8809	8809
LCL closing date	29 Jun.	6 July	13 July	20 July	27 July	3 Aug.	10 Aug.	17 Aug.	24 Aug.	31 Aug.
FCL closing date	1 July	8 July	15 July	22 July	29 July	5 Aug.	12 Aug.	19 Aug.	26 Aug.	2 Sept.
ETD Felixstowe	4 July	11 July	18 July	25 July	1 Aug.	8 Aug.	15 Aug.	22 Aug.	29 Aug.	5 Sept.
Halifax	12 July	19 July	26 July	2 Aug.	9 Aug.	16 Aug.	23 Aug.	30 Aug.	6 Sept.	13 Sept.
New York	14 July	21 July	28 July	4 Aug.	11 Aug.	18 Aug.	25 Aug.	1 Sept.	8 Sept.	15 Sept.
Baltimore	16 July	23 July	30 July	6 Aug.	13 Aug.	20 Aug.	27 Aug.	3 Sept.	10 Sept.	17 Sept.
Charleston	18 July	25 July	1 Aug.	8 Aug.	15 Aug.	22 Aug.	29 Aug.	5 Sept.	12 Sept.	19 Sept.
Long Beach	27 July	3 Aug.	10 Aug.	17 Aug.	24 Aug.	31 Aug.	7 Sept.	14 Sept.	21 Sept.	28 Sept.
Oakland	28 July	4 Aug.	11 Aug.	18 Aug.	25 Aug.	1 Sept.	8 Sept.	15 Sept.	22 Sept.	29 Sept.

Exports, Far East – Maersk Line

Vessel	Arild Maersk	Luna Maersk	Arthur Maersk	Anna Maersk	Maersk Rotterdam	Laust Maersk	Anders Maersk	Axel Maersk	Arild Maersk	Luna Maersk
Voyage No.	8807	8807	8807	8807	8807	8807	8807	8809	8809	8809

All Export Sailings from Felixstowe via the Maersk Tempo

LCL closing date	27 Apr.	4 May	11 May	18 May	25 May	1 Jun.	8 Jun.	15 Jun.	22 Jun.	29 Jun.
FCL closing date	29 Apr.	6 May	13 May	20 May	27 May	3 Jun.	10 Jun.	17 Jun.	24 Jun.	1 July

ETD Felixstowe	1 May	8 May	15 May	22 May	29 May	5 Jun.	12 Jun.	19 Jun.	26 Jun.	3 July
Rotterdam	2 May	9 May	16 May	23 May	30 May	6 Jun.	13 Jun.	20 Jun.	27 Jun.	4 July
Grangemouth	30 Apr.	7 May	14 May	21 May	28 May	4 Jun.	11 Jun.	18 Jun.	25 Jun.	2 July
Bremerhaven	3 May	10 May	17 May	24 May	31 May	7 Jun.	14 Jun.	21 Jun.	28 Jun.	5 July
Algercias	8 May	15 May	22 May	29 May	5 Jun.	12 Jun.	19 Jun.	26 Jun.	3 July	10 July
Singapore	23 May	30 May	6 Jun.	13 Jun.	20 Jun.	27 Jun.	4 July	11 July	18 July	25 July
Port Kelang	26 May	2 Jun.	9 Jun.	16 Jun.	23 Jun.	30 Jun.	7 July	14 July	21 July	28 July
Penang	27 May	3 Jun.	10 Jun.	17 Jun.	24 Jun.	1 July	8 July	15 July	22 July	29 July
Bangkok	25 May	1 Jun.	8 Jun.	15 Jun.	22 Jun.	29 Jun.	6 July	13 July	20 July	27 July
Hong Kong	26 May	2 Jun.	9 Jun.	16 Jun.	23 Jun.	30 Jun.	7 July	14 July	21 July	28 July
Manila	30 May	6 Jun.	13 Jun.	20 Jun.	27 Jun.	4 July	11 July	18 July	25 July	1 Aug.
Kaoishung	30 May	6 Jun.	13 Jun.	20 Jun.	27 Jun.	4 July	11 July	18 July	25 July	1 Aug.
Keelung	30 May	6 Jun.	13 Jun.	20 Jun.	27 Jun.	4 July	11 July	18 July	25 July	1 Aug.
Busan	29 May	5 Jun.	12 Jun.	19 Jun.	–	3 July	10 July	17 July	24 July	31 July
Kobe	31 May	7 Jun.	14 Jun.	21 Jun.	28 Jun.	5 July	12 July	19 July	26 July	2 Aug.
Moji	1 Jun.	8 Jun.	15 Jun.	22 Jun.	29 Jun.	6 July	13 July	20 July	27 July	3 Aug.
Osaka/Nagoya	1 Jun.	8 Jun.	15 Jun.	22 Jun.	29 Jun.	6 July	13 July	20 July	27 July	3 Aug.
Tokyo	1 Jun.	8 Jun.	15 Jun.	22 Jun.	29 Jun.	6 July	13 July	20 July	27 July	3 Aug.
Yokohama	2 Jun.	9 Jun.	16 Jun.	23 Jun.	30 Jun.	7 July	14 July	21 July	28 July	4 Aug.
Shimizu	3 Jun.	10 Jun.	17 Jun.	24 Jun.	1 July	8 July	15 July	22 July	29 July	5 Aug.
Otaru	5 Jun.	12 Jun.	19 Jun.	26 Jun.	3 July	10 July	17 July	24 July	31 July	7 Aug.

Exports, West Africa – Maersk Line

Vessel	Axel Maersk	Luna Maersk	Anna Maersk	Laust Maersk	Axel Maersk	Luna Maersk	Anna Maersk	Laust Maersk	Axel Maersk	Luna Maersk
Voyage No.	8805	8805	8805	8805	8807	8807	8807	8807	8809	8809
All Export Sailings from Felixstowe via the Maersk Tempo										
LCL closing date	24 Feb.	9 Mar.	23 Mar.	6 Apr.	20 Apr.	4 May	18 May	1 Jun.	15 Jun.	29 Jun.
FCL closing date	26 Feb.	11 Mar.	25 Mar.	8 Apr.	22 Apr.	6 May	20 May	3 Jun.	17 Jun.	1 July
ETD Felixstowe	28 Feb.	13 Mar.	27 Mar.	10 Apr.	24 Apr.	8 May	22 May	5 Jun.	19 Jun.	3 July
Rotterdam	29 Feb.	14 Mar.	28 Mar.	11 Apr.	25 Apr.	9 May	23 May	6 Jun.	20 Jun.	4 July
Grangemouth	27 Feb.	12 Mar.	26 Mar.	9 Apr.	23 Apr.	7 May	21 May	4 Jun.	18 Jun.	2 July
Bremerhaven	1 Mar.	15 Mar.	29 Mar.	12 Apr.	26 Apr.	10 May	24 May	7 Jun.	21 Jun.	5 July

Vessel	Maersk Bella	Maersk Bravo	Maersk Bella	Maersk Bravo	Maersk Bella	Maersk Bravo	Maersk Bella	Maersk Bravo	Maersk Bella	Maersk Bravo
Voyage No.	8807	8807	8809	8809	8811	8811	8813	8813	8815	8815
Algercias	12 Mar.	26 Mar.	9 Apr.	23 Apr.	7 May	21 May	4 Jun.	19 Jun.	1 July	16 July
Monrovia	18 Mar.	1 Apr.	15 Apr.	29 Apr.	13 May	27 May	10 Jun.	24 Jun.	8 July	22 July
Abidjan	21 Mar.	4 Apr.	18 Apr.	2 May	16 May	30 May	13 Jun.	27 Jun.	11 July	25 July
Lome	22 Mar.	5 Apr.	19 Apr.	3 May	17 May	31 May	14 Jun.	28 Jun.	12 July	26 July
Lagos	24 Mar.	7 Apr.	21 Apr.	5 May	19 May	2 Jun.	16 Jun.	30 Jun.	14 July	28 July
Cotonou	25 Mar.	8 Apr.	22 Apr.	6 May	20 May	3 Jun.	17 Jun.	1 July	15 July	29 July
Tema	27 Mar.	*	24 Apr.	*	22 May	*	19 Jun.	*	17 July	*

Vessel Voyage No.	Faith 8813	Faith 8815	Faith 8817	Faith 8819	Faith 8821	Faith 8823	Faith 8825	Faith 8827	Faith 8829	Faith 8831
Algercias	11 Mar.	26 Mar.	8 Apr.	23 Apr.	6 May	21 May	3 Jun.	18 Jun.	1 July	16 July
Dakar	16 Mar.	2 May	13 Apr.	30 Apr.	14 May	28 May	8 Jun.	25 Jun.	6 July	23 July
Freetown	18 Mar.	–	15 Apr.	–	16 May	–	10 Jun.	–	8 July	–

* 1988

A development of the modern container shipping company is found in the use of on line computer which enables the freight forwarder and major clients to gain access in terms of cargo reservations, sailing schedules, customs, rates, ports of call, container availability, monitor of containers and other traffic data. This computerization of on line equipment will become more extensive. Many such shipowners have all their key offices such as sales, ports, management linked by computer on a worldwide basis. Hence the paperless office obtains in such companies (see pp. 428, 433).

more efficient and produces the most productive container through-put. The most modern one would be computer-operated and handle double stack container trains. Basically there are three methods of container handling detailed as follows:

(i) Quay portainer crane working in association with van carriers.
(ii) Quay portainer crane working in association with tractor/trailer operation.
(iii) Quay portainer crane working in conjunction with tractor/trailer operation and container stacking cranes – the latter situated often some distance from the actual berth area.

The actual quay portainer crane may be of the type with long outreach over the water and a short landward reach behind or with long outreach over both water and quay. The latter is the more favoured type as it permits a stowage for containers under the crane structure. All the foregoing three methods involve the import landed container being moved away from the crane by van carrier/tractor and trailer to a container stacking area.

With increasing emphasis being given on quicker port turnround times, the most modern system uses a 336-ft long gantry crane which moves containers overhead to and from the berthed vessel instead of using the traditional straddle carrier. A notable saving is in the straddle carriers. The 500-tonne capacity gantry crane can handle five containers at a time. It functions like a huge cartridge and is fed continuously by rubber-tyred yard cranes. This transfer device enables both the shipside crane and the yard gantry to operate simultaneously but independently with an obvious saving in work time. Computerization plays an important part in the operation, controlling the delivery and pick-up of containers from the truckers as well as the movement and positioning of all containers in the terminal.

The container is then processed through customs clearance unless it is destined for an inland clearance depot in which case the container under bond is transferred to a rail or road vehicle for despatch. In the case of the locally cleared containers it may be despatched by road or rail to importers' premises/inland situated container base/or simply discharged locally through the port/berth container base. The process is reversed with exported containers. Straddle carriers are used extensively to move containers within the berth area.

The container berth varies greatly in size. Much depends on the anticipated annual through-put and vessel capacity. It can vary from

5 to 8 hectares for the second generation cellular ship, to one of up to 30 hectares with the fourth generation vessel. The critical aspect is the 'back-up' area accommodating parked containers. Stacking of containers in excess of three high is rarely exceeded as it creates many problems. Two high is usually the most common.

The loading of containers on board the vessel can create many problems particularly when a number of different container lengths and port destinations are involved. The vessel has to be properly trimmed by the stern and the loading plan must take into account dangerous cargo and those containers requiring special attention, e.g. it may be an open container with a commercial vehicle in excess of the accepted container heights and thereby requiring to be stowed on the upper or open deck. The formulation of the stowage plan is usually done on the computer.

Container ships usually carry substantial quantities of such cargo on the open deck where special equipment/fittings are provided. Stacking up to three high on open deck is quite common. Such a practice of open-deck container shipments enhances the productivity of such ships and is particularly ideal for distributing empty containers caused through imbalanced working.

The time spent in loading and discharging containers varies by port and circumstances. In very broad terms, one can attain 25/30 containers per hour for discharging cargo, whilst for cargo exports the figure falls to 20/25 per hour per crane of single container capacity. Many ports now have cranes of 2-container capacity with much improved loading/discharging rates.

A modern container berth handling third generation container ships with 7/8 vessels per month is likely to handle 22 000 – 26 000 containers. This is more than seven times a conventional berth handling capacity.

Container trades have emerged significantly during the late 1960s/ early 1970s in all parts of the world.

Details of some container routes are given below:

(a) The Australia/New Zealand – Europe Container Service (ANZECS) is a consortium of British, Continental and New Zealand Conference Lines operating integrated services between Europe and Australia/New Zealand maintained by a fleet of 16 container ships.

(b) BEACON (British and European Shipping Lines Joint Container Service) provides regular services between Europe and the Red Sea and East Africa and Mauritius.

Table 16.2(a) Extracts of Maersk Line transit times in 1988: Imports transit times – door to door worldwide

	Tokyo	Tema	Surabaya	Singapore	Penang	Muscat	Monrovia	Manila	Lome	Lagos	Kuwait	Kobe	Keelung	Karachi	Kuala Lumpur	Kaoshiung	Jeddah	Jakarta	Hong-Kong	Freetown	Dubai	Doha	Dammam	Dakar	Cotonou	Busan	Bombay	Bangkok	Bandar Abbas	Bahrain	Abidjan
Aberdeen	29	20	27	22	27	39	27	30	16	14	36	31	31	27	43	28	34	26	25	18	37	52	41	14	19	33	44	29	40	40	19
Birmingham	28	19	26	21	26	38	26	29	15	13	35	30	30	26	42	27	33	25	24	17	36	51	40	13	18	32	43	28	39	39	18
Bristol	28	19	26	21	26	38	26	29	15	13	35	30	30	26	42	27	33	25	24	17	36	51	40	13	18	32	43	28	39	39	18
Cardiff	28	19	26	21	26	38	26	29	15	13	35	30	30	26	42	27	33	25	24	17	36	51	40	13	18	32	43	28	39	39	18
Edinburgh	29	20	27	22	27	39	27	30	16	14	36	31	31	27	43	28	34	26	25	18	37	52	41	14	19	33	44	29	40	40	19
Felixstowe	26	17	24	19	24	36	24	27	13	11	33	28	28	24	40	25	31	23	22	15	34	49	38	11	16	30	41	26	37	37	16
Glasgow	29	20	27	22	27	39	27	30	16	14	36	31	31	27	43	28	34	26	25	18	37	52	41	14	19	33	44	29	40	40	19
Grangemouth	27	18	25	20	25	37	25	28	14	12	34	29	29	25	41	26	32	24	23	16	35	50	39	12	17	31	42	27	38	38	17
Leeds	28	19	26	21	26	38	26	29	15	13	35	30	30	26	42	27	33	25	24	17	36	51	40	13	18	32	43	28	39	39	18
Liverpool	28	19	26	21	26	38	26	29	15	13	35	30	30	26	42	27	33	25	24	17	36	51	40	13	18	32	43	28	39	39	18
London	28	19	26	21	26	38	26	29	15	13	35	30	30	26	42	27	33	25	24	17	36	51	40	13	18	32	43	28	39	39	18
Manchester	28	19	26	21	26	38	26	29	15	13	35	30	30	26	42	27	33	25	24	17	36	51	40	13	18	32	43	28	39	39	18
Reading	28	19	26	21	26	38	26	29	15	13	35	30	30	26	42	27	33	25	24	17	36	51	40	13	18	32	43	28	39	39	18
Southampton	28	19	26	21	26	38	26	29	15	13	35	30	30	26	42	27	33	25	24	17	36	51	40	13	18	32	43	28	39	39	18
York	28	19	26	21	26	38	26	29	15	13	35	30	30	26	42	27	33	25	24	17	36	51	40	13	18	32	43	28	39	39	18

Table 16.2(b) Extracts of Maersk Line transit times in 1988: Imports transit times – door to door from North America

	Atlanta	Baltimore	Boston	Calgary	Charleston	Cleveland	Dallas	Denver	Detroit	Edmonton	Halifax	Houston	Indianapolis	Jacksonville	Kansas City	Los Angeles	Memphis	Miami	Montreal	New Orleans	New York	Philadelphia	Phoenix	San Diego	San Francisco	Savannah	Seattle	Toronto	Vancouver	Wichita	Winnipeg
Aberdeen	16	12	12	18	14	17	19	26	15	18	13	19	15	15	18	24	17	15	12	17	11	13	26	24	25	15	29	12	31	18	16
Birmingham	15	11	11	17	13	16	18	25	14	17	12	18	14	14	17	23	16	14	11	16	10	12	25	23	24	14	28	11	30	17	15
Bristol	15	11	11	17	13	16	18	25	14	17	12	18	14	14	17	23	16	14	11	16	10	12	25	23	24	14	28	11	30	17	15
Cardiff	15	11	11	17	13	16	18	25	14	17	12	18	14	14	17	23	16	14	11	16	10	12	25	23	24	14	28	11	30	17	15
Edinburgh	15	11	11	17	13	16	18	25	14	17	12	18	14	14	17	23	16	14	11	16	10	12	25	23	24	14	28	11	30	17	15
Felixstowe	14	10	10	16	12	15	17	24	13	16	11	17	13	13	16	22	15	13	10	15	9	11	24	22	23	13	27	10	29	16	14
Glasgow	15	11	11	17	13	16	18	25	14	17	12	18	14	14	17	23	16	14	11	16	10	12	25	23	24	14	28	11	30	17	15
Grangemouth	15	11	11	17	13	16	18	25	14	17	12	18	14	14	17	23	16	14	11	16	10	12	25	23	24	14	28	11	30	17	15
Leeds	15	11	11	17	13	16	18	25	14	17	12	18	14	14	17	23	16	14	11	16	10	12	25	23	24	14	28	11	30	17	15
Liverpool	15	11	11	17	13	16	18	25	14	17	12	18	14	14	17	23	16	14	11	16	10	12	25	23	24	14	28	11	30	17	15
London	15	11	11	17	13	16	18	25	14	17	12	18	14	14	17	23	16	14	11	16	10	12	25	23	24	14	28	11	30	17	15
Manchester	15	11	11	17	13	16	18	25	14	17	12	18	14	14	17	23	16	14	11	16	10	12	25	23	24	14	28	11	30	17	15
Newcastle	15	11	11	17	13	16	18	25	14	17	12	18	14	14	17	23	16	14	11	16	10	12	25	23	24	14	28	11	30	17	15
Reading	15	11	11	17	13	16	18	25	14	17	12	18	14	14	17	23	16	14	11	16	10	12	25	23	24	14	28	11	30	17	15
Southampton	15	11	11	17	13	16	18	25	14	17	12	18	14	14	17	23	16	14	11	16	10	12	25	23	24	14	28	11	30	17	15
York	15	11	11	17	13	16	18	25	14	17	12	18	14	14	17	23	16	14	11	16	10	12	25	23	24	14	28	11	30	17	15

(c)   COBRA is a group of British and Continental lines operating container ships serving ports in India, Pakistan and Sri Lanka.

(d)   Trans Freight Lines is a leading Atlantic carrier operating a modern fleet of vessels between Europe and North America.

(e)   SAECS Southern Africa Europe Container Services offers container and Ro/Ro services between UK/North Continent and South Africa.

(f)   The Far Eastern Freight conference contains the TRIO Group which is a consortium of British, German and Japanese lines operating a fleet of 21 container ships on the Europe/Far East route.

Examples of transit times from UK involving P & O Container vessels are given below:

Far East and Jeddah:	Jeddah 8 days; Busan 23 days; Tokyo 27 days; Singapore 18 days; Kaohsiung 23 days; Kobe 29 days.
Australia and New Zealand:	Adelaide 35 days; Sydney 34 days; Christchurch 44 days; Melbourne 30 days; Auckland 38 days; Wellington 42 days.
North America and Caribbean:	Baltimore 16 days; Houston 19 days; Port Everglades 16 days; Charleston 14 days; New York 14 days; Boston 12 days.
Indian Subcontinent:	Bombay 40 days; Madras 30 days; Cochin 37 days; Colombo 30 days.

A significant feature of containerization involving the 'through-transport system concept' is the growing use of computers. With the use of data transmission systems often backed up by satellites, it is now possible to provide an instantaneous communications link between a number of container terminals and the ships on the high seas. Complete bills of lading, stowage plans and container terminal layouts may be quickly processed and transmitted, transforming a slow and laborious job into a moment's work on a computer keyboard.

A major development in the 1990s will be the rapid growth of the double-stack container train. This will be especially significant in the United States and Western Europe. It will result in a rationalization of ports of call by container tonnage. A modern doublestack container train of nearly one mile length is capable of conveying 820 TEUs. The double-stack container trains which are completely integrated with specific countainer shipping line sailings are called Mini Land Bridge and journey overland in North America by rail distances of between 2000 and 3000 miles. The trains convey 6.10 m or 12.20 m containers of 2.4 m width and 2.6 m height. The wagons are 60 or 80 ft long.

In 1988 modernization plans were under way to provide ten new water-front rail transfer facilities for double-stack operations at the West coast ports of Long Beach and Los Angeles. This is resulting in a recession of some US East Coast ports particularly those in the Mexican Gulf. Shipping Lines hitherto calling at these ports are now discharging containers in the US West Coast and sending the consignments on to the US South and Gulf destinations by rail.

An example is the Japan Line which has discontinued calling at all US East Coast ports and has inaugurated a pure inter-modal rail connection into US East Coast port destinations from the US West Coast. Four main West Coast ports, Los Angeles, San Francisco, Seattle and Vancouver serve as gateways for import entries while US exports move through the same ports plus Portland. This has resulted in a rationalization of the Japanese flag container fleet resulting in more productive use of container tonnage and further development of the next generation of container ships exploiting the economies of scale and further crew reductions attained through new technology. Other Maritime lines serving the USA and European seaboards are in process of doing likewise as the economic benefits of the double-stack container movement offering lower overland distribution cost and rationalization of ports of call by container operators are realized. By 1986 the US West Coast ports' share of the nation's container trade rose from 31% in 1981 to 41%. Conversely the East Coast ports have fallen from 35 to 30% in the same period. By 1988 60 double-stack container trains per week were operating from the West Coast ports and this figure is expected to treble by 1990.

As we progress through the 1990s the multi-purpose Container-Ro/Ro vessel will become more common primarily in the deep-sea trades. Such vessels will be capable of conveying a combination of both ISO containers and Ro/Ro units. The Ro/Ro units are usually unaccompanied trailers plus trade cars, lorries, etc. Advantages of this type of tonnage include flexibility of ship capacity involving a varying capacity of Ro/Ro units and containers. This facilitates the most productive use of ship capacity in a varying international market situation. Moreover, the vehicle traffic which is driven on and off the ship aids quick port turnround of the vessel. It also facilitates the shipment of the indivisible load which is very much on the increase.

Usually, such vessels do not require a portal ramp facility, but have their own ramp facility accommodated on the ship hydraulically operated.

16.2　CONTAINER TYPES

The range of container types tends to expand annually to meet the increasing market demands on this fast-growing international method of distributing merchandise. Basically the majority of containers used are built to ISO (International Standards Organization) specification thereby permitting their ease of ubiquitous use on an international scale.

Given below are details of some of the types of containers available and their salient features. Details of the container dimensions are found on page 396:

(a)　General purpose containers are closed and are suitable for the carriage of all types of general cargo and with suitable temporary modification for the carriage of bulk cargoes, both solid and liquid. The containers are basically a steel framework with steel, glass reinforced plastic or aluminium alloy used for cladding; the floors are either hardwood timber planked or plywood sheeted. Access for loading and unloading is through full width doors. Aluminium cladded containers have plywood lined interior walls. Cargo securing/lashing points are located at floor level at the base of the side walls.

With suitable temporary modifications solid bulk commodities, granular or powder, may be loaded into general purpose containers. These modifications, depending on the nature of the cargo to be loaded, usually involve the location of a bulkhead at the door end of the container, and in most, but not all instances the fitting of a polythene liner.

This method of transport has proved successful in reducing costs to both shipper and consignee due to the reduction of manpower involved in both loading sacks or bags and the stuffing and/or stripping of same into and out of the container, the cost of packaging, e.g. poly bags is of course eliminated.

The commodity payload may also be increased thus allowing an increased cargo to freight margin.

Before implementing a bulk movement system it is necessary to consider the following points:

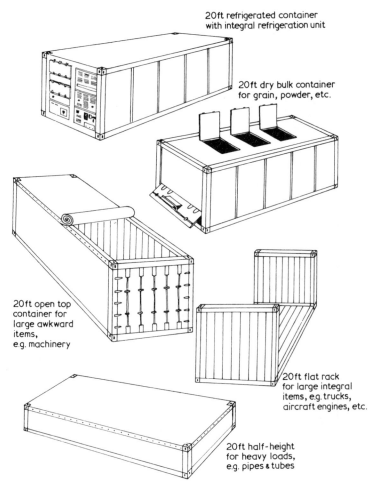

Fig. 16.1 Container types.

(i) Ensure that loading point is capable of loading bulk i.e. throwers, blowers, etc capable of end loading are available.

(ii) Ensure suitable receiving facilities are available, e.g. bulk silos, receiving hoppers, etc. and that premises are high enough to accept (if under cover) a container when in the tipping position.

(iii) Ensure that tipping trailers are available at the final destination.

It is also possible to transport certain non-hazardous bulk liquids in

Table 16.3 ISO container dimensions by type

Container Type	Overall Dimensions (ft/m)	Interior Dimensions (Minimum)			Door Dimensions		Cubic Capacity (Minimum) (m³)	Tare Weight (Maximum) (kg)	Gross Weight (Maximum) (kg)
		Length (mm)	Breadth (mm)	Height (mm)	Breadth (mm)	Height (mm)			
General Purpose	20×8×8½ (6.1×2.4×2.6)	5 890	2 345	2 400	2 335	2 290	32.7	2 450	24 000
General Purpose	40×8×8½ (12.2×2.4×2.6)	12 015	2 345	2 362	2 335	2 260	66.3	3 700–4 380	30 480
Insulated	20×8×8½ (6.1×2.4×2.6)	5 760	2 260	2 235	2 260	2 215	29.0	2 413	24 000
Fruit	20×8×8½ (6.1×2.4×2.6)	5 770	2 300	2 275	2 300	2 215	30.19	2 362–2 732	24 000
Refrigerated	20×8×8½ (6.1×2.4×2.6)	5 450	2 260	2 247	2 260	2 247	27.7	3 460	24 000
Refrigerated	40×8×8½ (12.2×2.4×2.6)	11 550	2 270	2 200	2 270	2 170	57.8	4 670–4 940	30 480
Bulk	20×8×8½ (6.1×2.4×2.6)	5 892	2 347	2 379	2 335	2 285	33.1	2 730	24 000
Ventilated	20×8×8½ (6.1×2.4×2.6)	5 892	2 303	2 380	2 305 Side Openings Length (mm)	2 273 Height (mm)	32.3	2 720	24 000
Flat Rack	20×8×8½ (6.1×2.4×2.6)	5 940	2 400	2 310	5 576	2 310	31.9	2 610–2 810	30 480
Flat Rack	40×8×8½ (12.2×2.4×2.6)	12 066	2 263	2 134	11 662	2 134	58.6	5 960–6 100	40 640

Container Type — Open Top / Tarpaulin Top Sliding Roof Bows

Container Type	Overall Dimensions (ft/m)	Overall Interior Dimensions			Door Dimensions		Roof Aperture		Cubic Capacity (Minimum) (m^3)	Tare Weight (Maximum) (kg)	Gross Weight (Maximum) (kg)
		Length (mm)	Breadth (mm)	Height (mm)	Breadth (mm)	Height (mm)	Length (mm)	Breadth (mm)			
Open Top	20×8×8½ (6.1×2.4×2.6)	5 890	2 345	2 340	2 335	2 260	5 712	2 175	32.4	2 093–2 513	24 000–30 480
Open Top	40×8×8½ (12.2×2.4×2.6)	12 025	2 247	2 305	2 235	2 200	11 832	2 150	63.47	3 949–4 650	30 480
Half Height	20×8×4¼ (6.1×2.4×1.3)	5 906	2 313	1 075	2 280	1 003	5 775	2 224	14.3	1 724	24 000
Half Height	40×8×4¼ (12.2×2.4×1.3)	12 010	2 235	940	2 284	980	11 900	2 073	25.2	3 656	30 480

Container Type — Tank

Container Type	Overall Dimensions (ft/mm)	Total Water Capacity (litres)	Tare Weight (Maximum) (kg)	Tank Material	Gross Weight (Maximum) (kg)
Tank	20×8×8½ (6.1×2.4×2.6)	24 000	3 150	Stainless Steel	30 480

Container Type — Open Sided / Bulk

Container Type	Overall Dimensions (ft/m)	Minimum Interior Dimensions Gates in position			Minimum Door Dimensions		Minimum Side Dimensions		Cubic Capacity (Minimum) (m^3)	Tare Weight (Maximum) (kg)	Gross Weight (Maximum) (kg)
		Length (mm)	Breadth (mm)	Height (mm)	Breadth (mm)	Height (mm)	Length (mm)	Height (mm)			
Open Sided	20×8×8½ (6.1×2.4×2.6)	5 895	2 310	2 300	2 335	2 180	5 602	2 235	31.1	3 365	24 000–30 480
Bulk	20×8×8½ (6.1×2.4×2.6)	5 892	2 347	2 379	2 335	2 285	–		33.1	2 730	–

general purpose containers which have been fitted with special flexible tanks. These tanks are laid out in the container and a securing harness attached. A bulkhead is then positioned at the door end of the container and the left-hand door closed. The tank is then ready for fitting.

(b) Insulated containers protect against heat loss or gain and are used in conjunction with a blown-air refrigeration system to convey perishable or other cargo which needs to be carried under temperature control. Internally the containers are equipped with an aluminium T-section floor and the inside face of the doors are fitted with moulded vertical battens to permit air flow around the cargo. It is important when cargo requiring temperature control is loaded in this type of container, an air space of approximately 7.5 mm is left over the top of the cargo to allow free air circulation. Securing points are positioned along each side of the floor, while lashing points to prevent cargo fall out are sited at the door end of the container by the corner posts.

(c) The fruit container has been developed to carry fresh, deciduous and citrus fruit, the internal dimensions being slightly larger than the standard insulated container to accommodate the packing of standard fruit pallets and cases. The internal structure of the fruit container is basically the same as the insulated container.

(d) Refrigerated containers are designed to operate independently of a blown-air refrigerated system and are fitted with their own refrigeration units which require an electrical power supply for operation. Each container is capable of being set at its own individual carriage temperature. The internal structure of these containers is similar to that of the 'port hole' insulated container with alloy T-section floor and securing points each side at the base of the side walls and fall out lashing points at corner posts. The container is of steel construction with the cladding of stainless steel lined or aluminium alloy. The electrical supply will usually operate on either 200 to 220 volts, single phase or 380 to 440 volts three phase at 32 amps both at 50/60 Hz.

(e) Bulk containers are designed for the carriage of dry powders and granular substances in bulk. To facilitate top loading three circular hatches (500 mm diameter) are fitted in some containers in the roof structure. For discharge a hatch is fitted in the right-hand door of the container. Full width doors are fitted to allow loading of conventional cargo. Constructed of steel framework with steel cladding, the containers are usually equipped with mild steel floors to enable ease of cleaning. Lashing points are fitted at the base of the sidewall and at the top of the container along the top side rails to enable the securing of polythene liners (if required).

(f) Ventilated containers are of steel construction. They are broadly similar to the general purpose container specification, except for the inclusion of full length ventilation galleries sited along the top and bottom side rails, allowing the passive ventilation of the cargo. The ventilation arrangement is such that the ingress of water is prevented. It is ideal for such products as coffee.

(g) Flat rack containers are designed to facilitate the carriage of cargo in excess of the dimensions available in either general purpose or open top containers. They consist of a flat bed with fixed ends, the external dimensions conforming in all respects to the ISO requirements. Suitable lashing points are fitted to the floor and/or side rails of the container within some cases four corner rings. A combination of two or more flat rack containers can be used to form a temporary 'tween-deck space for uncontainerable cargo moved on a 'port to port' basis provided the total weight and point loading the cargo does not exceed the static capabilities of the flat racks. It is ideal for uncontainerable cargo.

(h) Open top containers with their top loading facility are designed for the carriage of heavy and awkward-shaped cargoes, and those cargoes whose height is in excess of that which can be stowed in a standard general purpose container. The floor of the containers are of hardwood timber plank or plywood, and there are a number of cargo securing points in the floor or along the bottom side rail at the base of the sidewalls. The containers have a removable door header either removable or sliding roof bows to allow loading to be effected either directly through the roof aperture or through the door using overhead lifting equipment. Tarpaulin tilts are available to protect the cargo. Also there exists the overheight tilt for use with overheight cargo. It can also be described as an open sided/open top container.

(i) The half-height version of the open top container is designed for the carriage of heavy, dense cargoes such as steel, pipes and tubes, etc. It is ideal for shippers whose premises have a restricted height for loading or discharge. The steel containers have a tarpaulin top, a removable door header bar and securing points set into the floor.

(j) Tank containers are generally constructed with the carriage of a specific product or range of products in mind. It is usual for shippers to provide their own tanks. Such containers are owned or leased by the shipper. They are usually constructed of stainless steel and for liquid cargoes may be used for either dangerous goods or non-hazardous cargo. A wide variety of products are shipped in tank containers ranging from the wet to dry bulk cargoes. Many are dedicated to one product.

(k) Open sided containers are designed to accommodate the carriage of specific commodities such as plywood, perishable commodities and livestock. These steel containers have a fixed roof, open sides and end opening doors, the sides being closed by full height gates in 1.37 m wide sections, and nylon reinforced PVC curtains (the curtains may be rolled up to the top side rail when not in use) which meet TIR requirements. There are eight lashing points each side affixed to the bottom side rail (outside) below floor level, nine rings located in the floor and five rings vertically up each corner post.

(l) High cube reefer containers are of 12.20 m long 2.4 m wide and 3.0 m high (9 ft 6 ins). They are equipped in accord with the data found in item (d).

(m) Artificial 'tween-deck containers are without end walls, side-walls or a roof and also known as a platform carrier. They are 6.10 m long and 2.4 m wide or 12.20 m long and 2.4 m wide. These units are used for oversize and overweight cargo which cannot otherwise be containerized. By combining several artificial 'tween decks on board a vessel it is possible to obtain a very high payload. See also item (g).

(n) Hanger containers are used for dry cargo and are equipped with removable beams in the upper part. They are used for the shipment of garments on hangers. They are 12.20 m long, 2.4 m wide, and 3.0 m high, or 6.10 m long, 2.4 m wide and 3.0 m high.

A container developed and operated by Maersk termed a Super high cube of (45 ft) – 13.725 m long, 2.4 m wide and 3.0 m high (9 ft 6 in). It has a 27% larger cubic capacity (85.9m^3) than the general purpose container of 12.20 m long, 2.4 m wide and 2.4 m high.

(o) Bin containers have a cargo capacity of 21 600 kg and a tare weight of 2400 kg and a length of 6.06 m, a width of 2.44 m and a height of 1.30 m. They are ideal for heavy dense cargoes such as steel, pipes, etc. They have no doors.

(p) Bolster flat containers have a cargo capacity of 23 000 kg and a tare weight of 1940 kg and a length overall of 6.06 m, a width of 2.44 m and a height of 0.23 m. They are ideal for a variety of heavy cargoes. The average operational life of a container is 12 years.

As we progress through the 1990s, it is likely that a new generation of containers will be introduced under the approval of the ISO. Emphasis will be placed on higher capacity (for example the 9 ft 6 in high container).

The argument that you cannot put everything into boxes will always be valid but as most trades and ships are geared up to containerization so the box manufacturers are producing more specialized designs to increase the range of commodities which can be boxed.

To date, the 'specials market' has been responsible for the development of the flat, flatrack, folding-end flatrack, half-height, tank, reefer and bulktainer type of container and more variations on these themes are likely to be seen as the container builders respond to shipping demands.

The flatrack, folding-end flatrack and cargo platform market forms a considerable part of the whole 'specials' picture. Already used by 'combi'-vessel and Ro/Ro shipping operators, they are increasingly being utilized by pure container operators. They are now considered essential tools in international shipping since there is still a great deal of cargo unsuited for transportation in standard containers. For awkward cargo, the shipper or consolidator needs the alternative of either top or side loading.

Overwidth or overheight cargo can also be accommodated easily in units of this nature, permitting a high percentage of so-called 'non-containerizable' cargo to be shipped within a pure container transport system. Since a loaded flatrack can be top lifted – often even when loaded with overheight cargo – and can be incorporated within a container stack, it is almost invariably preferred over the cargo platform by lift-on/lift-off container operators.

In cellular container ships, it is becoming increasingly popular to provide a 'tween-deck within a hold by positioning two or more flatracks side by side in the container cells. Large items can then be lowered into the hold to straddle the units.

Equally, the fixed flatrack, which can be loaded to a height greater than the end walls, provides a valuable opportunity for Ro/Ro operators to maximize headroom on vehicle decks. The folding end flatrack, such as the Stakmasta 'Stakrak', has this same advantage, but complements it with the benefits of compact empty stowage.

This is often essential where, for example, wheeled or block-stowed cargo constitutes the return-leg loading. While the cargo platform provides both an overheight capability and compact empty storage, when loaded it cannot be stacked, other than on the top tier, and neither can it be top lifted. The cargo platform is therefore much more restricted in its operational capabilities, when compared to the Stakrak.

Stakrak units are favoured particularly for bulky, oversize cargoes, but accessibility from the side can be useful even for more normal sized pieces. Side access permits loading of a vehicle-mounted Stakrak by a fork truck, without recourse to loading ramps or special loading bays. Many shippers, especially of heavy cargo, find this feature invaluable, since many fork trucks are unsuited to end loading standard dry cargo containers.

Ship operators, too, have discovered the benefits when using Stakrak equipment. General cargo intended for shipment on multi-purpose vessels, Ro/Ro or container ships can be consolidated at the port prior to vessel arrival and then loaded aboard rapidly. Turnround times when loading general cargo are slashed. Should there be a lack of suitable back-haul cargo, the units can be shipped back empty, stowed compactly on the weather-deck.

The same benefits are applicable to any of the Stakrak range, but the range itself has evolved to meet particular needs.

The Stakrak Free Standing Leg Unit, for example, is a Stakrak with four folding end corner posts rather than end walls. Consequently, it is able to handle overlength cargo in the same way as a cargo platform, but can still be stowed within a container stack, either ashore or on board vessel.

Stakmastas are suitable to carry piping manufactured in copper and other materials. Much of this is overlength and so other types of equipment were not practical. When oversize cargo is not being carried, there is the possibility for the unit to be used as a standard container, within a stack, or in the cell guides of a ship.

The development of the Stakmasta Stakbed, a piece of equipment that offers the three-in-one capability of being a cargo platform (or flat), a fixed-end flatrack and a folding-end flatrack.

Whereas the Stakrak has solid end walls of pressed steel, the Stakbed has only the vertical corner posts with horizontal bracing pieces. Recesses in the cargo platform permit the end frame to stow, when folded, flush with the deck to provide an unrestricted surface area for cargo loading.

This arrangement, when compared to the Stakrak, allows for a reduced 'folded height' and allows four 40-ft Stakbeds to be stacked and locked together within a 7½ ft module height. These may then be top lifted, trucked, railed or shipped as one container.

When erect, the end walls permit the Stakbed to be used as though it were a fixed-end flatrack. Thus the container operator, regularly top lifting units and stacking them within a ship's hold or on a container park, can treat the Stakbed as a normal container.

A major advantage of containerization is the availability of through rates to be quote incorporating both the maritime and surface portions of the transit (see Chapter 9).

The task of stowing the contents of a container is an important activity bearing in mind the need to use the container capacity in the most economical way and prevent damage to the contents during the transit. Container stowage is fully explained in Chapter 6 of my book *The Elements of Export Practice.*

16.3 ADVANTAGES/DISADVANTAGES OF CONTAINERIZATION

The advantages/disadvantages of containerization can be summarized as follows:

(a) Advantages of containerization

 (i) It permits a door-to-door service being given which may be from the factory production site to the retail distributor's store – an overall distance of may be 10 000 km.

 (ii) No intermediate handling at terminal (port) trans-shipment points.

 (iii) The absence of intermediate handling plus quicker transits permits less risk of cargo damage and pilferage.

 (iv) Low risk of cargo damage and pilferage enables more favourable cargo premiums to be obtained compared with conventional cargo shipments, i.e. 'tween-deck tonnage.

 (v) Elimination of intermediate handling at terminal transfer points, i.e. ports, enables substantial labour savings to be realized, which in industrial high income per head countries can realize considerable attractive financial savings.

 (vi) Less packing needs for containerized shipments. In some cases particularly with specialized containers, e.g. refrigerated tanks (liquid or powder), no packing is required. This produces substantial cost savings in international transport.

 (vii) The elimination of intermediate handling coupled with the other advantages of containerized shipments, permits the cargo to arrive in a better condition when compared with conventional cargo shipments.

(viii) Emerging from the inherent advantages of containerization, rates are likely to remain more competitive when compared with conventional tonnage ('tween-deck) shipments. A significant reason is that containerization is in the main a capital-intensive transport system, compared with conventional liner systems which are very much labour intensive.

(ix) Transits are much quicker compared with conventional cargo shipments. This is achieved through a combination of faster vessels, the rationalization of ports of call and substantially quicker cargo handling. An example is the UK/Australia service where the round voyage time has been reduced from the twenty weeks taken by conventional services a few years ago to the five weeks (approximately) taken by container vessels nowadays.

(x) Emerging from faster transits and the advantages under items (vii) and (viii) it encourages trade development and permits quicker payment of export invoices.

(xi) Containerization has permitted fleet rationalization. On average one container vessel – usually of much increased capacity and faster speed – has displaced up to eight 'tween-deck vessels on deep-sea services. This development has been facilitated by the rationalization of ports of call.

(xii) Container vessels attain much improved utilization and generally are very much more productive than the 'tween-deck tonnage.

(xiii) Faster transits usually coupled with more reliable schedules and ultimately increased service frequency, are tending to encourage many importers to hold reduced stocks/spares. This produces savings in warehouse accommodation needs, lessens risk of obsolescent stock, and reduces importers' working capital.

(xiv) Containerization produces quicker transits and encourages rationalization of ports of call. This in many trades is tending to stimulate trade expansion through much improved service standards. Accordingly it will result in increased service frequency which will aid trade development.

(xv) Provision of through documentation (consignment note) – bill of lading.

(xvi) Provision of through rate. This embraces both maritime and surface transport cost. This factor and the one under item (xv) very much aids the marketing of the container concept.

(xvii) More reliable transits – particularly disciplined controlled transit arrangements.

(xviii) New markets have emerged through container development and its inherent advantages.

(xix) Overall a total quality service.

(b) Disadvantages of containerization

(i) Containerization is a capital-intensive project and as such is beyond the financial ability of many shipowners. In many cases container services are now operated by members of the old conference groupings finding a new consortium. Even so, the finance required is very great for not only has a specialized ship(s) to be built but at least three sets of containers. With regard to the latter, ownership has tended to be held by container hire operators, by industrial companies (who use containers not only to carry but to advertise their goods); and by the ship owning consortia. In all three sectors, however, there has been a good deal of leasing of containers with the operational control resting with the lessors. The expense does not end here for at the chosen terminals the authority has to bear the cost of providing specialized cranes, trailers, van carriers etc., as well as strengthening quays and creating stacking space.

(ii) Not all merchandise can be conveniently containerized. The percentage of such traffic falls annually as new types of containers are introduced. Nevertheless, it is a constraining factor and can involve the shipper in capital outlay to adapt his production processes/premises/packaging etc., to suit the restrictive dimensions/weights imposed by the container.

(iii) The container in itself is a high capacity carrying unit, and in consequence, exporters with limited trade are unable to fill the container to capacity, and thereby take full advantage of an economical through-rate, for example from exporters' factory premises to importers' warehouses. This situation has been largely overcome by the provision of container bases situated in industrial areas or port environs, where less than container load traffic (LCL) is stowed (stuffed) into a container with other compatible traffic of similar destination/area.

(iv) In some trades a very, very small percentage of the traffic is incapable of being containerized due to its nature such as certain livestock. This does involve the shipowner in providing specialized – non-container – facilities on the vessel which inflates the capital cost of the project, and sometimes results in poor utilization of such facilities on the return passage.

(v) The stratification of some trades varies considerably by time of year and direction. For example a trade may have a preponderance of perishable cargo in one direction eight months of the year, whilst in the reverse direction the cargo may be consumer goods. This situation has to be reconciled in an acceptable container type(s) for use in both directions. Another example is to have cargo in one direction with a low stowage factor, whilst in the reverse direction it is a high stowage factor. Such problems although *prima facie* diffficult, have been overcome by the co-operation of all interested parties, particularly shippers/shipowners. Technological development in recent years such as food storage/processing etc. have eased the shipowners' problems considerably and tended to level out the, hitherto, peak seasonal nature of the traffic in some trades.

(vi) The container-owning company, which may be a consortium of shipowners, or container operator has a complex task in ensuring full utilization of such equipment. Most shipowner consortia have computer equipment to monitor and control their inventory of containers. The task is an international one and involves many parties to ensure strict control of the container when it is in their hands. Some method of container control is essential to ensure good utilization of the equipment in the interest of maximizing revenue.

(vii) In some countries restrictions exist regarding the internal movement, particularly by road, of certain containers exceeding a certain dimension/weight. This has tended to restrict the full development of the larger container, particularly the 40(12.20 m)-footer, but long term the constraint is likely to disappear. Restrictions by canal/rail are virtually non-existent in many countries.

16.4 CONTAINER BASES

The function of a container base is to consolidate break-bulk cargoes (i.e. less than full container load consignment) into full container loads. The container base may be under the management of a consortium of ship container operators; a container operator(s) engaged in the freight-forwarding business; a consortium comprising freight forwarders, road hauliers, etc., and others engaged in such business, or a local port authority. It can be situated in the port itself; the port environs; or an industrial area which can support the facility in generating adequate quantities of containerized import/export traffic through it. The container base is road served and the larger ones often have rail facilities.

Overall the role of the Container Base can be summarized as convenient points to assemble LCL cargo; provide export packing and handling services for FCL and out of gauge cargo; provide inland customs clearance local to customers' business premises; provide totally secure storage and packing for empty and loaded containers together with cleaning and repair services; offer office accommodation on the spot for container operators, freight forwarders and other maritime service companies.

The object of the facility is to consolidate break-bulk cargoes destined for the same area/country into full container loads and thereby provide a service in that area particularly for the smaller importer/exporter. Consequently the process of stuffing (loading) and unstuffing (unloading) containers is performed at the container base. Many of the larger container bases are inland clearance depots which have the added facility of customs clearance for both import and export cargoes.

The major advantage of the container bases is to provide a service to the importer/exporter situated in the container base hinterland and relieve the port authority of local customs clearance of import/export cargoes. This latter advantage tends to reduce the problems of port congestion, i.e. containers awaiting clearance due to non-availability of documents, and enables the through-put of the container berth to be maximized. Ultimately it speeds up transit as no inordinate delay is usually experienced at the port and thereby encourages the development of international trade. Undoubtedly the number of container bases will increase as the container trades expand. The reader is recommended to study Chapters 5 and 12 of *Economics of Shipping Practice and Management*.

To conclude our examination of containerization, it is likely that, as we progress through the 1990s, the pattern of cargo liner trade featuring predominantly containers will change. Substantial growth can continue to be expected in the Far East markets. Moreover, container capacity is likely to increase featuring the 45 ft long and 9 ft 6 ins high container, especially in the North American market. The development of the intermodal transportation network is likely to grow to feature sea and air. The combination of these two transportation methods offers an economical alternative, and an average journey time is cut by approximately 75% when compared with sea freight. Transportation costs are reduced by up to 50% compared to pure air freight. Examples include the following:

Sea Transit		Air Transit	
Seaport	*Seaport*	*Airport*	*Airport*
Hong Kong	Sharjah	Sharjah	Frankfurt
Osaka	Vancouver	Vancouver	Frankfurt
Fukuoka	Vladivostok	Vladivostok	Leningrad
Valparaiso	Recife	Recife	Frankfurt
Caracas	Miami	Miami	Frankfurt

The air waybill and bill of lading documents are used. To aid faster development, compatible containers are being provided which go directly from the ship into the aircraft without the goods needing to be loaded. Boeing Jumbo air freighters with a payload of up to 103 tons, and capable of conveying pallets and containers are used. A number of other sea/air routes exist between the Middle East and North America, with the air transit commencing from the North American East Coast ports. High value, and perishable or urgent cargoes tend to use such services. In the container terminal area, the latest generation of the rubber-tyred gantry crane, of 35 tonne capacity, which straddles a seven-wide container block and can lift one container over a stack of four is being introduced.

16.5 INTERNATIONAL AUTHORIZATION

Emerging from the International Convention for Safe Containers sponsored by the International Maritime Organization and the UN in 1972, was the Health and Safety Executive. This was entrusted with the task of establishing an effective procedure for the testing, inspection and approval of containers. This was introduced in September 1982 whereby all international container movements had to be tested or otherwise approved by one of the accredited organizations appointed by the Health and Safety Executive. After approval each container is appropriately plated. Ship classification societies featured strongly in the accredited organizations. Lloyd's Register was one of the accredited organizations appointed. It operates a container certification scheme which provides for a system of quality control inspection during the manufacture of containers. The scheme ensures that all types of container are built to reliable and safe standards. It also ensures, through certification, compliance with the international conventions concerning container transport.

Details of the international authorization to issue certification for containers that comply with the appropriate requirements are given below:

(a) International Convention for Safe Containers (CSC) – operative from 1982.

(b) International Customs Convention.

(c) International Agreement for the Transportation of Perishable Foodstuffs (ATP).

Where the carriage of dangerous goods in tanks is involved, containers can be certified in accordance with the following:

(d) International Maritime Dangerous Goods Code for Sea Transport (IMDG).

(e) International Regulations concerning the Carriage of Dangerous Goods by Rail (RID).

(f) European Agreement concerning the Carriage of Dangerous Goods by Road (ADR).

(g) US DOT Regulations CFR49 for the Transportation of Intermodal Portable Tanks (IM101 & IM102).

(h) Canadian Regulations for the Transportation of Dangerous Commodities by Rail (CTC).

Tank containers, special containers or those manufactured in low volume production runs are inspected usually on an individual basis. When containers are manufactured in large production runs each container is inspected and certified. However, series production of general cargo containers can be monitored under a quality assured scheme. The scheme normally involves a review of the manufacturer's works by:

(a) assessing the quality manual and ensuring compliance with its requirements by a thorough audit of the works;

(b) advising, if necessary, how quality assurance programmes can be implemented;

(c) auditing incoming materials;

(d) verifying corner castings are obtained from approved suppliers;

(e) ascertaining that sub-contracted fabricated components comply with specification;

(f) reviewing production arrangements for orders to be certified;

(g) inspecting the works systematically to monitor quality control procedures during production;

(h) carrying out sample inspection of containers during production and on completion.

Any new design for a container must be type approved. This involves the following:

(a) appraising in detail the manufacturer's structural drawings;

(b) surveying the prototype container during construction;

(c) approving the testing establishments by reviewing procedures, test equipment, calibration records and methods of reporting;

(d) witnessing tests of the prototype in accordance with the ISO procedures applicable to the design including:

(i) lifting and stacking;

(ii) roof, floor, side and end wall tests;

(iii) base restraint;

(iv) transverse and longitudinal racking;

(v) weathertightness;

(vi) air leakage, thermal characteristics and refrigerating machinery capacity tests;

(vii) pressure vessel hydraulic tests, safety valve setting and leaktightness;

(e) issuing type approval certificates.

The International Container Safety Convention and the regulations relating to the transport of dangerous goods in containers also require in-service inspection at prescribed intervals throughout the operational life of the container.

The international consignment

Our study of shipping would not be complete without an examination of the international consignment in so far as suitability of transport modes, delivery trade terms of sale, and export documentation processing are concerned.

17.1 FACTORS TO CONSIDER IN EVALUATING SUITABILITY OF TRANSPORT MODE(S) FOR AN INTERNATIONAL CONSIGNMENT:

The following factors must be considered when evaluating suitability of transport mode(s) for an international consignment:

(a) Nature of the commodity, its dimensions/weight and whether any special facilities are required during transit. For example, livestock require special facilities, gold requires special security/strong room; meat requires refrigerated accommodation.

(b) The degree of packaging and the costs thereof. Air freight, containerization and through international road/rail services require less packaging.

(c) The degree to which the consignment presented aids cargo handling. For example, palletized cargo facilitates handling by fork-lift truck, whilst lightweight cartons are ideal for containers. Conversely, the awkwardly shaped package may require special facilities and/or handling arrangements, and may be subject to a possible freight surcharge.

(d) Any statutory obligations imposed relative to the transit. Certain products need special facilities both in the transport mode and terminal. This in itself restricts route/service and transport mode choice. For example, the movement of meat/offal etc. requires special facilities both by the operator to ship it and inspection facilities at the import terminal. Statutory obligations also can influence type of packaging as found for example in the Australian trade in the use of straw and case wood.

(e) Dangerous cargo. Again, regulations are stringent regarding its packaging, stowage, and mixture with other cargoes during stowage. This can restrict service/routing schedules.

(f) Terms of export contract. For example it may stipulate that goods must be consigned by a national or specified shipping line/ airline operator to save currency. This policy in shipping is called flag discrimination.

(g) Suitability of available transport services. For example, air freighters have limited capacity/weight/dimensions; weight restrictions may apply at a particular berth/shipping service, etc.

(h) The transit time and related urgency of consignment.

(i) The overall transport cost and evaluation of alternatives. This is an important item and will include rate; evaluation of transit time; cost of packaging and convenience/reliability of services. Additionally, one must consider frequent service requires less storage in warehouse; reduces risk of obsolescence of product; requires less working capital through less stock piling etc; facilitates smoother production flow; and helps to produce better customer relations. Service quality, risk of pilferage/damage, and marketing condition of goods on arrival are also relevant.

(j) Quantity of cargo available and period over which shipment to be made. It is desirable to undertake a transport distribution analysis of the options available, and thereby decide which is the most favourable in the light of the foregoing factors.

(k) Proximity and convenience, transport cost of the consignors/ consignees, promises relative to the seaport/airport, and the local facilities available.

(l) The range of shipping routes available, their cost, other costs, range of facilities, quality of resources, general availability, overall efficiency and convenience of operation.

(m) Distribution services used by the exporter's competitors, and their strengths and weaknesses.

(n) Likely changes in the foreseeable future, such as provision of modern tonnage.

17.2 DELIVERY TRADE TERMS OF SALE AND EXPORT CONTRACT

The basis of the price quotation depends on correct interpretation of the delivery trade terms of sale. Hence they determine the following:

(i) The charges paid by the buyer and seller.

(ii) Where delivery takes place in order to complete the export contract.

(iii) When the property and risk pass from the seller to the buyer. The following examples are relevant:

(a) Cash against documents – on payment
(b) Documents against payment – on payment
(c) Open account – payment by importer usually on receipt of merchandise
(d) Documents against acceptance – on acceptance
(e) Letter of credit – on acceptance of documents by bank

The financial aspects cannot be overstressed in the execution of the delivery trade terms of sale.

Details are given below of information found in a typical export contract in UK, but it must be stressed they can differ by individual country. This may be found in the export sales contract, or the commercial export invoice, and contains:

(a) Seller's name and address.

(b) Buyer's name and address.

(c) Confirmation that the document constitutes a contract of the goods sold to an addressee and that he has bought according to the terms and conditions laid down.

(d) Number and quantity of goods precisely and fully described to avoid later misunderstanding or dispute. In particular one must mention details of batches, etc. and reconcile goods description with custom tariff specification.

(e) Price – in UK often quoted in sterling – unless otherwise required. This may be US dollars or the buyer's currency. To counter inflation, particularly with long-term contract, it is usual to incorporate escalation clause therein; and to reduce the risk of sterling fluctuations, the tendency is to invoice in foreign currencies.

(f) Terms of delivery, e.g. CIF Lagos, FOB Felixstowe, ex works Luton.

(g) Terms of payment, e.g. letter of credit, sight draft.

(h) Delivery date/shipment date or period.

(i) Methods of shipment FCL or LCL, e.g. container routeing, train ferry, Ro/Ro-trailer, air freight.

(j)   Method of packing.

(k)   Insurance – cover note terms.

(l)   Import or export licence details or other instructions, such as certificate of origin, ATA carnet etc.

(m)   Shipping/freight/documentary requirements and/or details as found on the export cargo shipping instructions. Case marking instruction.

(n)   Contract conditions, e.g. sale, delivery, performance (quality) of goods, arbitration pre-shipment inspection (SGS), etc.

(o)   Signature – copy for buyer to return signed to seller.

Various forms of quotations exist in exporting and a study of them now follows. The more important ones are FOB and CIF.

(i) *CIF*. Undoubtedly the most popular quotation is 'cost, insurance and freight'. Under a CIF contract of sale the seller provides the goods; books cargo space on the vessel; pays freight to the buyer's port which is named, e.g. CIF Singapore; insures the goods on behalf of the buyer against normal marine and fire risks to that port, and pays all charges incidental in getting the goods onto the vessel. He is liable for any loss or damage before the goods reach the ship.

The seller is entitled to payment in exchange for the documents – including bill of lading and insurance policy – relative to the shipment. Hence the CIF contract is one to deliver documents rather than goods. If any loss or damage ensues after the shipping company has received the goods, and given a clean bill of lading, the buyer will take the necessary steps against the shipowner or underwriter. The seller cannot be held liable for any such loss or damage. The buyer will be responsible for the charges incurred in getting the goods off the ship to his warehouse, such as lighterage, dock dues and customs duties. It is often necessary for imported goods to be accompanied by special forms, e.g. consular invoices. In such cases it is usual for the CIF seller to defray the expenses of preparation.

(ii) *C & F*. Under Cost and Freight the exporter invoices the buyer for the cost of the goods and the freight, but not the insurance which becomes the responsibility of the buyer to arrange.

(iii) *EXW*. It may be – Ex works (EXW) cleared for export or – ex works (EXW) uncleared for export expected to be introduced in 1990. This quotation places the exporter's liability for cargo loss or damage and duties at a minimum especially in regard to EXW – Ex works cleared for export. Overall the seller bears all the cost and risks of the goods until such time as the buyer is obliged to take delivery of the consignment. To assist the buyer the option exists for the seller to clear the goods for exportation involving the seller obtaining all the requisite documents and presenting the goods/documents for customs clearance. The alternative of EXW – Ex works uncleared for export involves the buyer taking delivery as soon as the goods are placed at his disposal, pays all fees/charges of exporting and accepts risk from the factory gate. Title to the goods passes at the factory gates.

(iv) *FAS*. Under 'free alongside ship', the seller pays all costs incidental to getting the goods where they can be placed on board the vessel. The custom of the port may give FAS a special meaning such as 'goods placed in steamer's shed,' instead of the more usual meaning. There should also be provision for determining where the loss lies when goods are lost before they are actually taken onto the ship.

(v) *FOB*. This quotation, 'free on board', implies that the duty of the seller is to produce the goods, get them to the port and see they are actually placed on board the vessel which the buyer provides. Hence the seller meets all charges incidental to placing the goods on the ship, such as cartage, insurance, handling and lighterage. When the goods are placed on board ship and the seller has obtained a receipt for the goods, the seller's responsibilities cease. Thereafter the buyer pays all charges including insurance of goods from the departure port to destination and pays the freight. Usually the seller pays all port charges but this should be made clear in the quotation.

The seller still retains some dominion over the goods in particular circumstances. For example the right of stoppage *in transitu* is one which accrues to an unpaid seller when the buyer is insolvent, as soon as transit commences.

(vi) *FRC*. Under the free carrier term the exporter delivers the merchandise to a carrier at a named point on the same basis as found under the FOB term. However, the FRC is designed to meet the requirements of the multi-modal transport operation which may be a container or trailer movement under the Roll-on/Roll-off arrangement. In such a situation it is likely to be inland such as a warehouse, or inland clearance depot and not at a seaport as under FOB.

(vii) *DCP*. Under the freight, carriage paid term the exporter is required to pay for the carriage of the goods to name destination, but not the insurance.

(viii) *CIP*. Freight, carriage and insurance paid is the same as DCP except the exporter is responsible for insuring the goods. The terms FRC, DCP and CIP are becoming increasingly popular through the development of a multi-modal combined transport operation as found in containerization and Roll-on/Roll-off traffic.

(ix) *FOR*. This quotation 'free on rail', permits the seller to include in his price cost of goods, cartage and placing on railway wagons at the railhead from where the goods are to be despatched. Railway and other transport charges thence are paid by the buyer. Care should be taken to ensure the buyer cannot possibly misinterpret this quotation as free on rail at port of departure or at port of arrival. Thus if motor cars made at Luton are in question, the quotation would read FOR Luton. The terms FOW, 'free on wagon', and FOT, 'free on trucks', are synonymous with FOR.

(x) *Loco*. This quotation embraces price of goods including the cost of packaging and conveyance to the place named.

(xi) *Turn-key*. This arises where the export sales contract provides for the seller (exporter) to supply not only the goods but also commission it on the site defined by the importer. It thus involves the exporter providing the facility and also setting it up on the site. This is particularly common with large scale engineering projects where the seller is responsible for the entire operation to the point of construction and making it fully operational. It is particularly common in the Emirate States and in a consortia situation (see *The Elements of Export Practice*, Chapter 13).

(xii) *DDP*. Delivered duty paid or delivered duty unpaid quoting destination name and country of importation likely to be introduced in 1990. Under this term it places the maximum obligation on the seller regarding the cargo despatch arrangements. In such circumstances the seller is responsible for the conveyance of the goods at his own risk and expense to the named destination in the buyers (importers) contract of sale. The buyer accepts the goods at the named place of destination. He has the option to ask the seller to fund all the duty such as VAT/taxes on delivery, or undertake it himself for the buyers account.

Basically, the CIF contract is in many ways the best both from the buyer's and seller's point of view. As the seller is at the port of shipment or in country of origin, he is the better party to arrange and accept these liabilities. On the other hand, the buyer is responsible for arranging delivery, lighterage, cost of discharge, import duties in his own country, and loss or damage after the clean bill of lading has been issued.

17.3 RECEIPT OF EXPORT ORDER

Before dealing with the export order acceptance, it is appropriate to study the following check points which need careful scrutiny in any price list tendered. It emphasizes how important it is to ensure all the special costs which may enter into an export order are included together with the disciplined time scale to execute the order and ensure the goods arrive on time in a quality condition:

(a) Adequate clear – technical and not commercial – description of goods. Harmonized Commodity Description and Coding System (H/S).

(b) Goods specification – use metric.

(c) Quantities offered/available with delivery details including address and required arrival date.

(d) Price
   (i) amounts or per unit
   (ii) currency
   (iii) delivery terms which may involve part shipments over a scheduled period and/or transhipment – EXW, FRC, FOB, CIF, etc.

(e) Terms of payment including provision for currency rate variation.

(f) Terms of delivery, ex stock, forward etc., relevant estimate.

(g) Transportation mode(s), e.g. container, air freight, sea freight, road haulier.

(h) Insurance.

(i) Packaging and packing together with marking of the goods.

(j) Offer by pro-forma invoice.

(k) Identity of goods, country of origin and shipment.

(l) Specific documentation needs such as export licence, certificate of origin, preshipment certificate, etc.

(m) Tender bond to be followed by performance bond.

Prior to receipt of the indent/order a customer may need a pro forma invoice which is essential before a customer can open a bank credit in the supplier's favour. On receipt of the indent or order from the overseas client, the export marketing manager will check the specification and price in the order with the quotation together with its period of validity. Care must be taken to ensure the client is not trying to take advantage of an out-of-date quotation. For example where the quotation was FOB, the export marketing manager must note whether the customer wishes the supplier to arrange for freight and insurance on his behalf. The method of payment will be noted and checked with quotation terms. For example, where payment is to be made under a documentary credit, the documents the banks require must be carefully noted. The required delivery date will be particularly noted; if the delivery date is given and the client has been obliged to obtain an import licence for the particular consignment, the date of expiry must be noted.

Given below is a receipt of order check list:

(a) *Goods*
  (i) quality;
  (ii) quantity;
  (iii) description.

(b) *Payment*
  (i) price;
  (ii) method, i.e. letter of credit, open account, or documents against payment or acceptance;
  (iii) time scale;
  (iv) currency variation provision.

(c) *Shipment*
  (i) mode of transport/route/transhipment and whether buyer requests any specific carrier;
  (ii) any constraints, i.e. packing/weighing/dimensions/statutory and route restrictions;
  (iii) time scale enforcing despatch and arrival date;
  (iv) any marks, i.e. special marking on cases/cartons to identify them.

(d) *Additional requirements*
  (i) insurance;

(ii) preshipment inspection;
(iii) documentation such as certificate of origin;
(iv) specific packing – see item (c-ii);
(v) commissions or discount;
(vi) details of agent handling buyer's order and likely specific request.

(e) *Comparison with quotation*

A pro forma invoice is a document similar to a sales invoice except that it is headed 'pro forma'. It is not a record of sales effected, but a representation of a sales invoice issued prior to the sale. The pro forma invoice contains all relevant details, e.g. full description of goods, packing specification, price of goods with period of validity, cost of cases, and where relevant cost of freight and insurance. It is particularly used for quotations to customers and for submission to various authorities. Terms of payment are also always shown but it may not be possible to give shipping marks until a firm order is received. When used as quotation the pro forma invoice constitutes a binding offer of the goods covered by it, the price and condition shown.

As soon as the exporter receives the letter of credit, he should check it against his pro forma invoice to ensure both documents agree with each other. Usually, the contract will be in a more detailed form than the letter of credit, but it is important the exporter should be able to prepare his documents complying with both the contract and the credit. For general guidance the following check list should be adopted by the exporter.

1. The terms of the letter of credit which may be revocable or irrevocable.

2. The name and address of the exporter (beneficiary).

3. The amount of the credit which may be in sterling or a foreign currency.

4. The name and address of the importer (accreditor).

5. The name of the party on whom the bills of exchange are to be drawn, and whether they are to be at sight or of a particular tenor.

6. The terms of the contract and shipment (i.e. whether EXW, FRC, FOB, CIF, and so on).

7. A brief description of the goods covered by the credit.

Basically too much detail may give rise to errors which can cause delay.

8. Precise instructions as to the documents against which payment is to be made.

9. Details of shipment including whether any transhipment are allowed, data on the latest shipment date and details of port of departure and destination should be recorded. Advantage is gained to permit shipment 'from any UK port' thereby permitting the shipper a choice in the event of strike action. Similar remarks apply to the port of discharge.

10. Whether the credit is available for one or more shipments.

11. The expiry date.

It is important to check the reverse side of the letter of credit and any attachments thereto, the credit as further terms, and any conditions which form an integral part of the credit. Ideally both the seller (exporter) and the buyer (importer) should endeavour to make the credit terms as simple as practicable.

In situations where the seller (exporter) is uncertain of just how much of the credit he will draw, arrangements should be made with the buyer (importer) to have the value of the documentary letter of credit prefixed by the word 'about'. This will permit up to 10% margin over or under the amount specified. The word 'about' preceding the quantity of goods also allows a 10% margin in the quantity to be shipped. Alternatively the documentary letter of credit may specify a 'tolerance' – such as 7½% to 5% more or less – by which the seller (exporter) should be guided.

Documentation will usually involve the clean on-board bill of lading. For international rail movements it is the CIM consignment note, and for international road haulage transit the CMR consignment note. Particular attention should be given to pre-booking cargo space on the required sailing, and for container traffic booking a container suitable for the goods.

17.4 PROGRESS OF EXPORT ORDER AND CHECK LIST

In processing the export consignment one must bear in mind there are up to four contracts to execute. These include the export sales contract; the contract of carriage; the financial contract and finally the contract of cargo insurance. All these have to be reconciled with the processing of the export consignment.

To ensure the complex procedure of preparing the goods, packing, forwarding, shipping, insurance, customs clearance, invoice and collecting payment do not go wrong, it is suggested a check list or progress sheet be prepared for each export order. A suggested version is given below but it must be borne in mind there are many variations in processing a given export order:

Table 17.1   Processing export order

Order Cleared for Credit Worthiness: Terms of Payment	Sig- nature	Order Cleared for Distribution	Sig- nature	Order Cleared for Documentation Purposes	Sig- nature

(i) Customer's name and address
(ii) Customer's order number and date
(iii) Date of receipt and export department's serial number
(iv) Brief technical details of the order
(v) Import licence number and date of expiry – when applicable
(vi) Export licence number – when applicable
   (a) Date of application
   (b) Date received
   (c) Date of expiry
(vii) Method of packing
(viii) Shipping or airline – if prescribed
(ix) Type of insurance
(x) Terms of payment
(xi) Details of letter of credit, including full list of documents required
(xii) If FOB, who arranges and pays for freight/insurance
(xiii) Date order acknowledged
(xiv) Promised delivery date
(xv) Date order put in hand
(xvi) Pro forma invoices sent (often required by customer to open credit)
(xvii) Production department – completion date
(xviii) Goods inspected or tested
(xix) Packing ordered
(xx) Merchandise ready
(xxi) Shipping instructions ECSI complete
(xxii) Consular invoices completed
(xxiii) Certificate of origin or equivalent completed
(xxiv) Application for shipment/air freight space booking despatched/ accepted

Table 17.1   continued

Order Cleared for Credit Worthiness: Terms of Payment	Sig- nature	Order Cleared for Distribution	Sig- nature	Order Cleared for Documentation Purposes	Sig- nature

(xxv) Preshipment certificate process

(xxvi) Shipping marks

(xxvii) Shipment etc. instructions received/goods called forward/closing date/despatch dept instructed

(xxviii) Bills of lading/CMR/CIM/air waybill prepared and SAD

(xxix) Insured value declared – giving number of certificates required freight paid

(xxx) Bills of lading/CMR/CIM/air waybill and SAD received – document's serial number and date of shipment/despatch

(xxxi) Insurance certificates received – serial number

(xxxii) Draft and document lodged with bank

(xxxiii) Accounts' copy of invoice passed through books

(xxxiv) Payment received

In regard to items sent by parcels post or air freight, the credit and despatch arrangements may vary slightly in so far as the foregoing is concerned.

17.5   FUNCTION/PROCEDURES OF EXPORT DOCUMENTATION

We will now consider the processing of export documentation and the various procedures involved. Details of the salient points follow:

dated 10 March
(extracts from
original order)

Order received for delivery end April

All wool tissues
(Description of goods – wool and worsted piece goods)

Order No. B2
Market Lebanon
Port Beirut

Packing (type: 6 cases wood waterproof
paper-lined cases)

Marking LAS
Beirut 6

(a) Time scale of deliveries

15 March	Pro forma
1 April	Payment terms (L/C, etc.) received
2 April	Payment terms checked
5 April	Works stores promise
7 April	Shipping instructions ECSI
16 April	Preshipment certificate processed
18/22 April	Receiving/closing date of shipment
23 April	Insurance dealt with
25 April	Sailing date
28 April	Letter of credit – shipping date
4 May	Bill of lading required by this date
7 May	Completion of documentation to bank
12 May	Proceeds received
15 May	Letter of credit – expiry date

It must be recognized the number of documents given on p. 424 and their type vary by individual consignment, mode of transport, commodity, contracts of sale, importing country, customs within that country, statutory obligations, financial arrangements, etc. We will now examine briefly the salient documents involved:

(a) *Consular invoice.* A consular invoice may have to be prepared where the goods are consigned to countries which enforce *ad valorem* import duties. Such invoices have to be certified by the consul of the country to which the goods are consigned either at the place from which the goods are despatched, which is usual, or at the port/airport/ICD of departure. The forms upon which the details have to be inscribed are issued at the consular offices and a fee is payable on certification. The consul usually retains one copy, returns a copy to the shipper, and forwards further copies to the customs authorities in his own country.

(b) *Export invoice.* The exporter completes an export invoice

Table 17.2

Documents Required	Bank	Customer	Agent	Customs Clearance	Consulate	Total
Commercial invoices	–	3	–	–	–	3
Certified invoices	3	1	2	1	3	10
Certificate of origin	–	–	–	–	–	
Bill of lading	2/2	2	–	–	–	2/4
Preshipment certificate	–	–	–	–	–	
Insurance policy	–	–	–	–	–	
Insurance certificate	–	–	–	–	–	
Weight & contract note	1	1	–	–	1	3
Bank draft statement	1	–	–	–	–	1
Single administration document	1	1	1	1	–	4
ATA carnet	–	–	–	–	–	–
Dangerous goods note	–	–	–	–	–	–
Packing list	1	1	1	1	–	4
Preshipment certificate	1	1	1	1	–	4

The distribution of the documents will vary by transit and the carrier's needs, such as the copy of the Single Administrative Document for the carrier, which forms the movement certificate, must be met.

which embodies the date, name of the consignee, quantity and description of the goods, marks and measurements of packages, cost of the goods, packing, carriage, freight, postage, insurance premiums, etc. The actual form of invoice varies with the method of price quotation.

(c) *The invoice.* The invoice is a document rendered by one person to another in regard of goods which have been sold. Basically, it is a detailed list identifying the goods sold, specifying their nature, quantity, quality and price and other expenses incurred in delivering the goods. Its primary function is a check for the purchaser against charges and delivery. In the case of insurance claims and for packing purposes, it is useful evidence to verify the value and nature of the goods and in certain circumstances it is evidence as the contract between the parties, e.g. packing not up to specification may give underwriters redress against the seller. The invoice is not necessarily a contract of sale. It may form a contract of sale if it is in writing containing all the material terms. On the other hand it may not be a complete memorandum of the contract of sale and therefore evidence may be given to vary the contract which is inferred therefrom.

(d) *Certificate of origin.* Certificates of origin specify the nature of quantity/value of the goods, etc. together with their place of manufacture. Such a document is required by some countries, often to simplify their customs duties. Additionally they are needed when merchandise is imported to a country that allows preferential duties on British goods, owing to trade agreements. In order that goods from the UK may enjoy the lower schedules of duties, the customs authorities of the importing country must be satisfied as to the value of the goods, and they substantially represent British labour and British material.

Details of the four types of certificate of origin or their equivalent are given below:

(i) Those issued by a Chamber of Commerce or other official body: only required when specifically called for by the credit.

(ii) Commonwealth preference certificates of origin and/or EEC documentary evidence for Commonwealth EEC associates: usually contained on the back of a special invoice form or obtainable from outside approved bodies.

(iii) Exporter's own certificate of origin: may be used for any case where no special form is required by the creditor.

(iv) Single administrative document for EEC and Scandinavian countries.

(e) *Contract of affreightment.* This is found in the bill of lading/ CIM/CMR documentation.

(f) *Marine insurance policy/certificate.* This acknowledges the cargo value as declared has been insured for the maritime transit. The terms/conditions of such insurance are found in the Marine Insurance Act 1906.

(g) *Charter party.* This involves hire/charter of a ship.

(h) *Letter of credit.* This is a document enabling the beneficiary to obtain payment of funds from the issuer, or from an agent if the insurer complies with certain conditions laid down in the credit.

This document may be a commercial credit. It may be issued to finance international trade involving shipments of goods between countries, or non-commercial or personal credits for the use of individuals, e.g. consular letters of credit issued to tourists and holiday makers. The commercial credit may be a bank credit, i.e. drawn on an issuing bank which undertakes due payment, or non-bank credit, which although issued through a bank does not carry any bank undertaking. The letter of credit may be revocable or irrevocable.

(i) *Mates receipt.* Sometimes issued in lieu of a bill of lading. It has no legal authority but merely confirms cargo placed on board a ship pending issue of bill of lading.

(j) *Dock receipt.* Sometimes issued by port authority to confirm receipt of cargo on the quay/warehouse pending shipment.

(k) *Letters of hypothecation.* Banker's documents outlining conditions under which the international transaction will be executed on the exporter's behalf, who will have given certain pledges to his banker. It may be by direct loan, acceptance or negotiation of draft thereto.

(l) *Packing list.* A document providing a list of the contents of a package/consignment(s). In particular it will include the number and kind of packages, their contents, overall net and gross weight usually in kilograms, the dimension(s) of the package(s) including length, width and height and finally the cube of the package(s).

(m) *ATA Carnet.* An international customs document to cover the temporary export of certain goods (commercial samples and exhibits for international trade fairs abroad and professional equipment) to countries which are parties to the ATA Convention and cover reimport of such goods.

(n) *Pre-shipment inspection certificates.* An increasing number of shippers and various organizations/authorities/governments in countries throughout the world are now insisting the goods are inspected. This embraces their quality, quantity being exported and the price(s) proposed and market price(s), and the exchange rates comparison at the time of shipment. The organizations which undertake such work – which can extend to transhipment en route – are the Societe Generale de Surveillance (SGS) and classification societies (e.g. BV, see pp. 176–7).

The SGS representative will examine the goods at the place of manufacture or assembly prior to despatch. This is to ensure they comply with the description found in the export sales contract/bill of lading/export invoice. Subsequently the goods will be examined/ checked as they are loaded into the container or loaded onto the ship. In situations where a seller is at variance with SGS opinion, he may present his position to the SGS Principals, either directly or through his importer.

If everything is in order a clean report of findings (CRF) will be issued by SGS to their Principals. This is required together with other commercial documents such as bill of lading, letter of credit, invoice in order to obtain payment via the commercial bank and/or customs clearance import. If a non-negotiable report of findings (NNRF) is issued by SGS, the seller (exporter) may opt to discuss the matter with the Principal involved who remains the final arbiter. Such a situation arises where goods are shipped before SGS inspection has taken place. In due course SGS will issue the pre-shipment inspection certificate to confirm the goods have been supplied in accordance with the contract.

The SGS do not have the right to approve or prevent shipment of the goods. The opinion expressed by SGS is given after all the factors are provided to SGS by the seller. It is made in good faith but without any liability to the seller for any loss, damage, or expense arising from the issuance of report of findings. Currently some 60 countries require that both letters of credit and contract relevant to the import of goods contain a condition that a clean report of findings covering quality, quantity, price and exchange rates must be presented along with other documents required to negotiate payment. The system has been introduced for the following reasons.

(a) To minimize the loss of foreign exchange through over invoicing, concealed commission payments and illegal money transfers.

(b) To minimize losses of revenue and duty payments through under invoicing.

(c) To reduce evasion of import controls and help combat smuggling.

(d) To help control landed prices and therefore control local inflation.

(e) To avoid dumping of cargo through the incidence of shipping merchandise of sub-standard goods.

(f) To avoid the incidence of loss through shipment of underweight cargo or short shipments.

The reader wishing to know more about the processing of export documentation and the role of the individual documents, is recommended to read Chapters 12 and 13 of *The Elements of Export Practice.*

Elements of Export Marketing and Management deals with the professional techniques of export marketing from a practical viewpoint, including the development and expansion of the exporter's overseas markets and the 1992 Single European Entity's effects on marketing strategy.

17.6 DATA INTERCHANGE FOR SHIPPING (DISH) AND ELECTRONIC DATA INTERCHANGE (EDI)

During the past two decades a number of shipowners have developed computer systems as an integral part of their through transport operations to allow maximum control over complex cargo movement patterns whilst speeding up production of shipping documents. These include P & O Containers and Maersk Line. The area of the computer technology is called Electronic Data Interchange (EDI). It is concerned with the linking of computers to allow the electronic exchange of data and documentation. Such a facility speeds up communications; improves overall efficiency; reduces administration cost; eliminates double handling of information and the consequent risk of documentation error. It is especially ideal for the manufacture involved in the 'just in time system' of production and requiring accuracy, reliability, speed, care and total control of the cargo consignment.

A major problem inhibiting the extensive development of the EDI system linking the shipowner with the customer/shipper has been the wide range and variety of computers and systems in use worldwide today, and the complexity of interfacing with each of them on an individual basis. This has been largely overcome through the introduction in 1986 of Data Interchange for Shipping (DISH) which provides a standard means of electronic communication harmonizing different computers. It allows the shipping data and documents to be interchanged between the computers of companies and organization involved in international trade. Its long-term aim is to develop a data interchange system that would allow exporters and importers to exchange shipping information with Shipping Lines, trailer and Ro/Ro operators, airlines and freight forwarders dealing with both European trade, and trade between Europe and the rest of the world.

The DISH system permits information to be interchanged between the carrier and the shipper in the following five areas:

(a) *Bookings.* The bookings message is not intended to cater for initial bookings, i.e. reservation of cargo space with the carrier, but a confirmation/statement of a container, haulage, and service required by the exporter of the carrier.

(b) *Shipping instructions (ECSI/Shipping details).* The shipping instruction message represents the main transfer of information from the exporter to the carriers. It reflects all the information supplied on its paper equivalent. The message is also used by the carrier to prepare bills of lading and invoices and at this point the exporter warrants the information to be accurate.

(c) *Maritime Transport Contract (Bill of Lading/Waybill information).* The maritime transport message is sent by the carrier to the exporter and contains all the information relevant to the bill of lading or waybill. The basis of this message is that the exporter has the opportunity to check the details against the letter of credit requirement prior to receipt of actual bill of lading.

(d) *Accounting for freight (statement of charges/invoice details).* Accounting for freight messages reflect the detail charges incurred in the transaction. The exporter has the important benefit of early advice of actual charges incurred, often needed before his own paperwork can be finalized.

(e) *Sailing schedule changes.* The notification of the sailing

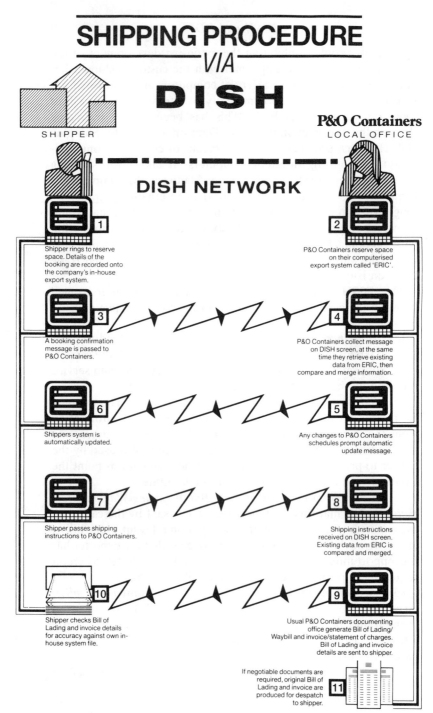

Fig. 17.1 The DISH system. (Reproduced by kind permission of P&O Containers).

schedule changes from the carrier or the exporter is confined to vessels port arrival/departure for the consignments in question. All the foregoing messages can be exchanged between each of the parties involved, i.e. exporter and carrier, exporter and forwarder, or forwarder and carrier.

The system operates on the basis that the exporter inputs banking information into his own in-house computer system. These data are transmitted onward via an interbridge facility – developed by SITPRO – which ensures all codes are correctly formatted prior to on-passing the information to the ICL Tradanet VAN (value added network). Once the message is received in correct format in the VAN, it is 'posted' through the Tradanet network to await retrieval in the shipowner's 'mail box'. The shipowner retrieves the information via another Interbridge facility which converts details into a code and format suitable for use in the shipowner's main frame computer. Outward messages from the shipowner to the exporter are handled in the same manner.

The benefits of the DISH system are given below:

(a) It reduces paperwork thereby yielding cost savings in administration through less handling of documents.

(b) It reduces overheads through elimination of all double handling of information or relaying of information into systems.

(c) Much improved accuracy is produced. The once only data entry process eliminates the need for repeated checking of information, reducing error tracing and correction procedures.

(d) Quicker receipt of information. This can result in savings in terms of lower stock levels in industry, quicker clearance by customs and the speedier production of statistics by Government.

(e) Speedier invoice/payment cycle plus presenting opportunities to the seller to reduce borrowings and interest payment on loans made to finance the movement of the goods.

(f) Greater control of transportation through speedier communications with a reduction in possible delays and consequent economies.

(g) A common type of data transfer based on internationally recognized standards.

(h) A more efficient service with faster up-dating and on-passing of shipping information.

(i)   More stable relationships between organizations leading to mutually more favourable terms of trading.

Attention is also being given to monitoring import cargo from the port of order to the final delivery in the warehouse. To facilitate the development of the DISH system a new association has been formed called the International Trade and Transport EDI Association. Its membership includes Customs, banks, insurance, shipping, freight forwarders, and so on. The DISH system was based on the European TDI syntax, but the new syntax to ensure compatibility on a worldwide scale is called Electronic Data Interchange for Administration, Commerce and Transport EDIFACT. It incorporates the requirements of America, Europe and the Eastern Bloc. New messages have been compiled using EDIFACT which include booking provisional, booking firm, transport order, contract status, charges invoice, charges (statement of charges) and response message.

The EDI system is used by the Maersk line which offers sophisticated documentation and container control systems from the point of origin to the cargo destination place. It has a worldwide network linking more than 100 Maersk line offices via satellite to track all cargo and container movements 24 hours per day around the world. It has established direct computer links to the public telex network, port and customs authorities, Maersk terminals and vessels. To the shipper requiring the direct computer interface to the Maersk worldwide information network the Maersk line provides the advanced global information concept which provides on-line connection of the cargo shipment details. It has a high degree of user friendliness. Such an on-line computer facility permits its shipper to obtain data on container specification, cut-off and pick-up times at Maersk terminals worldwide, and details of vessels and their schedules. Hence with an IBM or IBM compatible personal computer and basic dial-up equipment the shipper can gain access to the Maersk EDI system.

There is no doubt that EDI will play an increasingly important role in international trade and will include an increasing number of exporters, importers, carriers, forwarders and other companies in the shipping industry on a worldwide scale. It will incorporate links with banks, Customs and other organizations and networks. Moreover, it will develop electronic communication links covering many aspects of international trade including port community groups, Customs and Port regulations, pre-advice messages for import and air cargoes, payment instructions and confirmation through banks, damage and insurance assessment reports.

Major changes in shipping procedure and business practices are likely to result because of EDI. Alternatives to the traditional signed documentation such as bills of lading are being developed. Where non-negotiable waybills can be employed, paperless trading is already a reality. More and more manufacturers, wholesalers, and retail chain stores are adopting EDI and Community Network services and the shipping industry must play its part in the export contract order to the point of sale transaction electronic information chain.

CHAPTER 18

Ship management

Our study of shipping would not be complete without a brief review of the more salient aspects of ship management. Broadly ship management techniques fall into five divisions – commercial, operating, technical, financial and investment disciplines.

18.1 COMMERCIAL ASPECTS OF SHIP MANAGEMENT

The shipowner's commercial policy should be to maximize gross revenue to the service within any constraints imposed on him. The latter includes liner conference or other forms of agreements and governmental legislation. Other aspects include competition, and the cost to the shipowner of the service he provides. The latter is an important point in as much that overall the services should be profitable, and uneconomic ones discarded unless there are compelling reasons for their operation. This may be, for example, to keep out a competitor or operate a feeder service into a trunk route. The latter could arise through a major container shipping service being served by a number of feeder services. An example is Rotterdam being used as the major port of call for north west Europe including UK container service with a feeder service operating between Felixstowe and Rotterdam.

The tariffs should be so arranged as to maximize traffic flow throughout the year. For passenger traffic including foot passengers, coaches, motorist and accompanied cars, the two main tariffs would be one for the peak period and a lower one for outside the peak. For cruise passengers the rate would be a daily tariff varying by type of accommodation provided. Additionally a range of miscellaneous fares is likely to exist including 36/48-hour excursions on less popular sailings; limited availability tickets, e.g. 5 to 10 days; special fares for particular events such as trade fairs and inclusive tours and special reduced fares for group travel. The foregoing range of fares is particularly suitable for estuarial and short sea trade services, e.g. UK/Continental. An important aspect in such policies is to ensure the full-fare paying traffic is preserved and it is not eroded by the cheaper tariff traffic.

Much additional income can be obtained from the retail outlets on the ship such as restaurant, bar, shop, and revenue from cabin reservations. Special attention should be given to such facilities to ensure maximum income is obtained by retailing the products most favoured by the passenger. Market research techniques should be used. Additionally income can be sought from shipboard entertainment.

On the freight side the tariffs should be based on cost plus an element of profit. The latter may not always be possible due to the market situation. This could be particularly relevant to fixture rates found in chartering. Under liner conference rates the tariffs are agreed amongst members and regularly reviewed in the light of service cost and other factors.

Finally the shipowner, particularly the one who is engaged in liner-type services should prepare a marketing plan annually. It should embrace the following items:

(i) The nature of the service during the next 12 months giving details of ship disposition, sailing schedules, ports of call, etc.

(ii) The market the shipping route will serve and the nature of the traffic.

(iii) The tariffs and particularly any special concessions to attract new business and develop existing flows through possible more favourable rebate/discounts.

(iv) Any new features on the service particularly new tonnage, additional ports of call, improved transit, better customs clearance arrangements, simpler documentation, more attractive tariffs.

(v) Budgeted forecast of carryings on the route in the next 12 months by tonnage segregated into various commodity classifications and country of origin.

(vi) Any significant developments on the route foreseen in the next 12 months and how the service will benefit. For example a new industrial complex may be opening up in a country which could generate much additional business to the route.

(vii) Details of any promotional campaigns to sustain existing business and also obtain additional traffic. This may be through more advertising in shipping/trade journals, larger sales force, improved customer/shipper liaison, closer liaison with shippers councils trade associations, additional sales conferences, improved sales training, appointment of new agents, better literature, provision of a shipper's/exporter's advisory service, etc.

(viii) Technique to be used to measure route performance particularly carryings at regular intervals throughout the 12 months. This may involve regular monthly meetings with sales personnel to discuss results attained and sales strategy, particularly any new promotions.

(ix) Details of the sales targets for each sales sector. Regular reports should be produced to monitor results against the marketing plan forecasts and strategy.

(x) The plan should stress the competitive advantages the route has over other services, and the salient points the sales force should stress.

(xi) The plan should be flexible in its approach to take account of any changed situation which may emerge in the next 12 months.

(xii) The marketing plan must be devised to produce a profitable service and the strategy on tariffs: selling must be towards this sole objective. Its aim must be to increase the market share on a profitable basis particularly of those commodities which are viable or capable of becoming viable.

Overall its aim must be to provide adequate traffic to produce a profitable service. This should reflect the objectives for the forthcoming year both in terms of actual forecast carryings and the manner in which the traffic is to be secured.

18.2 OPERATING ASPECTS OF SHIP MANAGEMENT

The objective of ship management operation is to optimize the use of resources compatible with the commercial requirement, liner conference, or other agreements. Details are given below of some of the techniques employed.

(a) Crew manning levels to be at a minimum compatible with safety, statutory and market needs. This also applies to the number of crews of both officers and seamen per ship. For example, a passenger vessel may require more crew in the summer than in the winter to meet traffic needs and passenger certificate obligations, the latter being lower in winter. Additionally only one restaurant may be needed in winter compared with two in summer, thereby reducing crew levels on a passenger vessel.

(b) Critical continuous review of passage times to ensure schedules most economically timed, bearing in mind competition, market needs, fuel cost, crew expenses, port charges, etc. Again the situation can vary summer and winter.

(c) Fleet size to be at a minimum compatible with market requirement and long-term development. Additional traffic flows could be conveyed on chartered tonnage.

(d) Fleet composition should be as flexible as economically practicable thereby to cushion the effect of any sharp unpredictable variation in traffic flow. An example of flexibility of operation is the OBO tonnage and the multi-purpose Ro/Ro vessel, the latter found in the short sea trade. The Ro/Ro ship with a vehicle deck of varying capacity can meet a changing need on an individual sailing basis. Such decks, hydraulically operated, can convey some 300 cars, or 25 road haulage vehicles – the latter requiring high deck space. Another example is the SD-14s found in tramping or the Combi carrier (see p. 64).

(e) Vessels for which there is no work such as during winter or during periods of traffic recession should be placed on the chartering market or perhaps prepared for survey.

(f) Continuous study should be made of individual sailing carryings net revenue result, punctuality, outshipments, etc. to evaluate whether any change is necessary. For example, the type of vessel may be too small and a ship conversion to one having a larger capacity could be provided by stretching the hull or widening the beam.

(g) A continuous review should be made of all retail outlets on passenger ships to ensure they are profitable and/or fulfilling a market need.

(h) The merits of 'flagging out' should be examined in high crew cost maritime fleets. It would result in the shipping service becoming more competitive and produce beneficial crewing pattern changes.

(i) A continuous review of bunkering ports should be undertaken to ensure the most favourable bunker prices are obtained.

18.3   TECHNICAL ASPECTS OF SHIP MANAGEMENT

The maintenance and provision of ships forms a significant cost in the shipowner's annual budget. The aim is to provide a fleet which is compatible and economical to the market requirement at the lowest possible cost having regard to safety, statutory obligations and service standards. In consequence one must continuously keep under review the ship costs and the following points are relevant:

(a) Surveys to be conducted outside peak traffic period and to be of minimum duration compatible with market and economic circumstances.

(b) As much work as practicable prior to survey to be done during the time the vessel is in traffic use compatible with cost and other factors.

(c) Management techniques, e.g. work study, programmed maintenance replacement over specified period, critical path analysis, etc. to be used to keep survey cost to a minimum with clear specification to shipyards of what is required under fixed price terms. Computerization can help devise the survey specific requirements.

(d) A very few shipowners are opting out of maintaining vessels to voluntary Classification Ship Society standards, but merely maintaining the vessel to the statutory obligations defined in the regulations relative to the country in which she is registered.

(e) Vessels which have a passenger certificate valid 6 months may thereby reduce the annual survey/maintenance cost. This is particularly valid for estuarial services where such a policy is becoming more common as the winter service is either severely curtailed or discontinued.

(f) Vessels should be designed to keep maintenance expenditure to a minimum and likewise crew cost, with modern navigational aids and shipboard labour-saving devices. This is an important area of ship management in the context of new tonnage development and the need to ensure experience gained from existing vessels is translated into new ship design. This is in the interest of general ship efficiency, i.e. maintenance, crew manning levels, ship versatility of employment, general market trends/ needs.

(g) A number of options exist in regard to ship surveys and these should be carefully and continuously reviewed. It includes voyage survey, continuous survey, BIS notation involving 'built for in water survey', and planned maintenance system. The latter is becoming the most popular through the harmonized ship survey programme. Surveys include sighting survey; special periodical survey – hull and equipment; continuous survey – machinery; bottom survey; tailshaft survey; auxiliary boiler survey; EO class – 4-yearly survey; EO annual survey; loadline annual inspection; annual general survey; and safety radio certificate (see pp. 26–7).

(h) The development of shipboard management techniques should be explored (see *Economics of Shipping Practice and Management,* Chapter 14).

(i) Competitive tendering should be adopted regarding ship surveys and areas of particular attention to award the successful tender to the shipyard include timescale of work contracted; quality of work; industrial relations record; steaming time to and from the shipyard; payment schedule and any prolonged credit payment system; relations with the yard; currency used and the shipyard experience in handling the type of vessel involved.

18.4 FINANCIAL ASPECTS OF SHIP MANAGEMENT

Successful ship management depends on many factors, but an important one is adequate financial control to ensure the optimum use of the shipping company's resources. To achieve this there must be disciplined budgetary control embracing the revenue and expenditure budget on a service, ship, profit centre, divisional or other convenient basis.

This must be formulated with the consent of those responsible for revenue production, marketing and service managers, and embracing passengers, freight, accompanied cars, catering income, chartering income, miscellaneous receipts. In the case of expenditure it will include ship maintenance, port dues, crew cost, fuel, port agents charges, agents-passenger/freight commission, ship insurance, etc. The budget must be reviewed continuously to reflect variations in expenditure and revenue. This can be done at 3-monthly intervals with the actual results against budget being monitored monthly. A similar budget should be produced for capital investment programme and cash forecasts.

More recently Masters have been encouraged to become involved in budgetary control. It takes the form of the Master and his chief officers being responsible for an expenditure and revenue budget. Overall it is formulated on an annual basis and takes account of cargo to be conveyed, ship operating cost including fuel, crew, maintenance, port charges, etc. This type of budgetary control is likely to become more common and is dealt with more fully in my book *Economics of Shipping Practice and Management,* Chapter 14.

The object of budgetary control is to ensure maximum profitability of service/ships and it forms a very important part of ship management today (see also *Economics of Shipping Practice and Management,* Chapter 13). Usually with large shipping companies it is the practice to produce 1- and 5-year budget plans. Under the latter, sometimes called a business plan, it gives an indication of the future prospects of the company in financial terms and points to any defects in commercial/operating/investment policy. The business plan will embrace the following points:

(i) The shipping company investment plans in the next 5 years.

(ii) Traffic forecast in the next 5 years by route and the predicted financial results by service annually.

(iii) A brief commentary on each service results in the next 5 years and significant features which are likely to arise such as new ships, more competition, new pooling agreement under liner conference terms; expansion of flag discrimination, market developments, etc.

(iv) International events which could prejudice the company's 5-year developments. This may embrace more development of third world countries' fleets, more infiltration by Eastern bloc countries into cross trades, expansion of national fleets enjoying operating subsidies or some other form of state aid. Overall, such developments could reduce a shipping company's share of the market, reduce fleet complement or withdraw services.

(v) Statutory developments which may result in more training of sea-going personnel; provision of improved fire prevention equipment; more severe survey requirements for older vessels.

(vi) Future plans of the company particularly within the context of new services, rationalization of ports of call, reorganization of the company structure with more decentralization, etc.

(vii) Investment needs in the next 5 years and how it is to be financed. This may involve using existing company financial resources, obtaining government aid, selling older ships, realization of redundant estate assets, i.e. sale of a disused office block, using loan capital etc.

(viii) Assessment of how the major competitors will develop in the next 5 years, and how the shipping company will combat the situation. This extends to new competition. For example, one may rationalize the service to improve transit times and become more profitable involving fewer ships and ports of call. At the same time, more modern ships may be introduced to raise ship capacity productivity and service quality.

(ix) Political events must be assessed. This may embrace development of more free trade areas and expansion of existing ones.

(x) International trade forecast in the next 5 years and how the shipping company will feature in such developments. For example, liner trades on some routes may expand, whilst movement of crude oil may be stabilized. This will call for more investment in liner cargo tonnage which may be a multi-purpose type of ship capable of conveying both containers, as well as vehicular traffic, i.e. road haulage vehicles/trailers, trade cars, etc.

(xi) Any possible takeover of another shipping company or ancillary activity, i.e. shipbroking, freight forwarding, ports, etc.

Basically the business plan should point the way the shipping company is going in the next 5 years. It should greatly facilitate the company developing on a strong financial base with senior management well aware of its intentions and working towards its objective. The plan should be reviewed from time to time, updated and kept abreast of changed circumstances and other developments.

18.5 INVESTMENT ASPECTS OF SHIP MANAGEMENT

Ship investment today is an important function of ship management. One must bear in mind that international trade is a speculative business and subject to various fluctuations in the light of political events. For example the closure of the Suez Canal, the Korean War, the development of the Eastern bloc mercantile fleet, the expansion of flag discrimination practices, all have a profound effect on trade, and the shipowner must employ his fleet in the best way possible. Moreover, a vessel may take 3 to 4 years from the time the proposal to build is originated within the shipping company to the time she is launched. Moreover, she will have an economical operational life of between 12 and 15 years dependent on her type and use. Furthermore shipping has never been a very attractive investor's proposition and has usually only produced a modest capital investment return.

It is against the foregoing background that one must examine such capital investment which may involve new tonnage, converting existing tonnage, or buying second-hand tonnage. The following factors must be borne in mind as criteria for investment decision making:

(a) The actual market prospects of the trade or route both short term and long term. This may involve market research being undertaken; liaison with trade associations, engaging a consultant to formulate an assessment, or consultation with the Shippers' Council and Liner Conference.

(b) An analysis of the existing tonnage. This will embrace the ship's age; general suitability to the trade in which she is currently engaged; the running cost to include both voyage cost and survey/maintenance expenses; crew cost and method of manning; the resale value of the vessel; and the residual life of the vessel as an economic unit employed elsewhere in the fleet. All these items require to be costed.

(c) Account must be taken of existing competition and likely future developments. This will embrace subversive competition as found in flag discrimination practices, and the Eastern bloc countries' mercantile fleet infiltration into established liner trades taking a proportion of the cross-trade cargo flow.

(d) Any political factors relevant to ship investment facilitation. This may include government loans at favourable interest rates, or a subsidy to the shipyard. Additionally, cheap capital may be available from overseas banks/governments to sustain shipyard employment and encourage shipowners to scrap old tonnage and build new vessels. It may be a policy within a liner conference or large shipping company to have a rolling programme of continuous ship investment to spread the investment on a consistent annual basis. The alternative is to invest maybe for a 3-year period and then virtually have no investment for the following 5 years. This is not usually good financial investment management.

(e) Capital availability is a critical factor as many shipowners have difficulty in raising capital without resorting to available credit or subsidy facilities. It is due primarily to two factors: the low investment return on existing tonnage and the high rate of inflation experienced in ship construction in as much as a vessel built in 1960 may cost £2 million whilst thirty years later the figure is £30 million. The tariffs and ship productivity have not kept pace with the rise in shipbuilding costs. The cost of the capital ultimately sought must be closely evaluated and the usual technique is to use the discount cash flow. This gives on an annual basis the amount of cash the new tonnage will generate which in the early years may be a loss and later a profit. It should be related to the situation if no investment was undertaken.

(f) The method of financing may be through loan capital from the banks or government sources; raising capital on the stock exchange through the issue of share capital; utilizing existing funds which may be a combination of liquid assets and short-term investment; or the sale of displaced ships or other company assets such as an office block. It is usually a mixture of the foregoing.

(g) The economics of the new tonnage involves the evaluation of the direct costs embracing fuel, crew, maintenance, port charges, and the indirect cost such as depreciation, loan cost, etc. Such expenditure must be related to the revenue production. It is usual for a combined analysis to be done, embracing the existing vessel and the new one proposed.

(h) Any financial assessment the new investment should yield in taxation benefits and any other fiscal benefits provided by the government.

(i) An assessment should be made on the return on the investment. This should embrace the existing ship investment, the new proposed investment, and an alternative investment proposal which may involve buying second-hand tonnage, chartering vessels, or converting existing tonnage. A comparison between all three schemes should be made. A return on new investment of between 10 and 15% should be sought.

(j) The commercial factors should be closely examined particularly within the context of maintaining the existing market share on the route and securing/attracting new profitable business to the trade. It is important such traffic be conveyed in a profitable manner on the new ship through, for example, improved handling techniques and may be a capital-intensive service compared with a labour-intensive one hitherto.

(k) An assessment must be made of the available shipyard capacity and timescale of the project.

(l) Finally the investment memorandum should conclude by not only outlining the financial merits of new tonnage investment, etc. but also the financial effect on the shipping company if no investment took place and/or one resorted to chartering, buying second-hand tonnage or converting existing tonnage.

One must bear in mind that ship investment is very much a risk activity and of a speculative nature thereby reflecting the uncertainty of international trade and unpredictability of future development throughout the life span of the ships of 12 to 15 years. The investment objective must be to maintain and develop existing market shares and develop new ones to sustain and exploit investment profitability (see also *Economics of Shipping Practice and Management*, Chapter 4).

An increasing number of shipowners today obtain the advice and support of a merchant bank in the development of their business financially especially in the area of ship investment. Their expertise is able to evaluate the most advantageous financial package and propose realistic financial options.

To conclude our examination of ship management, one must bear in mind that to be effective it requires a continuous critical review of Company policy to ensure that the best financial results are attained. Where defects are found vigorous remedial measures must be taken. Thus for the liner conference operator – and in 1989 there were over 700 liner conference agreements operative – this usually requires consent from his partners within the agreement.

CHAPTER 19

Political aspects

19.1 FLAG DISCRIMINATION

Our study of the elements of shipping would not be complete without a look at the main political aspects of of the subject: flag discrimination, flags of convenience and subsidies, all of which are on the increase, except those for the flags of convenience.

Flag discrimination comprises the wide variety of acts and pressures exerted by governments to direct cargoes to ships of their own flag, regardless of the commercial considerations which normally govern the routing of cargoes. It also applies to directing their port authorities to offer most favourable rates to the national flag vessels and bunker charges.

Powers against flag discrimination in its various forms are now incorporated in the Merchant Shipping Act 1974 – part III of which enables the UK Government to take counteraction against foreign governments, where UK shipping or trade interests are affected, or where they are required to meet Britain's international obligations. Orders can be made to obtain information, to regulate the carriage of goods, to levy charges on ships, to refuse admittance of ships to UK ports, and to approve or disapprove agreements. The Merchant Shipping Act 1988 provided the government with powers of retaliation against unfair trading practices from overseas competitors.

Basically, flag discrimination dislocates the competitive nature of the shipping industry, because it often diverts trade to the less efficient carrier and obscures the real cost of the service. The more important forms in which it can be exercised are as follows:

1. *Import licences.* A number of countries including Chile, Brazil, Gabon, Malaysia, Peru, Sudan and India have used the granting of import licences to ensure carriage of cargo in ships of their own national flag.

2. *Discriminatory customs and other dues.* Preferential rates of customs and other dues are used to influence cargoes into ships of the national flag. An example is that of Guatemala where a customs surcharge of 50% is imposed on imports from certain countries but is waived if the goods are shipped in Guatemalian vessels. Discriminatory charges in harbour, lighthouse pilotage and tonnage dues, consular fees and taxes on freight revenue are other means of favouring the national flag. These charges are imposed in one form or another by Peru, China, Brazil and the Argentine.

3. *Administrative pressures.* Although in many countries there may be no statutory provisions reserving cargoes to ships of the national flag, the same result is achieved by administrative pressures of one form or another. The emergence of independent governments in Asia and Africa has meant that such official cargo is automatically routed by their own flag vessels.

4. *Routing of gift and other non-commercial cargoes.* An instance of this is the 50/50 rule in the shipment of US goods under their various aid programmes where half the goods are carried in American bottoms, and commercial considerations are completely disregarded.

5. *Direct legislative control.* This is the most damaging form of flag discrimination. In 1988 countries such as Argentina, Brazil, Chile, Ecuador, Peru, Turkey, Uruguay, Venezuela and Egypt resorted to direct legislative control in varying degrees. Uruguay, for example, has legislation which imposes virtually penal dues on a wide range of goods entering their country, unless the cargoes are conveyed in Uruguayan vessels.

6. *Exchange control.* The manipulation of 'exchange control' offers endless means of making shipment in national vessels either obligatory, or so commercially attractive that it has the same effect. Brazil, Colombia, China and Ghana have resorted to this control in the interest of their national fleets.

7. *Bilateral trade treaties.* In all, over thirty countries have entered into bilateral trade treaties, which include shipping clauses reserving either the whole of the trade between the two countries, or as much of it as possible, to the ships of the two flags. Most of

the countries indulging in such a practice are in South or Central America.

Many South American and developing countries who build fleets for prestige purposes and to reduce the drain on foreign exchange practice flag discrimination. They are usually subsidized and it is done in several ways as follows:

(a) Up to 50% of all goods passing through their ports must be carried in their own ships.

(b) A small concession in customs charges to reduce transport costs when charging full conference rates.

(c) A customs surcharge on goods carried by foreign ships.

Additionally other countries practice flag discrimination as under:

(i) Reserve all chartered tonnage to the national flag.

(ii) All coastal services to the national flag.

(iii) Development of a freight allocation agency favouring national flag and fixing rates.

(iv) Unfavourable pilotage regulations and higher bunker charges for foreign tonnage.

Flag discrimination prejudices the tradition of the effective and cheap shipping services which can only be provided if all ships, irrespective of flag, can compete freely for cargoes throughout the world. It gives rise to unnecessary ballast voyages and to the uneconomic use of tonnage. The problem of flag discrimination can only be tackled on an international basis, and it is to be hoped that the appropriate international shipping organizations can devise rules to promote fair international competition in shipping.

Flag discrimination by its nature tends to increase world mercantile tonnage and overall does not facilitate the most economical use of ship capacity. In consequence the national line of a developing country may be assured of some 50% of the trade available, whilst a Western bloc shipowner operating alongside would not have the same preferential trade treatment. Such a practice is contributing to the present serious surplus of laid up dry cargo tonnage.

There is no doubt that flag discrimination is one of the most serious problems facing the industry today, but because it takes so many forms and is inspired by diverse motives, there is no simple remedy. Compromise and expediency will offer no long-term solution. What is required is determined and concerted action by governments throughout the world. A catalogue of countries practising flag discrimination is found in *Economics of Shipping Practice and Management*, pp. 319–32.

19.2 FLAGS OF CONVENIENCE

Shipping companies, like any other undertaking, are subject to income and profits tax of the state where they operate, and the level of tax is very important to the shipowner. This problem is, of course, common to all industry, but for the shipping industry it is aggravated by the enormous cost of replacement which continues to rise as building costs increase.

Flags of convenience emerged when American oil companies became worried by political instability in Europe in the years leading up the 1939–45 war. The Panamanian flag enabled American oil companies to supply Britain despite American neutrality in the early years of the war. It also let them use British seamen instead of Americans on ships under the Panamanian flag. Liberia did not emerge as a flag of convenience until 1950.

British shipowners in particular, and indeed owners in any maritime country subject to similar taxation, are at a serious disadvantage when competing with tax-free or virtually tax-free national merchant fleets, under flags of convenience or Open Registries – as it is now often termed. Two countries which featured prominently in this practice are Liberia and Panama as confirmed in Table 19.1 given opposite.

The following points are relevant from an analysis of Table 19.1:

(i) Flags of convenience is an expanding fleet rising from 30 to 35% from 1981 to 1986.

(ii) A significant growth is recorded of those registries operating under the British system but with local conditions as found in Hong Kong, Gibraltar and Bermuda. Local conditions include relaxation of crewing requirements and favourable tax regimes.

(iii) The Liberia tonnage volume has declined temporarily.

(iv) The ban in 1987 on Cypriot registered vessels by the Turkish government will affect adversely the Cyprus Register as exemplified in 1988 of the transfer of the Thenamaris fleet from Cyprus to Malta.

Table 19.1 Analysis of flags of convenience within world mercantile fleet

Flag	1981 million GRT	Percentage of World Fleet	Flag	1986 million GRT	Percentage of World Fleet
Liberia	73.73	18.3	Liberia	50.91	13.4
Panama	28.93	7.2	Panama	41.61	11.0
Singapore	7.32	1.8	Singapore	6.89	1.8
Hong Kong	2.85	2.85	Hong Kong	8.89	2.2
Cyprus	1.96	0.5	Cyprus	13.38	3.15
Bermuda	0.44	0.1	Bermuda	1.95	0.5
Bahamas	0.28	0.1	Bahamas	7.56	2.0
Malta	0.26	0.1	Malta	1.77	0.5
Gibraltar	0.02	0.0	Gibraltar	2.60	0.7
% of World Fleet		30.95			35.25

Source: GCBS

A significant development in the mid 1980s onwards was the tendency for some UK shipowners to 'flag out' their fleets into the independent territory category of the Isle of Man. The Registration follows the British system and in addition to the tax haven status of the island, seafarers can be employed without payment of employers UK National Insurance, and pension contributions that would be payable under the UK rules and crewing agreements. Many shipowners from UK and Denmark for example have transferred to the Isle of Man and their crews offered new employment in the new Isle of Man articles by Manx based companies. By 1988 it had 2 million GRT registered in the Isle of Man.

The most recent development is the emergence of offshore registers which run in tandem with the mainland European registries from which they derive. An example is the Norwegian International Ship Registry (NIS) which was introduced by the Norwegian government in 1987. It is open to both Norwegian and foreign owners and permits shipowners to employ foreign crews other than masters. Foreign crews receive favourable tax treatment and in the case of salaries below a certain limit, are exempt altogether from Norwegian taxes. Certification and safety requirements are identical to those of the main Register, so that safety standards should not be prejudiced. By 1988 4.9 million GRT involving 155 ships had registered on the NIS register. A similar off-shore register is being set up by the Danish government and it is likely the German government will do likewise. This will bring back to the German flag many of the vessels flagged out to Cyprus and Singapore.

Opponents of open registry flags argue that the employment of Third World crews at lower than European rates of pay represents exploitation of the individuals concerned. They argue therefore that vessels should be flagged in the state of beneficial owner-ship, employing crews of the same nationality. This argument presupposes that every nation has a pool of trained and willing seafarers which is not always the case. Many emerging nations, such as Saudi Arabia, do not have a tradition of seafaring and are there-fore compelled to employ expatriate crews. A European deepsea shipping line must now compete with vessels employing low cost Far Eastern crews as well as many Far Eastern Lines with low cost indigenous crews. Since manning costs are related to the cost of living in the home country of the seafarer, there is a considerable variation throughout the world. The following table gives an indi-cation of the annual manning cost of a typical vessel.

Table 19.2   Annual manning cost of a deep sea container vessel

Flag	Officers	Crew	Cost (US$)
UK	UK	UK	908 000
Liberian	Korean	Korean	490 000
Bermuda	Phillipine	Philippine	481 000
Hong Kong	Hong Kong	Hong Kong	396 000

Source: GCBS

Hence Table 19.2 illustrates the cost advantage of flagging out to an open registry.

Shipping companies tend to pay for their new ships out of past profits, and it it those companies operating under the flags of countries of low taxation that have been able to expand their fleets, while the owners who are subject to high rates of taxation have not been able to expand their fleets to take advantage of increased demand. Under these circumstances, it is only to be expected that new tonnage will tend to be concentrated in those countries where profits are not subjected to especially high taxation.

It was an American who was credited with the invention of the term 'flags of necessity'. Such flags allowed US companies the chance of competing on the seas of the world without the burden of crippling wage costs which would otherwise be imposed.

For many years the British shipping industry has been opposed to flags of convenience as they impair the commercial freedom of the seas. But despite strenuous efforts to eradicate the practice, the industry has met with little success in this respect. In 1974 and 1975 the International Labour Organization (ILO) prompted a certain amount of trades union action against flags of convenience vessels in support of underpaid crew members. One such action led to a Cypriot vessel virtually marooned in the Manchester Ship Canal when tugmen and lock-keepers responded to an ILO call. Since most international trade either originates or terminates in industrial countries where the power of trade unions is strong, this may be the way that adherence to acceptable standards could be enforced.

A topic discussed at the UNCTAD V conference in Manila in 1979 was 'flags of convenience' of open registry fleets especially in the bulk cargo sectors where their participation is strong. It considered an *ad hoc* intergovernmental working group which had concluded that the continuing expansion of the open registry fleets had adversely affected the development of the national fleets of developing countries. Such vessels operated with foreign crews at low cost primarily from third world countries. The working group wished such open registry fleets to be phased out as soon as possible. Conference concluded and agreed to reconvene the working group to study the situation further and report.

UNCTAD V conference also discussed bulk shipping both dry and liquid, involving the rights of countries to participate in the carriage of bulk cargoes which they generate by their own trade. No overall agreement was reached as there was a major difference between the views of developing countries (the Group of '77') and those of the developed market economy countries over the fundamental nature of the problem. The latter argued that the bulk market was open to all carriers to compete under conditions of fair competition, while developing countries argued that the so–called 'free market' in the bulk sector was little more than a myth, and claimed that bulk cargoes were controlled by cartels, and locked into the vertically integrated operations of transnational corporations.

Ultimately the conference acknowledged the right of all countries to an equitable participation in the carriage of cargoes generated by their own trade and made the following recommendations designed to give effect to this right, emphasizing the need to take account of pragmatic considerations as detailed below:

(a) Equitable participation by the national lines of countries which have a regular trade in bulk terms.

(b) Use of bilateral treaties to govern participation in other trades.

(c) Stipulation in contracts for bulk sales of the right to transport a 'substantial and increasing portion of cargoes' by national vessels of developing countries.

To encourage foreign owners to register in Malaysia, the government introduced tax and other benefits which include a 12-year exemption on profit taxes for shipping companies and a similar exemption on dividend payments up to a maximum of 10%. The procedure for registration has also been simplified. This emerged from the UNCTAD V conference.

There is no doubt that the expanding flags of convenience fleet is posing many problems particularly to those Western nations which prefer to compete for trade strictly on commercial grounds.

Although the Conference recommendations were not agreed, it was decided that developing countries adopt unilateral measures to enter into a bilateral trading treaty with like-minded trading partner countries. Meanwhile a working group continues to study the question of phasing out of flags of convenience operations. Developing countries particularly do not favour open registries as they feel the trade should be carried in their own tonnage. Additionally they feel some of the crews of such tonnage come from third world countries and are thus exploited on low wage scales.

It is unlikely there will be any dramatic change in the near future, but the likelihood of flag of convenience fleet or as it is frequently termed today open registries surviving in their present form long term seems in doubt. By the early 1990s the development of the Isle of Man, NIS will signal a new era twist in the development of open registries.

19.3 SUBSIDIES

Since the First World War, many countries have decided in the interests of security or prestige that they must increase their merchant shipping. For the same reason, many countries, formerly not shipowning countries, have established merchant fleets. Many of these countries, because of higher wage levels or lack of ship management techniques, found themselves unable to compete economically. Such countries therefore solved the problem by subsidizing their fleets. For many years now the US government has made constructional and operational subsidies available to its shipowners, to cover the additional cost of labour, a result of the higher general level of American wages. Subsidies may also take the form of guarantees against losses, loans at less than market rates of interest, and mail payments at higher rates than would be paid on a strictly commercial basis. Here it must be remembered that many of the early British steam packet companies were built up by mail subvention. With the onset of the depression in 1929, subsidies became widespread until, by 1934, even the British Government was compelled to authorize a defensive subsidy of £2 million a year until 1937, to protect its tramp shipping. The enormous expansion of Japanese shipping since the 1960s was facilitated by subsidies.

Such subsidies distort the competitive structure of shipping and increase the cost of world shipping services, because they permit the use of vessels less efficient and more expensive than is warranted on an economic basis. However, it is difficult to see how a country like the USA can operate ships without subsidies, since the labour costs are so much higher than those of other countries. Of course, in a world where international specialization was fully used, and where no questions of national security were posed, shipowning would be undertaken only by those countries most fitted by their cost structures and efficiency to operate ships.

The British Government's decision in 1963, to make loans at low rates of interest for ships built in the UK yards, follows the action of other countries, with shortage of orders for their yards, who obtain fresh business by financing shipbuilders to make long-term loans below commercial rates of interest.

By the 1980s fleet subsidization was much on the increase in a variety of ways and reflected the increased tendency of nationalism and protectionism adopted by many maritime nations towards their fleet development and sustainment. Undoubtedly the UNCTAD V conference held in Manila 1979 stimulated the development of such policies particularly by third world countries. Details of the types of subsidization are given below:

(a)   Building subsidies may be a percentage of the total building cost or a fixed sum of the ship construction cost. It is usually given on certain conditions particularly as a means of sustaining the shipyard industry in the maritime country concerned rather than allow the vessel to be built in a foreign yard at maybe a lower cost and quicker time scale. This policy is particularly relevant to state-owned fleets and thereby seen as part of the nation's economy and facilitation of trade development.

In the case of non-state-owned fleets, building subsidies are likewise available in similar terms or with no constraints thereby permitting a subsidy to be afforded to a vessel built in a foreign yard. It must be recognized that not all maritime nations particularly third world countries have their own shipyards although the situation will become less common as their industrialization develops. It must be borne in mind that few shipowners today have the funds to provide new tonnage and rarely can more than one-third be found from the shipping company's own financial resources, the rest being provided from government and/or financial institutions.

(b)   Shipyard subsidies are much on the increase in a period of a depressed shipbuilding industry internationally. Hence governments would subsidize the shipyard both for new construction and repair work irrespective of whether the vessels are of foreign registration or of the particular maritime nation involved.

(c)   A further subsidy technique is to offer interest-free or low interest loans to their shipowners for new tonnage. Again it may be subject to various conditions such as the ship being built in the maritime country shipyard. Furthermore, it may be sponsored under a 'scrap and build' policy whereby, for example, three vessels in excess of 15 years old would be scrapped and two new ones provided in their place. A similar condition could arise in building subsidies.

(d) An operating subsidy arises when the shipping company is either granted a specified sum to make good the loss incurred each year or an operating grant. The latter is usually provided annually over a specified period.

(e) A convention arises whereby a shipping company provides a service which is essential to the economic and social well-being of a community. It may involve a group of islands served by the mainland in terms of a shipping service. Such a situation obtains in Scotland whereby the Western and Eastern Isles are small communities and their future well-being and economic development is conditional on relatively low freight and passenger tariffs. The convention is a sum granted annually by the government to the shipping company to keep such tariffs at a reasonable level to enable the islands to prosper economically. It is usually granted on certain conditions such as all-the-year-round service with maybe a minimum weekly service in each direction.

(f) Subsidies also arise in the form of fleet insurance being funded by the state as found in many Eastern bloc tonnage. It also extends to crew subsidization involving social security/insurance contributions being state-financed. Study Chapter 1 of *Economics of Shipping Practice and Management*.

Features of subsidies and their policies are given below:

1. It enables the maritime government to save hard currency in as much as if the cargo is conveyed in a foreign registered ship it would involve a hard currency outgoing payment. Likewise, the subsidized shipping company carries cargo for other countries and may even operate in a cross-trade situation. This earns invisible exports for the maritime country.

2. It tends to inflate the world shipping fleet capacity beyond the level which trade can support. Accordingly it destroys in some trades the commercial freedom of the seas and this is apparent when two competing companies seek the same traffic flow one of which is subsidized and the other not so. The former can usually undercut the latter in the knowledge that if he incurs a loss on the traffic, the government will still subsidize the service.

3. It encourages uneconomic ship operation as there is no incentive in some situations to reduce cost in the knowledge the

state will make good the loss and the service will not be withdrawn.

4. It develops further the policy of nationalism with fleets being built up not only for commercial reasons but also prestige and strategic considerations. Moreover, it is a means of saving hard currency and can develop the policy of flag discrimination in many countries.

5. It changes the financial evaluation approach when assessing the economics of a shipping service. For example, if a service is losing some £4 million annually and its invisible export contribution is £5 million, the State could decide that retention of the service is justified. Moreover, if the service were closed and it would cost some £6 million annually in hard currency for foreign carriers to convey such cargo for the maritime country, it would be justified to retain the service and subsidize it.

6. Countries having high wage scales find it increasingly difficult to compete with fleets with low wage scales relative to crew cost. Attempts have been made by industrial maritime nations to reduce their crew complement with some measure of success. Such nations to sustain their relative high cost fleet often provide some form of subsidy and foster the policy of flag discrimination. Alternatively some maritime nations are encouraging their fleets to flag out such as NIS (see p. 449).

7. It does not usually encourage efficiency as in some cases there is no incentive to keep ship operating cost to a low level in the knowledge the State will fund it.

The practice of operating subsidized fleets tends to be on the increase particularly by developing countries anxious to save hard currency by conveying their own trade. Moreover, with the majority of world shipyards in 1989 hungry for orders, various incentives are being offered to secure orders. Credit remains a dominant factor in any shipbuilding project negotiation. Banks are offering loans for new tonnage over a longer period. Governments are in many countries endeavouring to sustain their national shipyards by offering generous credit facilities and in many countries involving substantial subsidies both to national and foreign buyers. The situation was made more critical by the serious financial plight of many shipowners.

19.4 EASTERN BLOC MARITIME FLEET DEVELOPMENT

During the late 1970s the Eastern bloc countries have been expanding their mercantile fleets. In particular this involved the Soviet bloc general cargo fleet which in 1979 was of 10 million tonnes compared with the UK fleet of 7 million. This provides the Soviet bloc with between three and four times the capacity necessary to carry their national general cargo trade.

By early 1979 there were some 240 Soviet cargo liner vessels operating in cross trades in the international liner trades in competition with the established liner conferences where they charge freight rates which, by market economy standards, are so low as to be uncommercial. By 1988 the USSR tonnage totalled 23.8 million dwt (see Table 5.1) which confirms the growth of the USSR fleet now ranked at number seven position. Amongst the main trades affected are UK/Continent – East Africa, UK/Continent – Far East, the North Atlantic trades, the Trans-Pacific trades and, most recently, UK/Continent–Mediterranean trade.

The freight rates which Soviet operators charge are generally of the order of 15 to 30% below those of the conferences with which they are competing: in certain trades, the undercutting is even greater. This is possible because Soviet ships, which are all state-owned, enjoy low capital charges, no hull or machinery insurance and incur very low crew costs. In addition, costs of social services are not charged against shipping companies; (this is a considerable extra burden on the wages bill in the UK and other Western countries). Moreover, to the extent that their bunkers are obtained in their home ports, they benefit from rates well below world market levels.

The non-commercial undercutting tactics of Soviet lines have a dual effect on Western liner operators. They result, firstly in a loss of cargo to the Soviet lines and, secondly, they force conferences to depress freight rates for the cargo they do retain to levels which may be uneconomic.

The motives for Soviet expansion into the multilateral liner trades are partly economic, partly political and partly strategic. They have an urgent need to earn foreign exchange because of their massive balance of payments deficit with the Western world.

Their general cargo fleet, however, also provides the means of carrying military personnel and equipment to client nations, establishing a worldwide maritime presence and intelligence system and, in addition, gives the Soviet Union the potential to achieve a dominant position in the principal world trading routes.

The Soviet authorities have declared their wish to avoid a freight rate war and seek to operate within the established liner conferences, but this is clearly on the basis that their demands for conference shares are met. In most cases, it has not been possible to reach commercial agreement on the terms under which they could be admitted to conference membership and, in one case, when invited to join an open (US) liner conference, the Soviet line refused.

Whilst the outside activities of Soviet shipping may appear to be of advantage to shippers in the short term and whilst the UK Government is likely to continue vigorously to press for restraint in the growth of conference freight charges in all trades, it is in neither's interest to allow the undercutting tactics of Soviet operators to continue unchecked. In the shorter term, in the decline in the efficiency and regularity of the services on which so much of our overseas trade is dependent.

Consequently, as it has not been possible to reach agreement at commercial level, Western ship operators have called upon their governments to take appropriate concerted action to safeguard their shipping interests.

The EEC Commission introduced a monitoring system of carryings by COMECON ships within EEC ports with a view to determining whether there is a need for some form of control by quota or licence and that consideration be given by EEC Member States to the joint application of countervailing powers. Basically this is a surveillance system to monitor the activities of fleets whose practices are considered to be detrimental to the maritime interests of Member States. Negotiations are currently in hand between the UK and the USSR to obtain fairer shares of the UK/USSR non-liner trades for British operators, whilst formal monitoring by five European countries continues in three important trades.

It will be interesting to note how things develop particularly at a time when world trade is depressed and the growing Soviet mercantile fleet will only serve to increase the volume of world laid

Table 19.3 UK balance of payments: UK-owned ships

A. By year of contribution

£ mn

	Gross Earnings	Revenue from abroad	Net Direct Contributions[1]	Gross Import Savings[2]
1980	3 747	3 144	1 028	603
1982	3 183	2 527	457	656
1984	3 191	2 480	342	711
1986	3 260	2 519	537	741
1987	3 457	2 635	500	802

B. By Ship type

	Total Receipts (£ million)		%		Of which from cross trades		%	
	1985	1987	1985	1987	1985	1987	1985	1987
Liner*	2 007	2 363	80	69	854	1 087	43	52
Tramp	141	267	6	8	117	236	83	11
Tanker	348	807	14	23	294	761	84	37
Tanker	2 496	3 437	100	100	1 265	2 084	51	100

Note: [1] Gross earnings from abroad less disbursements abroad.
[2] Freight on imports, passage money collected in the UK and time charter receipts from UK non-shipowners.
* Includes cruise ships, ferries, container ships and cargo liners (refrigerated and others).
Source: GCBS

up tonnage. Moreover the long-established liner cargo operator subject to such Soviet mercantile fleet competition will find it increasingly difficult to operate profitable services unless measures are taken to redress the present situation.

19.5 SHIPPING CONTRIBUTION TO INVISIBLE EXPORTS

Shipping revenue as an invisible export can make an important contribution to the balance of payments of the chief shipowning countries. The contribution may arise in two ways:

1. A large volume of the country's trade may be carried in its own ships, so that foreign exchange is not required to pay freight on imports. Conversely, foreign exchange is earned where freight on exports carried in the country's ships is paid by the importing country.

2. Where a country's ships carry passengers and freight between other countries, substantial amounts of foreign exchange may be earned.

Table 19.3 shows the importance of the net contribution of British shipping to the UK balance of payments.

Table 19.4 UK-owned and-registered fleet (500 GRT and above)

	Dry Cargo		Tanker		Total		
	no.	*million dwt*	*no.*	*million dwt*	*no.*	*million dwt*	*dwt as % of world*
31 Dec. 1975	1 160	20.0	454	30.0	1 614	50.0	8.8
31 Dec. 1980	760	12.3	384	23.4	1 143	35.7	5.3
31 Dec. 1981	665	11.3	329	18.2	994	29.4	4.3
31 Dec. 1982	565	9.7	303	15.1	868	24.7	3.6
31 Dec. 1983	505	8.5	264	12.2	769	20.7	3.1
31 Dec. 1984	453	7.6	236	10.8	689	18.4	2.8
31 Dec. 1985	415	6.6	212	9.3	627	15.9	2.5
31 Dec. 1986	357	5.2	144	6.4	501	10.6	1.7
31 Dec. 1987	320	4.5	143	4.9	463	9.5	1.5
31 Dec. 1988	300	4.3	137	4.3	437	8.6	1.4

Table 19.5   World trading fleet (100 GRT and above)

	Dry Cargo		Tanker		Total	
	no.	million dwt	no.	million dwt	no.	million dwt
31 Dec. 1975	27 458	265	7 995	306	35 453	571
31 Dec. 1980	29 426	325	8 455	347	37 881	672
31 Dec. 1981	29 769	341	8 675	348	38 444	689
31 Dec. 1982	29 749	352	8 617	331	38 366	683
31 Dec. 1983	29 844	359	8 463	313	38 307	673
31 Dec. 1984	29 625	370	8 423	296	38 048	666
31 Dec. 1985	28 912	371	8 287	273	37 199	644
31 Dec. 1986	28 194	364	8 260	262	36 454	626
31 Dec. 1987	27 685	359	8 339	261	36 024	620
31 Dec. 1988	27 517	358	8 403	261	35 920	620

Source: GCBS

The net direct contribution to the balance of payments is derived after deducting expenditure overseas on essential items like fuel bunkers, cargo handling and port charges. Given in Tables 19.4 and 19.5 is an analysis of the UK-owned and registered fleet and the world trading fleet. It reveals a sharp decline in the UK fleet which has fallen from 9% of world tonnage in 1975 to 11% in 1988. It should be studied closely with Table 5.1 which traces the development of the ten largest mercantile fleets. The reasons for the UK fleet decline are numerous as given below.

(a) High cost of ship operation and low investment return encouraging shipowner to flag out.

(b) Little HM government support financially to aid ship investment compared with other maritime nations.

(c) Development of flags of convenience.

(d) Development of Eastern bloc countries' fleets.

(e) Adoption of liner conference code of 40:40:20.

(f) High crew cost compared with many other maritime fleets.

(g) Change in the pattern of world trade.

(h) Policy by many governments worldwide to develop their maritime fleets and their overseas trade to thereby improve their external trade balance.

All the foregoing points have been explained elsewhere in the book. It is dealt with more fully in *Economics of Shipping Practice and Management*.

19.6 CONCLUSION

The sixth edition of this book is published some 25 years after the first edition emerged in 1964. Throughout this quarter of a century great change has taken place in the industry. The subject has become more complex and the latest edition has been completely brought up to date in all its areas. The book preserves its lucidity of presentation for an international market now extending to over 200 countries. Each new edition has become more international in its content to reflect the needs of the reader worldwide.

Containerization and combined transport operation will continue to expand in the future. The world trading pattern will see accelerated growth in the Pacific rim of countries with more traffic in the Pacific Ocean than in the Atlantic Ocean – a situation obtaining since 1986. This trend will continue and widen.

New technology will continue to emerge in ship construction, operation and maintenance and also in the area of documentation. More emphasis will be placed on quality of service to the shipper and demanding higher professional standards at all levels of the industry. In 1988, GATT indicated the value of world trade increased by 8.5% compared with 5.5% in 1987. This performance marked four consecutive years of accelerated trade growth, and six consecutive years in which world trade grew more rapidly than world production. It is hoped that this trend will continue into the 1990s.

The outcome of these developments will be the need for more training and education throughout the industry. It will present opportunity and challenge coupled with professionalism. The sixth edition has been devised with this objective in mind. It is hoped it will facilitate the development of international trade through improved ship management and export/import practice techniques and thereby raise living standards worldwide.

APPENDIX A

Further recommended textbook reading

Branch, A.E. (1984), *Elements of Export Marketing and Management*, 1st edn, Chapman and Hall, London.

Branch, A.E. (1984), *A Dictionary of Commercial Terms & Abbreviations* (6000 entries), 1st edn, Witherby, London.

Branch, A.E. (1985), *Elements of Export Practice*, 2nd edn, Chapman and Hall, London.

Branch, A.E. (1986), *Economics of Port Operation and Management*, 1st edn, Chapman and Hall, London.

Branch, A.E. (1986), *A Dictionary of Shipping/International Trade Terms and Abbreviations*, (9000 entries), 3rd edn, Witherby, London.

Branch, A.E. (1988), *Economics of Shipping Practice and Management*, 2nd edn, Chapman and Hall, London.

Branch, A.E. (1988), *English – Arabic Dictionary of Commercial, International Trade and Shipping Terms*, (2200 entries), 1st edn, Witherby & Co. Ltd, London.

Branch, A.E. (1989), *Import/Export Documentation*, 1st edn, Chapman and Hall, London.

Branch, A. E. (1989), *Dictionary of Multilingual Commercial – International Trade – Shipping Terms in English – French – German – Spanish*, (13 000 entries), 1st edn, Witherby, London.

Mitchelhill, A. (1982), *Bills of Lading Law and Practice*, 1st edn, Chapman and Hall, London.

Packard, W.V. (1979), *Voyage Estimating*, 1st edn, Fairplay Publications.

Packard, W.V. (1980), *Laytime Calculating*, 1st edn, Fairplay Publications.

Schmitthoff, C.M. (1980), *The Export Trade,* 8th edn, Sweet & Maxwell, London.

Watson, A. (1985), *Finance of International Trade,* 3rd edn, Institute of Bankers, London.

APPENDIX B

Shipping terms and abbreviations

aa	Always afloat
ABS	American Bureau of Shipping Classification Society
Ad valorem	According to value
APT	Afterpeak tank
AR	Antwerp/Rotterdam ports range
ARA	Antwerp/Rotterdam/Amsterdam ports range
BA	Buenos Aires
BACAT	Barge aboard Catamaran
bb	Below bridges
bdi	Both days included
Back Freight	Freight incurred through cargo being returned from destination port
BH	Bordeaux/Hamburg ports range
BK	Bar keel
B/L	Bill of lading
BNA	British North Atlantic
Bonded warehouse	Accommodation under Customs' surveillance housing highly dutiable cargoes
BOTB	British Overseas Trade Board
Breaking Bulk	Commencing discharge
Broken Stowage	Space wasted in a ship's hold by stowage of uneven packages
BV	Bureau Veritas (French Ship) Classification Society
CAD	Cash against documents or cash after delivery
CAP	Common Agricultural Policy
Cargo Plan	Plan depicting space in a ship available for cargo
CB	Container base

C & F	Cost and freight
CIF	Cost, insurance, freight
CIF & E	Cost, insurance, freight & exchange
CIFCI	Cost, insurance, freight, commission & interest
CIM	International convention for conveyance of goods by rail, operative in the main in Europe
Closing date	Latest date cargo accepted for shipment by shipowner for specified sailing
COD	Cash on delivery
COGSA	Carriage of Goods by Sea Act
COP	Custom of port
C/P	Charter party
Cpd	Charterers pay dues
CSD	Closed shelter deck vessel
CTL	Constructive total loss
DBB	Deals, battens & boards
DBEATS	Despatch, payable both ends all time saved
DBELTS	Despatch, payable both ends on laytime saved
Dd	Delivered docks
DDA	Duty deposit account
DDO	Despatch, money payable discharging only
Dead freight	Space booked by shipper but not used
Demurrage	Money paid by charterer to shipowner for delay in loading or discharging of cargo as scheduled in charter party
Despatch	Money paid by shipowner to charterer for earlier loading or discharging of cargo as scheduled in charter party
DF	Direction finder
Disembarkation	Process of passengers leaving a vessel
DLO	Despatch, money payable loading only
D½D	Despatch, money payable at half demurrage rate
DSRK	Deutsche Schiffs Revision und Klassifikation, (German ship) Classification Society
DT	Deep tank
Dti	Department of Trade and Industry
dwt	Deadweight tonnes
ECA	Economic Co-operation Administration
ECCP	East coast coal port

ECGD	Export credit guarantee department
Embarkation	Process of passengers joining a ship
ESD	Echo sounding device
Ex works	Exports sold free of any transport, insurance and freight charges
Faa	Free of all average
FAS	Free alongside
FC & S	Free of capture & seizure
FCL	Full container load
FD	Free despatch
ffa	Free from alongside
FIO	Free in and out
FO	Free overside
FOB	Free on board
FOR	Free on rail
FOW	First open water or free on wagon
FPA	Free of particular average
FPT	Fore peak tank
Fwd	Forward
GA	General average
GAC	General average contribution
GCBS	General Council of British Shipping
GL	Germanischer Lloyd (German ship) Classification Society
GRT	Gross registered tonnes
GSSL	Ports of Genoa, Savona, Spezia & Leghorn
GSSLNCV	Ports of Genoa, Savona, Spezia, Leghorn, Naples, Civetta and Vecchia
GV	Grande vitesse
HH	Havre/Hamburg ports range
HR	Hellenic Register of (Greek) Shipping Classification Society
HHDWS	Heavy handy deadweight scrap
HWOST	High water ordinary spring tide
ICD	Inland clearance depot
ICS	International Chamber of Shipping
ID	Import duty
IDA	Import Duty Act
IMO	International Maritime Organization
In Bond	Goods liable for customs duty

ISO	International Standards Organization
IWA	International Wheat Agreement
JR	Jugoslav Register (Yugoslavian ship) Classification Society
LASH	Lighter aboard ship
Laydays	Period allotted in charter party for loading/discharging cargo
Lo/Lo	Lift on/lift off
LL	Load line
LR	Lloyd's Register Classification Society
LCL	Less than container load
LMC	Lloyd's machinery certificate
LNG	Liquefied natural gas carrier
LPG	Liquid petroleum gas
LOCO	Goods price includes packing and transport
LWOST	Low water ordinary spring tide
Manifest	Inventory of cargo on board a ship
MSA	Merchant Shipping Act, or Mutual Security Agency (USA)
ML	Motor launch
MV	Motor vessel
NAA	Not always afloat
NAABSA	Not always afloat but safe aground
NJ	New Jason clause
NK	Nippon Kaiji Kyokai (Japanese ship) Classification Society
Northern Range	US ports of Norfolk, Va., Newport News, Philadelphia, Baltimore, New York, Boston and Portland, Me.
NRT	Net registered tons
NS	No sparring
NV	Norske Veritas (Norwegian ship) Classification Society
OBOs	Oil/bulk ore carriers
OEC	Overpaid entry certificate
OECD	Organization for Economic Co-operation & Development
O/O	Oil/ore carrier
OSD	Open shelter deck

Out shipment	Passengers/cargo refused shipment as vessel already fully loaded
PC	Passenger certificate
P & I	Protection & Indemnity
PIM	International Goods Regulations, governing conveyance of goods by rail in Europe
PR	Polish Register (Polish ship) Classification Society
Pro rata freight	Freight charged on proportion of voyage completed
PS	Paddle steamer
PTL	Partial total loss
PV	Petite vitesse
Roads	Ports of Hampton Roads, (Norfolk, Newport News & Sewells Point)
RDR	Radar
Receiving date	Date from which cargo accepted for shipment by specified sailing
RI	Registro Italiano (Italian ship) Classification Society
ROB	Remaining on board (cargo/fuel)
Ro/Ro	Roll on/Roll off type of vessel
RS	Register of Shipping of the USSR
Shut out	Cargo refused shipment because it arrived after closing date
SHInc	Sundays & holidays included
SITPRO	Simpler International Trade Procedures Board
SITC	Standard International Trade Classification
SOLAS	Safety of Life at Sea
SS	Steamship
Stowage plan	Plan depicting location of cargo stowed in a ship
SWL	Safe working load
TBN	To be nominated
TC	Time charter
TEUs	Twenty foot equivalent units – term used in ship container capacity measurement.

TIR	Transport International Routier (Customs Convention)
TLO	Total loss only
TSS	Turbine steamship
UKHH	United Kingdom & Havre/Hamburg ports range
ULCC	Ultra large crude carrier
UNCTAD	United Nations Conference on Trade & Development
USMC	United States Maritime Commission
USNH	United States, north of Cape Haeteras (ports)
VAT	Value added tax
VLCC	Very large crude carrier
Weather working	Days on which – weather permitting – cargo may be loaded/discharged under charter party terms
WWDSHEX	Weather working days Sundays & holidays excepted
YAR	York Antwerp rules

Readers are urged in addition to study my (1986) Dictionary of Shipping/International Trade Terms and Abbreviations – (9000 entries), 3rd edn, Witherby, London.

Index